Journey into
MADNESS

The True Story of Secret CIA Mind Control and Medical Abuse

Gordon Thomas

BANTAM BOOKS

NEW YORK · TORONTO · LONDON · SYDNEY · AUCKLAND

JOURNEY INTO MADNESS
A Bantam Book
Bantam hardcover edition / June 1989
Bantam paperback edition / June 1990

Library of Congress Cataloging-in-Publication Data

Thomas, Gordon.
Journey into madness / Gordon Thomas.
p. cm.
Bibliography: p.
Includes index.
ISBN 0-553-28413-4
1. Torture—Case studies. 2. Human experimentation in
medicine—Moral and ethical aspects—Case studies.
3. United States. Central Intelligence Agency.
4. Terrorism—Lebanon—Beirut—Case studies. I. Title.
HV8593.T48 1989
365'.643—dc19
88-39375
CIP

Bantam Books are published by Bantam Books, a division of Bantam
Doubleday Dell Publishing Group, Inc. Its trademark, consisting of
the words "Bantam Books" and the portrayal of a rooster, is
Registered in U.S. Patent and Trademark Office and in other
countries. Marca Registrada. Bantam Books, 666 Fifth Avenue,
New York, New York 10103.

PRINTED IN THE UNITED STATES OF AMERICA

RAD   0 9 8 7 6 5 4 3 2 1

THEY JOURNEYED INTO MADNESS . . .

Allen Dulles—As director of the CIA in the late 1950s, he first became aware of the effectiveness—and illegality—of mind control as a means to political ends, backing a terrifying and dangerous program of medical abuse north of the border.

Dr. Donald Ewen Cameron—An internationally renowned psychiatrist, he used ordinary citizens to develop a radical technique he called depatterning: the systematic destruction of a patient's personality through electroshock, drugs, and radical surgery.

William Buckley—Described as a journalist and a "political attaché," he was in fact CIA station chief at the time of his kidnapping in Beirut. Ironically, his death was the result of protracted medical torture once researched and funded by his own country.

William Casey—As the reluctant successor to Stansfield Turner, he was determined to rebuild the power and prestige of the CIA—and to hunt down the murderers of William Buckley at any cost.

Dr. Aziz al-Abub—One of Dr. Cameron's most "talented" pupils, he is one of the most feared and powerful men in Beirut today. Carrying a medical bag of horrors, he moves from safehouse to safehouse "tending" his victims, many of them Americans held hostage by the fanatical Muslim Hizballah.

"THERE IS NO ESCAPING THE GHASTLINESS OF THE MESSAGE AND THE POWER OF THIS INDICTMENT LEVELED AGAINST ALL WHO COLLUDE, CONNIVE, AND COLLABORATE IN THE GREATEST MISUSE OF MEDICAL POWER SINCE THE NAZI FACTORIES 50 YEARS AGO."
—Anthony Clare, *Sunday Times*

**For
Nicholas and Natasha**

*My hope for the future;
one free of the horrors in these pages*

Contents

I swear by Apollo Physician and Asclepius and Hygieia and Panacea and all the gods and goddesses, making them my witnesses, that I will fulfill according to my ability and judgment this oath and this covenant. To hold him who has taught me this art as equal to my parents and to live my life in partnership, and if he is in need of money to give him a share of mine, and to regard his offspring as equal to my brother in male lineage and to teach them this art, if they desire to learn it, without fee and covenant; to give a share of the precepts and oral instruction and all the other learning to my sons and to the sons of him who has instructed me and to pupils who have signed the covenant and have taken an oath according to the medical law, but to no one else. I will apply dietetic measures for the benefit of the sick according to my ability and judgment; I will keep them from harm and injustice. I will neither give a deadly drug to anybody if asked for it; nor will I make a suggestion to this effect. Similarly I will not give to a woman an abortive remedy. In purity and holiness I will guard my life and my art. I will not use the knife, not even on sufferers from stone, but will withdraw in favor of such men as are engaged in this work. Whatever houses I may visit, I will come for the benefit of the sick, remaining free of all internal injustice, of all mischief and in particular of sexual relations with both female and male persons, be they free or slaves. What I may see or hear in the course of the treatment or even outside the treatment in regard to the life of men, which on no account one must spread abroad, I will keep to myself holding such things shameful to be spoken about. If I fulfill this oath and do not violate it, may it be granted to me to enjoy life and art, being honored with fame among all men for all time to come; if I transgress it and swear falsely, may the opposite of all this be my lot.

—The Original Oath of Hippocrates

I solemnly swear to devote all my knowledge and strength to the preservation and improvement of the health of man, to the curing and prevention of diseases, to work conscientiously wherever the interests of society demand; to be ever ready to render material aid, to be attentive and thoughtful of the patient, to maintain medical confidence; constantly to perfect my medical knowledge and physician's skills; to further by work the development of medical science and practice; to turn, if the patient's interest demand it, for advice to my professional colleagues and that I myself will never refuse advice and help to them; to preserve and further the noble traditions of our native medicine; and that I will in all my actions be guided by the principles of Communist morality, ever to bear in mind the high calling of the Soviet physician, and of my responsibility to the people of the Soviet state. I swear that I will be faithful to this oath throughout the rest of my life.

—Physician's Oath of the Soviet Union

I swear by God, the Great; to regard God in carrying out my profession; to protect human life in all stages and under all circumstances, doing my utmost to rescue it from death, malady, pain, and anxiety; to keep people's dignity, cover their privacies, and lock up their secrets; to be all the way, an instrument of God's mercy, extending my medical care to near and far, virtuous and friend and enemy; to strive in the pursuit of knowledge and harnessing it for the benefit but not the harm of mankind; to revere my teacher, teach my junior, and be brothers to members of the medical profession joined in piety and charity; to live my Faith in private and in public, avoiding whatever blemishes me in the eyes of God, His Apostles, and my fellow Faithful. And may God be witness to this Oath.

—The Islamic Physician's Oath

1

Perspectives:
A Note to the Reader

The dead only count when they leave a testimony.

—Joel Filartiga,
father of a son tortured to death.

In his memorable account of the Plague, Albert Camus described how Dr. Rieux was determined to complete his chronicle, "so that he should bear witness in favor of the victim, so that some memorial of the injustice and outrage done to them might endure. He knew that the tale he had to tell could not be one of final victory. It could only be the record of what had had to be done, and what assuredly would have to be done again in the never-ending fight against terror and its relentless onslaughts."

I can think of no better reason for telling the story in these pages.

While political terrorism has been capturing widespread attention for some time, almost nothing has been made public of how doctors today use their knowledge and skills in its support. Yet they regularly medically examine political prisoners before questioning to assess the degree of torture to be used. They attend interrogations to treat the direct physical effect of the torture they have approved so that investigation can continue. They recommend how much further torture can then be applied. Physicians employed in state-sponsored terrorism also falsify autopsy reports and provide fake medical certificates for persons those doctors know were tortured to death. A common description is "cardiac failure" or "pneumonia" on those certificates. Physicians who are members of terrorist organizations provide, or themselves use, drugs to force hostages into video recordings—confessions, exhortations, and genuinely pathetic pleas that have become a regular feature of TV newscasts. These stage-managed appearances are aimed at exerting worldwide psychological pressure designed to achieve the aims of the kidnappers.

All such routine malpractices violate medical ethics as defined by one of three oaths sworn by every physician before he or she starts to practice: to do no harm, provide assistance to all in need, and only treat with the consent of the patient.

Yet every day these pledges are flagrantly abused by doctors whose actions conform to the generally accepted definition of torture produced by the United Nations, Amnesty International, and other human rights organizations: the deliberate infliction of pain by one person on another in an effort to break the will of the victim.

In 1988 this gross and pervasive violation was occurring in over ninety countries; a quarter of the world's population were living in areas where abuses have long become habitual, particularly in the Soviet Union, Latin America, Asia, Africa, and the Middle East.

The nonmedical perpetrators of physical and mental violence, such as prison guards and interrogators, are steadily being joined by doctors prepared to put aside all professional ethics to advise upon or perform torture. Psychiatry, in particular, is highly vulnerable to being used by the state to maintain power and control the thoughts and actions of its citizens. George Orwell's *1984* and Aldous Huxley's *Brave New World* continue to exist within all those countries where a person's intentions and actions are interpreted by the state in a manner designed to destroy legitimate political dissent. In a high proportion of those instances psychiatrists provide the clinical label—and the veneer of legitimacy—that allows the state to incarcerate opponents. Doctors, therefore, are increasingly used to discredit and silence all those who oppose official policies; the description of political dissent as "insanity" would have no credence without their active support. In Russia, glasnost has done nothing to significantly reduce the number of dissidents languishing in closed institutions. There, as elsewhere, they continue to be tortured psychologically and physically by physicians trying to induce a change of political views. There are no firm figures for the number of doctors involved. Some human rights workers suggest the global number could run to many thousands. More likely it is in the hundreds, at least for those actively engaged in daily torture. It is manifestly impossible to arrive at any accurate figure for the number who discreetly play a supportive role in torture. But one, surely, is too many.

What is certain is that not since Hitler understood that doctors were an integral and indispensable part of his final solution have physicians become so involved in torture. Yet, dismissing them as simply mad doctors intent on satisfying their own sadistic whims is no more convincing than it was concerning Nazi clinicians involved in the death camps program. Many such physicians appear normal, offering a reminder that certain behavior does elude our full understanding. Indeed, much of what is described in this book cannot be explained by a comforting resort to psychological explanations, where personality and motivation interlock perfectly. All that can be safely claimed is that, because this account is authentic, there can be no simple explanation for the way these doctors behaved—and continue to behave.

In writing this book I had access to written testimony from prime sources, which can be assessed in the following descending order of importance: reports by human rights organizations of fully verified medically sponsored torture; properly attested affidavits by those who were subjected to medical torture; statements by defectors, either from a terrorist organization or from state-sponsored terrorism, about the use of physicians to design methods of abuse or who act as torturers themselves; and authentic documents, gathered by security forces, which offer proof of cruel, inhuman, or degrading treatment administered directly by doctors or at the behest of those security forces.

That evidence was supported by interviews. Thirty-five years of researching other subjects has convinced me that the only way to fully understand an issue is to talk to those directly involved. For this book I traveled extensively in North America, Europe, the Middle East, and beyond to Asia and, finally, Latin America, during which I had to ponder many versions of truth and untruth.

I spoke to more than a hundred persons either directly employed or working indirectly for intelligence agencies. They ranged from desk men to field agents, from academics to physicians employed in prisons and interrogation centers. I conducted multiple interviews with over fifty of these people; some seventeen prime sources were each questioned a dozen or more times. Their patience is something at which I still marvel—that and their willingness to talk. The only guarantee they asked for, and received, was that their anonymity would be protected.

To those who do not toil in the fields of investigative journalism, this is sometimes the moment when hands are thrown up and the question is put: "If they won't be named, how can we believe them?" The only sensible answer is this: Men and women who work in intelligence generally will not discuss security matters without an absolute guarantee of not being identified. However, that does not mean their words are any more, or less, believable; it simply requires that a reporter does not lower his guard.

In addition I followed the rules laid down by two of the great editors of this century, whom I had the good fortune to work for: Arthur Christiansen of the *Daily Express,* London, and Ed Thompson of the *Readers Digest.* Both were absolutely firm on such matters as wherever possible using two sources for an important fact, and that when writing someone was said to have "felt," "sensed," "thought," "understood," or "believed," such reactions must genuinely reflect the essence of a particular portion of an interview with that person. Both editors were insistent on the need to reproduce as accurately as possible the attitudes and personality of an interviewee, even when he or she was not directly quoted.

Bob Woodward of the *Washington Post* has rightly reminded all of us of the need to try and distinguish between what should genuinely be kept secret for the sake of national security and what officialdom tries to hide under the guise of security, when what is really at stake is the uncovering of inept decision-making and unethical behavior. In his own book, *Veil: The Secret Wars of the CIA 1981–1987,* Woodward quoted the guidelines of another veteran of our business, Ken Auletta. He has synthesized the complex business of prime and secondary sources, on- and off-the-record conversations, and recreating an event or happening with the use of memoranda, documents, letters, diaries, and notes-to-file. Auletta wrote that "no reporter can with 100 percent accuracy recreate events that occurred some time before. Memories play tricks on participants, the more so when the outcome has become clearer. A reporter tries to guard against inaccuracies by checking with a variety of sources. But it is useful for a reader—and an author—to be humbled by this journalistic limitation."

Auletta's reminder was certainly constantly in my mind during the interviews for this book. And just as *Veil* is among the first to illuminate the world of modern intelligence, so mine is an early entry into describing the field of medical torture. Like Woodward's stated attitude to his work, I freely recognize that the story in these pages cannot be the final word; instead, I see it as an encouragement for others to pursue the trail, to turn what is essentially today's reportage into the substantiality of tomorrow's history. Sometimes, such as that day in May 1987 in Beirut, as on previous occasions, I had no alternative but to simply be my own prime source—to enter the story and describe what I saw. I'm not enthusiastic about such intrusions; after all, it is the story and not the teller who matters. But at those times there really seemed no other way.

When *Veil* was published in the autumn of 1987 it was attacked largely on the grounds that the one-time director of the Central Intelligence Agency, William Joseph Casey, would never have given the interviews Woodward claimed, let alone be so forthcoming—or if he had, it had simply been to use Woodward to shape Casey's place in history and spread disinformation. It's the old story of trusting a source. Personally, I have no problem in believing that Woodward spoke, as he wrote, close to fifty times with Casey and that the director was as frank as *Veil* suggests.

I met Casey on two occasions in Washington in March 1986. My path to him had been cleared by senior U.S. diplomats and members of the CIA in the Middle East whom I had gotten to know through the hostage situation in Beirut. They said the only person who could begin to answer some of my questions was Casey.

The first occasion we met was in the International Club in Washington, D.C., on Friday, March 21; the second time was at the same venue four days later. On both occasions Casey wore the same dark blue suit, clearly custom-made because of his size. He seemed considerably bulkier than in his television appearances—and older, too. He looked physically unwell, his skin gray and taut around the eyes and jaw.

He wasted no time on small talk, getting down to business at once. I gave him a brief account of what I had learned in the Middle East about the hostages. He listened carefully and said some of it had to be "just goddamn speculation." Then he proceeded to substantially reduce that element by explaining in some detail why the CIA believed the hostages were being held under appalling conditions, including being ill-treated by a doctor. He suggested further ways I could "look into that aspect."

He was courteous and helpful, to a certain point—that point being that he told me he was "working with another writer," and consequently could only be of limited assistance. That writer, of course, was Bob Woodward.

But Casey did provide me with confirmation of a number of key matters relating to medical torture, speaking candidly after he had been satisfied that anything he said would not be attributed to him. His death on May 6, 1987, freed me of that agreement and I can simply say that this book owes a debt to Casey—even though I am certain he would not have wanted many of the revelations about the CIA's own behavior to emerge; it was very clear from our discussions that the director had a fierce protective feeling about not only the agency he then headed but the one he had inherited. I learned of his death back in the Middle East while pursuing one of the leads he had given. His passing came at the very time Congress had begun its public hearings on the Iran-Contra fiasco, whose ramifications arose directly out of the hostage-taking that forms a theme of this book.

The director, like my other interviewees from the intelligence world, would not be taped and would not allow notes to be taken at the time; those had to be written up immediately afterwards as background, that catchall phrase that means information provided could be fully used but not directly attributed. Surprisingly, it worked; cross checks invariably showed my sources were not only in a position to know, but what they were saying was the truth. I am not one who subscribes to the idea that intelligence services spend their time and money running a continuous international conspiracy to deceive journalists and authors. All, undoubtedly, do spread disinformation some of the time among the gullible and unaware. But all the time? No.

Yet, that said, I should also add that sometimes attempts were made to dismiss medical torture as no more than harsh but essential treatment of dangerous suspects—and that, indeed, the very presence of a doctor should be seen as that of a physician ready to intervene, rather like a boxing referee, when a victim's life is in danger.

Such arguments take no account of the long-term effects on the emotional stability of those who endure *any* form of violation of their basic human rights. Accounts by victims of torture are filled with trauma: recurrent nightmares and phobias, increased anxiety, and often impotency. Some of those symptoms are a direct result of medical abuse, itself not always easy to pinpoint, let alone assess, because its practitioners are often greatly skilled in its application.

Again, it was claimed that some of the doctors who were engaged in physical ill-treatment or psychological mind control were forced into such behavior because of threats to their own careers, and possibly their lives and those of their families. The most effective rebuttal to this suggestion is that the great majority of doctors—whether in totalitarian states or living amid terrorist enclaves—refuse to participate in such practices. Indeed, they are often prepared to risk their jobs, lives, and the safety of loved ones to avoid taking part in the violations of human rights that have become so systematic and efficient as to create a growth industry whose tools include drugs, electroshocks, mouth gags, garrots, blindfolds, and branding irons, with methods ranging from sexual abuse to sham executions.

Nor is the defense of self-preservation new. It was advanced by some of the twenty-one German physicians charged with medical crimes at Nuremberg. Disclosures during their trials led to the Hippocratic Oath having an addendum: "I will not permit consideration of race, religion, nationality, party politics, or social standing to intervene between my duty and my patient."

Forty years after that edict was framed, medical cooperation forms an integral part of torture in many countries; the demands of state-sponsored terrorism, or the organizations that deal in terrorism, require no less. Just as the Nazi doctors standing at the ramps of Auschwitz and other camps represented a kind of omega—what Prof. Robert Jay Lifton likens to "mythical gatekeepers between the worlds of the dead and the living"—so their successors continue to represent the use of the healing hand for harm. Lifton's lifetime investigation into Nazi medical malpractices is an invaluable tool for anyone trying to unravel subsequent medical torture.

What remains for me the most disturbing aspect of my investigation is that even as I write, and later when it is read, there are physicians who continue to participate in torture. Their behavior poses a continuous threat to all those of us who still possess that most precious of all gifts: the right of the human spirit to choose. In working on this book I have had to come to terms with my own emotions—disbelief, bewilderment, disgust, and anger and, more than once in the early stages, a feeling that the subject was simply too evil to cope with. Nothing I had researched before could have prepared me for the dark reality of doctors who set out to deliberately destroy minds and bodies they were trained to heal. The realization that physicians are part of a killing machine provokes a special horror. Throughout the interviews I worked through much of my personal conflict—whether to stop or go on—knowing that at every turn there would be further personally unsettling revelations. I survived by constantly reminding myself of a professional obligation to be balanced about doctors whose actions in the end raise a fundamental question: How did they become the way they were and are?

For the most part they did not give the impression, outside their work, of being totally evil; certainly they rarely filled the popular imagery of demonic figures. Equally, it must be said it is demonic that they are *not* demonic. And, without doubt, there is a deeply disturbing psychological truth that what they do does not require personalities anywhere close to sadistic: their behavior confirms that what can be properly called *ordinary* people, nurtured and tutored to find places within the oldest caring profession, can perform acts of authentic wickedness. To reveal their capacity to do so, I felt, like Dr. Rieux, a powerful need to complete a chronicle that has its beginning, though not its roots, in the predawn, neither light nor darkness, the hour the Moslem faithful say when night properly ends and another day starts in Beirut—4:30 A.M. on my watch on a morning in May 1987.

Major Sayad al-Hussein of the Syrian Army continued to survey through night glasses part of the fortified rubble that dominated the city. The barricade was the inappropriately named *La Ligne Verte,* the "Green Line" that separated the city's Christian and Moslem communities. This particular section was of tumbled buildings and their contents of old bedsteads, cookers that would never cook again, and cars the Shiite bombers found unsuitable for their lethal business.

This was the third day the major had brought me here, each time a journey made against the sights and sounds of tracer gunfire—the routine pyrotechnics that made Beirut probably the most dangerous city in the world. Snipers with infrared scopes on their rifles had a commanding field of fire from the windows of the surrounding ferroconcrete buildings.

We had come to attempt to glimpse a person who interested us both. The major would have liked to interrogate the man, but knew he could not until he received orders from higher authority. In the sensitive and uneasy atmosphere of Beirut, any move that was not fully thought through could lead to more bloodshed.

I wanted to look upon the face of the man who caught the attention of analysts in Washington, London, Paris, Vienna, Wiesbaden, and Tel Aviv. They were trying to assess him from afar, creating their fascinating psycho-profiles from the reports of undercover agents and informers. What they had let me read only intensified my desire to see the object of their intensive studies in flesh and blood. I realized that to see him in his own milieu would not make him easier to understand, but it would help to explain him in a way all the information I had accrued could not.

As the light strengthened, the major switched to fieldglasses. Abruptly he handed them to me, pointing to where people had started to appear on a street beyond the Green Line about a hundred yards away, in West Beirut, the Moslem sector.

In the strengthening light the man hardly looked like he did in the photograph Major al-Hussein had shown me earlier: the face was thinner and no longer young; only the pockmarks were a reminder of a childhood ravaged by ill health. He was also taller than his picture suggested, close to six feet, a wiry body in a dark three-piece suit. His only concession to local sartorial custom was the absence of a tie and wearing his trousers tucked into combat boots. He had a physician's bag in one hand.

There was nothing about Aziz al-Abub, sometimes known as Ibrahim al-Nadhir, to show he was a doctor who tortures. Yet a good starting point in trying to understand precisely what was meant by that was to continue to observe him as he crossed the street, walking quickly. . . .

Book One

AT THIS TIME

Modern medical knowledge and technologies are such that those with special skills know exactly how to use them to assault the physical and psychological constitutions of their victims.

> —excerpt from author's interview with Dr. Frederico Allodi, Canadian psychiatrist and member of Amnesty International Medical Group, in Toronto, April 1–3, 1987.

There's a doctor in Beirut who epitomizes what is meant by medical torture. He drugs the hostages to make them easier to handle, so that they can be moved from one safe house to another with less problems. He knows how long to keep them hooded and when to isolate them. That sort of thing. He's genuinely evil.

> —excerpt from author's interview with Arial Merari, Director of Studies into Terrorism at the Jaffee Center for Strategic Studies, in Tel Aviv, May 7, 1987.

1

The Doctors
of Terror

On Friday morning, March 16, 1984, William Buckley awoke
in his penthouse apartment in West Beirut, the three hundred and forty-third day he had spent in the city.

At that early hour Beirut could be seen at its best. Below
him, stretching into the distance, were over a hundred spiral-
ing minarets, the filigree on each iron-rimmed balcony already glinting in the sun. From them the faithful would soon
be summoned to their first prayers of the day. There were
streets that ran long and straight, magnificent boulevards, a
reminder of the time France was the dominant influence
upon the city; its language remained, but was spoken only in
the Christian quarter. In the streets around the apartment
block—curved, narrow, and frequently winding back on
themselves—guttural Arabic dominated.

Within an hour or so, the peace would once more be
broken by a roar of voices and traffic; just as the *tufo* gave
Rome its distinctive sound, Buckley remembered Beirut's
unique character was made up of the tidal wave of human and
mechanical sound reverberating against the building. At full
vent it made it impossible for Buckley to enjoy one of the
little rituals that had always filled his adult life.

He placed a classical album on the stereo turntable at the
side of his bed and carried one of the speakers on its extension flex to the door of the bathroom. He shaved and show-
ered, listening to the music, timing his ablutions so that they
were completed by the time the music stopped. He then
turned over the disc and dressed. That morning he selected a
short-sleeved shirt, silk tie, and a gray lightweight suit. Clothes

13

were another of his unbreakable habits. The shirts had the correct cotton texture and cut, the collar with old-fashioned points.

For the past thirty years he had bought them from the same shop, picking them up by the dozen, long- and short-sleeved, whenever he happened to be in New York; otherwise he ordered them from Brooks Brothers by mail from wherever he was posted. As for suits, he bought four every year, two lightweight, two medium-worsted. In all the years he had been a customer he remained a perfect Brooks 38, so he bought from the rack. His tie came from the Brooks classical range of plain or muted stripes. He liked the fact that the store was unfailingly prompt in fulfilling his orders, mailing them to the most remote places; it was a comforting reminder that, in his uncertain world, some things did not change.

Buckley moved the speaker from the bathroom to the kitchen as he prepared a breakfast of orange juice, cereals, toast, and coffee. He had enjoyed an identical start to the day for as long as he could remember.

Beirut had been a challenge from the beginning. Although no one actually said so, it was a way for him to try to come to terms with his own immediate past and his future. Since Saigon his career had stagnated. He had one or two operations in Africa but nothing as important as those days when he had run several networks halfway across Vietnam. Beirut was the Agency's way of giving him a break, a chance to prove himself anew, to show that this trade was still a second skin.

He had been told as much by Chuck Cogan, the Agency's operations chief for the Near East. Buckley had never forgotten, or forgiven, how the tall, spindly legged operations division chief had stroked his mustache and announced in that unmistakable Harvard accent, "This is a big one, Bill. Make it work."

Afterwards, Buckley had mused how a desk job could change a person. Not so many years before, Cogan had been out in the field, running some very stunning operations in the Congo, Sudan, and Morocco, where he had become the station chief who had recruited the CIA's second monarch— King Hassam II of Morocco. But Cogan had come in from the field. On that last meeting he had been very much head-of-division: formal, brusque, no pleasantries. Leading Buckley to his office door, he had repeated, "It's big, Bill. Don't you ever forget that. You're back in the driver's seat. Don't go off the road."

It had taken time to settle in, and in doing so Buckley had used up a great amount of healthy skepticism and endless hours spent meeting contacts in apartments and cafes that spilled on to the alien streets. Between meetings he occupied himself taking a crash course in Arabic and reading everything available in English on the history of Islam. The bookcase in the living room was testimony to his effort. Its shelves included a well-thumbed copy of *Islam and the Logic of Force*, propped beside the small selection of European classics he carried from one post to another: Maugham, Thackeray, Joyce. There was also Mailer's *Naked and the Dead* and the complete collection of Le Carré and one or two biographies, all of which he regularly reread.

As he ate, the sun was already warm on the kitchen windows. Through them he had another magnificent view of Beirut. Yet even from up here it was possible to see the hatred that engulfed the city and, beyond, all of Lebanon. Wherever he looked there were new gaps in the skyline: an office block collapsed by dynamite; an apartment dwelling demolished after a truck bomber rammed his lethal cargo into its foundation. In the past month over twenty new gaps had appeared, each a home or workplace destroyed in the endless destruction.

In the past two years hundreds of buildings that had stood for decades had been blasted away. A local newspaper had estimated the cost of a week's fighting in Beirut: around two million U.S. dollars in property losses alone. Buckley could not recall a week when there had not been trouble. Yet—and he found this incredible—a brand-new building would appear, occupied before it was even completed, testimony to the strong gambling instinct in most Lebanese.

Nevertheless, no one seemed capable of eliminating the anarchy and healing the divisions. Many people had told him it could not now be otherwise. He had listened carefully. It was part of the job.

Only two days before, another painful reminder of the threat everyone in Beirut faced came literally crashing in upon the private world he had constructed high above the city. A car-bomb had detonated in the street below while he was fixing cocktails for a colleague and his wife. The shock waves blew out all the apartment windows, showering them with glass. After attending to their cuts, he and his guests spent the remainder of the evening sweeping up the shards. Buckley cooked dinner, listening attentively to news of home— the couple had just returned from a vacation in the United States—and afterward, sensing the wife's reluctance to venture into the streets after the explosion, he insisted the couple stay in one of the guest bedrooms. Next morning he telephoned the embassy and a Marine patrol escorted the couple home.

Over many years William Buckley had developed his own special relationship with the world, displaying a quality of mind marked by good manners, unfailing courtesy, and detachment. Most people said he was brighter than brave, but he was also a man who accepted that in his line of work there were still dues of danger that simply had to be paid. Living in Beirut, he had come to say, used up both the principal and interest in emotional stress. Within that closed circle where he could speak openly about such matters, he had added that after this assignment it might be time to consider coming inside for good, making his way from one Langley desk to another; then with that honesty which also marked him, he would grin and say that everyone who had spent time in the field felt like that, and if nothing else, intelligence work was a continuing education in coping with human weakness.

One of Buckley's weaknesses was his housekeeping. Yet he insisted, from the beginning, on doing the work himself; he saw that as part of the security that went with the job. Unwashed crockery, pots, and pans were a feature of the kitchen, clothes were scattered casually about the living area, the laundry bag was overflowing. His friends teased that he enjoyed a masochistic pleasure from the chaos of his rented accommodation. His usual reply was that he never found a woman he would allow to take care of his creature comforts permanently; that, in any event, the worst failing of his work was to expect too much of people, especially where women are concerned. Besides, his way of life simply did not allow for continuous friendships, let alone constant, passionate fidelity. He had even ventured, within the confines of the small circle who knew precisely the business he was in, and who regularly invited him over for Saturday dinner or Sunday brunch, that love made people sometimes act irrationally. No one had been known to press the subject with him; he had a cutoff point people sensed. After almost two years in Beirut as America's most senior spy in Lebanon, William Buckley remained, by choice, an outsider.

Not even those who felt they were close to him asked questions about the woman in the framed photograph on a side table. She was wearing a crème de menthe–colored solar topee and a skunk skin jacket bought with $600 Buckley once gave her for a French World War I victory poster she had found. Her name was Candace Hammond. They had met in between his tours, when he was working out of Langley in 1977, and he was assigned to be the CIA's observer at Exercise Robin Sage, a biannual war game run out of Fort Bragg in North Carolina. For a short while a vast tract of the area known as Pineland was deemed to be under the control of an evil dictator, whose troops were played by the 82nd Airborne Division. Green Beret detachments dropped from Fort Bragg into Pineland, where they attempted to make contact with a civilian resistance and set up safe houses and arms caches. Sometimes genuine civilians were enrolled in the exercise. Candace was portraying a nurse when Buckley met her. They soon became lovers, and their relationship had been a surprisingly easy one between two very different souls. In the photograph she appeared a striking rather than a beautiful woman; she had fine angles, but they did not quite come together to make a whole. The couple corresponded regularly, and he sometimes telephoned her at her home at a crossroads called Farmer-in-the-Carolina backwoods. He kept all her letters, carrying them with him to the office in the very special briefcase that went with his position.

Buckley was described on the protocol list of diplomatic appointments at the U.S. Embassy as a political officer. No one, for a moment, had been taken in by this cover. Try as he might to disguise his work habits, to be vague in conversation about his responsibilities, to attempt and hide behind his pride in obscurity, it was common gossip in the city that he was the Agency's head-of-station. Just as there was popular agreement about his private life, so those people shared an understanding as to why he was in Beirut. He had simply been lucky enough to have been buried in Africa during the purge, the famous Halloween massacre in October 1977, when Admiral Stansfield Turner, President Carter's choice as director, had cleared out the Agency: almost two hundred employees had either been fired, transferred, or had taken early retirement. Buckley, like everyone else, had heard the corrosive stories coming out of Washington, of good agents in disgrace and fine careers ruined. But he remained unscathed. His reputation as a methodical field officer, utterly reliable—and not only in his loyalty to the Agency but also in the way he conformed to what was expected of him during any purge, keeping his head down. He was known as a man who never filed a report that was not properly identified as to its dependability and who never made an evaluation that was not at least grounded in probability. That had all helped to save him as the atmosphere in Langley grew more poisonous. As with all purges, the darkness had lifted. Nevertheless, he had had to wait patiently before emerging from Africa to run one of the most important listening posts within the Agency.

Long before coming to the city, Buckley had heard of its pleasures and pitfalls from an old friend, Robert C. Ames, the Agency's most senior Middle East analyst. Their friendship went back many years. Sartorially opposite—Ames was a flashy dresser, favoring cowboy boots and tinted pilot's spectacles and seersucker suits—both men shared the same passion for good food and literature. Beirut, Ames insisted, was still the finest city in the region in which to dine out. That had been toward the end of their last night together, when Buckley was still in Cairo supervising the training of President Anwar Sadat's bodyguards and adding to the Agency bugs that had been planted all over the presidential palace, a job his friends in "Division D" had cheerfully allowed him to do. Everyone in Langley knew Buckley was simply the best at such covert activities. Ames had come fuming into town that he was still suffering repercussions from the Mossad's car bombing of a priceless asset—Ali Hasan Salameh, head of intelligence of the PLO. Over dinner at the Semerimis, Ames had painted an evocative portrait of Beirut as being at the crossroads of all the double crosses. He said he loved the place: "It's the only checkerboard in this business worth playing on."

When they had finally made their way to their beds, Ames had said to Buckley that "when they call me back in, I'll do my damnedest to make sure you get the job." Buckley still remembered those words.

This Friday morning, Buckley would make the usual rounds of the Foreign Ministry. Over coffee, and when the polite chit-chat could be safely put aside, he planned to continue probing to discover how long the Lebanese government could survive. The signs were ominous: another minister had resigned; there was talk of a new financial scam; Sheykh Fadlallah had issued further warnings to the prime minister to close the American university in the city, on the grounds that its teaching was aimed at undermining those of Islam.

He planned to round off each meeting with a polite, though by now largely meaningless, inquiry about how the authorities were progressing with their investigation into the car bombing of the U.S. Embassy. Twelve CIA and Defense Intelligence Agency officers attending a regional conference on terrorism were killed. Ames was one of the victims.

Buckley knew that his selection to be head of station had been received with incredulity among senior colleagues. They pointed out that his experience was largely in Vietnam and later Laos, where he had organized several of the hill tribes into private armies for the Agency. From Asia he had gone to Zaire to act as paymaster for British, French, and American mercenaries fighting Marxist forces in neighboring Angola. He had then traveled north, to Cairo, to train Sadat's bodyguards, only to see them fail in the face of a suicide attack that led to the assassination of the president. It was Buckley's first experience with the awesome power of religious fanaticism. In Beirut he learned a great deal more about the phenomenon.

In one way this posting was like any of his others. Essentially, he lived in a world where he could not share many of his experiences with anyone. In such conditions a man became more vulnerable where exercising vigilance was concerned: It is only human, if only for a short while, to want to step outside a universe filled with special incantations and signals and codes. It was even more human in William Buckley's case on this Friday morning, weeks away from his fifty-eighth birthday and in a debilitated condition, after almost two decades of continuous service in the tropics.

Buckley may even have been aware of the judgments that had begun to surface: that he was more in the mold of one of

George Smiley's old men than someone James Bond would choose as a partner in a tight corner.

Before leaving the apartment, William Buckley performed one last ritual. He got his briefcase, which had been designed by the technicians at Langley. It was a burn bag, intended, at a twist of the key clockwise, the usual way of locking, to incinerate the contents in seconds by means of gas-filled flames emerging from a ring of jets built into the base. To secure the case the key had to be turned in the opposite direction. Buckley, being the man he was, would have checked each jet carefully to make sure their nozzles were free of dust before filling the briefcase with paperwork, some of it stamped TOP SECRET, other papers marked SECRET, and all of them warranting the minimum security classification, CONFIDENTIAL. Candace's letters also went into the case. He locked the case and attached it by a chain to a bracelet on his wrist.

He deadlocked the apartment door behind him—the only other key was held by the ambassador—and walked to the elevator. It stopped at a floor below. A man entered. He was young, well dressed, and carrying a briefcase. A few floors further down the elevator paused again. This time a woman tenant joined them. Buckley exchanged polite greetings with her. The man did not speak. At the ground floor the woman stepped out, wishing Buckley a nice day, no doubt proud of her grasp of American idiom. The two men rode down to the basement garage where Buckley kept his car. Normally his embassy driver would have been waiting. But this morning Buckley had decided to drive himself to his appointments. He had told no one at the embassy of this violation of security; following the car bombing of the embassy it was an unbreakable rule that no American official traveled alone in the city.

As he walked toward his car Buckley's first inkling of disaster may well have been the fierce blow from the man's briefcase to the back of his head, probably powerful enough to send him sprawling and leave traces of blood and hair on the hide. The attacker dropped his briefcase—when it was later recovered it was found to contain several rocks—and most likely grabbed the stricken intelligence man. From somewhere inside the garage a white Renault appeared. There were two men in the car, the driver and his companion in the rear. He may well have assisted Buckley's assailant to get him and the burn bag into the back of the car. With Buckley half-sprawled on the floor and the other two men squatting on top, the Renault roared out of the garage, its rear door flapping open dangerously.

The woman who had exchanged pleasantries with the CIA station chief moments before was standing at a bus stop near the garage exit. She glimpsed what had happened and started to scream for help.

If he heard her shrieks, they were almost certainly the last entreaties William Buckley would have heard on his behalf.

2

The Madness Network

Buckley's apartment block was now pierced with shell holes so that it looked, if anything, like a towering kitchen grater. The view from the roof was magnificent, offering panoramic vistas of the city, the mountains, and the sea. Understandably it must have been one of which William Buckley would never have tired. It might—who knows?—have lulled him. Even so, the gang had moved swiftly and surely in a ritual of their own: observe, grab, and vanish. Only the size of their catch might have given them a nervous feeling.

In reconstructing what had happened to the station chief, the CIA investigating team concluded that the white Renault, with maximum acceleration, roared through the Moslem quarter, and was waved past several checkpoints before reaching the well-prepared safe house. Buckley was probably dragged out of the rear, his brain still allowing him no time to remember events or begin to react for his own safety. That he was alive and relatively uninjured was a tribute to the skill and detailed planning of his kidnappers.

Waiting at the entrance to the house were the men who, because they had no known identity, were called by the Israelis the *keepers*. With them was Dr. al-Abub.

To perform his duties, Dr. Aziz al-Abub had received special training in the techniques of mind control. A growing number of his colleagues nowadays worked in Soviet psychiatric hospitals where Jewish refuseniks and political dissidents of all persuasions are detained; in the multiplying prisons of Afghanistan, Ethiopia, Iran, and Syria; in specially built centers from Albania to Angola. There were also physicians trained by right-wing regimes for similar work throughout Latin America and Asia, from the southern tip of Africa to the thirty-eighth parallel, which divides one oppressive Korea from another. In all those places, as well as others, doctors routinely created the same dread in their victims: the knowledge they were beyond the help of family, friends, or lawyer, out of reach of the due process of law and at the mercy of those whose work it is to show no mercy. Dr. al-Abub could draw comfort, should he ever need it, that the work he did was elsewhere state-sponsored and allowed to discreetly flourish under governments who are signatories to international law.

In Beirut there was, anyway, now little law. Once the pride of French colonialization, the city was slipping daily, and visibly, into the Third World. Black marketeering and inflation were rampant. The Lebanese pound had become more worthless than the Weimar Republic scrip. The virtual collapse of living standards had left a powerful and permanent aftereffect on a population that had tried to integrate the civil conflict into its life-style. But finally, over Hamra Street in the west to the Rizak Tower in the east, along the seafront Corniche, among the laneways of Kantari, over every twist and turn hung something to rival the stench of death—that of the defeated living, a sour and pervasive smell that spoke more of hopelessness than any words could.

Dr. al-Abub's presence showed how complete the Hizballah's hold was on Beirut—the real power rested now in the hands of the Shiite Moslems. For them financial wealth and prosperity held little appeal; they were long used to poverty. They were ready, even eager, to see the city, indeed the whole of Lebanon, lurch into an irreversible depression. From its depths they would rise to claim forever the land on behalf of Iran. Dr. al-Abub was there to help make that more possible.

When he walked down this particular street, part battleground, part demolition site, he saw a sandbagged barricade spread across half the road. Any car approaching the emplacement had first to negotiate a number of oil drums filled with rubble, the route between them linked with black streamers, the color of the Hizballah. Beyond the emplacement was a group of youths in kaffiyehs and remnants of khaki fatigues. Their accents revealed they were from the rural south, a land of villages and fanaticism. Now they had made a village in the street; behind the barricade were a brazier, cooking pots, boxes of fruits and vegetables, and bedrolls. The youths lived and slept here and, if need be, would die defending the post. For this they each received the U.S. currency equivalent of $300 a month, a vast salary amid the economic collapse of Lebanon—and far more than the $75 the Israelis paid each member of the South Lebanon Army militia.

Dr. al-Abub, it was widely rumored, received ten times that income, along with an apartment and a car to drive out to the Bekaa Valley where some of the foreign hostages were held. Such status symbols, together with his education and authoritarian manner, further distinguished him in the community. Everybody knew he had the power of life or death over the hostages; all accepted that if he was ordered to, he would exercise it without a moment's hesitation.

To show their own loyalty and challenge the Syrian army order forbidding such displays, the youths had covered a nearby wall with posters. One L of the green Arabic lettering for Hizballah was in the outline of a Kalashnikov rifle. Spaced among the posters were color photographs of dour, bearded faces. They were some of the young martyrs, the truck bombers and snipers, who died. Each wore the same Hizballah symbol stitched to their dull brown combat jackets. In a further act of defiance, the youths flew the Iranian flag, nailed to a pole and bedded in a pile of rubble. Sometimes when they were bored they posed for each other, rifle at the ready, feet planted firmly on the pile, chanting slogans about the glory that came from killing their enemies. Somehow, their very youth made them all the more frightening, and the future for Beirut, and Lebanon, even bleaker. The eldest was no more than fourteen years old.

They nodded at Dr. al-Abub, staring silently at him. Their task was to resist any attempt to rescue the hostages. The boy soldiers knew that on the other side of the Green Line, no one was certain how many had survived incarceration, punctuated by having a pistol cocked to a temple, or undergoing the meticulous procedure of mock execution by firing squad. In the years of strife, hundreds of Lebanese hostages had been kidnapped by various factions and tortured and killed. But among those who still survived were now twenty-four foreigners, some of whom had already spent nearly eight hundred days in captivity. Those were the men Dr. al-Abub visited without fail every morning. His bag contained a variety of Soviet- and American-manufactured drugs capable of reducing the will to resist of the strongest-minded hostage. Nor was there always a need to inject the drugs: a capsule or vial mixed into their food was a simple and effective way.

Drugging was part of a sophisticated campaign whose very visible and harrowing apex was the video and cassette recordings of the hostages regularly released to the world's media. The tapes conveyed an attitude of hopelessness and often sheer fear which had been deliberately induced, and the videos were designed to arouse popular sentiment to force governments to accede to the demands of the hostages' captors. Dr. al-Abub's techniques had left administrations like that of the United States and Britain impotent and enraged; the *force majeure* at his command, his skill as a mind-controller, had shown itself as more than a match for all the diplomatic and military power of the West. The knowledge would not lessen Dr. al-Abub's wish to hide what he did. In that respect he was also no different from his fellow practitioners elsewhere: Wherever it was carried out, medical torture was secretive and performed by doctors who had the expertise to conceal what they did.

The CIA specialists would guess that as Buckley was manhandled out of the car one of the keepers stepped forward holding a sack coated with several layers of black paint. It was thrust over Buckley's head and pulled below his shoulders, pinioning his arms. He was bundled into the house. A trapdoor led down to a cellar, into which he was maneuvered. His wrists were bound and another restraint placed around his neck, pulling taut the sack around his head, until he might have suffocated but for the small opening cut with a knife so that Buckley could breathe through his mouth. The neck halter was tied to a shackle in the wall. If Buckley tried to make any sudden, violent move he would strangle himself.

The specialists suggested that Dr. al-Abub would have pulled a stethoscope from his black bag, opened Buckley's shirt, and listened to his breathing. He then could have produced a syringe and ampoule, inserted the needle in the vial, and drew up the colorless liquid. A keeper probably used his knife to open up a seam in Buckley's coat sleeve. Dr.

al-Abub strapped on a rubber tourniquet, waiting for the
veins to show. Then he had slid in the needle, concentrating
on a slow, even delivery of the liquid. William Buckley was
unconscious in a few moments. As he slumped to the floor,
the halter was loosened. It was a common way to treat a
hostage.

The skills of Dr. al-Abub had largely supplanted more
violent actions. His approach was far more subtle. That was
why he was a respected figure. Without resorting to an ounce
of explosives he had achieved far more, proving that the most
effective violence was that which came from using the contents of his physician's bag.

The justification for his behavior was buried within the new
morality accepted by all physicians engaged in torture. Mikhail
Bakunin, the nineteenth century Russian anarchist, formulated the broad ethic: "Whatever aids the triumph of revolution is ethical; all that hinders it is unethical and criminal."
Today, revolution included the defense of a dictatorship and
allowed, for example, the doctors at the Detention Command
Center in Seoul, Korea, to continue with their regular practice of using stomach pumps to force water through prisoners'
nostrils while they were suspended by their feet from hooks
in the ceiling; by the physicians in Kroonstad Prison, deep in
the South African veldt, who used drugs and electroshocks on
inmates; by the doctors at the Central Revolutionary Interrogation Department in Addis Ababa, Ethiopia, who deliberately burned parts of prisoners' bodies with scalding water or
boiling oil and then injected them with various drugs supplied by the Soviet Union, to see which one healed tissue
more effectively. Or by those physicians registered with the
Colegio Médico de Chile, whose daily task offered a medical
assessment on how to most effectively brutalize prisoners. All
those medical tortures were carried out with the same belief
that no doubt sustained Dr. al-Abub: the transcendent ethics
of the new morality meant people could be ill-treated and, if
need be, destroyed. A proof, at least for him, of the effectiveness of the ethic was that it had forced the enemy to stop its
destruction of West Beirut.

Dr. al-Abub's expert eye identified damage from either
high or low explosives, the difference discernible by the
shattering effect of low—what the stolen U.S. Army training
manual at the terrorist boot camp called *brisance*. Most of the

devastation in the city had been caused by low explosives deflagrating. A perfect example of its cratering effect was the toppling of the American Embassy and then, a few months later, the U.S. Marines headquarters and a French military barracks. Both had been attacked almost simultaneously by young men driving trucks, each packed with one thousand pounds of explosives. Two hundred and forty-one U.S. servicemen and fifty-eight French paratroopers were killed.

The men who planned those attacks, somewhere in this warren of narrow streets and alleys, were the strategists who could study a photograph of a target and decide exactly how much hexagon, a popular explosive in spite of its volatility, must be added to the equally unstable nitroglycerin to produce a required effect. Like the alchemists of old, they worked by experience and instinct, and their language was rich with the words that brought death: oxidizers, desensitizers, plasticizers, and freezing-point depressants. They knew to the exact ounce the quantity of hexagon—which they differentiated, like all explosive experts, as either RDX or PETN—that was needed to level a high-rise, collapse an underground car park, use in a car bomb, or be molded into a booby trap designed to detonate in the face of the unwary. For the Marine HQ and the French barracks they had used Composition-B, a standard mixture of sixty percent RDX, thirty-nine percent TNT, and one percent of wax, used to coat and desensitize the explosive long enough for the teenage drivers to hurtle into the target.

Those people, *his* people, had thought of it as a high point. Surely, after that, wouldn't they achieve victory? The question was a logical outcome of a piece of common knowledge. Borrowing a phrase once used by a leader of the most hated of their enemies, Israel, they told each other: "I fight, therefore I exist."

When victory did not come, their fury surged through the streets like a boiling sea, lifting and cleansing them. But, through his medical training, the doctor never allowed it to take control of him entirely; there was always that little gyroscopic figure, professionalism, which deep inside him managed to remain upright, allowing him never to be swerved by emotions. This attitude had helped to bring victory, if not in clear sight, then that much closer.

There were no rules to the struggle they waged: they said

there could be none against enemies who had, for them, broken all the sacred tenets of their God.

So it was with hostages: Anyone could be taken without consideration of race, sex, or creed. The morality of terrorism must never be prejudiced by definition. That had undoubtedly helped make it possible for Dr. al-Abub to perform his work, to cloak violence with the respect his profession normally attracted. This was also what made him different from all those around him who dealt in more conventional terrorism.

Long ago Dr. al-Abub had embraced the basic premise that this society must be destroyed. Accepting that, the logical conclusion seemed flawless: Any action was permissible in the name of righteous rage. That, above all, was almost certainly what also sustained him and fulfilled his search for identity.

People stepped out of his way. Almost never did he return the traditional greeting—*salaam aleikum*. Such discourtesy would usually draw a rebuke, perhaps even a violent response. But he could be sure no one would raise a hand or voice against him because of who he was and, most important of all to these uncultured and poorly educated people, the skill that allowed him to control the minds and bodies of at least a handful of their enemies. His doctor's black bag was a more potent symbol of approaching victory than the most spectacular act of destruction.

The sight of the tall, slightly stooping physician was a reminder of how far events had moved since that turning point five years earlier, Sunday evening, May 30, 1982, when a handful of men made their way through the crowded streets of the western suburbs to attend a meeting.

Like Dr. al-Abub the people in those streets could remember it now as the last complete week of freedom they had enjoyed. Despite the civil war entering its seventh year, a normal life had then been still possible in Beirut. The better educated, and optimistic, among its population said it was written in the ancient books of Islam that the city, having survived so much, would be safe.

While those around him now respectfully stood aside for Dr. al-Abub, almost certainly few would have done so on that Sunday. Then he had been a newcomer, only two months among them and, for all his sympathy for their aims, still an outsider. Instead, they had reserved their salutations for each of the clerics walking purposefully through the covered bazaars and across the small open spaces that served as playgrounds and parks.

They had all timed their journeys to arrive at the same time at an apartment situated almost in the center of West Beirut. It was in the Fakhani district, where Arab music was played through loudspeakers attached to the lampposts and the last vestige of Western influence had been removed at the command of the most militant of all the Shiite clerics who had sent for them. One by one he greeted them, his voice low, in the manner of those who knew each other well. They were all dressed in identical robes and tarbooshes; the tassels on their garments signified they were graduates from one of the most prestigious of Islamic universities, the campus in the holy city of Najaf in Iraq.

There, in an atmosphere of pious fastidiousness, they had studied sacred law, theology, and philosophy, following a pedagogical curriculum that had not changed for a thousand years. Central to it was that, following the death of the Prophet Muhammad in the year the Christian calender calls A.D. 632, a schism engulfed Islam that was even greater than the Reformation was to produce. Its two great forces, the Sunnis and the Shiites, became irrevocably divided. The Shiites insisted that the leadership of Islam should have remained in the Prophet's family and, upon his death, they had pledged their support to Muhammad's cousin, Ali, who became Caliph or successor to the Prophet. Ali was murdered in A.D. 661. But, in the Shiite theology, Ali and his descendants were Imams—divinely guided leaders and mediators between God and man, Christ-like figures on earth. There were twelve Imams before the last disappeared in A.D. 940. It is a fundamental Shiite belief that he is hiding in one of the vast Arabian deserts, awaiting the right moment to reemerge and establish a purified Islamic government of justice. In some ways there are similarities with the Christian belief in the Second Coming, but with one significant exception: the Imam, on his return, would launch a *jihad*, more violent than any before fought over the centuries by his Shiite disciples. This inherent belief in the cleansing power of violence is what separates the Shiites from the Sunnis, who have grown and prospered and account for more than eighty percent of the world's 800 million Moslems. The Shiite movement, some

160 million, has remained dominant only in Iran, Iraq, and Bahrain. There they maintain the essentials of their faith—self-flagellation, atonement, and martyrdom—while waiting for the Imam to reappear.

At Najaf in the early 1960s, a new threat was perceived to fulfilling this miracle. There was intellectual ferment as the teachers warned that Western influence—its cinema, theater, television, fashion, and above all its moral code—had become an unbearable threat to Islamic Shiite values and religious autonomy. It was hampering the return of the Holy One.

The clearest and most dire voice raised in warning was that of Ayatollah Ruhollah Khomeini; he had arrived in Najaf in 1965 after being expelled from Iran for plotting against the Shah's foreign and domestic policies. During the thirteen years he spent in Najaf, Khomeini delivered the most important lectures ever given to its students. Each several hours long and enveloped in allegories and parables, they contained at their core a bold and visionary claim: True Islamic government was only possible if the faith's clerics held the exclusive right to political rule.

Those who gathered in the apartment were indoctrinated with that ideal. Among their hopes was that the Imam would mark the one thousand and fiftieth year of his disappearance by returning to live among them. That would mean that by 1986 they must have created a suitable environment for him to emerge. By such calculations were their expectations kept alive. Their readiness to further these expectations was due not only to personal and ideological ties forged at Najaf, but also to the man who had summoned them to the uncared-for apartment, which served as his home and political office.

Sheykh Mohammed Husayn Fadlallah was unconcerned about the acquisition of personal comforts; he regarded them as yet another Western evil that diluted the stark purity of Islam. The room where he had assembled his fellow clerics contained a number of hard-backed chairs set against olive-green walls, bare except for a portrait of an unsmiling Ayatollah Khomeini, who had imbued Fadlallah with an unquenchable fire to promote revolution.

For that Sunday meeting, Fadlallah had prepared his ground with the same thoroughness he showed as a student. Each man's record—his sermons, standing in the community, his total fidelity to the daily observance of his faith, and much else—had been carefully studied before an invitation was extended. Fadlallah was close to his forty-seventh birthday, while the others were in their late twenties or early thirties. His superiority was reinforced by a copy of a book, closed, on top of the only other piece of furniture in the room, a circular beaten-brass table on low legs. Every one of those around him could quote verbatim lengthy passages from *Islam and the Logic of Force*. Its arguments for armed struggle and confrontation rather than submission regularly formed the basis for the Friday evening preaching not only in the mosques of West Beirut but in thousands of others throughout the Middle East. The book's author was Fadlallah. He had written it in 1976, the second year of Lebanon's civil war. It became a best-seller in the Moslem community, surpassed only by the sale of copies of the Koran. Fadlallah's work was bought even by illiterates, who stared uncomprehendingly at the text while it was read to them by a cleric.

Fadlallah's intellectual supremacy compensated for a lack of physical charisma. He was barely five-feet-six, and even a voluminous robe could not completely disguise a potbelly. His beard was ill-kempt and streaked with white; his lips thick and his teeth and fingers stained with tobacco from the Gauloises he chain-smoked through a long, slim holder, the only sign of affectation he permitted himself. His eyes protruded beneath an unusually wide expanse of forehead, with the hairline visible under the tarboosh. He bore a striking resemblance to Grumpy, one of the Seven Dwarfs.

His voice was hoarse and coarse, the authentic accent of the street-corner demagogue.

The clerics Fadlallah had chosen were not only bound to him, and each other, by the shared formative experience of Najaf; they were also proven religious leaders in their local communities.

Also present was Dr. Aziz al-Abub. He was then a few weeks short of his thirty-first birthday, but his face and bearing were of an older man: a stoop had developed and his hair had started to thin; there was little about him to show he had once been a leader of the Pasadaran, the revolutionary guards, in the medical school at Tehran University. His suit had been purchased in Moscow after he qualified and went to the Soviet capital for postgraduate studies at the Patrice Lumumba Friendship University. Founded in 1960 by Nikita Khrushchev, nominally to train intelligentsia cadre for the nations of Asia, Latin America, and Africa, the university's real mission was to educate students from underdeveloped countries so that they could return to their homelands and promote pro-Soviet activities. Its faculty included a number of senior KGB officers and agents. What they had taught Dr. al-Abub helped explain his presence at that meeting. He had come to Lebanon versed in the latest Soviet pharmacological techniques for keeping a person passive over a lengthy period and reducing the will to resist.

What was decided at the meeting was unequivocal. All those present left the apartment pledged to recruit every Moslem they could to create a new Lebanon, to make the country an Islamic polity and society that would mirror Iran. They willingly accepted that to do this required the Hizballah to declare total war on all those who opposed that aim.

So, indeed, it began.

Within weeks Hizballah had fired the imagination of the deprived and fueled a dormant belief that only Islamic law and justice was pure: all else was evil and must be destroyed before it devoured Islam. Inside a year there were tens of thousands of followers, each spreading the word with missionary zeal throughout West Beirut, into the fertile Bekaa Valley and the hinterland, and out to the stark Shiite villages in the rural south of the country. There the message was carried to the very border with Israel: the hour of Islamic retribution was at hand.

First Hizballah propagandized through rallies and speeches: then, from funds provided by Iran, it founded its newspaper and a radio station. Later came training bases to create a well-armed militia. Its fighters challenged and increasingly overcame other factions: the defeated were absorbed into the ranks of Hizballah. Despite a different political theory, an alliance was informally entered into with the PLO.

With the weeks in West Beirut passing in darkening pessimism under a relentless siege by Israel's forces, who cut off even the staples of life, bread and water, the will to resist grew.

The high priests of the Hizballah remained unsatisfied. They knew they must create a further visible proof that deliverance was at hand, that the old order of the West which had held sway in Lebanon was about to be destroyed before the eyes of the faithful. A direct result of that decision was the presence of Dr. al-Abub and his briefcase filled with syringes and drugs walking through a warren of streets, souks, and alleys in West Beirut.

Back in America, the CIA investigating team was certain that one of the men unclipped the briefcase from Buckley's wrist and searched his suit pockets for the key. Just as the burn bag locked counterclockwise, so could it be opened.

Nowadays Beirut's kidnappers had refined their methods, knowing exactly when to use a girl, or for that matter a boy, as bait, and how to use backup cars to block pursuit. They knew now that it was harder to grab someone from a Mercedes, because it had central door-locking; easiest of all was simply to walk up on either side of a target and then, with the getaway car at the curb, literally grab a victim by the elbows and hurl him into the backseat. Sometimes they injected a fast-acting tranquilizer, jabbing the needle through clothes into a buttock or upper arm. Such things had become routine.

Dr. al-Abub could be certain there were any number of people in the Moslem quarter and beyond who still agreed with the sheer speed of the Buckley operation. Even while the woman's screams turned the first heads, the car had hurtled down a side street, heading east toward the Fakhani district. While it was a common belief that the snatch team had long disbanded—a persistent rumor held that its members had died a few weeks later in an Israeli air strike—the memory of what they achieved was enshrined in West Beirut, and was a continuous cause of cold rage elsewhere.

In the cobweb of streets where Dr. al-Abub did his work, the details told were not so much how a hated American fell victim to his own laxity, but rather glorified the daring of his captors. Men continued to remind each other over their cups of *chai* that it was never easy to get close to any foreigner. The foreigners were always doing the unexpected, such as changing their routes to work, and the times they came and went from home or office. Those random movements must have made "the American"—in West Beirut William Buckley was rarely spoken of in any other way—very hard to catch. What the team had done was a matter of great community pride, the more so because by now everybody knew exactly whom they had captured.

No one, least of all Dr. al-Abub, could possibly have known all the details of the effects, both immediate and less immediate, that the kidnapping had. But from the beginning the importance attached to the recovery of the American was clear.

In spite of all that had happened in the intervening three years, no one in West Beirut would easily forget how the foreigners tried to penetrate into every nook and cranny of their homes and places of work. They had offered money, huge sums, American dollars or any currency of choice, for information, the merest of clues. Sheykh Fadlallah and the other clerics let it be known that anyone taking a cent of the foreign money would be betraying the struggle and would be severely punished. Everyone still remembered how, after the American had been wafted from view and the warning promulgated at the end of Friday evening worship, the very next day a couple of youths—lads, really, one eleven, the other barely twelve—had come back through Museum Crossing, the main checkpoint in the Green Line. They had walked untroubled past the Christian militia. But at the Hizballah checkpoint they were stopped and searched. Each boy had a new Walkman cassette player, the very latest, fitted with Dolby and automatic reverse. In the younger boy's pocket was discovered a few Lebanese pounds. After a severe beating the children, having admitted everything, led their guards to the place where they had buried the rest of the money, under a pile of rubble near the Hippodrome, the racecourse where horses no longer ran because the track was littered with shrapnel splinters. They repeated their confession to a more senior Hizballah man. There was little enough to admit: a chance encounter with an Arab from the Christian sector, who had asked some questions about the car people had seen roaring through the streets of Fakhani. The boys had felt no wrong in accepting the money he had offered for their information. They may have still been protesting their innocence when successive bullets in the head silenced them. News of the executions had quickly circulated, so that within an hour there was not a person in the entire sector who was unaware of what, and why, this had happened. There had been no further need to remind anyone of the penalty for such treason.

The foreigners had even joined forces. The Americans had actually gone so far as to enlist the support of the Russians, who drove from their embassy along the much-bombed Corniche Mezraa to a meeting at the Hotel Alexandra in East Beirut. Afterward the Soviets put the word out among their contacts in the PLO that they were interested in the American; but the silence had been impenetrable. In all the places where it was still possible for foreigners to listen to the heartbeat of the Moslem community, not a whisper was detected.

Dr. al-Abub now knew that this had not deterred the enemy, *his* enemy. Just as they produced the most effective weapons—the American cluster bombs that turned a Beirut street or an entire Shiite village into bloody pulp; the Zionist booby traps in the shape of children's toys that left so many of a growing generation half-blinded, legless, or armless; the heat-seeking rockets that homed onto the most securely hidden sniper in a pile of rubble—so it was they who had the most effective intelligence. The enemy had the money—enough to rebuild this ruined city—to spend on learning the truth. It had continued to use it to probe, subvert, exploit a human weakness. Dr. al-Abub would accept that in every cause there was always someone—and just one was sometimes enough—who, for a reward, would talk.

It was common knowledge now, for instance, that a few months after the kidnapping of Buckley, a trusted West Beiruti, a man who had lived among them for years, who had run arms for the PLO and was ready to do the same for the Hizballah—that man, a Shiite Moslem, had, despite Sheykh Fadlallah's warning and the example of the boys, almost certainly betrayed the revolution. He had not returned from a mission in Europe and Greece, had gone to forge further links with groups there. His last appointments had been in Cyprus. When he failed to arrive on the short flight from Larnaca, checks had been made. He *had* kept his final meeting and had been driven to the airport. There, somewhere between passing through immigration and boarding the plane, he vanished. The most careful inquiries failed to reveal his whereabouts. It was manifestly clear that only the most powerful intelligence services—the ones that Sheykh Fadlallah constantly warned the faithful to be aware of—had the resources to spirit him away. In Cyprus that meant the Americans and British. No one in these streets now doubted that in their hands the traitor had talked.

That, of course, explained so many things: the arrogance of the enemy; the way it still tried to make deals highly favorable to itself; the manner in which it had so often identified something the Hizballah believed was secret. The enemy knew. It could only have done so with prior knowledge.

At times the process of sifting possibility from probability demanded the delicacy of hostage negotiating. Among the specialists goodwill was matched equally with disagreement over such basics as to who had kidnapped William Buckley. The CIA and SDECE were sure it was the PLO, a typical Yasir Arafat response, violent and vindictive, to his latest military humiliation at the hands of the Israelis.

The Italian DIGOS, using its considerable network of informers among Rome's Middle Eastern community, were the first to pinpoint the snatch squad. On Tuesday, March 20, 1984, a teletype was sent from Rome police headquarters to Interpol in Paris. The agency immediately relayed confirmation to all member forces that the kidnappers were Hizballah. In Washington an FBI operative keyed the information on to Langley.

The CIA team flown in from Washington, working out of the embassy annex in East Beirut, had used the spare key to Buckley's penthouse kept by Ambassador Reginald Bartholomew. The agents made a detailed inventory of the apartment, reconstructing Buckley's last hours, before allowing his personal possessions to be boxed for shipment to the United States. A statement was taken from the woman eyewitness, more for form than for any real hope of a lead. But once the Italians pinpointed the kidnappers, the CIA, working through Mossad, was quickly satisfied that the Hizballah had dared not risk taking Buckley out of the encircled city. He remained somewhere in the sprawl of West Beirut, between what remained of the heavily shelled port in the north and the Hotel Sands to the south, near the international airport. There were simply not enough Green Berets in the world to rescue Buckley from probably the most hostile conglomeration on earth.

Just as many people in West Beirut remembered exactly where they were and what they were doing when the white Renault roared past or news of the mission reached them as it spread like a flashfire to the remotest parts of the sector, so Dr. al-Abub could have vouchsafed that the initial excitement had also been followed by mounting tension. The Americans were bound to react, if only to demonstrate to the world that no one trifled with the Great Satan—since Sheykh Fadlallah had used the description, President Reagan had been known by no other name in West Beirut. Lookouts were posted at the port to warn of the approach of the Great Satan's armada, the Sixth Fleet, a precursor to Marines wading ashore. The bomb makers worked feverishly preparing stockpiles of Beirut Hand Grenades and booby traps. Boys were placed on the roofs to watch for approaching aircraft. Everyone waited. Nothing happened. It remained one of the most talked-about mysteries in the Moslem quarter that there was no military response. At the time, the idea took root that perhaps the Great Satan was planning some other move. No one could imagine, though, what that could be. But at least they were thankful he had not unleashed his awesome military power. The intense speculation as to what could be happening in Washington continued.

In Langley, men who should have known better lent their names to foolish and dangerous suggestions. Deputy Director of Operations Clair Elroy George, who was running the investigation and who had been station chief in Beirut in 1975 when two American hostages were snatched and later released unharmed, chaired a meeting at which it was suggested that a short-acting nerve gas, one with no known permanent effects, should be sprayed across the entire Moslem quarter, momentarily paralyzing everyone on the ground while rescue squads dropped into the area. One of those present would remember how the idea died under the remorseless reminder by George that for a start, the United States had just delivered a strong protest to Iraq about the use of chemical warfare in the Gulf War, and in any event, there would be no way of containing the gas within the sector. There was also the matter of the Soviet Embassy sited in West Beirut. George had witheringly asked what Moscow's response might be to having its diplomats gassed—even momentarily.

CIA director William Casey faced an unprecedented crisis. He had lost two heads of station in Lebanon—something that had not happened anywhere else, not even during the worst days of the Cold War. To cap it all, a member of the investigating team he had sent to Beirut had taken leave of his senses. The Lebanese security police had handed over several Hizballah suspects. The team member had ordered them driven to a safe house in East Beirut. There he had used a portable electroshock machine—borrowed from the American University Hospital in the city—and, in the presence of a medical technician, proceeded to electroshock the suspects. Several had received multiple shocks through the night. One man had died. Others had suffered severe physical damage. When a horrified embassy official informed the State Department of what had happened, DDO George sent an encoded message to the embassy ordering the immediate return of the CIA operative. He had been fired as soon as he returned to Langley.

It was not, Casey said to George, that he was squeamish about such methods; it was that they clearly were not appropriate for the situation. What was needed, he told his deputy, John N. McMahon, was old-fashioned human resource intelligence. He ordered McMahon to fly to Tel Aviv. Peter Mandy, senior Israeli intelligence man, received the deputy director in his office in a drab high-rise in an eastern suburb of the city with a magnificent view of the distant hills of Judaea. McMahon pleaded forcefully that just this once, Mossad should put the recent past behind them. There was a matter of professional pride here; heads of station just could not get killed or kidnapped and the matter be allowed to rest. At the end of the day Mandy pledged the involvement of Branch-40, the most secret of all Israel's intelligence services. But, added the Mossad man, it would still take time. And no promises —Okay?

McMahon had forced a smile: Okay.

In the meantime, suggested Mandy, there was some immediate assistance at hand.

It was then that the specialists—an amalgam of psychiatry and other disciplines—were called upon.

Starting with virtually no hard information about the Hizballah other than that it was Islamic and demonstrably extremist, the scientists followed a standard procedure based upon the old and proven principal of studying the situation from the subject's viewpoint. From that they learned there was no justification on moral or legal grounds in Islam for kidnapping. But they also accepted that probably much of the motivation of the Hizballah, like the Koran, could not be translated into a totally accepted Western framework, as could, for example, the driving forces behind Europe's terrorist organization, or even the PLO.

The CIA turned to those closest to grasping the inimitable words of the Hizballah clerics, the very sounds of which moved men to tears, ecstasy, and then rage and violence. They sought the help of the analysts at the Dayan Center and the Jaffee Center for Strategic Studies. Both institutes were sited within the campus of Tel Aviv's university, but were far removed from conventional academic studies.

Here, men who had spent years combatting terrorism in the field used their accumulated experience to study terrorist logic and methodology. They had compared, for instance, the rhetoric of the IRA with that of Italian terrorist groups, seeking common roots. They searched to find why some were more attracted to left- rather than right-wing groups, or the reverse: was it simply a class distinction, or a rebellion against all class—or something else? They still remained uncertain of this, one of the many imponderables of their work. They continually probed the critical question of whether certain individuals became terrorists primarily in order to have logistical support for committing acts of violence. They tried to assess the ego-boosting effects on a terrorist who found his or her name on MOST WANTED posters. They attempted to estimate the effect upon followers of terrorist leaders who had become media personalities, like Yasir Arafat and Abu Nidal. They read transcripts of every terrorist trial, seeking clues the court might have missed, and studied the often fragmentary but always fascinating tidbits, supplied by undercover agents and brought by men of the Mossad, who plodded through the shabby corridors of both centers, past the locked doors with no outside handles and behind which worked some of the sharpest minds in today's intelligence world. On their computers were stored data about Middle East terrorists in particular that was unrivaled: their given names, aliases, birthmarks, fingerprints, or tiny surgical scars left by even the most skilled of plastic surgeons. Also recorded were a terrorist's professional hallmark: any distinctive approach to committing acts of barbarism, such as shooting a victim on one particular side of the head or priming a bomb in a certain way.

The researchers endlessly updated every facet of terrorist personality, discovering, among so much else, that seventy-nine percent of those in custody admitted to severe conflict

with their parents. And that one in three of European terrorists had been convicted in juvenile court before joining a
group; until then their lives had generally shown a failure,
both emotionally and vocationally, to integrate into society,
and terrorism seemed the only appealing opening left. Such
information made it possible for the scientists in Tel Aviv to
make sense of the many millions of disparate facts available
through their computer terminals about each living terrorist:
the teenagers of Londonderry who hurled petrol bombs; the
men of the Red Army Faction in West Germany who dyna-
mited cars of businessmen working for the Americans; the
Italian groups who booby-trapped a restaurant or home of a
political figure they opposed; the terrorists of Central and
South America; those of Asia; and those of all those countries
where terrorism exists, either as a state-sponsored evil or as
anti-state.

Both the Dayan Center and its companion behavioral laboratory were in the forefront of continuously reevaluating the
prospect of the ultimate act of terrorism—a group threatening
to detonate a nuclear weapon. At both centers men of tight
reasoning and an impressive grasp of the mentality of terrorists watched with mounting unease the growing criminal activity in the nuclear arena. Since 1970 there had been sixty
threats made against American cities in which the callers
claimed to possess nuclear materials—and the incidents were
seen to be sufficiently serious to have involved all the nation's
law enforcement agencies in operations never yet made public.

The claims in the end proved to be hoaxes. But each threat
showed that terrorists were moving down the nuclear path.
Precisely how close they had come was still one of the many
guarded secrets on the Tel Aviv computers; those with access
merely confined themselves to saying that the further away
the last incident, the closer they were to the next.

The computers also held details of how between 1966 and
1977, there were ten terrorist incidents against European
nuclear installations. Members of the Red Army Faction were
arrested in 1986 with maps and drawings of West Germany's
nuclear sites and security patrol routes. That year the U.S.
Nuclear Control Institute admitted there were 9,600 pounds
of enriched uranium and plutonium now unaccounted for in
the United States—enough to create more than two hundred
Hiroshima-type explosions. Also stored on the Tel Aviv com-

puters were the details, never to be made public, of how the Mossad monitored Qaddafi's search for a nuclear weapon, beginning with his attempt to buy one from China in 1970; his pouring of 100 million British pounds into Pakistan's nuclear energy program, hoping to benefit; and how the CIA, nudged by Israel, persuaded President Zia, when he came to power in 1977, to cut Qaddafi out of the spoils. Much of the work at both the Dayan and Jaffee institutes was top secret, for the eyes of Israel's spymasters only.

The pooled wisdom of, among others, Arial Merari, director of terrorist studies at the Jaffee Center for Strategic Studies, a psychologist who had made a close study of the Shiite mentality, and the research of Martin Kramer, the Dayan Center's resident expert on the Hizballah, was, within hours on the way to Langley.

The Jaffee data included a comprehensive review of how the Shiites fit into the long and colorful chronology of the Moslem faith. Kramer's findings concentrated on the Hizballah, showing how the organization was formed, why it believed it alone was now the chosen redeemer of Lebanon, and how this pervasive sense of a divinely sanctioned mission was continually evoked by the Hizballah clerics to fire the fury of the mob. Kramer predicted that the kidnapping of Buckley would be followed by others, but that each case would create a growing unease in the Hizballah hierarchy until there was a clear-cut statement from Sheykh Fadlallah, the movement's supreme conscience, on the morality of kidnapping. But, that said, cautioned Kramer, it should also be remembered that Sheykh Fadlallah had responded to his initial doubts about suicide bombing missions by creating a moral logic that justified the attacks. Therefore, it would be wrong to draw consolation from there having been no *fatwa* forbidding hostage-taking.

Accompanying that opinion was still more background, pieced together by Mossad's own experts. This included the service's evaluation of the virtual impossibility of mounting a rescue mission. It was based on the very latest ground intelligence from Beirut, some of it only days old. Along with that very secret material went a photostat of the *mushaf*, the first known lithograph copy of the Koran, written in Turkey in 1246; attached to the text was a commentary by a Mossad Arabist on the verses the Shiite movement has taken as revealed truth. The title of each tract could have been of no comfort to Casey and his staff. As the director said, there was something indeed messianic about passages called: THE EMISSARIES, THE TIDINGS, THE OVERTHROWING, and THE CLEANSING.

While the Tel Aviv material was en route, aboard an El Al jet, couriered as part of a diplomatic pouch to the Israeli Embassy in Washington, analysts at Langley were trying to assess how Buckley would react to captivity. Working with the findings of Dr. Martin Symonds, a psychiatrist consultant to the New York Police Department and recognized as probably having the widest experience within North America on how kidnap victims respond during their ordeal, the Agency specialists believed that Buckley's reactions would follow an almost immutable pattern, characterized by four distinctive steps. It would make no real difference in the end that he was a trained intelligence officer trained in ways to resist interrogation. Because he would be in close and prolonged contact with his kidnappers, Buckley's psychological responses would be little different from any other kidnap victim; there is no actual way to prepare a person to cope with the stress of being taken hostage—any more than a woman can be preconditioned to endure rape. While the duration and intensity of each stage would depend to some extent on Buckley's willpower, they would follow the predestined pattern which Dr. Symonds had discerned in almost a hundred victims.

Even while Buckley was reeling under the blow from the briefcase, he would have experienced a feeling of disbelief, an instinctive denial that what was happening was actually occurring to *him*. That feeling may have remained until his arrival at the hiding place his captors had prepared. At that point the second phase would have taken over, and that desperate denial—the only immediate psychological defense open to him—was probably overwhelmed by a sudden and shattering reality. *It was happening to him.* At that point Buckley's reactions could have included frozen fright, clinging to his captors and, most disturbing of all for his superiors, compulsively needing to talk to his kidnappers, if only to try and convince them he should be freed. It was then that the head of station could unwittingly have done the most damage: in his stressful situation he might have made serious admissions about his work. At that stage, Dr. Symonds's findings

suggested, kidnappers invariably uncovered valuable information about a hostage's background.

For properly trained terrorists, that period was also of
crucial importance for sowing the first seeds of indoctrination—
preparing a victim to collaborate. At first Buckley's kidnappers would alternately abuse or ignore him. Then gradually
they would begin to feed back information they had earlier
gleaned from his confused speech, creating in his already
strained mind a feeling that his captors were all-knowing and
therefore all-powerful, that to resist them would be pointless.

The Agency specialists knew how effectively the technique
had been used on American prisoners captured in the Korean
War, and how the methods had been refined at, among other
places, Patrice Lumumba Friendship University. A computer
search began at Langley to discover who, if anyone, was
listed as having been trained in any of these Communist
centers and was now known to be in Lebanon. It was a long
shot, and no one really expected it to turn up a name.

No one could be certain when the next stage of Buckley's
ordeal would have set in. Days could have passed, though in
Dr. Symonds's view it would unlikely have stretched into
weeks. But then it would have surfaced, that invisible seep-
age traveling through the deepest recesses of Buckley's brain,
a destructive unleashing of a chemical through some still
barely understood electrolytic imbalance. This imbalance causes
intermittent bouts of apathy and sudden rages, along with
insomnia, when the sleepless hours are filled with self-
recrimination and an endless and exhausting reexamination of
the traumatic events that brought on the depression. Such a
depression could be seen in bereavement, divorce, sudden
poverty—or being taken hostage.

The psycho-profile of Buckley at that stage of his captivity
showed a man bowed down by despair, suddenly aged, his
face haggard, slowed up physically and mentally, his voice
monotonous, and with every word and movement, like living
itself, a terrible burden. He would feel constantly tired and
any sleep would leave him entirely unrefreshed. He would
become most depressed in the small hours—and then be at
his most vulnerable, when his moral stamina to resist the
slightest pressure would be at its lowest.

That would be the time he would find it hardest to remember that generally those who refused to cooperate were in

less danger of seeing their defense systems swept away; conversely, those who showed the slightest sign of giving in were doomed. It was often at that time, usually between three and five A.M., that a skilled captor would awaken his prisoner to try and bring about total inner conflict and basic fear, so that the captive experienced one of the most primitive and terrifying emotions he could know—the belief that he was powerless to avoid his annihilation as a person. That was the stage when physical and psychological integration broke down and the prisoner seemed to be left with two alternatives: going mad or dying. That would also be—in William Buckley as with anyone else—when self-accusation would be at its most destructive and his lack of hope at its peak; when he would be locked in some terrifying inner struggle to on one hand refuse to cooperate, and on the other accede to the compulsion to do so. It could be the time when Buckley's thinking would be delusional, when he might well imagine he had caused huge damage to those he loved—and his employers. He may have wanted to weep, but could not do so; in any event, crying would not purge his emotions. Then once more that inner rage would take over.

William Buckley, like the prisoner in Kafka's *The Trial*, like the victims Dr. Symonds had examined, would at that stage feel stupid both for allowing himself to be snatched and for behaving the way he had so far—that initial disbelief, followed by paralyzing fear and, probably most upsetting of all to Buckley, those periods of compulsive talking. Even while those struggles raged within him, he would almost certainly wonder—as his superiors themselves pondered—what had he given away, whom had he compromised, who was at risk because of his stupidity.

Buckley's mental agony could be accompanied by further physical symptoms: a decrease in sexual desire, loss of appetite, and constipation, followed by perhaps a growing feeling that the only solution for him would be suicide, that only by taking his own life could he pay for all the harm he had done to others. No one could say how long this period would last. Any estimate would depend on how the Agency psychiatrists had rated Buckley's previous personality patterns and reactions during his annual medical checkup. A sign of hope was that he had never been a person excessively dependent on others. That should, in theory, make him less prone to develop some of the phobic responses common to this phase of kidnapping.

Then, just as suddenly as the depression had come, it would leave him. Buckley could be filled with a wondrous feeling, convinced he was strong enough to fight off any further victimization. Then would come another shattering self-discovery; in the light of this newfound clarity he would see that not only was resistance manifestly impossible, but so was escape. His captors had blocked all possible potential for freedom. That would be the point when he might take a new look at cooperating.

The Langley team began to make their first cautious predictions. If Buckley's captors were sufficiently clever, they would notice and capitalize on his latest psychological shift. They would recognize that Buckley's mood changes were part of a continual carving out and refilling of that inner void created by his kidnapping. Under their carefully instilled guidance, they could channel what was fundamentally his guilt away from himself, so that he would come to believe that his mistake was not so much what he had done—failing to avoid the kidnapping—but what he had been: a hated Western Imperialist.

The team expected that this condition, known as *logical dishonesty*, would manifest itself on video, in which they confidently expected to see a contrite Buckley revealed to the world's media. They would not be unduly shocked if Buckley would appear to condemn his colleagues and government. It had happened before.

No video came. No one really continued to believe William Buckley would soon be freed.

When the Tel Aviv material had been perused, senior CIA officers understood that one of the many differences between the Hizballah and other organizations was that it did not automatically claim immediate responsibility for its actions. Other groups needed such international recognition to enhance their reputations, to make them seem more terrifying in the eyes of their targets. Public gratification had no place with the Hizballah. Another important difference was that within the Hizballah morality was proclaimed by the clerics; they provided their cadres with a sacred mantle. Where other groups often justified their actions as attacking a colonialist morality, the Hizballah was not interested in such political semantics. The question was not where to draw the line between what was a legitimate target and what was not; there was no line to be drawn. In its creed there were no innocent victims.

Once more the intelligence officers bowed to the knowledge of their medical colleagues. They accepted that Buckley would next display, in that progression Dr. Symonds had indicated, a separation of his motor and cognitive functions. His behavior may then, on the surface, have appeared still calm; he could even have begun to be friendly with his captors. But that could have been no more than a masquerade to conceal the continuation of his inner destruction, while at the same time he would focus all hopes for survival on the terrorists. They would have exploited that feeling.

On Monday morning, May 7, 1984, fifty-two days after the kidnapping, the U.S. Embassy in Athens received a packet posted in the city and addressed to the ambassador. It was routinely passed through the bomb scanner in the mail room. When everyone was satisfied the package contained only a video, the wrapping, with its boldly printed name and address, was carefully undone and placed to one side. The video itself bore no identity mark as to the contents. But the VHS tape was a cheap, common German make. What one of the staff saw after he began running the cassette made him stop the film and summon more senior diplomats. When they had watched for a few minutes, the ambassador was sent for, together with the Athens head of station. They reviewed the tape's entire two hours. The CIA officer called Casey.

Next morning a junior embassy official drove to the Athens airport and used his diplomatic passport to avoid even the lackadaisical Greek security checks before boarding an Olympic Airways flight and traveling business class to Rome. From there he took a Pan Am jet to Washington. He was met on the tarmac by a car with a government registration, its driver having clearance to bypass immigration and customs and taking his passenger out through a gate in the airside perimeter and onto the parkway. After a short drive a big green sign above the road proclaimed: FIRST RIGHT. CENTRAL INTELLIGENCE AGENCY.

The tape and wrapping were taken at once to the office of the director. Waiting with Casey were McMahon and George.

A technician took the wrapping away for laboratory analysis. The three senior Agency men sat down to view the tape.

The video showed William Buckley undergoing torture. The absence of sound made it all that more shockingly obscene—that and the way the camera zoomed in on and then away from Buckley's nude and damaged body. He held before his stomach a document marked MOST SECRET. It was proof that the burn bag had failed.

The cassette was handed over to the technicians. They enlarged selected frames in an attempt to establish the background against which Buckley had been filmed. In the end they decided it was rough-plastered stone, suggesting the filming had taken place in a cellar. That was the only clue they would offer as to his whereabouts. The paper was of the kind Mediterranean shopkeepers used to wrap groceries. The handwriting had been carefully copied out, either to disguise the writer's identity, or by someone unfamiliar with English.

The Agency's medical specialists took over. They produced more information, all of it highly disturbing. Buckley showed symptoms of being drugged; his eyes were dull and his lips slack. His gaze was that of a person deprived of daylight for some time; he continually blinked owlishly as if he had great difficulty in adjusting to what appeared to be weak lighting used for filming. The doctors were almost certain that Buckley had been hooded. They noted his wrists bore chafe marks; so did his neck, as if he had been tethered at both points, either with a rope or chains. A careful study of every inch of skin, enhanced section by section, revealed puncture marks, suggesting he had been injected at various points. Suspicions grew. Only a doctor or a person trained in paramedic techniques would know where and how to inject without killing him.

The second video came twenty-three days later. This time it was posted to the U.S. Embassy in Rome. This tape too was brought to Washington. Once more, the wrapping yielded no clue except that a different hand had penned the address and the paper was of Italian manufacture, the sort probably used by one of the boutiques in the city.

The video had been shot against a very similar, if not the same, background as the first. It revealed that Buckley continued to be horrifically treated, and evidence that a physician's hand was involved in his torture was much more discernible. There was sound on this tape. Buckley's voice was slurred and his manner noticeably more egocentric, as if not only the world beyond the camera, but his immediate surroundings held increasingly less interest for him. Clinically speaking, he was assessed as seeming to be in an induced stupor, as if he had received psychotropic drugs.

The Agency pharmacologists found it impossible to decide which drugs had been used. Buckley may have been injected with one of the phenothiazines. Any of a dozen of those powerful agents could have suppressed the physically energizing systems in his body and made him sedated and stupefied.

The pharmacologists called his condition "snowed," and believed it explained why his voice was so fuzzy and he appeared often unable to shape words or focus his blurred eyes. That chemically induced fog had not only affected his speech but also his bodily movements. His hands suddenly shook and his legs beat a wild tattoo on the floor as he mumbled pathetic pleas to be exchanged under a guarantee that the United States would remove all of its influences from Lebanon and would persuade Israel to do the same. The shock was not so much the demand he was relaying but the way he made it, in a voice that the specialists could best describe as zombie-like. They were positive that his condition had come about only through the intervention of a properly qualified physician, able to judge exactly the amount of the drug of choice to inject.

Then, acting on one of those hunches that made him a good counterintelligence officer, Director Casey ordered another search through the Agency's data bank. It took days for the computers to locate the photograph of Dr. al-Abub and the cross reference to the Hizballah. It was a good example of harnessing technology to draw fact out of darkness.

Copies of the transcript of Buckley's words were sent to the White House and State Department. With them went a lengthy position paper written by an Agency analyst, Graham Fuller. The thrust of his argument was that while there should be no full-scale U.S. or Israeli withdrawal from Lebanon, it might be possible to obtain Buckley's release by using Iran as a broker—in return for secretly providing the regime with arms to wage war against Iraq. Fuller's thesis was that, with the Soviet Union making inroads into Iran, it was time for the United States to relax Operation Staunch—the code name for the embargo President Reagan had encouraged his European allies to reluctantly enforce against Iran. A deal on this level could also be a positive way of encouraging those elements of Tehran's ruling theocracy deemed by Fuller to be moderate, an important consideration for the day when the Ayatollah Khomeini would die and the United States would once more be able to try and regain a footing in the region.

Upon reading the transcript and position paper, Secretary of State George Schultz summoned the Israeli ambassador to discuss the situation. The diplomat asked for time to consult with Tel Aviv. Within hours he was back, this time in the Oval Office, informing the president and the secretary that Israel would not object to the United States opening a dialogue with Iran, even if that included equipping them with the latest weapons. According to Casey, who had been asked to join the meeting, the ambassador said he and his superiors well understood the underlying motive—Buckley's safe return. Israel would always make a similar effort to secure the return of one of its men. No one mentioned the fact that Israel was also anxious to see its Iranian and Iraqi enemies continue to bleed each other white on the Gulf battlefield— that, with Iran's military power in decline, this plan could redress the balance, allowing more of the enemy to be killed. Thus were planted the seeds of what was to become known as the greatest Washington scandal since Watergate—the shenanigans of Irangate.

Among others who worked in the White House, news reached Lieutenant Colonel Oliver North of what had happened to Buckley. North was a junior member of the NSC, answerable to the president's National Security Advisor, Robert C. McFarlane, or his deputy, Vice-Admiral John Poindexter. In his Marines uniform, North cut a dashing figure in the corridors of the White House and elsewhere in Washington. He spoke well and forcefully about how the president was making America great again after all the years of what North called "Carter-fuck." His first response to the kidnapping was that "we should send in a snatch team and I'd be more than proud to lead it." It drew a smiling response. Everyone knew the lieutenant colonel was gung-ho. No one queried his courage; they only doubted his ability to reason matters through.

But then he was way down the ladder and couldn't really do any harm.

Among other instructions, Casey ordered that the videos be studied with an eye toward proving his suspicion that a doctor had played an important part in torturing Buckley.

Physicians with the appropriate Agency security clearance reviewed the films and tried to formulate opinions as to how Buckley would survive. There was a cautious acceptance that with his training and personality type he could endure quite severe treatment. His Agency medical record indicated he possessed enough self-esteem to withstand considerable battering before he collapsed. He also had a natural stoicism. No one could be absolutely certain about how his defense mechanisms would respond to every challenge—those periods of gross anxiety attacks, nightmares, the overwhelming sense of helplessness, followed by bouts of rage and then periods of black resignation. But there was agreement among the psychiatrists that, horrific though it was, what he was undergoing had essentially been tried before and had largely failed. No brave new world of precise human control existed; the mind remained too complex and the techniques too crude.

While drugs could produce an enormous impact on Buckley's mood and behavior, and probably his memory, and were certainly strong enough to have terrorized him, their application might leave no permanent damage—if he was recovered soon enough.

The knowledge gave added impetus to the machinations beginning to take shape elsewhere within the Agency, the Pentagon, the State Department, and ultimately the White House as the groundwork for trading arms for Buckley went ahead. Both Casey and George repeatedly told colleagues that they should see Buckley's release as the Agency's personal crusade; as one Agency man, George Carver, remembers, "It was partly a matter of esprit de corps—we looked after our own."

Others were lending a helping hand. The BND computers came up with Dr. al-Abub's stopover in Frankfurt; the Israelis produced what they hoped was "probably quite useful input based upon our direct experience with the Hizballah mentality"; and the Italian DIGOS and French SDECE offered what Casey described as "helpful bits and pieces."

The information would still not answer the philosophers'

unanswerable doubts. But it satisfied those who spent their days in a world of stratagems that sought to frustrate the truth as well as uncover it. They began to believe they were coming closer to discovering more about what had happened to William Buckley at the hands of Dr. al-Abub.

3

The
Specialists

Beyond the Moslem enclave were psychiatrists, psychologists, behavioral scientists, and psychoanalysts intent on outwitting the doctor. When they had completed their work, intelligence operatives would use their findings to try and kill Dr. al-Abub.

The focus of the specialists' work was Washington, D.C. There, the organizations primarily involved were the CIA and the National Security Agency (NSA). The CIA had assigned the task to its Political Psychological Division, headed by Dr. Jerrold M. Post. The fastidious, soberly dressed psychiatrist also held a senior teaching post at the capital's George Washington University.

The division produced personal and political profiles of world leaders and, increasingly nowadays, of leading terrorists. The assessments were regularly routed through the office of the director of the CIA, William Casey, and passed on to President Ronald Reagan. In the White House he and his wife, Nancy, spent hours studying what Dr. Post and his staff made of the private habits of, among others, Prime Minister Margaret Thatcher and her relationship with her husband. Of more interest and concern to the president and his first lady was Dr. Post's profile of Colonel Muammer Qaddafi. They were convinced the Libyan leader was determined to assassinate the president; their fears had been stoked by Casey. The raw research upon which the director based his views, and which Dr. Post and his team translated into psychological terms, had been gathered by CIA stations abroad and sent to the Agency's deputy director of operations (DDO), Clair Elroy

George, who had spent more than a quarter of a century conducting covert operations. Behind a relaxed wise-cracking manner, George was a hard-bitten intelligence officer, capable of swift and ruthless action, including, if ordered, the assassination of a man like Dr. al-Abub.

Much of the material George received he classified as SCI—Sensitive Compartmented Information—which meant that its distribution within the Agency was severely restricted. SCI material had allowed Dr. Post to continually update the personality profile of Qaddafi. One of George's field agents in Libya had discovered that, in the privacy of his tent, Qaddafi liked to put on Max Factor makeup and Gucci high-heeled shoes and cuddle a teddy bear. Dr. Post had suggested that Qaddafi was "a transvestite-type personality . . . highly unpredictable." After receiving the psychiatrist's assessment, President Reagan had told Casey: "If it helps to make that loony-tune even crazier so that his people will kick him out, Qaddafi can take a peek in Nancy's closet any time."

Increasingly, the division's staff had concentrated upon psyching out Dr. al-Abub.

The division was helped in its work by the sophisticated eavesdropping technology of NSA, itself the most ultrasecret arm of U.S. intelligence. NSA gathered its information through satellites and ground listening posts strategically placed across the world. It used U.S. Navy submarines to tap into undersea telephone cables around Russia and spy planes to reinforce its surveillance of the Soviet Bloc. It had also planted bugs in every diplomatic mission in the Middle East, friendly or otherwise, to increase its knowledge about terrorists. These listening devices had been actually positioned by a CIA team put together by DDO George. The men were specialists in breaking and entering, the best burglars on the Agency's payroll. They had their own Agency designation—Division D—and an open expense account to case a target. On missions in the Middle East they generally posed as businessmen.

All the NSA intercepts were processed by banks of computers working around the clock at its headquarters. In a twenty-four-hour period the computers isolated, transcribed, cross-checked, and identified as many as a hundred million spoken words. Those working on Middle East intercepts separated various Arab accents, the Farsi dialects of Iran, and the French patois of Beirut. NSA satellite cameras regularly filmed the city street by street and, back in Washington, using the most advanced photographic techniques of enhancement, more computers isolated every face and produced an acceptably recognizable photograph. But so far there had been no positive identification of Dr. al-Abub.

However, his tentative psycho-profile along with those of numerous other terrorists were sent to the National Foreign Intelligence Board (NFIB) on which sat the heads of all U.S. military, police, and secret intelligence. They met regularly under the chairmanship of Casey. The profiles were also sent to the National Security Planning Group, the most important of the decision-making bodies in the Reagan administration. It included the president's senior foreign policymakers, Secretary of State George P. Shultz and Secretary of Defense Caspar W. Weinberger. Casey also had a seat on the NSPG. It placed the director firmly at the center of all covert operations conducted by the United States.

Like the president, Casey had become obsessed with men like Dr. al-Abub. The latest snippet of intelligence on their behavior would deepen the furrows around the director's mouth and cause the loose skin to tighten and whiten around his jaws. Then he looked far less the forgetful professor and more the most deadly of spymasters the Agency had had for years. Reading those snippets, Casey would mutter: "The goddamn sonofabitch. We've gotta get those motherfuckers."

Others shared a similar sense of urgency about Dr. al-Abub.

Overlooking the Thames, on one of the floors of Century House, London, the high-rise headquarters of Britain's Secret Intelligence Service (SIS), analysts also worked up their psycho-profiles of the physician. They were supplied with information gleaned by the British Embassy in Beirut, some of it so sensitive that it was hand-carried to London by a Queen's Messenger, the Foreign Office's most secure way of transporting secrets. Among those whose work helped the SIS analysts formulate their conclusions was that of Dr. John Gunn, professor of forensic psychiatry at Maudsley Hospital. His pioneer study into the mentality of those who took hostages was widely recognized. Identifying the still more direct contributions of his colleagues to the SIS was banned under Britain's archaic Official Secrets Act.

In Paris, the physicians of the Service of External Documentation and Counterespionage (SEDC)—known throughout the intelligence community as the "swimming pool" because its complex on the outskirts of the capital is near the Tourelles bathing pool—had also been given the top-priority task of piecing together Dr. al-Abub's background. To help them they had recruited a number of Parisian psychiatrists and psychologists.

Within the sprawl of buildings near Wiesbaden that houses the BND, the West German secret intelligence service, like-minded doctors worked along similar lines. They, too, were assisted by outside medical sources, including Herr Professor Jo Groebel, one of the country's leading experts in the psychology of terrorism.

Further east, in Vienna, Austria's small but highly efficient security service had mobilized virtually the same team of specialists who had put together a psycho-profile of Mehmet Ali Agca, the Turkish-born Moslem fundamentalist who had tried to assassinate Pope John Paul II, in May 1981. In a second floor suite of the service's headquarters, the physicians worked under the direction of a burly, hard-drinking lawyer whose contacts in the Middle East were legendary. He had made his reputation for his detective work into the Austrian connection to the papal shooting.

In Rome, at the drab headquarters of DIGOS, the Italian national antiterrorist squad, doctors tried to fit together their mosaic of Dr. al-Abub. They were helped by Dr. Franco Ferracuti, Professor of Criminological Medicine and Forensic Psychiatry at the University of Rome, another world-ranking expert on the behavior and states of mind of terrorists.

At the opposite end of the Mediterranean, in Israel, the search for clues about Dr. al-Abub was closely monitored by David Kimche, who had been deputy director of Mossad before taking a senior position in the Israeli Foreign Ministry. Among other moves, Kimche had mobilized the considerable intellectual resources of the country's two "terror laboratories" at the University of Tel Aviv.

Between all these groups there was a constant interchange of information. Some of the more interesting originated from surprising sources. A portion of it came personally from King Hussein of Jordan. Despite the fact that in 1977 it had been disclosed that the Hashemite ruler had been a CIA-paid agent for twenty years, the king continued to supply high-grade intelligence data to the CIA. The information was classified within the Agency as "back channel," indicating that no direct Agency approach must be made to a source, and placed on Langley's list reserved for the most sensitive of intelligence and circulated only to a select few. The royal data had included invaluable insights into Qaddafi, Arafat, Mubarak, and the condition of the foreign hostages in Beirut. In a recent report the king had described how the hostages were routinely threatened with summary execution, subjected to repeated torture by being hooded and kept in lengthy isolation, often in chains, regularly had their night's sleep broken by being moved from one safe house to another, and were frequently drugged by Dr. al-Abub to make them more malleable. King Hussein's report confirmed what the Agency already knew. But it had been deemed of sufficient importance to be hand-carried from Amman to Washington by a U.S. Embassy official.

Other information about Dr. al-Abub had been passed to Chuck Cogan, the Agency's operations chief for the Near East, by the then–Saudi ambassador to the United States, Prince Bandar bin Sultan. The son of his country's defense minister, the gregarious, high-living Arabian diplomat had also been an Agency asset for years. He enjoyed reminding Cogan that he received some of his hottest information when he entertained his Middle East sources in his private office— serving them catered McDonald's Big Mac burgers on solid silver plates with McDonald's milk shakes presented in hand-cut crystal glasses.

Cogan, another Agency veteran, processed Bandar's tidbits on to Clair George, who in turn sent them to Dr. Post and his fellow doctors. They passed the information on to their colleagues around the world, on a strictly need-to-know basis.

Thus were the links forged to discover everything possible about Dr. al-Abub.

The specialists were sure Dr. al-Abub had no need of a defense mechanism fostering faith. He had seen too much of death to fear its presence. Death, after all, was an integral part of his life; in that respect he was no different from the suicide bombers. Those who plotted his end strongly suspected his wish must be that before they destroyed him, he would kill as many of his enemies as possible. The interdisciplinary hunters, however, were almost certainly beyond his reach in their protected, unadvertised places of work.

In Washington the specialists sometimes met in a safe government brick townhouse on Jackson Place, where Reagan had stayed before assuming office in 1981. In that same four-floor century-old building a commission had met in 1974 under the chairmanship of Vice President Nelson A. Rockefeller to investigate the way the CIA had itself used doctors to commit highly unethical acts, including the torture of patients. Reagan, then governor of California, had been on the committee. When it delivered its censorious report he had been the only member to defend what the CIA had done. The specialists, meeting in 1987 to review progress over Dr. al-Abub, had been previously put on notice by Casey that they should not waste time rummaging through the account of CIA-approved medical malpractice. In the director's view, "it had nothing to do with what was happening in Beirut."

No one really believed that. But no one, not even the strong-minded Dr. Post, was prepared to debate the matter.

Everyone in the intelligence community knew that Casey had, on taking office on January 28, 1981, made it an article of faith not to resurrect the past. To do so, he had mumbled, was bad for morale and gave comfort to America's enemies. So: no probing; no attempt to see how Dr. al-Abub's methods were a logical extension of what the CIA's own doctors had done twenty years earlier. To even suggest such a connection, Casey had said, was unthinkable. He could not have been clearer. Only a fool, prepared to be labeled unpatriotic, would have gone against the director. To a man the specialists were neither foolish nor unpatriotic.

On the organization charts the media from time to time tried to piece together and publish, the specialists remained among the empty spaces. They protected their anonymity zealously. They knew each other well, through attending the same closed conferences on security and through a continual exchange of information. Some, no doubt, were trusted more than others. But they were all enjoined by a common desire to establish a suspect's background and motive, to tease fact out of the darkness. It was work to which many were attracted but few were called. Those who were formed part of an international task force on terrorism, and their combined intellectual reasoning had been brought to bear on what Dr. al-Abub was doing in Beirut.

To begin with, they had a little background: no more than a

single snapshot and a handful of biographical details. The shah's secret police originally passed both to the Central Intelligence Agency.

In half a dozen countries every centimeter of the print showing Dr. al-Abub had since been enlarged and studied for evidence of plastic surgery that would make him harder to identify. Glasses and various shapes of beard had been superimposed on the snapshot by computers to suggest how he might look now. But the original photograph was old, taken when he was twenty-two years of age and culled from a group snapshot during his freshman year as a medical student. On the day he posed he was beardless, his plumpish cheeks pitted from the aftereffects of a childhood pox, his eyes clear and innocent.

But the hunters were not discouraged. They had often started with less. Gradually, working within their own constraints, they began to create an idea of him, getting to know a little more about his body and his mind. Using a technique called remote in-depth analysis, but generally referred to as RIDA, they took on, and continued with, the task of mapping out who al-Abub was and why he behaved as he did. They evoked a great deal in their search: God and the devil and the role they played in his mental life; and whether he was also one of those who possessed what sociobiologists term a genetic predisposition to become both a terrorist and a medical torturer through what they describe as an abnormal amount of genes favoring spite. Much of what they felt was intended to remain only between them, as verbal signposts along their road of trying to discover what Dr. al-Abub was like.

One of the Agency's few remaining Lebanese assets in Beirut had risked his life to get close to Dr. al-Abub in late 1986, tailing the doctor through the streets of the Moslem sector. His physical description of the physician had provided further clues.

The specialists now knew that years of hard living had whittled down his face, making his nose appear longer and his chin more pointed. His eyes had long lost any semblance of innocence. They were usually red-rimmed, each iris bloodshot, the pupils dark and watchful and suspicious. They would continue to scan each approaching person—a swift, appraising look, then on to the next face. It was one of the survival techniques he would have been taught in training camp—that an enemy's face will generally give him or her away: there will be invariably a tension, perhaps lips clinched too tightly, an eyelid that flickers out of control, maybe no more than a tiny facial tic. His instructor would have drummed for hour upon hour upon those basic facts until they became ingrained.

The specialists were also coming to understand the complex psychological forces that motivated men like Dr. al-Abub, who do not easily fit the typology of crusaders, criminals, and crazies.

He had never, as far as the specialists knew, displayed the anger that in many ways was parallel to guilt. It would be satisfying, at least for the behaviorists, to show that at the root of his behavior was rage. It was there, of course. But it was not an all-animating and life-energizing force. He was, they thought, psychologically both a compact and complex man, perhaps with what they called a strong streak of masked violence, which allowed him to use his skill in a businesslike manner on those he did not wish to recognize, in the usual sense of the word, as people. Instead, to maintain order within his immediate psychological universe, he needed to equate his unspeakable actions to his own concept of virtue, to feel he was doing no more than responding to a threat to his own culture, his own environment, his own people, his own entire life. Treating the hostages the way he did not only gave him a sense of purpose and of being alive, but was his response to what he most certainly saw as the victimization of himself and his people by a corrupt Western society that had not, so he might have thought, begun to understand the moral and psychological intensity of a faith that would not recognize his work as atrocity.

On that last point Dr. al-Abub would have been wrong.

Increasingly, the tangled skeins of the psychology of Hizballah itself were under intense study in places as geographically apart as Tel Aviv and Washington, London and Los Angeles, Jerusalem and Paris. In those and still other cities, researchers employed directly by intelligence services, paid through substantial grants by those agencies, or working independently were trying to charter how Hizballah moved from a pure calling to an increasingly structured, centralized, and accountable organization—a prime force in international terrorism. In 1985, the Shiite movement produced fourteen percent of all terrorist acts in the world; three years later its percentage had almost trebled, each act performed in the name of dogmatic religious ideology and a dichotomous view of the world, one that sanctioned the spilling of the blood of nonbelievers. State support, particularly from Iran, continued to provide a virtually unlimited supply of money, weapons, and expertise, as well as the protection of diplomatic cover to mount operations. While Israel remained the prime target, Hizballah cadres had penetrated ever further into Europe; Spain, France, and Denmark had all felt the blasts of bombs planted by men who had learned their skills in the Moslem quarter of Beirut.

To combat this unprecedented terror, scientists of many disciplines were pooling their skills and discoveries, along the way writing the first lexicon on terrorism based on psychiatry, history, and cultural influences. They looked for differences and similarities between the Hizballah and other organizations; they analyzed such complex matters as Hizballah's concept of revolutionary heroism and how it varied from that of other groups: they examined the perplexing question of the sense of significance a person felt in simply belonging to the movement; and they studied, line by line, the rhetoric of the Hizballah and other groups, seeking common threads. They tried to assess whether it was possible to convincingly place Hizballah into one of the two categories where almost all other terrorist groups could be confined: those intent on destroying the society they lived in, the world of their parents; and those dedicated to continuing the revolutionary mission of their fathers. Within that classification operated more subtle and still not always fully understood motives. For some, becoming a terrorist was an act of revenge for real or imagined personal injury done to them by society; for others, terrorism seemed the logical way to obtain redress against a society that had done some injury—real or imagined —to their family; for still others, becoming a terrorist was the final act of rebellion against parents loyal to society.

Yet, in confronting Hizballah, the researchers found none of the criteria exactly fitted; the Shiite organization slipped through the net in a number of areas. In other groups the path to terrorism followed a consistent strand—from sympathizer, to passive supporter, to active supporter, and finally to full member. But Hizballah continued to enroll entire communities who could not be compartmentalized, either in composition or ideology, nor identified with other common reasons for joining a terrorist group.

In 1987 the researchers turned elsewhere, seeking to grasp the theological concepts the clerics used to justify their activities; how they were able to adapt holy writ to wage holy war. The first tentative evaluations suggested that, stripped of its religious underpinning, the messianic aspirations of Hizballah bore a striking resemblance to those that launched the French Revolution and, in this century, the upheavals in Russia and China. All endowed terror as a justification to create a new and ideal society.

Yet, unlike those revolutions, Hizballah had developed one particular method to achieve its aims. Dr. al-Abub was an integral part of a strategy that had been thought of as the moral logic of extraordinary means.

In July 1982, less than a month after presiding over its formation, and with Israeli forces encircling West Beirut, the leaders of the Hizballah, along with Dr. al-Abub, once more assembled in Sheykh Fadlallah's apartment to discuss a further momentous step—the taking of hostages from among the foreign community in Beirut. No other Lebanese faction had done so.

The precise thrust of the discussion remains uncertain. It can, however, properly be reduced to a few key elements: kidnapping foreigners would insure immunity from further attack as long as Israel believed the captives remained alive; it would insure worldwide attention to the demand for a pure, Islamic, Hizballah-controlled Lebanon; a concerted campaign of kidnapping would collapse sectors of the country's economic, cultural, and social structure that depended on foreign investment and support; hostages would guarantee a powerful bargaining factor to obtain military, political, and economic concessions from hostile governments; and hostages would provide a persuasive incentive for enemies to hand back captured Hizballah fighters.

The decision to take foreign hostages was to confirm Hizballah's preeminence as Lebanon's most ruthless organ of terror.

The specialists recognized it would be easy for Dr. al-Abub to rationalize his role in such a decision, just as they agreed that the beginning, for him, was when he was told to change his name.

Until October 1977 he was known as Ibrahim al-Nadhir, the first son of the widow Muzzeyene. When he was twelve his father had died of a heart attack in the service of the shah's imperial army. The specialists wondered how great had been the effect on the boy's sense of family continuity. Knowing nothing about the daily relationship within the family, the specialists assumed it probably was no different from that of any such family. The father, they assumed, had a strong sense of family honor, was concerned with maintaining the family's place within the existing social and economic strata, and was prepared to instantly avenge insults to the family name.

The specialists then considered the extent of the boy's grief when his father died; how much he may have identified not only with the loss of a loved one but with death itself. Dr. al-Abub's father's death occurred during the era when boys of his age came into the city, planted their little bombs, and ran for safety. If they managed not to be caught by the shah's army or police the first time, they were generally grabbed when they next tried to blow up a street kiosk, water hydrant, or mailbox. By seventeen, it was different; the youths who had somehow evaded capture were then men. They knew how to obey orders, how to avoid informers, cover their tracks, and insure they had safe houses and secure routes to them after a mission. They chose their targets with care and increasing boldness: a police station, a supermarket that served a barracks, then the barracks itself, planting a bomb in its officer's mess, killing and maiming the shah's men. That was the beginning. Within a year no soldier was safe hitchhiking home on leave from one of the military installations around Tehran.

In the city itself it was common knowledge who was behind the outrages. The newspapers, radio, and television were filled with denunciations of Ayatollah Khomeini and the other clerics in Najaf. But no longer could they be dismissed as Mephistos to impressionable youths. Within the Shiite community they were heroes, with the Ayatollah himself cast as a people's general, the great impresario of violence who had finally come to fulfill the ancient promise. With each attack on the shah's forces the excitement grew; and with it the expectation that perhaps, after all, the long-hidden Imam was coming out of the desert, himself appearing in the guise of an urban guerrilla. From then on there was not a Shiite unwilling to provide food and shelter for their brothers and sisters in arms.

The specialists conceded that one of the many imponderables was how great an influence the steadily gathering momentum of revolution had upon the doctor. One factor in drawing people into terrorism was the need to imitate the actions of others against society, performing in a way which the behaviorists called a break in the lifeline and the psychiatrists added that what was severed was the experience of life, and that becoming a terrorist allowed the construction of a new sort of life vitality. Perhaps understandably, those who fought terrorists on the ground were not overly concerned with such subtleties of human function; for them it was enough to know that Dr. al-Abub was now what he was.

His past was punctuated by considerable gaps. Because of his mother's death early in 1977 the rest of the family scattered, a younger brother and three sisters, went back to one of the Shiite villages in northern Iran. Shortly after his mother's death the doctor entered medical school at Tehran University, where he made steady progress.

His student years remained virtually unknown; such important details as his friendships and any sexual experiences were unknown.

However, the loss of both parents at such an important stage in his life could only have heightened his need to protest, and perhaps, suggested the psychiatrists, heralded the onset of numbing violence. His anger toward society would have increased, filling him with a renewed urgency for ways to not only punish it, but also to reassert his own vitality. The principal of cause and effect was familiar to those who studied the mentality of terrorists: through violence, terrorists saw an opportunity to apportion blame and restore meaning to their lives. The behaviorists thought it significant that a high proportion—in some groups as many as a quarter— had lost one or both parents by the time they were fourteen.

The specialists were working with very little personal data— really no more than an Israeli interrogation report of the only surviving member of a Hizballah bombing mission into Galilee who had met Dr. al-Abub, and a Soviet defector's debriefing by the CIA in which he dimly recalled coming across him. Dr. al-Abub could be placed in either of two personality categories. With his self-centered individualism and lack of regard for the feelings of others, he fit the extrovert mold. That would make him seek and enjoy the dangerous life of the terrorist, with the additional bonus of the extra recognition that went with his special skills. Yet, just as convincingly, he could be typed as paranoiac, suspicious, and aggressive, sensitive to any slight, always prepared to defend himself.

By late 1977, the world Dr. al-Abub had known was on the edge of totally crumbling. The more SAVAK, the shah's murderous intelligence service, was unleashed, the greater the opposition grew. Ultimately, nothing could have halted the inexorable advance of the Islamic fundamentalism promulgated from Najaf. There was common agreement among the specialists that this would be the most logical explanation as to why, on the last Thursday in October that year, he decided to attend a rally addressed by one of the authentic heroes of modern terrorism.

Raised and nurtured in Nablus, then in Jordan but now part of Israel and still a hotbed of Arab activism, Abu Nidal was the new type of terrorist: well-educated, a cool strategist, capable of bold and imaginative planning, with the charisma to make others execute his schemes. On September 5, 1973, five of Nidal's men had occupied the Saudi Arabian Embassy in Paris and held eleven members of the staff hostage in the name of a group he created for the occasion—the Revolutionary Organization of Socialist Moslems. The French government allowed the gunmen to go free, a concession that overnight made Nidal's a household name in the Moslem world. He went on a tour of the more radical campuses in the Middle East, preaching violence and recruiting those prepared to further it.

Nidal's visit to Tehran University was disrupted by the shah's security police, and he barely escaped arrest. Ibrahim al-Nadhir was among those who helped Nidal escape, guiding him to a safe house in the city suburbs. Though there was no earthly way of knowing any of this at the time—it first emerged later through the questioning of a Hizballah bomber in Khaim Prison in South Lebanon by Israeli army interrogators—in their brief time together, Nidal had urged the student to devote himself to the cause of revolution. The first step would be to assume an appropriate nom-de-guerre. Nidal suggested "Abub." In Arabic it means punishment.

Every Western intelligence agency, as well as the KGB, had its ever-lengthening computer printouts on Nidal. They were once more pored over. A SAVAK officer, living in retirement in Paris, was questioned by the SDECE. His continued cooperation was part of an arrangement he had with the SDECE: He would be allowed to live untroubled in France as long as he was available for consultation. No one expected he would much longer have any value, as the growth of terrorism had been so swift. When his usefulness was over, a decision would have to be made about whether to deport him. But to everyone's surprise, he remembered that Thursday, how close he had been to grabbing Nidal. His recollection of the terrorist dovetailed into what the SDECE knew. Nevertheless, the SAVAK man's account was Telexed to Washington. There, Dr. Post and his men tapped the information into their computer terminals. It strengthened the Israeli account of what the Hizballah prisoner had admitted, and which had also been forwarded to Washington.

Faced with the worldwide threat from terrorism, such cooperation between intelligence services was routine. It had further helped to reduce the professional animosity between the Israelis and the CIA. A once close relationship had been ruptured after Israel invaded Lebanon, surprising the Agency and the world. But the official coolness between the Mossad and the CIA was also a direct result of the religious beliefs of President Reagan. Just as the Hizballah had invested Lebanon with a divine purpose, the chosen site of the Imam's second coming, so was the president a committed believer that the ultimate showdown between a returned Christ and what Reagan called the forces of darkness would result from events north of Jerusalem—in Beirut. Reagan had brought to the White House a small shelf of books that predicted no less. One was the *Scofield Reference Bible*, first published in 1909 and since then selling millions of copies to the born-again Christian movement. Its gospel of impending apocalypse was preached daily by the president's favorite evangelists, Jerry Falwell, Pat Robertson, and James Swaggart. They, too, regularly implied that the end of the world was not only close and to be welcomed because the good would survive, but that Lebanon was almost certainly going to be the cause of Armageddon. The president's library also contained a copy of *The Late Great Planet Earth* by Hal Lindsey, who predicted events in Lebanon would lead to the end of the present world.

When Israel's forces swept out of Galilee into Beirut, the president and Nancy had sat transfixed before their television set watching Pat Robertson say that this was "the beginning of the end," that soon those forces of darkness would indeed be swept from the entire face of the earth and in its place would come what the president and his first lady, like all good Christians, yearned for—that utopia the Scofield Bible called Rapture, in which "God returns, brings Peace and Joy to the Raptured Ones." The president was convinced he and Nancy were among those to be so blessed.

When the Israelis failed totally in their mission to Lebanon, the president had not bothered to hide his disappointment from Casey, Shultz, and Weinberger. Reagan had said, "We should cut and run from those guys who promised so much." Casey, sensing the need to do something, had canceled the cozy relationship in which Mossad and CIA men dealt directly with each other. Instead he had set up a structure in which only DDO George dealt with his counterpart in Tel Aviv, the Mossad's Peter Mandy. In the past year both men had worked well together and the result had been, among many other exchanges, important tip-offs on terrorists and their activities.

It was Mossad that had produced the real clues enabling Dr. Post and his staff to see how Nidal became the pivotal force in Dr. al-Abub's life. The specialists were certain that there had been an immediate bond between the two men, that Nidal provided the final impetus for Dr. al-Abub to accept what Freud had defined as "the aggression of the unconscious instinctual impulses." It had enabled Dr. al-Abub to equate Nidal's murderous philosophy with a new ideology of commonly shared concerns. This fit with what was known about Nidal. He was the great stage manager of terrorism; the giver of hope through using up the lives of others; an extraordinary taskmaster but never one to expose himself to the return fire his actions produced.

The next certainty about Dr. al-Abub was that he graduated in late 1978, swearing his physician's oath to the sound of a dying dynasty. The shah had only weeks of rule left. Entire cities were already closed citadels, controlled by the clerics of the Ayatollah Khomeini. In a last desperate act of savagery the shah continued to fill the prisons with the suffering innocent. Perhaps that encouraged the doctor, who had just sworn to harm no one, to decide to play a direct role in the anarchy. Dr. al-Abub joined a revolutionary group and, upon the arrest of its leader and other members, he was appointed leader.

That was seen as another important step in shaping his future. Within any terrorist group, leadership carried certain special responsibilities: a need to motivate others, and to continuously remind them that their thwarted goals could only be achieved through violence. There was a requirement to stress constantly that the world outside the group was filled with decay and was a fitting subject for destruction, just as Nazi ideology embodied the Jew as the personification of physical perversion, ascetic corruption, and spiritual putrefaction.

Dr. al-Abub had driven past the soldiers on duty at the entrance to the airfield outside Esfahan in Iran, wearing a flight mechanic's overalls, which were stolen, like the toolbox on the seat beside him. Parking the truck, he walked to a Learjet and stowed the toolbox beneath an inspection hatch in the aircraft cabin. Later, through binoculars shared with the rest of the group, he watched from a distance as, late in the afternoon, the crew and their passenger boarded the plane. It taxied toward the runway. Still some way from its takeoff point several things occurred simultaneously: a vivid flash, brighter than the setting sun, emerged from within the belly of the fuselage; chunks of metal were wrenched from its top; and still moving forward, the plane lifted vertically from the tarmac, defying for a moment the laws of aerodynamic stress. The fuel tanks in each wing exploded with a roar that drowned the cheering. They felt the heat on their faces over a quarter-mile distance. From within the fireball a section of the tail shot into the sky, and one of the engines careened along the taxiway spitting molten rivets at the approaching fire trucks and ambulances. Finally, a pall of smoke obliterated the scene. Another of the shah's officials had been removed from the list of targets passed to the group from Najaf.

The analysts wondered if that was when Dr. al-Abub would have begun to suppress the dualism within himself, that struggle between taking life and remorse. Some terrorists admitted they never quite settled the conflict; others said it went with the first death. If the latter was so in Dr. al-Abub's case, it would not necessarily have made him more directly aggressive and violent, but it would have nurtured the evil that now made it possible for him to torture.

For those trying to discover the psychodynamics of Dr. al-Abub's behavior, the plane episode continued to serve as a useful reference point. It was the only time the physician was known to have resorted to what they termed traditional terrorism.

A little more had become known about his life after the destruction of the plane.

In late 1979, with the shah finally deposed and the Ayatollah Khomeini installed in Tehran, Abu Nidal had sent word to Dr. al-Abub, who was approaching the end of an internship in a hospital in the city suburbs, that he had been given a scholarship to Patrice Lumumba Friendship University. In return for free tuition and other financing, he must first serve as a doctor at a training camp run by the Fatah Revolutionary Council, yet another group founded by Nidal. A week later Dr. al-Abub was in the northern desert of Iraq. There, for six months, he treated wounds and ailments, attended political lectures on the evils of Zionism and the threat of Western imperialism, learned about explosives and survival techniques, and lived and behaved like any other terrorist, sharing a common belief system reinforced by distinct dress and customs. In March 1980, he took a flight from Baghdad to Moscow to enroll for the spring semester at the Patrice Lumumba campus. The next two years were spent in the university's postgraduate medical school.

Among its many courses were those on the techniques of persuasion, political indoctrination, and the still mysterious black art known as brainwashing, itself a translation of the Chinese colloquialism, *hsi nao*. The lectures drew upon the successful methods used to brainwash Allied prisoners during the Korean War in the 1950s; the episode remained a benchmark in how to change, with small chance of reversal, personal value systems. It had also been a high point in the Russian use of medical torture techniques—and had driven the CIA to try and emulate them, with disastrous results, which had finally led to the humiliating Rockefeller Commission. But that was all part of the Agency's past which Casey had ordered to be buried. In the end the CIA specialists had told themselves that on this occasion it was probably not theirs to reason why, and that there was, after all, so much other pertinent material available.

The most comprehensive files in any Western intelligence agency were on Soviet intelligence techniques. The specialists had read far into the night or had sat before their computer terminals summoning information from a data bank until their eyes ached.

They learned that Dr. al-Abub, like other students at Patrice Lumumba, was taught that brainwashing rarely involved physical cruelty. Instead, it depended on carefully calculated psychological pressure. This included the use of repetition, harassment, and humiliation. At the Soviet academy students took turns acting out the roles of interrogators and prisoners under the watchful eye of instructors drawn from the ranks of the KGB's own medical corps. Those cast as prisoners were made to memorize lengthy and increasingly complex Communist tracts and then questioned, hour upon hour, alternately asked to recite portions or comment on meaning.

The first sign of weariness, lack of cooperation, or inability to answer correctly was dealt with by the harassing technique. A prisoner would be summoned from his meal and lectured on the necessity of paying attention; when he returned to the table he would find it bare. His sleep was disrupted in the small hours and he was asked to recite or comment on portions of text he had earlier failed with. The more compliant he became, the more he was harassed. Finally, he was subjected to humiliation, a technique aimed primarily at turning his fellow students against him. The instructors explained that they were made to suffer because of the student-prisoner's mistakes; the student-prisoner then became, at least momentarily, the object of hatred by the rest of the class. Only when the instructors decided he had been driven close to mental collapse was the exercise stopped.

Russian behaviorists analyzed the responses of each student and showed how, with a little more pressure, they could have been manipulated to the stage of serious mental damage. The students were then instructed on how to achieve such an effect.

A seminar was devoted to the deliberate and active steps

required to strip an individual of his selfhood, and how to
build up something new from the bare psychic foundation
that remained. In this assault upon identity a key factor was
to create a state of infantile dependency, so that a person
became disorientated until finally, like a young postulant
entering a religious order, he "dies to the world." Only at
that stage, lectured the KGB psychiatrists, was the victim
ready to receive the salvation of those who now controlled his
every action.

The techniques were taught for establishing guilt in a victim's mind and how from that should come self-betrayal, the
denunciation of long-cherished ideals, which in turn would
create still more genuine guilt and a growing compulsion to
confess. The students were told that when a person had
purged himself of his past, he should be encouraged to accept
new substitute beliefs. There were lectures on how to prepare a person at that stage to make a videotape recording, in
which he admitted guilt and appealed to the world to recognize the justice of the demands of the captors. Faculty doctors explained how the process could be accelerated by the
use of drugs to create rapid disorientation, induce fear, produce confusing stimuli, and cause fatigue and physical debility.

The specialists patiently creating their psycho-profiles of
Dr. al-Abub were increasingly convinced that it was in Moscow where he had learned the techniques of medical torture.

4

Connections

Dr. al-Abub would not have to look far in West Beirut to find men ready to swear by Allah, the Beneficent and Merciful, that the treatment of the American was proof of what was revealed to the Prophet at al-Madinah and set down in the Surah XXIX: "O ye who believe! Spy not!" The word had gone forth from Sheykh Fadlallah to the other clerics and, after Friday evening prayers, they urged it should be spread through the bazaars and sidewalk cafes to all who could hear. The American had been allowed to live among them; yet, all the time they had tolerated his presence he had been working secretly to destroy all they knew was sacred.

In those weeks following his kidnapping the rumors had been many and varied. The American had sent lamp signals from his penthouse to the ships of the Great Satan which, under cover of darkness, had steamed over the horizon before vanishing again before dawn. There was a transmitter in his apartment so powerful that he could not only communicate with Tel Aviv, but also directly with the home of the Great Satan in Washington. No one had asked why, with such a powerful radio, he needed to use a flash-lamp to signal the fleet. Instead, the stories proliferated. The American had been planning to poison the water supply in West Beirut. Discovered on him had been plans of the underground sewers through which he intended to lead his forces to murder all the clerics.

Men would pause on their way to answer the summons of the muezzin and exchange the latest news. The American had been plotting to bring about division between the PLO and

71

the Hizballah. He had been supplying Iraq with the chemicals with which it burned the skins from the bodies of their Shiite brothers-in-arms in Iran's jihad. A rocket had been found on his apartment roof which, when fired, would have been a signal for the Great Satan's ships to once more rain ruin from the air upon them. Women preparing the evening meals interrupted their keening to tell their children, again, that what was happening would help to redress the death of a loved one killed by a Zionist bomb or shell. After the meal the children once more poured through the streets, chanting the slogans of total victory before playing a new game: captors and hostage. There was increasing difficulty in persuading a boy to undertake the role of prisoner because it meant being questioned and then punched and beaten with sticks and spat upon.

A favored place for the game was around the Basta jail in the northern end of the sector. The Hizballah had turned the ancient building into a headquarters. What provided further excitement to the play was knowing that the American was the first hostage to have been kept in one of the underground cells.

Others had taken his place, hated foreigners all—but none more so than the American. Even now, after all that had been done to him, they still could not bring themselves to feel even a mite of pity. Allah had made plain to the Prophet in that divine moment before the battle of Badr that forgiveness would be totally inappropriate in a case like the American's. Instead there was, and remained, common agreement that his fate embodied the essentials of jihad.

During his first weeks in captivity William Buckley was hidden in a succession of cellars, each soon filled with the stench of his body waste, misery, and fear. Most of the time he was drugged and kept hooded. On the occasions when the sack was removed he stared vaguely at the men behind the video camera and his face had drawn in upon itself. They had promised him freedom if he cooperated in the filming, explaining what they wished him to say. He had refused.

Dr. al-Abub had brought to bear the techniques he acquired in Moscow.

Few people in West Beirut could begin to understand the precise nature of his intervention—what injections he used, their quantity and strength. The contents of his black bag remained as mysterious to them as always. The American belonged to a society that, for them, daily used violence and suppression. Therefore he could only expect similar treatment.

No one saw any need to protest against the imported skills of Dr. al-Abub.

The curriculum at Patrice Lumumba had covered all aspects of the techniques of persuasion. A Soviet anthropologist had explained at the outset of the course Dr. al-Abub attended that attempts to change opinions were older than recorded history and most certainly originated with the development of speech. A social historian lectured on how the United States had developed first the most powerful advertising industry in the world and then, in time of hostilities, adapted the techniques of Madison Avenue to psychological warfare.

There followed a thorough grounding in the principles of religious conversions and the lessons to be learned from what was essentially a Western phenomenon of withholding food, physical discomfort, and even extreme pain to arouse powerful emotions of guilt, anxiety, distress, conflict, and finally nervous exhaustion before the stage was reached when a person was at the height of suggestibility and ready to convert. Dr. al-Abub had watched films of modern American evangelists, men like Oral Roberts and Billy Graham, which illustrated the point. His lecturer had gone back in time to examine the techniques of John Wesley and his ability to create emotional tension, and how the key to the preacher's success had been his intuition, his skill at singling out one member of his audience, knowing that if he could establish a sympathetic relationship with him he would win over the crowd—and the day. The KGB psychiatrist had explained how Wesley's technique could be applied to suit the doctor-prisoner relationship.

The doctor was lectured on Catholicism's rite of confession, and was told that behind its exaggerated language and penances was an effective means to control minds. Just as Rome inculcated belief by affirmation of repentance, so could cooperation in secular areas be instilled. Another tutorial examined the manipulative effects of voodooism. While voodoo achieved this through its deities, the same result could also be induced by hallucinogenic drugs, including mescaline, which had the unusual effect of translating noise into visual stimuli—a sound become color. It was an effective way to create in a person the feeling of being on the edge of madness. The KGB doctor explained that someone who refused to cooperate should be threatened with remaining forever in a state of chemically induced insanity.

Dr. al-Abub had been reminded that, as a doctor, he must always look upon every person as possessing a large number of complexes that normally were repressed deep within the unconscious to maintain mental balance. Yet so often it required no more than acute observation combined with the basic technique of isolation and, if needed, a selective use of drugs such as lysergic acid diethylamide, LSD, to release those complexes—generally with devastating effects.

Considerable time was devoted to probing the mechanism of personality, not only to understand it as the meeting place of all relationships, but to learn that it could be dramatically affected by drugs that, for example, altered the function of the thyroid, reducing a person to near imbecility, or caused joints to become inflamed or shrink from bones, created temporary blindness, impaired speech, produced incontinence, resulted in loss of hair, and led to a frightening rise in body temperatures. Dr. al-Abub was initiated into how many of the discoveries of the major pharmaceutical laboratories in the West, like Sandoz and Eli Lilly, could be adapted to assist in mind control. It was explained to him the effect of isolating a person from the outside world for lengthy periods in total darkness; how it rapidly produced hallucinations, phobias, and allowed terrifying fantasies to appear real; how sensory deprivation could traumatically transform the goals, values, and ideals of a lifetime.

He had studied the common factor in the confessions of Allied prisoners of war in Korea. No matter how severely the captives were treated by the North Koreans and Chinese, the ultimate terror came from within their own minds. No technique, no drug, nothing could ever achieve the mind control that resulted from creating such inner conflict. To achieve that, Dr. al-Abub was lectured to never forget that personality was not only largely bound up with role behavior, but was also dependent on role perception and, most important of all, self-perception. The crucial factor was to distinguish between someone playing a role and someone accepting the reality of a situation. The distinction could only be made by partially probing for a weakness in personality and, when such a weakness is located, ruthlessly attacking it. In the beginning, it may be no more than the tiniest of wedges in a person's psyche, but by careful manipulation the gap would widen until ultimately the victim surrendered.

Finally, Dr. al-Abub was instructed that those who were most susceptible to an appeal to their emotions—sexual offenders, those with drinking or drug problems—were the easiest to persuade. The most difficult were his medical colleagues, policemen, and above all intelligence officers. Invariably, they needed more preparation, more isolation, more pressure to break their wills to resist.

It had meant more horror for William Buckley.

The specialists knew the Soviet techniques were designed to create a feeling of helplessness that some Western psychiatrists called basic anxiety and others termed traumatic psychological infantilism. The symptom common to both was that a victim became compelled to turn to the very person who was endangering his life. They wondered how far Buckley had experienced this feeling. At that point he could not only have felt his captors wielded total power of life and death, but would then have begun to reveal other significant behavioral changes that Dr. al-Abub would have most certainly been trained to notice.

Buckley could have come to see his kidnappers as good people. The phenomenon was called pathological transference. It could be seen, for instance, where parents seriously abused their children, even threatening their lives, yet when their offspring were rescued, perhaps by social workers, the children almost never complained about their treatment: they were overwhelmed with gratitude that their parents had let them live.

Dr. Symonds had, however, found that when kidnappers shot at their victim prior to abduction, pathological transference never took place; gunfire or any form of direct violence at that moment destroyed the delicately balanced mechanism that created transference in a victim's mind.

To further gauge how Buckley might have continued to respond to his captors, the American specialists were helped by the research of Dr. Frank Ochberg at St. Lawrence Hospital, Lansing, Michigan. In the aftermath of the kidnapping of the U.S. Embassy hostages in Tehran, the first foreigners to be held in such circumstances, the psychiatrists made a pioneer study of one of the most extraordinary effects of being taken captive—the bond created between hostage and abductors, the Stockholm Syndrome. The term originated in Sweden in 1974 when a bank robber held hostage a girl teller. During the siege she fell deeply in love with her captor. Dr. Ochberg concluded that the response was common to many hostage situations—that the stress of a shared experience overcame the normal barrier of captor and victim, allowing them to form a united front against a world that had brought them both into the situation. The criminal or terrorist claimed he or she was driven to take a hostage because there was no other way of achieving set goals; the hostage believed he or she had been placed in the situation by a society that did not give sufficient protection. Dr. Ochberg concluded that such complex psychological interaction occurred early on in a kidnapping, and arose from a pathological transference based on terror, gratitude, and a redefining of normal defense systems on the part of the hostage.

Buckley had been routinely counseled by CIA psychiatrists to avoid making any attachment to captors. He was told that while it would be tempting to give way to the normal urge to do so, he must always remember the desire was deliberately fostered by captors to create more support for their demands—such as having a hostage cooperate in making a video or audio tape. Most important of all, he had been ordered to accept a fundamental difference between the role of an Agency employee taken captive and that of an ordinary person. In dealing with civilian kidnap victims, the policy of all American law enforcement agencies was to encourage the development of a bond between captive and captor as a means to ensure the survival of the victim. Buckley, however, was instructed that it would be an unacceptable security risk for him ever to enter into such a relationship.

The troubling question of whether he had managed to avoid doing so remained unsettled, until the third video.

Its arrival in Washington on Friday, October 26, 1984, two hundred and twenty-four days since Buckley was kidnapped, came at a time of high drama. Only a week before, the IRA had almost succeeded in assassinating Mrs. Thatcher and her cabinet colleagues while they slept in their party conference hotel in Brighton, England. There was a deepening concern in Langley that other subversive groups would be encouraged to make a similar attack against the Reagan administration, perhaps even an assault on the president in the White House. An Agency analyst produced a sobering update of the activities of the forty terrorist groups who, in that year alone, had left a trail of bombings, murders, and kidnappings. The CIA, along with other agencies, was fully mobilized to combat any action terrorists contemplated in the United States. Within the Agency there was a firm belief that a long-expressed fear of terrorist groups forming a worldwide alliance was about to happen.

In Paris an Agency employee had discovered evidence of connections between the new Italian Red Brigade and the Revolutionary Cells Movement in West Germany. In Athens the CIA station had uncovered similar ties between the Greek Revolutionary Group for International Solidarity and French Action Directe. All the groups used explosives provided by Libya.

In the Middle East various Arab factions were co-producing terrorism out of Damascus and Cairo. Overshadowing them all was the Hizballah, daily growing more powerful and sinister. It too had begun to expand its links with Europe's terrorists.

The sense of a global conspiracy primarily directed against the United States was heightened by news from Cairo that another video of Buckley had been mailed to the U.S. Embassy from the city's Heliopolis post office. While Beirut was only a short flight from the Egyptian capital, it nevertheless showed that the Hizballah moved with impunity. If its couriers passed undetected through the immigration systems of the Middle East and Europe, might not they be emboldened to enter the United States and post a bomb instead of a cassette?

The knowledge of a third video increased the anger that had never left some veteran Agency officers since that day four years earlier—Sunday, November 4, 1979—when the Tehran Embassy had been overrun and sixty American staff members had been taken hostage. Those officers had argued strongly at the time for a response along the lines of Israel's successful rescue of its nationals hijacked to Entebbe. The CIA men had said a similar full-scale operation, involving both the Agency and all three American armed services, delivered with speed and determination, would have scattered the Revolutionary Guards and safely extracted the Americans from Iran. President Carter had hesitated, and there were men within the CIA who would never forgive him. Worse, when he had authorized a mission, it had ended in the debacle in the Iranian desert—with rescue helicopters crashing in sandstorms. The disaster had particularly infuriated the Agency, as its own agents had behaved bravely in gathering the essential prior intelligence. One had infiltrated into Iran by posing as a German businessman. His passport had been forged in Langley. However, a vigilant Iranian immigration official had pointed out he had never seen a German passport where the holder's middle name was not printed in full. The quick-witted agent explained that in his case he had special permission to only have an initial H because his parents had named him after Hitler, and that since the war he had been allowed to conceal the name.

Now, under a very different president, Ronald Reagan, the Agency felt more was being done to recover one of its own. The moves to trade arms with Iran had begun gathering momentum. The nagging question was whether a deal could be secured in time to save Buckley.

The Cairo video, if possible, was more harrowing than its predecessors. Buckley at times was close to a gibbering wreck. His words were often incoherent; he slobbered and drooled; and, most unnerving of all, he would suddenly scream in terror, his eyes rolling helplessly and his body shaking.

From time to time he reached off the camera frame for one of the documents that had been in his burn bag. These he would display to the camera. Then, his voice momentarily clearing, he would launch himself on a pathetic defense of his captors' right to self-determination in Lebanon.

Once more the way he spoke was carefully observed for further insights into Buckley's mind—to judge, for instance, whether he was already resigned to inevitable death at the hands of his captors.

Another issue that mattered to the men who reviewed the video was whether there were clues from Buckley's behavior to show he had not forgotten a carefully instilled principle of his training: to put aside the normal Christian abhorrence to suicide. To do this he would have to overcome the memory of his formative years when, as a devout Catholic boy, he would most certainly have listened to his priest speak of the Hell that faced those who took their own lives. But Buckley had been told his work permitted suicide as the ultimate means to protect the secrets he was privy to; he had been encouraged to see that if he ever had to kill himself, it would be the supreme act of courage; that for him committing suicide was a human and honorable option.

There was no indication that the ruined figure on the video remembered what he had been told. The specialists continued to study, sometimes rerunning a portion of the film over and over. They noted the way Buckley's hands sometimes unconsciously moved across his private parts as he repeated his pleas to live in exchange for the patently impossible demands of his captors. In that movement was he displaying something more than modesty? Was it a physical glimpse of something deeply significant going on inside his head? The specialists knew that a fear of castration was a common response in a hostage, that a deep concern about emasculation actually surpassed fear of death. Even in his dire circumstances, William Buckley might still consciously find his death too abstract a concept, yet castration would be only too understandable. Despite days reviewing those portions of the film where Buckley's hands moved across his pelvic area, the specialists remained uncertain as to whether the movements were consistent with an unconscious acceptance of his inevitable death.

Director Casey's understandably urgent question was, could they judge from Buckley's condition how much he could have revealed? The specialists studied the video from another angle, trying to estimate the level of anxiety in Buckley's voice. At times it was virtually impossible to distinguish anything through the slur of words. But gradually, using computers to isolate phrases, they began to assess the anxiety Buckley was experiencing. Hoping to determine his level of helplessness, they worked within a clearly defined Freudian framework— "the subject's estimation of his own strength compared to the magnitude of the danger and his admission of helplessness in the face of it; physical helplessness if the danger is visible and psychological helplessness if it is instinctual."

It was clear that Buckley could no longer confront the sheer terror of his situation; its magnitude had, from what the specialists saw on the video, overwhelmed him. Isolated and engulfed, he would have felt little different from a child unable to cope; he would have experienced the same mental disintegration and a sense of being on the edge of the abyss. Just as an infant cried for its mother to rescue him, so would Buckley have turned to his captors. In return for his being saved, he would almost certainly have told them what they wanted to know.

The specialists considered whether part of his tension on the video arose directly from what they termed his level of guilt anxiety, what others call conscience. There appeared to be signs—the movements of his eyes, mostly—that while he delivered the demands of his captors, deep within his mind he was waging a struggle to retain his moral integrity. For hours the specialists considered whether this was true guilt or neurotic guilt. They used a language no outsider could readily comprehend to make distinctions over how much his human order of being was disturbed and how far he might have experienced existential guilt arising from a specific act, in his case his revelations to his captors. That knowledge would have left him blank with despair. Then the specialists again considered whether Buckley not only accepted but yearned for the inevitability of his death—and yearned for it to come quickly.

They noted, too, his physical condition. Between the second and third videos he appeared to have lost between fifty and sixty pounds. The sinews on his neck, arms, and legs stood out, so did his ribs. There were further signs of bruising from injections; his eyes continued to display the effect from being hooded.

When the two-hour tape had been viewed it was turned over to the technicians. Again, they could offer no worthwhile leads as to where the film had been shot; the printing, like the wrapper also offered no clue.

The winter months were a time of waiting in West Beirut and, in some quarters, of mounting impatience as the warm rains of December gave way to chill January nights and hardened men huddled over charcoal fires and voiced a view that the time had come to empty the secret supply dumps of explosives, load them on to the growing fleet of hijacked trucks, and end the frustration of the young men and women waiting to be called upon to drive themselves into paradise.

Those militant voices urged that a concerted attack upon every surviving foreign-owned or occupied building in East Beirut would cause the last of their enemies to depart.

From Sheykh Fadlallah's apartment came a call for patience, one that was repeatedly relayed by the other clerics at evening payers on Friday.

The *ulama* also began to explain that through questioning the American, it had been discovered that their enemies had developed terrible tortures that they would not hesitate to use. Sheykh Fadlallah had himself addressed a rally on January 22, 1985, the day deliberately chosen, he said, because it marked the eleventh anniversary of a plan by the Great Satan to introduce into his state of California a special center where their brothers, the Moslems of North America, would have parts of their brains removed and electrodes implanted in their skulls so that the Great Satan could control them. It was against such evils, Sheykh Fadlallah concluded, that they were forced to resist.

When he had been governor of California, Ronald Reagan had lent his considerable authority to promote what he termed a violence center for the state. He intended it should be established on an abandoned nuclear weapons test site in the Santa Monica mountains. Reagan had tirelessly lobbied President Richard Nixon, the Secretary of Defense, and numerous federal agencies to approve the center and made it a theme of his 1974 State of the State message. He was genuinely mystified at the outrage the proposal drew. When the state legislature canceled the project on the grounds that public opinion was too sensitive, Reagan continued to reflect the view of some of the country's leading physicians and brain surgeons that the center was desirable as a means to bring under control the violence in the cities. The project remained on the governor's active file until he became president.

In Langley, Casey at the outset had asked the Agency specialists a basic question: How could a doctor, trained to heal, behave like Dr. al-Abub?

The director was told there was no simple or single answer. Any meaningful response must realistically begin with the Nazi doctors and their Japanese counterparts, and include those Soviet psychiatrists who treated dissidents, as well as the Chinese physicians and the doctors in South America who worked within the framework of state-sponsored torture.

Casey, when he read this evaluation, shook his head. The world, he told some of his senior colleagues, was becoming a darker place by the day.

Something, he added, had to be done—not just about men like Dr. al-Abub, but about "all those bastards who make it possible for the likes of him to operate."

The director's list of those enemies was almost as lengthy as the list of hatreds compiled by the mullahs.

The question some of the specialists found uncomfortable was this: Could Dr. al-Abub claim that he really had not behaved any differently from those other doctors? He, too, had been imbued with a strong moral certitude and driven by a fanatical self-righteousness. Neither had he shown even for a moment that he knew, let alone cared, where essential suffering in the cause of medicine ended and torture began.

Before those doctors, it had been that much easier to draw the line: to promise, for instance, that what the Nazi doctors had done, what Chinese physicians had managed to do in Korea, what Soviet doctors still did in their psychiatric hospitals, and what was carried out elsewhere, Beirut included—that all that could never be allowed to happen in a civilized city, let alone one in North America. But this could no longer be said. Not after what had happened in an old mansion overlooking the St. Lawrence River in Montreal once upon a recent time.

To be exact, what the doctor had done had not even started there; rather it could be said to have properly begun in the setting of a fine house on Q Street in Georgetown, among a carefully chosen group of Washington's politicians, diplomats, career officers, scientists, intelligence officers, and, for their host, some of the city's most beautiful women. The doctor liked to say that gatherings like that were a perfect example of the by-product of the area's only industry: government. Such remarks attracted Dr. Donald Ewen Cameron to the man who invited him to the party—the most powerful spymaster in the Western world before Casey.

Book Two

TO THIS TIME

The room had a long hall. It was a room and a long hall, because the bathroom was built-in. And I heard him saying to the residents outside my door: "We'll give her shock treatments"; what, what? He did not come near me. He did not enter the room. He discussed nothing. He was cruel, savage, inhumane. He did not come near me—then . . . unknown to me they had taken out the consent forms so he could do his malicious, malevolent work without interference from anyone . . . My memory is being in a deep, dark, pitch-black hole with no sense of appendages, like a worm. There was no sense of solidity, like I was not on the ground and I was not on water. It was like being suspended in an eerie, black hole. . . . But I was aware of existence, being. I was also aware that there had been no beginning, that this seemed to have been going on forever. There was also no awareness that there was no end to this existence. But somehow, in some part of my brain that hadn't been at least temporarily destroyed, there was that wondering: I'm here, where have I come from?

—excerpts from the deposition of Dr. Mary Matilda Morrow, psychiatrist and neurologist, plaintiff in the case of Mrs. David Orlikow, et al., v. United States of America; sworn before Scott T. Kragie, Assistant U.S. Attorney; Barbara A. Rubino, paralegal office of general counsel, Central Intelligence Agency; and James C. Turner, counsel for plaintiffs, on June 19, 1986.

The patients would be staggering and semi-doped, trying to listen to the voices coming through the speakers in their regular football helmets. I didn't like to work in the Sleep Room. But he used to say, "Girlie, that's what you're here for. Do it." He used to call every woman "lassie" or "girlie." Maybe he thought it made him a little bit more human. I didn't think to speak out against him because for me he was a very authoritarian figure and it would not have come into my mind to doubt him.

—excerpt from author's interview with Nurse Peggy Edwards (née Mielke), Toronto, March 4, 1987.

5

Sowing the Seed

There was always an excuse to have a party, Allen Dulles never tired of saying to his wife, Clover, providing the host understood only the finest foods and choicest wines were to be served. That was why he did not enjoy going to the White House for one of the folksy gatherings, when the president assembled his wartime cronies and their wives, and he would reminisce about how he had put the Russians, British, and French in their places. The new director of the Central Intelligence Agency had no quarrel with those reminiscences; what Dulles objected to was that Mamie Eisenhower, the first lady, clearly did not think it mattered whether the wines were of the correct vintage and the cheeses imported and not processed somewhere in the Midwest.

By contrast, Clover had established a reputation in Washington for providing the very best food. Items out of season in local shops were flown in specially, like the Russian sturgeon that formed the centerpiece of the buffet in the dining room in their home in Georgetown on that March evening in 1953. One or two of the guests, who claimed to know the difference between a fish caught in Soviet waters and one hooked off closer shores, wondered whether the sturgeon lying in state on its wooden bier was her husband's way of expressing satisfaction with the news from Russia. A few hours earlier Moscow Radio had announced: "The heart of the inspired continuer of Lenin's will, the wise leader and teacher of the Communist party and Soviet people, Joseph Vissarionovich Stalin, has stopped beating."

Though the Russian ambassador had canceled his invitation

to attend the party, which Clover had organized to mark Congress's confirmation of her husband's appointment to head the most powerful intelligence organization in the world, the Dulleses agreed it would be unthinkable to not go ahead with the celebration just because Stalin was dead. Besides, there was a more personal reason to rejoice. After months of being close to death—the victim of a bullet in the head from leading a charge against a North Korean machine gun nest—their only son, Allen Macy Dulles, Jr., had turned the corner. He had recovered sufficiently to make the long flight from Japan, and they had gone to Andrews Air Force Base to meet the incoming plane. Photographers were on hand as the boy, on a stretcher, was disembarked. The next day most newspapers carried a picture of Allen Dulles leaning affectionately over his son and kissing his bandaged head. The best-placed cameraman had caught the tears glistening behind the father's spectacles.

Moving among his guests, pausing to greet here a senator, there an admiral and, over by the fireplace, a group of Foreign Service officials, Allen Dulles was the epitome of the attentive host, emitting that soft laugh some people said was not really a sign of amusement but merely a means of expressing the tension he often felt. Occasionally his face would genuinely light up with pleasure when he met an old wartime acquaintance, such as William E. Colby, who had parachuted into Occupied Europe to lead French Resistance teams on sabotage and assassination missions. In his steel-framed spectacles and neat haircut, Colby now looked like a small-town businessman, not a killer. The bond between him and his host was close, forged by commonly shared danger. Colby was one of the Agency's gray men, with that knack of melding into a crowd, seeing everything, saying as little as possible. He was pure spy.

Dulles continued to go from one group to another, sometimes squeezing the elbow of one of several beautiful women invited for their looks. It was the only intimacy he permitted himself in public. No party was complete for the middle-aged spymaster without its quota of models, television starlets, and the most elegant of the long-legged secretaries working on Capitol Hill. Flirting with all of them, seeing how far his intellectual superiority could seduce them, helped him relax. There was endless speculation on the city's embassy party circuit over who would be the next girl, young enough to be his daughter, he would bed. No one could be certain. He was, in every sense, a man of secrets.

Another group consisted of lawyers, sober-faced and -suited, one or two of the older men with fob chains across their vests, and all with what Clover called courtroom eyes. Allen had also always insisted that no party was complete without its quota of attorneys. In a rare confidence he had told her they knew how to reach out and connect all kinds of people: the rich and powerful, the clever, the reckless, those who lived on the fringe of the law, and even beyond it. The lawyers knew most of the skeletons in all the society closets, keeping Dulles as informed as J. Edgar Hoover's FBI was on the domestic front. Clover partly rated her success as a hostess by the number of out-of-town lawyers who found a reason to be in Washington on business and then stayed over to come on to the house. She sometimes wondered if some of the New Yorkers billed their clients for overnighting in the capital; she had heard horrendous stories about the way some Wall Street law firms charged.

But she doubted that the imposing lawyer commanding the attention of the group would do such a thing. Leonard W. Hall was probably not only the wealthiest attorney present but also one of the richest men in the room. Part of his fortune came from his New York practice; the balance came from stocks. He was also chairman of the Republican National Committee. Every time he came to a party he brought with him a different associate, a lawyer Hall felt was a rising star in the profession and could benefit from rubbing shoulders with the elite of Washington. Clover, however, had been surprised at Hall's companion on this night. When he had shook her hand, he had not looked his hostess in the eye, and mumbled his name so badly that Hall had to say, "This is Bill Casey. You ever got a problem with investments, he's the one to sort it out."

She had nodded vaguely, mentally telling herself she knew a hundred lawyers she would consult before even thinking of going to this awkward, heavy-jowled man with fleshy lips and gaps between his teeth.

Yet her husband had greeted Casey like an old friend, fetching him a drink, taking his arm, guiding him into a corner of the room where they had stood, heads close in deep conversation, oblivious to everyone else.

William Casey, like Colby and some of the others in the room, was a World War II veteran of the Office of Strategic Services (OSS), the forerunner of the CIA. When Casey had left the OSS to enter law practice, Dulles had predicted, "You'll be back. Once this business is in your blood there is no letting go."

After a while Dulles had taken Casey over to where Hall stood, sipping his whiskey, saying little, watching the crowd. Clover remembered that her husband, in his preparatory briefing on some of the guests, had described Casey as pure New York. She disliked New Yorkers. Besides, there was something about Casey she found positively menacing.

One of the groups was dominated by a congressman, Lyndon Johnson of Texas, the Senate's new minority leader, who was describing the latest move in the deepening crisis between the White House and the Republican leaders on the Hill over taking a tougher line with Moscow. They wanted to renounce all wartime agreements made at Tehran, Yalta, and Potsdam. President Eisenhower had prevaricated, finally agreeing to a draft that fell short of what the Republican mastodons demanded. The document had been written by Allen's brother, John Foster Dulles, Secretary of State, and based largely upon the analysis of their sister, Eleanor Lansing Dulles, in charge of the Berlin Desk at the State Department. The family triumvirate effectively created and controlled the foreign policy of the United States for Eisenhower. Johnson made it clear he was going to have to tell the president that Democrats were equally unhappy about his conciliatory attitude toward the Soviets, but he would not embarrass the White House and further divide the country by voting against the draft. Johnson could be certain "that before sun-up Foster and Eleanor would know. Allen's parties were a conduit. Everything got sucked up, everything got passed along to the right places."

Dotted among the guests were a number of young men in dark lounge suits. They were the pick from the latest crop of Agency recruits. Their role was to take care of the unattached girls until Dulles made his choice. They were known as the stud detail. Clover intensely resented their presence. They were a reminder that her husband remained feckless. There was, however, one exception: a slim man whose looks reminded her of Montgomery Clift—the same pensive, slightly hunted look, and eyes that concentrated hard on what was being said. William Buckley had become the one "stud squad" member she accepted ever since they had met at an Agency Christmas party.

The foreign spies were outnumbered by the senior officers of the Agency and their wives, the men mostly drinking twelve-year-old bourbon, the women sipping iced champagne. Presiding over the buffet was Natalie, the family cook and household treasure, who had not only prepared the sturgeon but had created a sumptuous display of exotic foods from the Caribbean, South America, and the Far East to consecrate Clover's theme for the evening: Springtime on Q Street. Sometimes her husband would confide to his closest friends that his wife had no sense of money and frittered it away on trivialities. No one took the complaint seriously; most people agreed that Dulles was a big spender as well as a big thinker.

After a distinguished career in American wartime intelligence, Allen Dulles had reached the peak of his profession. As director he controlled, with the absolutism of a medieval monarch, an organization with an annual budget larger than some European countries and one with unrivaled technical facilities to gather intelligence and the manpower to conduct espionage operations. Neither Hitler's Abwehr, the KGB, nor Britain's Secret Intelligence Service came near to matching the resources at Dulles's command. He had in excess of $100 million a year to spend, which he could dispense with at only the most notional of accounting; neither Congress nor the president had any real idea of how or where the money went. Without consulting anyone outside the Agency, and acting usually upon his own discretion, he would dispatch agents against any nation, friend or foe, neutral or potential enemy. Within the Agency it was said that he had a spy in place close to the center of every major government in the Western world and a growing number within the Soviet empire. Only the Chinese had reputedly so far proven impossible to infiltrate. To support an army of field officers he had his own agronomists, economists, meteorologists, and, of increasing importance to him, his own psychiatrists. He depended on their clinical reports to help him arrive at any number of decisions, including who would fly the Agency planes on secret missions, who would command the Agency's private armies, and who would lead the Agency's military campaigns.

Dulles continued to move gracefully among his guests, leaning slightly forward as he listened to a conversation, then, when he moved on, straightening himself. Those little movements were the only sign of the club foot he had been born with and that, in spite of corrective surgery, had left him with less than perfect balance: in quiet moments he still brooded over the deformity and some people said this had affected his nature. The family had all sworn a solemn oath the matter would never be discussed with outsiders. Some said that silly business marked Allen's entry into the world of secrets.

On this cold March evening there was another and far more serious matter deeply troubling Allen Dulles. Only a handful of men around him had any idea what it was and how he intended to deal with it.

Guests were arriving by the minute and Clover had lost what her husband once described as "that look of a terrified doe before the hunter plugs her right between the eyes." Instead the tension lines around her eyes had relaxed and she wore the satisfied face of a hostess who knows the party will be a success. In her youth Clover had been a hauntingly beautiful woman and the smile she wore as she greeted each guest was a reminder of that. She knew little of the details of her husband's work, and so next to nothing about some of the guests he greeted.

Theirs was a marriage where she had finally steeled herself not to question—not why her husband needed the comfort of adoring women, or why he enjoyed going to salons, back parlors, and political caucus rooms, or how he managed to span the Washington political spectrum, adroitly balancing friendships with senators and congressmen so that virtually the entire legislature was wholly fond of him. On those occasions, as on this evening, he would conceal the darker, ruthless, and totally unscrupulous man and display only the cheerful, worldly, and witty side of his personality.

Yet Clover sensed that something was troubling her husband as he eased himself in and out of groups. She recognized the signs: the soft laugh came a little too often and he was having his glass refilled faster than usual. But above all, she had not seem him single out one of the women for a later assignation. That was unlike him; it could only mean something really serious had, at least momentarily, subdued his strong sexual drive.

Clover had come to terms with her husband's philandering. Partly it was because the bitter recriminations she had unleashed in the first flush of discovering about his behavior had left her both exhausted and terrified at her own anger; it had been strong enough to have driven her to contemplate suicide. At those moments she salved her misery the only way she knew, by making her husband pay where it hurt him most. Each time she discovered a new adultery she had gone to Cartier. She had filled a jewel box with expensive baubles marking his infidelities.

Over the years Clover had also consulted several psychiatrists who had prescribed drugs that only momentarily masked her pain. It had been an Agency doctor, a kindly man, who had finally taken her aside during a reception at the French Embassy for Bastille Day and said she could benefit from seeing a Dr. Cameron.

He explained that Dr. Cameron had a reputation for dealing with emotional problems in women and that his work was respected throughout the world of medicine, and his hospital in Montreal drew patients from all over North America and beyond. She had said it would be impossible for her to go to Canada. The Agency physician said Dr. Cameron frequently came to Washington. Desperate for help, Clover had agreed to a meeting. A few weeks later the CIA doctor had called and said Dr. Cameron would like her to have lunch with him at the Mayflower; sensing her surprise, he had added that Dr. Cameron had no office or hospital facilities in Washington and that, besides, he felt she would find it easier to relax in more informal surroundings. Over the meal she had told Dr. Cameron about her husband's affairs and their effect upon her.

Dr. Cameron had spoken about the tensions of working in a clandestine world, saying that intelligence work was like no other; that it filled even the strongest of men with doubts and uncertainty; and that she should try and see her husband's sexual transgressions as those of a man seeking to remind himself of his masculinity. The doctor suggested that because of the complexities of his personality, he had to do this outside the marriage—though she should never feel that her husband did not love her. He did, but on terms she would have to try and accept. To instill that acceptance, Dr. Cameron suggested she should come to Montreal, where he could treat her. "It's the only way, lassie." He had stared at her fixedly, and though she could not think of any reason, she had felt uneasy.

Nevertheless, Clover had spent days closeted in her bedroom, weeping, wondering whether she should go. But in spite of the continuing pain of lonely nights knowing her husband was in the arms of another woman, she had decided against going.

She felt that entering a mental hospital would destroy what was left of her marriage. It would also do immeasurable harm to the Dulles name she bore so proudly. Even if they would not show it, for public emotion was not their way, the family would be devastated. John Foster was a brother-in-law she greatly admired, though her husband's attitude toward his elder brother was ambivalent, a combination of begrudging admiration and dismissal, of moments of real affection followed by lengthy spells of unexplained resentment. She admired Eleanor because her sister-in-law had also endured much unhappiness, yet somehow had managed to rise above it. Eleanor's husband had been an important Jewish scholar who, when she was pregnant, could not accept the idea of fathering a baby in whose body gentile blood would be mixed with his own, a constant reminder of how he had betrayed the purity of his own strict faith. He had gassed himself shortly before the child was born on a September morning in 1934.

Almost twenty years later, Clover had learned to accept another Dulles family tenet: pain was something to be endured. Rather than go to Montreal, she had remained in Washington, slowly learning to live with her anguish and carving a niche for herself as the capitol's best partygiver.

Clover had discovered when she had met Buckley quite by chance, at the Agency Christmas party, that Dr. Cameron was a friend of her husband. Someone had mentioned that, in a typical gesture, Allen had sent a bottle of his favorite malt whiskey as a seasonal gift to Montreal through the State Department's diplomatic pouch. Curious, she asked who merited such treatment. Perhaps sensing her surprise at the answer, William Buckley had steered the conversation to other topics. Afterward, she wondered whether somehow he knew she had seen Dr. Cameron professionally and did not wish to embarrass her, or whether he felt there was a matter of security involved in revealing her husband knew the psychiatrist. Whatever the reason, she had been grateful to Buckley for displaying such tact.

Since then he had been a regular party guest, causing Dulles to have joshed his wife over whether the invitations were a prelude to her taking young Buckley as a lover. Clover had blushed furiously and said he should not judge her lack of morals by his own. But she always enjoyed Buckley's presence. He was gentle and courteous and always respectful, reminding her of those days when her own son had doted on her.

Just as Clover Dulles never told her husband about her consultation with Dr. Cameron, she had naturally not probed into his relationship with the psychiatrist. She had assumed that the doctor was part of that other world from which her husband virtually excluded her—and which, anyway, she really did not want to be involved with. As usual, because Dr. Cameron was making another of his visits to Washington, Allen had invited him to the party. Never would Clover have connected the physician's presence with those little signs that indicated her husband was deeply worried.

Dulles continued to steer late arrivals toward the bar. Several of them were diplomats of nations their host deemed to be unfriendly, and against whom the Agency waged relentless war. Yet their presence was also part of his own philosophy for heading such a powerful organization. Where other secret service chiefs shielded their names from the world, he had made a calculated decision to keep in the public eye throughout his professional life. Even during those wartime days in Switzerland as station chief of the OSS he had boldly fixed a nameplate to his office door, alerting all visitors who he was and what he did. Cordially greeting guests who would not hesitate to destroy all he believed in was Allen Dulles's special way of showing he was so powerful he did not have to make a mystery out of common knowledge—that, in the end, he could outspy them all.

A slightly bowed figure with bushy eyebrows and a pipe clutched firmly between his lips, he presented the same avuncular appearance that constantly filled the newspapers, showing him at baseball games, film premieres, and big fights.

The worry Clover had sensed had been gnawing at him for almost three years, arising from what had happened after that last weekend in June 1950 when, on the distant 38th Parallel, North Korea had launched an all-out attack against its southern neighbor. The United States had moved swiftly to combat the naked Communist aggression. The United States was once more at war, less than five years after its atomic might had finally brought to an end World War II. Then, Americans had felt invincible. But in that summer of 1950, they were faced with the greatest shock since Pearl Harbor. Within forty-eight hours of the first American troops being taken prisoners, some of them had made extraordinary broadcasts from behind Communist lines, bitterly attacking their government and their homeland in a language filled with the rhetoric of Moscow and Peking.

The president had demanded to know how this had happened. How could the enemy have taken control of the minds of red-blooded Americans? How could the cream of the country's youth, including officers who had graduated from the nation's finest military academies, sound like the rabble-rousers of Eastern Europe? How could superbly trained soldiers allow themselves to become traitors, urging those in the front line to defect to communism? There were many questions—and no immediate answers.

Finding them had become a top priority within the Agency. In the past three years its experts had studied letters sent by prisoners in North Korea praising life under communism to their bewildered families, who could only wring their hands and say they sounded so totally unlike the sons and brothers they had seen off to the Far East. The Agency had collected hundreds of articles by prisoners attacking America and extolling the virtues of communism, articles that appeared in the left-wing press in Europe, India, North Africa, and Indonesia. Agents had worked with the FBI in checking on the authors: almost none of them had shown any previous aptitude for writing, yet the articles were well-written and filled with intimate details of the life they had known in the United States and that they now appeared to totally reject.

Further shocks followed. The enemy began to repatriate small groups of prisoners. Upon their return to the United

States, the nation had been stunned to see that the veterans made it clear they had no wish to live again in America, but yearned to return to be among the Communists. Most frightening of all, they wanted others to come with them. Former POWs began to appear on the streets of the country's major cities, handing out leaflets urging people to support North Korea's efforts to win the war. There was uproar, violence, and a mounting sense of fear. Everybody agreed that what was happening was evil—that this could be the greatest threat the United States had faced. If somehow the enemy had managed to change the minds of the present generation, then if not checked it must lead to the corruption of future generations. People even predicted there would be no future unless this malignant mental enslavement could be countered.

The possibility had haunted the Agency since its creation in 1947. Dulles was among those who remembered the notorious Moscow purge trials of 1937 and 1938 when hard-bitten *apparatchniks* had momentarily diverted world attention from Hitler by the astonishing manner in which they had stood before their judges and confessed to crimes they clearly did not commit.

During his years in Switzerland Dulles had spoken to some of the leading chemists employed by the Sandoz drug and chemical company. They had said that almost certainly the Russians had used drugs and hypnosis to elicit such performances. In the post-war years the Communists had resumed staging show trials in which the defendants again appeared to be zombies. Dulles remembered his discussion with the Sandoz chemist, Dr. Albert Hofmann, who had created the drug LSD. The brilliant young researcher described how, on testing the substance on himself, he felt he would have confessed to anything to escape from the fear unleashed in his mind.

Were the Russians using LSD to prepare victims for trials? Dulles recalled that at Dachau, Nazi doctors had experimented with mescaline, a drug so lethal that it induced prisoners to reveal their most intimate secrets. Was that how the Soviets guaranteed their public confessions? Such questions became crucial when, in 1949, Cardinal Józef Mindszenty stood before the bar of Communist justice, his eyes glazed, his movements robotic, and delivered a devastating monologue of treasonable acts that were clearly beyond his capability to have committed.

The cardinal's trial had galvanized the Agency. Its Scientific Intelligence Unit was expanded to become one of the largest departments within the CIA. Plans were laid for the training of an elite team under Dulles that would, in the words of a memo dated June 14, 1949, "apply special methods of interrogation for the purpose of evaluation of Russian practices." The intent was to duplicate the suspected Soviet use of drugs and hypnosis on refugees and repatriated German prisoners of war.

Even before the Korean War and the unnerving sight of Americans behaving as if they, like the cardinal, were controlled by some unknown force, the Agency set up its first full-scale behavior control program. On April 20, 1950, CIA Director Roscoe Hillenkoetter authorized a virtually unlimited use of unaccountable funds for the project, which was given the code name Bluebird—chosen, it was said, when the director saw a bird soaring into a blue sky beyond his window. Two months later North Korea struck, followed by those abject broadcasts that stunned Americans.

On July 20, 1950, the Agency took its first practical step to test behavioral controls on humans. Two members of Scientific Intelligence, doctors, flew to Tokyo with Dulles under the strictest security. They set to work in an annex of the U.S. Embassy. Their subjects were four Japanese, who had been employed by U.S. Army intelligence but were suspected of also working for the Russians. They had so far refused to admit to being double agents. Each man was injected with sodium amytal, a powerful depressant. Then, an hour later, each received an injection of Benzedrine, a stimulant. The alternating injections were repeated over a twenty-four-hour period. Dulles then questioned the visibly disoriented suspects. The records of the interrogations would remain buried in the vaults of the Agency—though the rumor would persist that the Japanese finally confessed and were taken out to sea at night, shot, and dumped overboard as shark bait. In late October that year, the team traveled in the utmost secrecy to Seoul and, this time working out of a U.S. Army intelligence compound in the city, used similar techniques on twenty-five North Korean prisoners of war. The results were far less successful. Not one of the prisoners was prepared to denounce communism. Discouraged, Dulles and the doctors returned to Washington. They arrived in the midst of national turmoil.

In September 1950, the *Miami News* had published an article under the headline BRAIN WASHING TACTICS. It was the first formal use in any language, and the term brainwashing immediately became common. No one knew then that the Agency had created the phrase and fed it to an operative who worked under the cover of a journalist. Already stunned at the behavior of the prisoners, Americans were aroused to fury at what the term implied: from the brains of wholesome young men had been washed all that was good in America and in its place had been poured all that was bad in communism. How?

One senior Agency employee, Morse Allen, had no doubt. He believed the enemy was using an electrosleep machine that put subjects to sleep without shock convulsions. As they were drifting into one of the various levels of slumber, a semi-conscious stage known as the twilight zone, they would be susceptible to autosuggestion and their interrogators would indoctrinate them, perhaps also using an advanced form of hypnotic therapy to ensure new ideas remained locked in the subconscious of each prisoner. Fantastic though the concept sounded, Allen pointed out that there was nothing very unusual about the machine. It was being used in a hospital in Richmond, Virginia, to help mentally disturbed patients. In a memo to his superior, Paul Gaynor, Allen recommended that the Agency should purchase a machine: "Although it would not be feasible to use it on any of our own people because there is, at least, a theoretical danger of temporary brain damage, it would probably be of value in certain operations, such as the interrogation of POW's or those of interest to this Agency."

The matter was not pursued. Perhaps it was rejected because Allen did not specify why, exactly, it could not be used on our own people and what precisely was temporary brain damage.

Nevertheless, by the time Dulles was back in Washington, Allen was pursuing an even more radical answer to how the North Koreans brainwashed. He had discovered, talking to psychiatrists in Scientific Intelligence, that electroshock treatments not only produced amnesia in patients for nonspecific periods, but when their memories started to return, patients often provided important information about themselves and their backgrounds. At that stage it would have been possible for the Chinese and North Korean doctors to implant anti-American values. Further, the Agency psychiatrists had told him that by lowering the setting on an electroshock machine, a patient would experience excruciating pain. While there was no possible therapeutic value in such pain, it could be an effective method of coercion, and it was quite possible that the prisoners had been subjected to such pressure.

But even if they had, it still did not explain how that pressure worked.

It became clear to Dulles that Scientific Intelligence had too intellectual an approach, that its scientists were preoccupied with pure research and not prepared to test out their theories. After the Far East missions, Scientific Intelligence had shown no stomach for further work on humans. However, the Agency's Office of Technical Services Staff (TSS) had no such qualms. It provided gadgets for field agents—fountain pens that could shoot, coins that exploded, and poisons that left no trace, along with the disguises they needed and forged passports and travel documents. Most important, TSS was not only staffed with scientists equally as brilliant as those at Scientific Intelligence, but they were men with operational experience. They would have no reservations about testing ideas on unsuspecting subjects, especially in such a vitally important and urgent area as brainwashing.

In late 1952, Project Bluebird was renamed Operation Artichoke —a vegetable Dulles was partial to—and was placed, at his behest, under TSS. The department immediately set out to recruit doctors and scientists of all disciplines. Apart from their proven professional qualifications, they must also fit a criteria Dulles had defined: "Each person's ethics must be such that he would be completely cooperative in any phase of our program regardless of how revolutionary it may be." There must be no hesitation over taking part in lethal medical experiments.

TSS also set about finding subjects to be used for what from the outset were acknowledged would be mind-control experiments to try and discover the enemy's methods. The Agency sought individuals of dubious loyalty, suspected double agents or plants, subjects having known reason for deception—anyone, in effect, whose fate would not be commented upon. In Agency terms they were expendables, who ultimately could be terminated. In plain language, they were persons who could be killed.

The search had produced a few expendables. Their fate would remain another closely guarded secret. Some undoubtedly died from drugs or having their brains burned out with electricity. The file on the terminals remained in a safe in the director's office.

Yet despite all the money spent, the projects begun and abandoned, the subjects terminated, the answer as to how the enemy brainwashed remained as elusive as ever.

For the past three years, while the nation had grown more appalled at the sight of the elite of its armed forces making unbelievable, cliché-ridden confessions the Agency had become increasingly frantic in its search for the answer.

The doctors at TSS ignored their medical oath to do no harm to anyone, and repeatedly crossed well-known ethical lines. National security outweighed all other considerations. Professional and—most important of all, perhaps—personal morality ceased to matter. There was at times a sense of madness in the Agency's corridors. Dulles arranged for Sandoz to airfreight a quantity of LSD. It was tried on a small number of subjects: volunteers from TSS. The results were startling. The guinea pigs seemed to literally go out of control in minutes after taking the drug, behaving like madmen. Yet LSD did not seem to be any help in restructuring human behavior. Mescaline was experimented with. It, too, seemed unable to reproduce the effects the Nazis had obtained in Dachau. The sense of desperation increased.

Agency chemists consulted old almanacs to find if there was a witch's potion to explain what had happened; archivists consulted the records of the Inquisition for clues; Orientalists searched their domain; Arabists theirs. There was nothing, not a hint that would point to how the North Koreans were getting such bizarre and lasting cooperation. The psychiatrists, psychologists, and transculturalists all agreed that what had happened was psychologically rooted. But how? Through drugs? Hypnosis? All the prisoners had been physically examined by the country's leading neurologists and neurosurgeons upon their return. There had been no sign of any surgical intervention. Yet, it appeared that parts of the prisoners' brains had been interfered with. But how?

Gradually over the past year there had developed within the Agency a sharp rift. There were those who believed there was no magic in what had happened, that the prisoners were really latent Communists whose beliefs had simply surfaced in response to their captors' prompting. Other Agency employees countered that the brainwashed soldiers had often been pillars of their communities: conservative, church-going youngsters imbued with their parents' old-fashioned values. They could not be dismissed as malcontents who had been simply waiting for a chance to reveal themselves.

Something very peculiar had happened to them in North Korea. But what? What had made them really seem no different from the zombielike figures who appeared in the Soviet show trials? It was clear those persons had been drugged. But there was no evidence that the returning veterans had been doped. Was it possible that there existed in North Korea a drug that the West did not know about? The Agency archivists combed accounts of the Russian Revolution and read the transcripts of war crimes trials at Nuremberg and in Tokyo. They found ample evidence of horrific treatment of prisoners, but nothing to suggest that either the Russians, Nazis, or Japanese had managed to brainwash their victims.

Volumes had been produced offering theories that, in further reams, had been demolished. Finally, it became clear to Dulles that the only possible way to find the truth would be to duplicate everything the Communists could have done. Only by discovering the exact methods used to brainwash would it also be possible to produce an antidote. But to conduct such clinical trials almost certainly would require a hospital and patients.

For months, pending his confirmation as director, Dulles had hesitated. The risks for him and the Agency were enormous. If it ever became known that the United States government had funded what would be unprecedented clinical trials—ones beyond all ethical acceptability—it would most certainly lead to the sudden end of his remarkable and brilliant career. Not even John Foster could save him in such a situation. Forgotten, then, would be all those other triumphs he had masterminded; the way he had out-maneuvered single-handedly foreign governments, removed dictators and monarchs, and established that the Agency's writ ran from the tip of South America to the edge of the Arctic Circle. It would all count for nothing if it was ever hinted at that he had authorized the brainwashing of Americans.

Yet, that streak of adventurousness that sometimes bordered on the reckless drove him on. Gradually all the doubts came down to one question: Did it have to be Americans who would be used as guinea pigs?

Trying to determine the answer had created in her husband the signs Clover had detected.

As with all Dulles parties, what Clover disliked most had happened: little groups were forming, inward-facing conclaves of the sober-suited and well-informed. Beneath a portrait of her husband's father in severe clerical garb—the Reverend Allen Macy Dulles had been a minister of the Presbyterian Church in New York and was remembered within the family for casting doubts on the Virgin Birth—was what Clover called the first team. She knew a few of them by name but nothing of what they did. She only knew her husband regarded them with fondness. There was Dr. Sydney Gottlieb, who like Dulles had been born with a club foot, as well as a stammer. He had dealt with the physical defect by taking up folk dancing; the stammer had been eradicated by sheer willpower. He lived in a former slave cabin and kept goats on his fifteen acres in Maryland. She knew he was a chemist and a graduate of Cal Tech; she would have been astonished, and perhaps alarmed, to know that nowadays Dr. Gottlieb spent part of his time conducting dragnet searches through the jungles of Latin America to find new poisons for Agency operatives to use to murder and leave no trace. With him was Richard Helms, who still liked to impress people by dropping he had gone to Le Rosey, the Swiss preparatory school the Shah of Persia had also attended and that, during his days as a correspondent with United Press in Berlin, he had obtained a remarkably frank interview with Hitler. She would have been probably even more surprised to know that the smooth-talking Helms was very much concerned with the question preoccupying her husband.

Grouped around the pair were others from the Agency, men and women, whose names she always forgot. She only remembered Dr. James Monroe because he was one of the politest Agency persons she had met; for the most part the others tended to be cool or even downright distant. She would have been quite staggered to have learned that nowadays Dr. Monroe spent his days trying to find ways to successfully break and rebuild minds.

Clover knew better than to intrude on their discussions. In the past they had displayed an unnerving habit of abruptly breaking off in midsentence when she or anyone else who was not a member of their charmed circle approached. Then they would make polite small talk, something Clover really hated. At those times she had felt like a stranger in her own house. Yet she could still count this party as a huge success. Couples were lining up to reach the buffet and emerging from the dining room with laden plates. It was a fork supper so that people could still drink while eating. She would touch nothing; she never did at her own parties until the last guest had gone. Then she would pick at the remains of the buffet. Her husband was nowhere to be seen and for one sickening moment she wondered whether he had, after all, picked out a girl and sneaked her upstairs. Then she saw him, in the midst of yet another camp.

She recognized two of its members at once. Talking earnestly was Dr. Harold Wolff, a tiny man with the most dominating personality she had ever encountered. Even Allen did not interrupt when Dr. Wolff spoke. He was one of the country's leading neurologists and was on the faculty of Cornell University Medical College. But of far more importance to Clover, Dr. Wolff was also successfully treating Allen, Jr., for his head wound. Standing beside the neurologist was Dr. Cameron. He was not only tall, but imposing. When he was not speaking, his palest of blue eyes were fixed intently on the person addressing him; he could stand so perfectly still that not a movement disturbed his custommade blue suit: she could not remember him ever coming to the house in anything but that sober dark two-piece. When he spoke there was the softest of burrs, as if he wished to remind people that his ancestors had fought at Culloden in the Highlands of Scotland when America was still being roamed by Indians. He invariably greeted her formally but as the evening lengthened he called all the women lassie. She didn't know why, but he still made her feel uneasy.

Dr. Cameron had brought with him another psychiatrist, an Englishman, who had reminded her they had last met at a banquet given by the American Psychiatric Association: Dr. William Sargant. The *Post* had carried an item that he was in town to attend a medical conference. Just as the capabilities of her other guests would have astounded her, so she would have been amazed to learn that among his other skills, the strong-faced Dr. Sargant was regarded by her husband as Britain's leading medical expert on eliciting confessions.

Nor, of course, did Clover know that Dr. Sargant did not approve of all the techniques of Dr. Cameron—for example, his idea of keeping patients asleep for weeks at a time, during which they were regularly electroshocked, often twice a day, in an effort to restructure their minds. Dr. Sargant had sharply expressed his disapproval of such medical madness. Despite such disagreements, the two most renowned psychiatrists in the English-speaking world remained good friends, often sharing the results of each other's research into mental illness.

On this visit to Washington Dr. Cameron had told the Englishman that government was making the usual wooing sounds for him to get involved. Naturally, understanding how such matters worked, Dr. Sargant assumed that Dr. Cameron's invitation to the Dulles party was part of that courtship. In Dr. Sargant's mind there was "no doubt that Ewen was being fished for by the CIA."

Like most Washington weeknight parties, the Dulleses's gathering was over by ten-thirty; government went to bed early and rose accordingly.

Clover was therefore surprised to see her husband lead Dr. Wolff and Dr. Cameron to his den after arranging for another guest to give Dr. Sargant a lift back to his hotel. The two doctors were then joined by Dr. Monroe, Dr. Gottlieb, and Richard Helms.

After nibbling at one or two dishes while Natalie organized the hired help to tidy away, Clover retired to bed, unaware that her husband had found the answer to his problem.

The Agency doctors would continue committing serious breaches of their sacred oath; would still, if need be, use treatment methods that were reckless and dangerous to life; and would, in the final analysis, be present at, take part in, or even be solely responsible for bringing their work to a terminal stage—medically killing under the cover which the CIA provided. But the director had decided that he need not use Americans for the full-scale trial he proposed to arrange and finance in a still more determined effort to unlock the secrets of mind control. He would instead look north, beyond the borders of the United States, to Canada, to Montreal, to Dr. Ewen Cameron. The psychiatrist and his unsuspecting Canadian patients would be the Agency's flag bearers into the unknown world of influencing memory, changing personality, and disturbing the mind.

6

The
Unsuspecting

She awoke, certain she had sleepwalked during the night
and turned on the central heating, even though it was June.
This was why the sheets were wet and wrinkled. Madeleine
Smith's nightdress clung to her body and the perspiration
made her feel cold. The bedside radio, Eddie's present for
her twenty-seventh birthday, had come on at its preset time,
a few minutes before six A.M. Madeleine had been a broad-
caster in local radio until the morning when she refused to go
into a studio because the Wise Men were sitting on the
microphone. She had fled from the station. That was two
years ago. She had never returned to work.

Since then she had been unable to sleep beyond six, and
often she would already be half-awake, listening through the
drug-induced fog for the voice of the newscaster. He had
been on duty the morning she refused to broadcast and had
smiled at her sympathetically, and said that after all these
years in the business he still experienced sudden moments of
panic. When he had gone to another station, she had followed him, by moving the radio dial. She didn't know why,
any more than she could have explained why something
inside her urged her to get up and begin another day of
pacing and searching through the apartment after Eddie left
for work.

She had told Dr. Cameron she could best imagine it to be
like being driven from deep within by a powerful spring.

Dr. Cameron had looked at her across the spotless, orderly
desk, not saying a word, sitting upright in the high-backed
leather chair, waiting for her to continue. Finally, he asked,

"Lassie, do you have more to say?" She had shook her head and he had waited a moment longer, to be quite sure, before motioning her out of his office. As she crossed the large room he began to speak into a dictating machine. She couldn't understand the words, but the tone was unmistakable: she had somehow once more managed to irritate him. But how could she begin to tell him how she wished she could be a wife to Eddie, yet every time he touched her she became stiff and frightened and the only way she could ever allow him to make love was for her to imagine Eddie was her father. Sometimes he was also one of the Wise Men. She had told no one about them.

Dr. Cameron had prescribed tablets that he said would help lessen the driven feeling. It had meant increasing the Thorazine to three at bedtime, each capsule two hundred milligrams. Eddie counted them out once he was certain she was in the bath, leaving the shiny green cylinders which reminded her of caterpillar larvae, beside a glass of warm milk on her side of the bed. Then he would return the bottle to its safe hiding place.

Madeleine would fall asleep planning how she would spend the next day searching for the bottle. The Wise Men kept urging her to find it.

The newscaster said it was June 19, 1954, and the top story of the day was the execution of Julius and Ethel Rosenberg for betraying some of America's atomic secrets to the Russians. She wondered what it would be like to die from electrocution. Would it be quicker than the tablets? She wondered whether the Wise Men would allow her to try.

Sometimes the Wise Men frightened her. Then she would refuse to listen to them, rushing from one room to another, clutching a floor mop, determined to find them and drive them out of her home. But they were smart, like Eddie was clever in the way he hid the bottle. She would never find either the Wise Men or the capsules. Defeated, Madeleine would allow the Wise Men back into her mind.

Eddie was curled up in his boxer shorts on his side of the bed, his body bronzed from weekends on their balcony overlooking the city. Even asleep, she had told Dr. Cameron, her husband looked so strong. When he came in after a long day on the road from making calls on all the hardware stores in and around Montreal he would be exhausted and famished.

She would have been too busy pacing and searching to have prepared dinner, but even then he would not complain. Instead, he would hold her tightly, while she shook and tried to cry.

The tears never came; they seemed to stop at some point just behind her eyes, just as something, even at that moment, made her stop from telling Eddie about her feelings for her father. Then, trying to banish them, she would bury herself in his body. But when he tried to do more than hold her, she would draw away, panicked. Those were the moments she especially felt she was being unfaithful to her father.

Eddie would cook dinner—mostly out of cans—and they ate on trays before the television. While he cleared away the trays, she would try to concentrate on the screen. But it was difficult, especially when the Wise Men suddenly appeared and danced back and forth across the top of the set. Once she had laughed so loudly at their antics that Eddie came in from the kitchen and looked at her peculiarly. The early evening movie had been a murder mystery.

Every night by nine o'clock, drugged and drained, she would fall asleep, bringing to a close a day that had been like any other.

Madeleine remembered now why her side of the bed was so soggy. She had lived through an old nightmare of being put in a baker's oven and slowly roasted alive. She always managed to kick open the door just as her skin started to drip fat. That was when she woke up, clammy and shivering.

She had told Dr. Cameron about her dream. He had asked her all sorts of questions. Who had put her in the oven? When she came out of her nightmare did she hear noises like blowing, roaring, humming, rattling, shooting, thunder, music, crying, or laughing? She had shook her head. He had gone on. Had she heard whispering, a voice or voices calling out to her, a person or persons she could not see but knew was there?

As he asked the questions, his eyes never left her, as if he could somehow look into her mind. She had thought for one dreadful moment that he knew, after all, about the Wise Men and how they talked to her. She had remained silent, staring back at him, imagining that the Wise Men had built an invisible wall across the desk that protected her from him.

He had gone on asking questions. Did she ever, for instance, imagine she was being struck by molten rain drops? Fire or bullets? She had shook her head, bewildered at such questions. When the allotted fifty minutes were up, he had spoken into his microphone.

The telephone on Eddie's side of the bed rang: six-thirty. His brother, Andy, always rang at this time, five mornings a week, to make sure Eddie would be ready to begin another day's calls. She hated the telephone, convinced its ringing angered the Wise Men, their fury building while Eddie shaved and dressed and was out of the apartment, pausing only to kiss her good-bye and leave her daytime tablets beside a glass of water in the kitchen.

After Madeleine swallowed them she started once more to empty cupboards and drawers, searching for the bottle. The Wise Men in their long gray robes and mist around their bare feet followed her, first balancing effortlessly on top of the coffee grinder. Then, with a hop, skip, and a jump, each of them moved to the plate rack before dancing from one spice jar to another, all the time taunting her that she would never, ever find the bottle. That drove her to tip out drawers onto the floor until the center of the kitchen was a pile of napery, cutlery, crockery and old bills. There was no sign of the bottle. Madeleine moved to the living room.

The Wise Men were sitting on the large wooden framed mirror over the mock fireplace. The mirror was a wedding gift from her parents; its heavy carved oak frame was more suitable for one of the large houses up on Redpath Crescent rather than this midtown apartment. She started to walk toward the mirror, but the oldest of the Wise Men, the one with the beard that flowed from just below the large eye where his mouth should have been, waved her away.

While they were sitting in a row on top of the mirror, it was hard for her to know who was who. Their faces were identical: no nose or mouth, only that unblinking solitary eye above a rounded chin; they each had a fringe cut, like monks. Their beards, she had decided, indicated their age: the youngest had a goatee and the beards of the others were increasingly longer until the oldest Wise Man, the one who had shooed her away, had a beard that reached his toes.

In the past she had begged them to help her find the bottle. But they had only taunted her the more, saying she was useless to herself and worthless for anybody else. She felt the spring tightening inside her. The room was becoming brighter, not with the morning sun but the glow of certainty radiating from her. The bottle was somewhere in this room.

Madeleine began to take down the books, their spines imitation leather, each embossed in gold leaf with a title of the works of William Shakespeare. It had been her prize for winning the debating competition in her final year at school. The bottle was not hidden behind the volumes. She turned to another shelf containing Eddie's textbooks for the business management course he had taken. She dropped them onto the carpet, listening to them thud, watching the pages fly open. The shelf was finally empty. She tipped out a third, then a fourth shelf, sweeping the books to the floor, club editions and novels she had bought second-hand, along with the paperback thrillers Eddie liked. The shelves were finally empty and there was still no sign of the bottle.

The Wise Men sat on the top shelf, laughing at her, saying if she could not even find a bottle how could she expect to be anything but worthless.

Dr. Cameron had asked, during one of the first sessions, whether she loved herself. Or did she feel that was impossible? Perhaps because she felt like a victim of some terrible plot? She had stared at him. He had asked if she ever felt people like the Jews, or the nuns who had taught her at school, were persecuting her, mocking and slandering her, threatening her, even to the point of wanting to torture her. She had shook her head, her black curls bobbing. That day he had not spoken into his dictating machine. Instead he had said she should check into the hospital. "Lassie, it's the only way you can be made well again." She had not believed him then; she did not now.

The Wise Men were still laughing. Kicking the books from under her feet, she went to the cabinet that held her parents' other wedding gift, a collection of porcelain figurines her father had bought before he returned from Japan at the end of World War II. He had promised them to her when she married. Never for a moment had he suspected no man would ever measure up to him.

The bottle must be behind the dolls. The Wise Men's words came fast and faster, silently rushing through her head. *Behind the dolls*. Turning from the cabinet, holding a figurine in her hand, Madeleine suddenly felt a compulsive need to block out the words. She clenched her lips and pressed her hands to her ears to escape the dreadful chant. *Behind the dolls!*

The figurine lay on the floor, shattered. For a moment there was silence in the room—a long and terrible moment while she stared down at what she had done. She had broken the doll, broken one of her father's dolls.

Suddenly, with renewed fury, the chanting resumed. *Break them all! Break them all! Break them!*

She stood shivering in her nightdress before the cabinet. The shrieking filled her head. *Break them all! Break them!*

She reached forward and, with one sweeping motion of her hand, smashed the figurines against the sides of the cabinet. She snatched at those that remained and began to hurl them across the room at the mirror, shattering the glass. Then, like a child's rag doll she folded to the floor, covered with tears and splinters of porcelain.

Finally, Madeleine fell asleep.

When she awoke, a new voice was coming from the bedroom radio. A woman was talking about the latest scientific discovery—that smoking was linked to heart disease. The Wise Men reminded her she could not smoke herself to death—but she could find peace when she located the bottle.

She dragged herself off the floor and went to the bedroom. The telephone was ringing. She looked at her watch. It was almost one o'clock. While she had been asleep Eddie would have rang twice from his calls, at nine and eleven; he called her every two hours to see how she was. She picked up the receiver and heard the relief in his voice. He talked, she listened. If she wanted, he could cut short his day and be back by early evening. In the meantime, she should phone her mother to come over.

No! In her head she screamed the word *No! No! No!* She hated her mother; she had stood between Madeleine and her father.

Eddie said once more that he loved her and asked again if she was okay, and if she was okay, and she said she loved him and that she was fine. She put down the telephone. He would call again at three. That left two undisturbed hours. Sensing her new resolve, the Wise Men no longer mocked. Instead they told her to be calm and to think logically, step by step—and then she would surely find the bottle.

Before he prescribed the pills, Dr. Cameron had questioned her. Had she ever felt like killing herself? Had she ever heard anyone tell her to do so? Apart from that nightmare, did she have other dreams about death? Did she think it would be nice to die? Did she fear, as a good Catholic lassie, that if she took her own life she would go to hell?

She had shaken her head to each question.

After a final stare he had written out the prescription. Then, when she had felt he was ready to trust her, he insisted Eddie should call him. Standing outside the closed bedroom door she had caught snatches of Eddie's side of the conversation. "I appreciate it's a risk we have to take. . . . I'll make sure they are kept in a safe place. . . ."

Madeleine looked around the room, her determination growing. She began to search systematically. She went to the bathroom and returned with a stool. Balancing, she reached the top of the wardrobe, running her hands across its dusty surface. Nothing. She began to search inside the wardrobe, pulling out the clutter of shoes and handbags, looking inside each item. Nothing. She checked the rail of clothes, divided equally between Eddie's suits and sports jackets and her dresses and winter coats. She carefully patted each garment and checked their pockets. Still nothing. At one end of the rail, wrapped in a plastic cover, was the two-piece costume she wore for the honeymoon to Vancouver, 2,500 miles each way by train; she had loved every mile of it. She lifted off the cover and began to pat the costume. Nothing. She was about to turn away when she noticed a string hanging from the hanger. She pulled it and drew out a paper bag that had been suspended inside the jacket. She opened it.

Madeleine had finally found the bottle.

Behind her she heard a low concerted whisper of satisfaction and relief from the Wise Men.

She looked at the bottle, turning it over in her hand and then holding it up to the light, shaking the capsules so that they danced inside the glass. The Wise Men circled around her, hovering in midair, chanting. *Do it! Do it! Take them! Take them! All of them!*

"No!"

Madeleine's scream silenced the voices in her head. She slumped to the floor, staring at the bottle. The Wise Men said she must allow nothing to weaken her resolve. She felt her heart beating, so fast that she felt faint.

When he had first seen her after an internist had completed a physical examination, Dr. Cameron had looked at the results and asked about her weight. Did it fluctuate a great deal? Did she suddenly feel hot and sweaty? Did she have spells of constipation followed by diarrhea? He had inspected her wrists, the palms of her hands, the soles of her feet. He had asked about her periods. Were they irregular and scanty? He had put so many questions. She had answered them all.

Madeleine went to the bathroom and washed her face and combed her hair. Then she stepped out of the nightdress and put it in the soil bin behind the door. She felt very calm.

She must write Eddie a note. She went to the kitchen. There were tears on her cheeks. She could, after all, cry—she really could. That was wonderful. She sat at the counter, where she used to breakfast with Eddie, and took a sheet of paper from the pile he kept in the kitchen to jot down details of new customers to be followed up or orders to be phoned through to head office.

During that first consultation, Dr. Cameron had told her to copy out a passage from a book. He had silently watched her write. For what seemed a long time he studied her work. Finally he asked how long she had written like this, using flourishes for capital letters, contracting some words, leaving others out. She had not answered. He had not pressed the matter.

Madeleine stared at the paper. She knew what she wanted to say, but somehow could not find the words. Instead she began to doodle: flowers, suns, and then flames all over the paper. She wrote over the artwork. "Dear Eddie, I am happy you want . . ."

She tried again, still jumbling up the words so that the next sentence read, "Dear happy, you want to be Eddie."

That was followed by: "You dear, I Eddie . . ."

The Wise Men once more began taunting. *You can't do it. You can't do it! You can't!*

Madeleine put down the pen and picked up the bottle and walked over to the faucet, filling a glass of water. She placed the tumbler on the drainer. Then she unscrewed the bottle top and tipped a handful of capsules into her hand. The Wise Men were grouped behind the glass, watching her carefully, the way Dr. Cameron had done. In one irreversible movement, she shoved the capsules into her mouth, crushing their shells in her anxiety to swallow them. She washed them down with water and refilled the glass. She swallowed more pills and drank again. She could taste the bitter powder in her mouth and felt the bits of plastic sticking between her teeth.

Finally, the bottle was empty and the Wise Men had gone. She felt suddenly alone and frightened. This was not an attempt; she was going to kill herself.

She walked to the bedroom and lay on the bed, closing her eyes, imagining what was happening inside her, the poison slowly spreading from her stomach through her body and into her brain, coating it, finally blocking out all the pain. There was a ringing sound. She felt heavy and sleepy. The ringing was far away. She imagined her brain was curling up, shriveling until it was the size of a pea. The ringing had stopped. She was dying.

That must have been why she felt so strange. This was the onset of death. But why was it shaking her, rattling that pea inside her head? She could not open her eyes. There were voices, not those of the Wise Men, yet urgent and commanding voices. First Eddie's and then strangers'. Hands lifted her off the bed and onto a stretcher. She was rushed over the carpet, crunching over the mess in the living room, out of the apartment, and into the elevator. Eddie knelt beside her, holding her hand, asking over and over again. "Why? Why did you do it?" Out in the street, more voices, shocked and surprised voices, asking if she was dead.

Madeleine was lifted into the ambulance. Eddie climbed in beside her and the attendant. The driver switched on the siren and raced through the late afternoon traffic to the Allan Memorial Institute on the lower reaches of Mount Royal, a hill that rises sharply from Montreal's downtown area. Madeleine was unloaded and rushed to a treatment room where she was transferred from the gurney to a table, fitted with straps. Her legs and arms were secured. A doctor thrust a long metal and sponge tube down her throat and began to pump out her stomach. When he had completed the task he telephoned Dr. Cameron.

Mary Matilda Morrow had always wanted to be a doctor. She wanted to be respected, admired, and loved like her father had been by his patients. Encouraged by him, she had studied the medical history of the past century, during which all the great advances of medicine were achieved, beginning in 1846 with the discovery of anesthesia, which led to painless surgery. Everything that went before, her father said, was part of the age of ignorance, of torture and a fruitless stumbling in the dark. Reading not only about that first operation performed under gas in the Massachusetts General Hospital in Boston, but also about how Louis Pasteur identified the microbial killers under his microscope and how Joseph Lister used the first carbolic spray in the operating room, the harbinger of still higher surgical standards, she was confirmed in her belief that a career in medicine was the only one for her.

While surgery and the other disciplines of her father's profession were well served in Montreal, the city was no different from any other in Canada in its attitude toward the mentally ill. The two great custodial institutions in Montreal were Verdun Protestant Hospital and St. Jean de Dieu Hospital for Catholics, a place so large that it had its own private railway to transport its six thousand inmates from one monolithic depository to another. Her father had told her there was almost no treatment provided and that the government allowed only seventy-five cents a day to clothe, feed, and shelter a patient.

That furthered her desire to be a doctor—even if it meant working in one of those grim, gray stone buildings. She was certain that, just as a hundred years earlier, men had taken surgery out of the environment of the abattoir, so others would do the same for psychiatry and its complementary disciplines of neurology and neuroanatomy.

It did not quite work out as she had planned. With the family unable to afford the fees for medical school, Mary had enrolled in a nursing course. Her second year of studies was marked by one of those bitter controversies that periodically surfaced in Montreal's medical circles. A small psychiatric hospital had opened in the very center of the city, amid the fine mansions of important businessmen and doctors. It was the first time she had heard of the Allan Memorial Institute or its director, Dr. Cameron, recently from the United States. What upset local residents was that there were no bars or windows or locked doors in the new hospital. Patients, it seemed, could come and go as they pleased. In a community with a strong Victorian attitude toward the insane, that was seen as dangerous and foolhardy. Mary, however, thought it a good idea to abolish bars and locks.

She scrimped and saved to finally enter the most prestigious medical school in Canada: McGill University in Montreal. She had qualified in 1951. She was, she sometimes admitted to herself, obsessed with the idea of making a success of her life—but then, many of the heroic figures in medicine had the same single-minded purpose.

On this September morning in 1955, Dr. Morrow reflected that what her father had often said of Montreal was still true: next to Quebec, it was the one Canadian city where a doctor, to get along, needed to know the rosary as well as how to read a blood pressure gauge. Not only did the Catholic Church physically dominate the city as the largest landowner, but it also reached deep into the minds of its people. Many of the patients she saw were filled with the anxieties and guilt that came from being unable to live by their faith. For the most part they came from the rural world beyond Montreal, drawn to the city by the promise of high salaries. They brought with them a lifetime of being taught by their priests, for example, to take baths in their undergarments to avoid the sin of exposing their own flesh.

In her laborious climb up the medical ladder, Mary Morrow had been driven on by the idea that Paracelsus was right when he had said the highest of all qualifications a physician should pursue is wisdom; without that all her degrees and qualifications meant nothing. Wisdom could not be found in books, nor could it flourish alongside the bigotry, backbiting, and the machinations of doctors who knew, for instance, how to write subtly damning references that made it that much harder for her to be accepted. She sometimes wondered if their opposition and resentment was because, unlike them, she had begun her career as a nurse in the hospital where she now held an appointment as a neurologist: St. Mary's, one of several Catholic teaching hospitals in the city.

The workings of the human brain and the nervous system continued to fascinate her. She hoped one day to make her own contribution to understanding more fully the limbic system, which controlled emotions and the process of learning; the cerebellum, responsible for all bodily muscle movements; the occipital lobe, which controlled sight; and the temporal lobe, which regulated hearing.

In the past four years she had held a number of junior appointments in the United States. But the urge to return to Montreal and prepare for the day she hoped to have her own department at St. Mary's had been strong.

Misunderstood, she continued to go her own way. She never turned down a chance to expand her knowledge and she saw patients late into the evening. At times she could be brusque, but gradually she had even brought that under control by adopting a rather impersonal coolness to those she worked with.

She asked herself questions about treating brain malfunction, which increasingly troubled her. Was lobotomy really the ultimate answer? Every year thousands of the depressed, violent, schizophrenic, and alcoholic, when all else had failed, had their frontal lobes severed. Even children's brains had been cut in the United States to make them good American citizens. She was convinced there had to be a better way than hacking out both amygdala—the clusters of cells in the temporal lobes, thought to control emotional responses. But she had not enough experience to begin to suggest an alternative.

Nor was she enthusiastic over electroconvulsive therapy, in which an electric current was jolted through the brain. No one yet knew the precise effect it had. Its proponents—and there were many in Montreal—said it was therapeutic. But, given a choice she would prefer some other way. Those treatments simply did not fit into her concept of how patients should be managed.

To further her career, Dr. Morrow had recently accepted a part-time post at the Montreal Neurological Institute, while continuing to see patients at St. Mary's. She was also doing highly specialized research on the nerve supply to the carotid arteries, blood vessels in the brain. She also managed to find time to attend clinical conferences and read the publications in her field. At times she felt anxious and depressed, wondering how she could continue to cope with such a workload.

Dr. Morrow was now planning yet another career move, which she hoped would bring her that much closer to her dream of being St. Mary's first woman chief of neurology. Achieving that goal, she hoped, would put an end to a terrible sense of inferiority, which arose from the fact that when she transferred any of her own patients from St. Mary's to the Neurological Institute for more sophisticated investigation, she had no authority to do anything for them. With her own department at St. Mary's, which she intended would lack for nothing in equipment, she would have total control over treatment. Only when that happened would the debilitating sense of failure stop. The question of her future had begun to prey on her mind.

She decided the best way to achieve her ambition was to add psychiatry to her other qualifications. Surely, then, St. Mary's would recognize she was exceptionally talented and give her a department. She had decided to study for her diploma in psychiatry under Dr. Cameron. She remembered his lectures to medical students on the rudiments of psychiatry only because he had seemed nervous, ill-attuned, and unable to really communicate. Yet she had recently read some of his clinical papers; they were fluent and persuasive and at times almost messianic. It was clear he saw psychiatry almost as the new religion of medicine.

Encouraged, believing she may have misjudged Dr. Cameron, she looked forward to joining his staff. She also had to admit that in less than a decade, he had turned the Allan Memorial Institute into one of the most renowned psychiatric teaching hospitals in North America—some said the world. There was a behavioral laboratory that specialized in studying human responses by means of sound and visual recordings. The experimental therapeutics unit was under the direction of Dr. Robert Cleghorn, one of the most respected researchers in Canada. The electrophysiological laboratory was run by another renowned physician, Dr. Lloyd Hisey. There were departments for vasulographic, pharmacologic, and transcultural studies. From what she had heard, every nook and cranny of the old mansion on Mount Royal was occupied with research, testing, and treatment.

From what she had gleaned from snatches of conversation in the medical staff room at St. Mary's, some of the treatments were radical. Dr. Cameron prescribed large quantities of drugs, repeated courses of electroshock, and a technique he had developed called psychic driving, repeatedly playing back selected words to a patient to break down psychological barriers and open up the patient's unconscious. The staff room consensus was that it sounded like something the Russians or Chinese would have used to brainwash American prisoners rather than a treatment to be given in the psychiatry flagship of the McGill University medical complex.

Following one of the many principles of her father, Dr. Morrow avoided medical gossip and decided she would defer judgment until she had firsthand knowledge of the situation. In the meantime, she had another, more pressing problem. In spite of all her hospital appointments, she was desperately short of money. It was not that she was extravagant—in many ways she lived a frugal, almost monastic life, not from choice but because her schedule left her almost no time to relax and socialize. What little free time she had was given over to coaching students in her speciality, neuroanatomy. Often she taught them without charge. At the end of a week she would be hungry and yet not have a dollar to satisfy that hunger. She wondered if that could explain why she felt so tense. She was close to forty years of age, alone, dedicated and ambitious. So where had her life gone wrong? Whenever she asked the question, there was no time to consider it. She plunged back into work, if only to try and ward off the anxiety attacks that left her feeling so low.

Like a thief in the night it had come again, taking away Jeannine Huard's fragile peace, filling her mind with dread and shame, reminding her of what had happened the last time she had been hospitalized under Dr. Cameron's care. Five years later, the horror of it was something she could not share even with her husband. Yet she knew that what had been done was as frighteningly real as the despair that once more gripped her on this March day in 1956.

No one—not her husband, family, or friends—really understood what it was like to be burdened with such depression, so powerful that it affected her speech, her movements, kept her awake at night, filled her with self-recrimination, kept her from eating, took away her sexual desires, disrupted her menstrual cycle, and physically stripped pounds from her already slight frame.

Outsiders only saw a wan-faced young woman with a caring husband and a healthy baby daughter. How could she begin to tell them about what had happened that time she had trustingly placed herself in the hands of Dr. Cameron?

She had undergone an appendectomy in another hospital and had never fully recovered. Her family doctor thought she was anemic and prescribed a tonic. It did no good. She had lost her interest in normal pleasures and became apprehensive, and finally alarmed, when she lost five pounds in one week. She wondered whether she might have cancer.

Because Jeannine could not afford private treatment, she went to a public clinic at the Royal Victoria Hospital in Montreal. The doctor referred her to the Allan Memorial Institute. In the admissions room a nurse had filled out various forms and asked her to sign one headed CONSENT FOR EXAMINATION AND TREATMENT. The nurse dated it April 4, 1951.

Jeannine was escorted to her room. For days nothing happened. She lay in her bed, staring at the ceiling or trying to sleep, wondering why she had been asked to sign a form when no treatment had followed. Finally, a doctor came and asked numerous questions about her life. She answered as best she could, though she felt increasing anxiety under the probing.

The doctor returned after a few days, this time with a tall, virtually bald man with unblinking eyes. He called her lassie and inquired if she sometimes felt her heart racing and wanted to faint or had throat spasms. He asked if she became easily irritable, wanted to be left alone, or became quickly upset. Jeannine felt frightened. The questions made her wonder if the doctors thought she was really crazy.

One day they started to drug her. She thought she swallowed up to forty pills a day. The antidepressant drugs soon began their biochemical work. Suspended between being half-awake and half-asleep, her mouth dry, her eyes heavy— some of the side effects of her tablets—soon her memory began to play tricks. She'd been unable to remember which day it was, and then which part of the day it was; morning, noon, and night all became the same hazy blur. She felt restless and unable to complete even the slightest thought.

One morning she was taken to a treatment room. A doctor stood beside what looked like an electric chair. She was strapped in. A metal hat was placed on her head. Suddenly, a dazzling spotlight flashed into her eyes, so bright and powerful that she thought she'd been blinded. She could not remember what else had happened.

Next day, she was taken to another treatment room. This time she was ordered by another doctor—like all the others, she never was able to learn his name—to stand before him. He injected her in the arm. Next he fitted goggles with thick-hinged plastic lenses over her eyes. Jeannine felt fingers lift a hinge so she could peer out with one eye. What she saw petrified her. The physician was holding a gun close to her face. It had a tube running from its butt to a cylinder. Before she could beg him not to fire, he squeezed the trigger and a powerful blast of compressed air was shot into her eye. She recoiled, and was about to slump to the floor when the doctor caught her, pulled her to her feet, and commanded her to stand still. He lowered the lens, leaving her in trembling darkness. Then he lifted the other lens and, again at point-blank range, shot another jet of air into her eye.

Reeling from the shock and pain, her eyes inflamed, she was once more strapped in a chair, again similar to one in an execution chamber, with wires embedded in its arms and legs. The wires were taped to her fingers. Standing behind the chair, the doctor began to question her. She was spared nothing—from childhood fantasies to her wedding night; from schooldays to the birth of her baby. Had she always been a poor eater? Did her mother force her to eat? Did her father allow her to clear her plate? Had she wet her bed? Did she love her father more than her mother, or the other way round? Did she love her husband more than her child? Or her daughter more than him? Or equally? Did she love herself? Did she think she was a failure as a wife and mother? Did she get angry over little things? Did she like to keep her home immaculate, or didn't she care about housework? Was she scared of being alone? Did she like being alone? Did she like making love? Did the prospect of sex sometimes frighten her? Had she enjoyed her wedding night? Did she have sexual dreams?

It seemed the questions had gone on for hours. Finally she reached the point where she was "so upset that I couldn't do anything."

The wires were removed and she was taken back to her room and given another injection that sent her into deep unconsciousness. Years later she discovered what had caused that—insulin coma treatment, which she found every bit as terrifying as being confronted by a gun and blasted in both eyes.

No one ever explained the purpose of what had been done. After weeks of such treatment she left the hospital, feeling no better.

Over the past five years she had tried—God, how she had tried—to cope, to fend off a feeling of having failed her husband and her responsibilities.

"Oh God," she would whisper. "Please help me. Please . . . please . . ."

Once more her depression returned, filling her with a crippling despondency, leaving her in torment that, after all, she would have to return to what she now thought of as the house of horrors on the hill.

For Jeannine and the hundreds of other patients who had been admitted to the Allan Memorial Institute, there had been many additions and changes to the treatment regime. Dr. Cameron's almost uncanny ability to raise money had led to increased experimental research on those often too ill to know what was happening. A new wing had been added, increasing the bed capacity to a hundred.

As 1956 drew to a close, the world had grown a little darker in the aftermath of the Suez Crisis and the Hungarian uprising. Both the People's Republic of China and the Soviet Union looked somehow more menacing that winter, despite the size of the vote that had returned President Eisenhower to the White House. The aged war hero seemed a poor defense against encroaching communism.

Few knew—least of all Madeleine Smith, Dr. Mary Morrow, and Jeannine Huard—that Dr. Cameron was finally ready to oblige an old friend, Allen Dulles of the Central Intelligence Agency, to discover the seemingly effortless way in which the Communists brainwashed people. His patients would be his weapon.

Dr. Cameron knew what he must do, believing there was no other way and, above all, that he was totally right.

7

Beyond All
Reason

On a bitterly cold January morning in 1957, the sun still aglow behind the snowscape, a black Cadillac drove along icy Highway 87, heading north out of Lake Placid in upper New York State. Despite the treacherous road conditions, Dr. Cameron drove fast, one gloved hand on the wheel, the other gripping a microphone. On the seat beside him was a portable recorder fitted with a long-life Dictabelt. In the two hours it would take him to reach the Canadian border and, shortly afterwards, Montreal, he would have used up a dozen belts.

All would be transcribed before nightfall by his team of secretaries. One would type his comments on the detailed case notes he had reviewed over the weekend at his home in Albany while his wife, Jean, and the children, three boys and a girl, played chess. Another secretary handled administration, a third his publications—books, articles for the academic journals, lectures, and statements to the press. He knew the value of publicity and also when to avoid it.

There would be absolutely no publicity concerning what he was dictating as he drove. It would be transcribed by the secretary who handled his most confidential work, the indefatigable Dorothy Trainor.

. . . application for grant to study the effects upon human behavior of the repetition of verbal signals. One: General purposes. We are requesting a grant to support studies upon the effects upon human behavior of the repetition of verbal signals. Our present interest is directed towards both (a) the production of changes in behavior and (b) changes in physiological function, the major emphasis to be upon the latter because of the greater ease of measurement. Two: Background . . .

Long experience in applying for research funding had taught Dr. Cameron to immediately engage attention. The committees that approved grants were frequently swamped by applications, and often did not look beyond the first page of a proposal. During the past thirteen years he had already raised more money than any other Canadian doctor. It had begun with $40,000 in 1943 from the Rockefeller Foundation to create the Allan Memorial Institute. Further substantial sums were raised to extend the institute and hire some of the leading figures in North American medical research. No source was too great or small for him to overlook: government agencies, philanthropic foundations, wealthy businessmen, down to the proceeds of bring-and-buy sales, raffles, and even school collections.

Now, on this ice-bound road, Dr. Cameron was dictating another request for funding.

. . . the effects upon human behavior of the repetition of verbal signals have been under study at the Allan Memorial Institute for Psychiatry since June 1953. The early investigations were based upon the observation that repeated playback of particularly significant statements made by the patient during psychotherapy elicited a number of phenomena: (a) increased productivity by the patient of material of dynamic significance; (b) the material was related to the statement repeated (or driven); (c) increased identification of significant components in the repeated material; (d) this increased identification, or recognition, of significant components was particularly marked in the patient. It was evoked in the therapist . . .

That brief background note, he could be certain, would still not alert anyone to question, for instance, whether there was any significance in that June date. No one, of course, could know—Dr. Cameron had made sure—that what he had begun on that day over three and a half years ago was his first contribution to the Central Intelligence Agency's search for methods of mind control.

Significant developments had occurred since the meeting in Allen Dulles's study following the party to celebrate his appointment as director.

On April 3, 1953—the day the Pentagon pronounced that any American prisoner in Korea who refused to come home when offered repatriation would be immediately classified as a deserter and shot on sight—Dulles once more displayed his penchant for big spending and a schoolboy enthusiasm for using cryptonyms. He authorized $300,000 to be put at Dr. Gottlieb's disposal for "ultra-sensitive work in the use of biological and chemical materials." At the same time, Operation Artichoke became Project M-K-Ultra. The first two letters designated it as a Technical Services Staff (TSS) operation. The word "Ultra" was a reminder for Dulles of the great Anglo-American intelligence coup of World War II, which had broken almost all of the German military codes.

Absorbed into M-K-Ultra was Project M-K-Delta, which had been investigating how the Agency could best make use of chemical-biological warfare. A CIA team, directed by the tireless Dr. Gottlieb, was working closely with the Special Operations Division at the Army's biological research center at Fort Detrick, Maryland, producing a lethal line in aerosols. Each can was filled with toxins that killed in seconds or, if termination was not required, would leave a victim paralyzed or at least incontinent for weeks. The men of M-K-Delta, some of them physicians on the register of the American Medical Association, were currently engaged in developing a shellfish toxin that would kill instantly. The poison was intended for use by agents sent on what the Agency called no-hope missions. Before leaving Washington, each spy would be given a "lucky silver dollar" coated with the substance. If captured he was supposed to clamp the coin between his teeth. The inventive Dr. Gottlieb had not explained how an agent would persuade an enemy to let him do that.

Dr. Gottlieb's new brief for Project M-K-Delta was "to investigate how it was possible to modify an individual's behavior by covert means." He would work closely with Richard Helms, an inspired combination of the physically malformed scientist with a passion for folk dancing and the smooth former newspaperman who knew all about killing. They became known around the Agency as Beauty and the Beast.

Both men were still furious over the Agency's involvement in a Navy experiment the previous summer. Project Chatter had made Dr. Gottlieb wince. The project was the brainchild of Dr. Richard Wendt, chairman of the psychology department at the University of Rochester, who had received $300,000 worth of Naval Intelligence money to investigate mind control. After two years' research Dr. Wendt told his controller in Washington that he had created a potion that could make anyone talk. The Navy had informed the CIA. The Agency asked for the ingredients. Dr. Wendt refused, except to say his concoction was "so special that it could make a dumb man talk." It was hardly the sort of scientific judgment to endear the psychologist to Dr. Gottlieb, but no amount of pressure by the Agency could persuade the diminutive, middle-aged Dr. Wendt to reveal the contents. Dulles finally ordered it should be tested on expendables, those who could be terminated. The director, in a moment of pique over Dr. Wendt's behavior, ordered the operation to be renamed Project Castigate.

Because of its ultrasensitivity—all those involved on the Agency side had accepted this would probably end up as a terminal job—it was decided to conduct the tests abroad. West Germany was chosen because, in the words of a memo, "there is the proximity of subjects." The defeated Rhineland was still one of the places in Europe where refugees and suspected double agents could be plucked out of internment camps with no questions asked. The Agency's field office in Frankfurt was told to find expendables and keep them in isolation.

On the point of departure, the Agency team received an astonishing demand from Dr. Wendt. Perhaps emboldened over his success in keeping secret the contents of the drug, he insisted that his beautiful young assistant accompany him to Frankfurt. Morse Allen, who had moved on from promoting electrosleep as a means to brainwash and had been placed by Dulles at the head of Project Castigate, was outraged. There were numerous heated telephone calls from Washington to Dr. Wendt. He was adamant; he would not make the trip without his assistant. Once more, in spite of increased misgivings, the Agency gave way. In the utmost secrecy, the psychologist and his companion flew with the Agency and Navy teams to Germany.

Arriving in Frankfurt, the intelligence operatives received an unpleasant shock. Dr. Wendt suddenly decided to confide to them the components of his wonder drug. It consisted of Seconal, a depressant, Dexedrine, a stimulant, and tetrahydrocannabinol, best known as the active ingredient of marijuana. Not only had all three drugs been exhaustively tested by the Agency's chemists and found useless in effecting mind control, but they were already on the open market, combined in a pep pill known as Dexamyl, soon to be called by the streetwise as the goofball.

But, having come so far—the $300,000 expended by the Navy, the costs the Agency had accrued in setting up the operation—it was unthinkable to return home empty-handed and face the wrath of Dulles. Dr. Wendt was separated from his companion and taken to a safe house outside Frankfurt, which the local CIA office had prepared. It had a sound-proof treatment room, equipped with microphones and two-way mirrors for the intelligence men to observe Dr. Wendt at work. Wendt's first subject was a man identified as possibly a Soviet agent, forty years of age, possessing a reputation as a Don Juan. For the next three days the man's food and drink was spiked with an increasing amount of the three drugs. He was soon woozy—but to the renewed fury of the intelligence men, Dr. Wendt announced that the subject was unsuitable.

Four more men were brought in over the next week. The first three were also rejected after a few hours of treatment. The fourth was deemed to be such a potential source of information that he was awarded his own special code name, Explosive.

He was a Soviet KGB officer, who according to the file "was hard boiled, with an ability to lie consistently but not very effectively." Dr. Wendt, perhaps sensing he was stretching the patience of his colleagues, set about Explosive with a vengeance. The Russian was pumped full of drugs—an astonishing combination of fifty-milligram shots of Dexedrine followed by twenty-five-milligram injections of Seconal and equally large amounts of the marijuana derivative. Explosive went into a dreamlike trance, giggling happily to himself for hours on end. Dr. Wendt turned to his colleagues and tried a joke. "Guess it's back to the drawing board."

He was lucky, Morse Allen would remember, not to be "throttled then and there."

Dr. Wendt retreated to his assistant; he would sit for hours playing her the same lullaby on the safe house piano while the Agency and Navy teams tried to salvage something from the disaster. Dr. Wendt's sessions at the piano ended when his wife abruptly arrived in Frankfurt, seeking her philandering husband. He had thoughtfully left his address in case of any family emergency.

Mrs. Wendt was not amused to discover her husband's assistant. Dr. Wendt, perhaps reacting to what had been a stressful time, ran from the safe house to a nearby church. He was overpowered by the Agency men on the point of jumping from the bell tower. Sedated with some of his own supply of Seconal, the psychologist and the two women in his life were secretly flown back to the United States. Dr. Wendt never recovered from losing his government funding. He died a few years later, still convinced he had been shabbily treated. Dulles had written the final epitaph for Project Castigate: In the future no doctor used by the Agency in drug research would, under any circumstances, take part in field tests. The fate of the subjects would be discreetly left unrecorded.

Dr. Wolff, a veteran of numerous military and intelligence panels, had been briefed to begin work with his colleague at Cornell University, Dr. Lawrence Hinkle, an equally brilliant neurologist. With the full consent of Cornell's president, Deane W. Molott, and the university's most senior administrators, the two doctors were given full access to Agency files on 7,190 American prisoners brainwashed during the Korean War. They also examined the extensive data the CIA had on Soviet methods of mind control.

For the first time, important distinctions were made by the doctors between the techniques used by the Russians and Chinese. Both systems began with a prisoner in solitary confinement, continually harassed by rotating shifts of guards telling him when to stand and sit, and disrupting his sleep if he made the slightest move during the short spells permitted; both systems excluded all outside contact, newspapers, letters from home, or listening to the radio. Time itself was denied the prisoner: his watch was taken away and he was kept in a cell with no windows and a constant overhead light.

However, the Russians rarely extended this initial period of sensory deprivation beyond six weeks. The Chinese maintained it far longer, often keeping a prisoner under these conditions for three months, and adding lengthy periods of total darkness to the incarceration.

The interrogation techniques were also different. The Soviet approach was to confront a victim with specific accusations, and to demand a full and immediate confession to those crimes. The method depended on telling a prisoner that he knew what wrong he had done and the interrogator was merely there to record any admission of guilt. In this Kafkaesque situation of not knowing what he was accused of, but being invited to admit to some crime, a prisoner invariably found himself struggling to prove his innocence. The Chinese interrogator would point out how manifestly absurd it was to make such a claim; the fact that he was a prisoner must surely suggest to him that he had committed some offense.

While the prisoner continued to try to reason and plead, the interrogator would sit clearly bored with such unbelievable protestations. Abruptly, the mood would change. A prisoner would be invited to accept a last chance to recant by helping the interrogator to review the accused man's entire life. Confused, yet sensing there may yet be a way out, a prisoner would eagerly seize the opportunity. Captive and captor would move forward toward what the prisoner believed was a common goal, an end to this relentless probing. But, as he was once more taken through the details of previous interrogations, the slightest departure from what he had said then would be seized upon. The Chinese interrogator would say, often with a sigh of regret, that the offender was not yet ready to tell the truth. Further weeks of isolation would follow. Then, once more, the questioning would resume.

The American neurologists suggested this was the point where the prisoner invariably felt something must be done to end this. He must find a way out.

In Soviet hands it meant signing a blanket confession of a list of itemized crimes for a show trial that was followed either by execution or exile to a labor camp.

But the Chinese went further. They wanted to reeducate their prisoners. This was done at special centers where the teachings of Marx and Mao were instilled, along with self-criticism and all the other trappings of conversion.

The Cornell doctors concluded that neither the Russians nor the Chinese depended totally on drugs, hypnosis, or any of the standard methods of behavioral control known in the West.

Their report to Dulles—so sensitive that it would never be fully declassified—led to a conclusion only remarkable to those unfamiliar with the director's thought process. In the years he had spent in wartime Europe—his daily life filled with spies and counterspies, secret police, emigrés and exiles, saboteurs, professional assassins, agents provocateurs, Fascists and anti-Fascists, Nazis and anti-Nazis, Communists and anti-Communists, all being encouraged by him to intrigue against and, where need be, kill each other—Dulles had survived by following one rule: Nothing is what it seems.

The director was convinced that neither neurologist had fully understood what happened in North Korea. Accepting that the Communists did not depend on known behavioral methods of mind control, Dulles had persuaded himself that the enemy must possess a method unknown in the West. It was therefore all that more urgent to move forward on that assumption.

Dr. James Monroe was told to set up a research foundation to provide a cover for further clandestine research involving doctors and scientists. It would be called the Society for the Investigation of Human Ecology and was headquartered in a townhouse on East 78th Street in New York, close to Cornell. Dr. Wolff agreed to be the new foundation's president, lending it immediate prestige and removing it from any suggestion of suspicion. Dr. Monroe was the executive secretary. With a staff of four bureaucrats, he would handle the administration of funds, laundering them through the foundation so that they could not be traced back to the Agency.

Finally, Dr. Cameron had been asked by Dulles whether there was any way he could help. It was not an order, or even a request. Long ago, the director, like many others, had realized Dr. Cameron was not the sort of man who could, in the slightest way, be coerced. Rather, it was if anything an old friend diffidently asking for assistance in difficult times.

Driving through the winter morning Dr. Cameron continued to map out his first application to the society, taking up the offer of Agency money that had always been available to him. The proposal would seal his Faustian bargain.

> . . . by continued replaying of a cue communication, a per-
> sistent tendency to act in a way which can be predetermined
> with respect to its general characteristics can be established.
> In other words, by driving a cue communication one can
> without exception, set up in the patient a persisting ten-
> dency for that cue statement, and other components of the
> community of action tendencies from which it was drawn, to
> return to his own awareness . . .

No one would ever know—Dr. Cameron had also seen to
that—all the events that had led to him placing his patients,
himself, and his reputation, together with the integrity of the
institute and finally, that of McGill University, at the disposal
of the Agency.

> . . . the dynamic implant thus established, and especially if
> reinforced by repeated driving, tends to activate more and
> more of the components of the relevant community of action
> tendencies. Those components tend to appear in the pa-
> tient's awareness. This materially contributes to problem
> identification by the patient and the therapist and, hence,
> facilitates the process of therapeutic reorganization . . .

Dr. Cameron could be certain that Dr. Monroe would
grasp the significance behind the jargon. They had spoken
several times in the past year, each time Dr. Cameron taking
the greatest care to insure the conversations were not overheard at his end. He had locked the office door and used the
direct-line telephone on his desk, avoiding going through the
hospital switchboard. Dr. Monroe found the conversations
encouraging; he reported to Dulles that Dr. Cameron was
working on a promising line of inquiry.

It was one with a curious history. In March 1948, Dr.
Cameron had clipped an advertisement from a New York
newspaper promoting the Linguaphone Company's latest invention, a gadget called the Cerebrophone, which was hailed
as "a revolutionary way to learn a foreign language while you
sleep." It consisted of a rather cumbersome phonograph fitted with a time switch that could be preset to activate the
record player. Linguaphone's brave new world suggested that
not only would language students learn while they slept, but
that the entire educational system of the world could be

revised, with schoolchildren learning their lessons in this
novel way and "tomorrow's university would be at the bedside." The company had glowing testimonials to support its
claim. A German woman said she lost her accent completely
after repeatedly listening to *The White Cliffs of Dover;* a
Spanish opera singer insisted he mastered perfect Italian
while sleeping. At $120, the Cerebrophone included an under-
pillow speaker so that "sleep teaching" could continue without disturbing others. But five years later, in 1953, the gadget
was a loss leader for Linguaphone.

Returning from Washington, Dr. Cameron had decided it
nevertheless offered a promising start for his adventures in
the world of mind control on behalf of the CIA. With an
inventiveness Linguaphone would surely have envied, he
recognized sleep teaching would sound more scientifically
impressive if it was called psychic driving. A Dormophone—in
a last desperate attempt at marketing the company had renamed the product—was prepared for use on a patient in
June 1953. Dr. Cameron had first taped a therapy session
with the manic-depressive, a woman of forty. Then he had
edited the tape, selecting a key passage. This had been
assembled in a sequence that would be repeatedly played
back to his patient.

Heading toward Canada through a frozen landscape of ham-
lets and small towns, Dr. Cameron continued to dictate.

. . . the dynamic qualities of the implant are a function of (a)
the amount of and repetition of driving; (b) the intensity of
the response; (c) the defenses; (d) stress tolerance; (e) especially for desensitization. The major continuing effects of the
dynamic implant are (a) progressive problem identification;
(b) resulting reorganization of behavioral patterns; (c) nega-
tive evaluation of neurotic patterns present in the cue communication used in driving . . .

The words conveyed nothing of the excitement he felt that
June morning when he had sat down with the woman and
began to play the tape with its endlessly repeated sad remi-
niscence from childhood when her mother threatened to
abandon her. Dr. Cameron was convinced that threat lay at
the root of his patient's depression; it had been created
because she could not cope with maternal rejection.

After he repeated the tape seven times, the woman asked him, "Do you like to do it all the time?"

He continued playing the tape.

After eleven repetitions she cried out, "I hate it when you do it all the time!" He had persisted. After four more repetitions she suddenly burst out, "It is the truth."

When the tape had been played nineteen times the woman began to tremble and cried out she hated the sound of her own voice. After thirty repetitions she began to breathe rapidly and shake uncontrollably and moaned that she hated her mother. On the thirty-fifth repetition she chanted, "I hate! I hate!" After three more revolutions she begged for the tape to be stopped. When Dr. Cameron ignored her, she threatened him with her hands. But the inexorable sound of her voice continued. She began to whimper and plead. Only then, on the forty-fifth repetition, had he stopped the recording.

Afterwards, Dr. Cameron had noted how completely the woman's defense system had been penetrated. Was that what the Communists had done? Was that the way they destroyed existing belief systems and replaced them with others? The question obsessed him.

The Canadian border was close. Inside an hour, in spite of the weather, he would reach the hospital, plunging himself into another week of twelve-hour days and longer. No one, he knew, understood how he could maintain such a relentless pace at his age. He would be fifty-six this December, yet he had the energy of a man half his age. It had been another reason for his success; where others had flagged, he would always drive himself on.

A number of the medical staff and senior nurses at the institute disapproved of the man Dr. Cameron had hired to develop specialist equipment needed for more intensive psychic driving. Dr. Cleghorn, his deputy, had not bothered to hide his anger that Leonard Rubenstein, an Englishman with a Cockney accent and with no formal medical training, should be in charge of a research and development behavioral laboratory. Yet in spite of the protests, Rubenstein, a tall, stringbean of a man who wore a doctor's white coat, loped through the hospital corridors in a commendable impersonation of Groucho Marx, delivering one-liners in a bass voice that made Dr. Cleghorn cringe.

He was usually accompanied by his assistant, Jan Zielinski,

a Polish-born engineer who also had no medical qualification
and rarely spoke to anyone, peering owlishly at desperately
sick patients. Dr. Cameron had explained to no one why he
had recruited a former member of the British Army's Royal
Signals Corps and a Pole who struck Dr. Cleghorn as better
suited to mending an engine rather than dealing with minds
in torment.

Dr. Cleghorn was one of those who still failed to always
understand that his chief was a man who rode roughshod over
the conventions, who was not impressed with professional
titles, wealth, or position and the social trappings of Montreal
society. He was only concerned with results. For him
Rubenstein and Zielinski promised success: that was his only
criteria in employing them. It mattered not a whit to Cameron that neither man had no business on the wards, let alone
having direct contact with often severely disturbed patients
who required the most skillful of medical management. Dr.
Cameron had made it clear that he would, if forced, defend
the two technicians against the entire medical and nursing
staff.

So far, no university official had dared challenge him. It
would mean risking losing the doctor who had brought more
prestige to McGill than any other psychiatrist on the faculty.
Dr. Cameron was president of the all-powerful American
Psychiatric Association, was soon to be president of the Canadian Psychiatric Association, and was to accept the supreme
honor of his discipline, the first presidency of the World
Association of Psychiatrists. Already he had founded the Canadian Mental Health Association and had served as chairman of the Canadian Scientific Planning Committee. No other
psychiatrist on McGill's faculty had published so many scientific papers so widely; no one had given so many lectures, was
so well known in the medical world, and had brought so
many students to the campus.

He continued to dictate.

. . . our studies now turned to attempts to establish lasting
changes in the patient's behavior, using verbal signals of a
predetermined nature and of our own devising. After considerable experimentation, we have developed a procedure
which in the most successful case has produced changes
lasting up to two months. The procedure requires (1) the

breaking down of ongoing patterns of the patient's behavior by means of particularly intensive electroshocks (depatterning); (2) the intensive repetition (sixteen hours a day for six or seven days) of the prearranged verbal signals; (3) during this period of intensive repetition, the patient is kept in partial sensory isolation; (4) repression of the driving period is carried out by putting the patient, after the conclusion of the period, into continuous sleep for seven to ten days . . .

Dr. Cameron's methods had attracted criticism in the highest circles of Canadian medicine. Dr. Osmond M. Solandt, chairman of the Canadian Defense Research Board, a highly sensitive post that brought him into regular contact with the CIA and British Intelligence, had said after seeing the effect Dr. Cameron's treatment had on the wife of one of Dr. Solandt's colleagues that "this (treatment) was something the Defense Research Board would have no part in." Dr. Solandt had never wavered from the belief that Dr. Cameron "was not possessed of the necessary sense of humanity to be regarded as a good doctor." He had bluntly told Dr. Cameron not to bother to apply for any Defense Board grants.

Dr. Donald O. Hebb, chairman of the Psychology Department at McGill, who was also working closely with both Canadian intelligence and the CIA on sensory deprivation research, had voiced the opinion that not only were Dr. Cameron's methods ethically deplorable, but they verged on "the irresponsible—criminally stupid."

Powerful though such opponents were, they did not bother Dr. Cameron, either—no more than he was troubled by the icy driving conditions or completing his application, detailing how he planned to use the money to develop better methods of inactivating the patient; how he would administer a number of drugs, including curare; how LSD would be used to break down the ongoing patterns of behavior; and how he would not take a penny salary for overseeing the project. However, among others who would be paid was Leonard Rubenstein. Dr. Cameron proposed he should receive $2,500 for creating and supervising the "message-repeating mechanisms" that would be an integral part of a proposed project that would be spread over two years.

Under the terms of his McGill contract, Dr. Cameron would not have to clear the application with anybody. He was his own master. His entire life had been devoted to achieving such independence, to live up to a precept of a dominating father—that, to succeed, a man needed only the support of God.

Ewen Cameron was born on the evening of December 24, 1901, the son of the Reverend Duncan Cameron, minister to the good people of Bridge of Allan, a small town some twenty miles to the north of Glasgow. On Monday, wash day, the wind often blew the city's industrial grit over the low rolling hills and speckled the carefully pegged clotheslines. On those days the Reverend Cameron gathered up his golf bag, leaving his wife to bemoan the fate that made her live in such an inhospitable climate. When Ewen was old enough, his father took him along as a caddy, so saving the penny a day of hiring a boy to carry his bag. He grew into manhood hating golf.

What survives of his first years suggests a solemn-faced child with startlingly clear eyes, the son of a marriage of convenience. If there had been passion, it had died in his mother from a life of unremitting weekday toil and Sundays listening to his father delivering uncompromising sermons on Calvinism. The knowledge that his parents' union was a joyless one had a marked effect on his personality.

Ewen was fiercely competitive, hating to lose at sports and bitterly disappointed if his marks did not consistently place him at the top of his class. He was also insular and moody, had few friends, and spent most of his time reading. He particularly found endless pleasure in Mary Shelley's novel about Victor Frankenstein and the creature he created. In time, Ewen Cameron would come to see that the monster and its creator were the antithetical halves of a single being: Dr. Frankenstein represented the intellect and his nameless creature, the emotions. That concept would also play its part in the path young Ewen Cameron chose to follow.

He grew up against the bugle call and drumbeat summoning his near elders to the Great War. Some would return, medaled, blind, and maimed. This had a profound effect on him. So did the stories that circulated, told over and over in and around his father's kirk: the Kaiser was slicing off the right hand of Belgian school boys and had British corpses boiled down into soap or edible fat. The Kaiser—stomping, glowering, and threatening—was the ultimate in evil. This would sow the seeds of Ewen Cameron's feelings about all Germans. At the close of the Great War, having graduated from the Glasgow academy, he studied medicine at the University of Glasgow.

He was quickly fascinated by the brain. In the mid-twenties, steeped in the psychophilosophy of Freud, Jung, and others, the newly graduated Dr. Cameron decided that solving the complex problems of human behavior was to be his chosen career. After interning at the Glasgow Western Infirmary and then the city's mental hospital, he took a postgraduate course at the University of London. He received his diploma in psychological medicine, and in 1926 he left Britain to join the faculty of one of the most progressive hospitals in North America—Johns Hopkins in Baltimore. There he began developing the skills to trap the brain into releasing some of its secrets and formulating his own rules to explain patterns of human behavior.

But the first signs of overdriving ambition ensured he would not remain in Baltimore, waiting for promotion. He made a career move that colleagues believed would see the tall, angular, soft-voiced Scot disappear beyond the medical horizon. Dr. Cameron joined the staff of Manitoba's Brandon Mental Hospital.

The Canadian prairie asylum was a repository for the rejects of local society, a place of brutality, depersonalization, and filth, a closed institution whose nursing custodians made no distinction between the definitions and categories of madness. Brandon was at the end of the line for the Manitoba social transgressor, an institution of fear to equal the state prison; a person could disappear into either, never to be seen again.

To this unappetizing world, Dr. Cameron brought a reformer's zeal. He had what seemed an improbable dream—that one day the helpless, the forgotten, and the wretched would cease to be held behind bars and would be free to return, when ready, to society. In his mind was the beginnings of an idea for a day hospital system where patients came in the morning for treatment and went home at night. He also visualized a community health care program. He was exploring the shell of a grand vision in which the control and management of all kinds of madness turned solely on psychiatric decisions. But as yet there was nothing available to make that possible. The pharmacopoeia for controlling mood and behavior still depended on the few snake-roots and hallucinogens that had been used for centuries for subduing tor-mented minds. The chemistry of liberation—and scientific mind control—was still almost two full decades distant.

Yet behavior control, of a crude kind, was used at Brandon. The nurses knew how to get patients to do their bidding by using what few mood-altering drugs there were available; some belonged properly to the era of Tristan and Isolde and were the stuff of witchcraft and magic potions that had formed part of the happy hunting ground for the Church's inquisitors and their tests for loyalty. Dr. Cameron realized the answer must be to find a more effective means of controlling persons who could then be safely returned to society. At Brandon he began to create the rationale of authority—his—to justify the means.

With his already notable background—Glasgow and Baltimore, two of the great centers of applied psychiatry—Dr. Cameron, in remote and impoverished Brandon, made another important discovery. Barely twenty-eight, he virtually had a free hand to study the various schizoid mechanisms, psychotic fantasies, and the strange world of the paranoid where inner and outer realities are continually split—a world of the oscillation between love and hate, the breakdown of defense systems. He had never been more content. The seeds of mind control had taken root and were germinating in the unlikely environment of Manitoba.

In that first long Canadian winter he lost himself in the empirical imagination of Frederick Winslow Taylor, the founder of scientific management and the high priest of the cult of human engineering. Taylor had published, in 1911, a massive work primarily designed to show managers how to get more from their workers. Dr. Cameron realized it could be adapted to make patients function more efficiently. He began to carry out the first psychological tests at Brandon, an amalgam of Taylor's teachings and tests the U.S. Army had used during World War I. He began to see that a set of questions could be used to determine psychological responses, that such obtuse states as dangerous, violent, uncooperative—the common labels attached to the sick at Brandon—could be quantified. The tests were also useful because they justified all kinds of experimental medical intervention, such as isolating patients or denying them privileges when they refused to work after the tests showed they could. It was Dr. Cameron's first plunge into behavioral science, and he became a committed convert. His search to bring a new order to Brandon brought another important discovery: The science that could be applied to behavior made it respectable to manipulate his patients.

Viewed through the prism of his tests, those patients came into sharper focus. A disproportionate number were foreign-born, from Eastern Europe, human flotsam who somehow ended up in Manitoba—Poles, Russians, Bulgarians and Lithuanians and Russians who had fled the Revolution. They had found life in the new world equally hard and broke under the strain. Clearly, he saw that his tests could be extended to immigration screening, to keep out such people before they infected the community. He became fervent in his belief that science—especially psychiatry—could be used to identify and remedy the problems of society. This could all be changed by a radical approach to treatment. Brandon was a good place to begin, to test out his beliefs on those who had no future. The helpless would help him create the New Jerusalem.

He began to publish in the journals, coolly reasoned papers that suggested that if North America had been able to create affluence out of poverty, enlightenment out of ignorance, and citizens out of the dispossessed, so could mental health be structured out of illness. Because so little had been achieved, he believed that the mandate for reform was unlimited. He dusted off the principles laid down at the first Conference of Race Betterment at Battle Creek, Michigan, in 1914, where many of his aging peers had gathered to endorse resolutions that the future of mankind depended on robust attention to the mentally ill—their brain cells must be aroused to activity and restored to their normal freedom. This would only be achieved, in Dr. Cameron's view, by earlier intervention. Nor was Freud the answer; every city may have its psychoanalytic clinic, but psychoanalysis was only a weapon in the attack he envisaged. No condition—whether it was irregular menstrual syndrome or migraine—was described without a reminder that proper scientific management was the only solution. In those dust bowl years at Brandon, he laid down another tautological rule: His faith in effective results justified the diagnosis and the treatment; the treatment justified the faith. Behavior control, in all its guises, was the real veil of power. He would never swerve from such belief.

In the cold winter nights of Manitoba he continued to read about how such control could be attained and justified. Taylor had put it succinctly in one sentence that Dr. Cameron took as his leitmotiv: "In the past the man had been first; in the future the system must be first."

From Italy in 1938, he had learned of a dramatic extension of that creed. Just as the story of Frankenstein had thrilled him as a boy, so Dr. Cameron was excited by the widely reported account of what happened in the early April morning in Rome at the University Hospital for Nervous Diseases. Umberto Castelli was forty years old, described in the medical notes one of his attendants carried as built like an ox and unaware of his physical strength. He was also clinically assessed as a catatonic schizophrenic—an illness that had started in his late teens, with increasing symptoms: insomnia, depression, and an increasing withdrawal from contact with life. Castelli had developed the strange grimacing and twitching that is common to the illness. There were still other symptoms: hallucinations and delusions, his muteness and refusal to eat, his sudden eruptive anger. Often he would repeat a single phrase for hours on end. Other times he would hold out his arms for hours as though crucified. For months Castelli had been under the care of Professor Ugo Cerletti. The doctor planned to use his patient for a revolutionary experiment.

Castelli was brought to a small, brightly lit room, placed on a trolley, and secured by heavy leather straps. One attendant stood at his feet, the other at his head. Castelli could only stare into a bright white light that shone from the ceiling. The professor stepped forward, holding what appeared to be two flatirons attached by flex to a machine. He positioned the metal surfaces against Castelli's temples and ordered a nurse to hold them in place. The professor pressed a button on the machine. Castelli's mouth opened and his body lurched against the straps as a contortion, a convulsion of ripping, searing pain coursed through his body. The low dosage—eighty volts for one-fifth of a second—produced a petit mal reaction. Professor Cerletti immediately prepared for a second treatment, this time with a higher voltage. Suddenly, in a rational voice no one heard him use before, Castelli spoke. "Please! No more!" Professor Cerletti ignored the plea and increased the voltage; the electroconvulsion was repeated. Castelli went into a second classic epileptic seizure. Then, after a short time, he sat up, calm and smiling.

The episode left a lasting impression on Dr. Cameron.

From his reading he knew that shock therapy was among the oldest psychiatric techniques in existence. An ancient Roman had tried to cure his emperor's headaches with an electric eel; in the sixteenth century a Catholic missionary reported that the Abyssinians used a similar method to expel devils out of human bodies. At Brandon he himself tried combinations of camphor, carbon dioxide gas, insulin, and the latest wonder drug, Metrazol, to induce comas and convulsions in schizophrenics and depressives. He also experimented with the tranquilizer chair, in which a patient diagnosed as suffering from torpid madness was strapped in and rotated at high speed until unconscious.

It did not matter that Professor Cerletti had offered no explanation as to how electroshock actually worked. It was enough for Dr. Cameron that it produced a result. He decided to use electroshock as his treatment of choice in schizophrenia. The decision coincided with important career moves. He finally moved from Brandon back to the United States, to Worcester State Hospital in Massachusetts, where he was appointed director of research. Still restless and ambitious for more experience, in 1938 he became professor of psychiatry at the Albany Medical School in New York State.

In New York State he became an enthusiastic proponent of another new form of mind control. Three years earlier—on November 12, 1935—in a Lisbon hospital, Dr. Egaz Moniz, a neurosurgeon, had drilled two holes on either side of the forehead of a mental patient. He had then injected the holes with pure alcohol, plunging the needle directly into the frontal lobes of the woman's brain. The operation was only partly successful in curbing her violence. He experimented on seven more of his patients. Then, for his eighth operation, the surgeon radically altered his intervention. Instead of trying to destroy nerve cells with alcohol he inserted in turn into each hole an instrument he made specially for the operation. It resembled an apple corer. He used it to crush all the nerve fibers in its path. Dr. Moniz called his new technique prefrontal leucotomy, from the Greek leuco, the white nerve fibers, and tome, knife. After twenty operations he called it lobotomy and, more formally, psychosurgery.

Dr. Cameron began to refer patients for the procedure who had severe disturbances that made them uncontrollably violent. Often he would stand in the operating room and watch a neurosurgeon sever the frontal lobes around the ventromedial region, which regulated emotional experience. Destruction of this area sometimes produced marked changes—violence gave way to stupor. The clinically ill found themselves with new symptoms: forgetfulness, withdrawal, a complete lack of spontaneity. With scar tissue from the burr holes, vacant stares, and a monster-like gait, they often resembled zombies, or Frankenstein's creature. But they were manageable; they could fit into the general scheme of hospital society; and that, in the end, was what mattered—not that their imagination, their sexual responses, their planning ability, their logic, or their skill to make judgments had been diminished or often completely removed. Dr. Cameron could rationalize, as indeed many of his colleagues did, that as institutional mental patients, they had no need for such responses; for them, what they had lost was unimportant. Another guiding principle had been laid down for the New Jerusalem.

Yet Dr. Cameron looked with horror on what was happening in Europe. There, Nazi doctors were preparing for their work in Auschwitz, Bergen-Belsen, and Dachau, places that would become the testing grounds for inhumane experiments on a scale unknown and unimaginable. Yet those German doctors found comfort that eminent colleagues across the Atlantic and also in Britain believed, for instance, that all born criminals can be identified by certain physical characteristics, and that the solution, in the words of America's Professor Henry H. Goddard, was "to sterilize them, allow them to perform only lowly jobs, confine them to ghettos, discourage them from marrying outside their race, and create a pure, American, superior intelligence to control them."

Dr. Cameron saw nothing wrong with Professor Goddard's solution—even though it had a striking similarity to the Final Solution Hitler would soon implement.

Shortly before Pearl Harbor, Cameron became a member of the Military Mobilization Committee of the American Psychiatric Association. His appointment coincided with two developments that greatly alarmed the Roosevelt administration. The first was the increasing number of conscientious objectors, mostly Quakers, who were prepared to endure the brutality of American mental hospitals rather than enlist. The second was the number of men rejected or discharged from military service for neuropsychiatric reasons. In all, two million of the fifteen million inducted into the U.S. Armed Services would be rejected on such grounds—almost twenty percent. No other nation in World War II would have such a poor record.

For Dr. Cameron the solution was clear. Not only did such rejects require treatment, but there was an urgent need to further prepare the ground for his ideas of psychiatric evangelism. He began a series of genetic, biochemical, intercultural, and neurological studies designed to identify the electrochemical processes in the brain that could offer a solution to mental illness. There was no shortage of patients; the great custodial hospitals of the United States were filled with those who refused to serve their country. At Albany they began to serve in another capacity—as Dr. Cameron's guinea pigs.

It was the Age of New Light—of new labels, new theories, and a new jargon that turned the unscientific and unsystematic into a lingua franca designed to confuse and keep at bay those not within the magic circle. Psychiatric screening procedures became standard; symptoms and definitions proliferated. No ailment was too great or small to study or argue over in the academic journals. Nowhere were the battle lines drawn more than in psychiatry, and especially in the study of schizophrenia; endless attempts were made to define, specify, and categorize the illness. Dr. Cameron had little interest in such debate. For him, his research showed that in schizophrenia the patient *was* the disorder.

The first years of war saw huge strides in the assessment of all the depressive disorders. There was a coming together of the psychological, psychiatrical, and medical support industry, of the manufacturers of electroshock machines, of restraint jackets, of drugs and chemicals. The distinctions between voluntary and coerced treatments were blurred and often merged. Almost every month further syndromes, symptoms, and mental illnesses entered the professional catalogue. There was little time, or patience, for controlled studies into treatment methods. Psychiatry, like everything else, was subservient to the cry, "There's a war to be fought." Mentally ill people had, if at all possible, to be gotten back to the shop and factory floor and the front line. The scientific measurement Frederick Winslow Taylor had created thirty years earlier was implemented with a ruthlessness that might even have made the great behaviorist blink. For Dr. Cameron the early 1940s were not only a time for bold decisions in handling patients but also in deciding his own future.

Albany was no longer enough. There, he still was answering to superiors. In Montreal, there was an opportunity that he sensed, correctly, might never come again. McGill University, already developing a reputation under Wilder Penfield, the distinguished neurologist, needed someone to chair its department of psychiatry. At Professor Penfield's suggestion, the post was offered to Dr. Cameron. He accepted in 1943.

He had been given one assurance and was offered two pieces of advice by his sponsor: He would have a free hand; in return he should try and learn French and apply for Canadian citizenship.

Fourteen years later, crossing the Canadian border on this wintry January morning, having dictated his proposal to the Society for the Investigation of Human Ecology, he knew that the promise of independence had been kept—even though he blithely ignored the suggestion of giving up his American citizenship and learning French. Turning off Pine Avenue West, he parked before the mock Italian Renaissance-style mansion in limestone, which had become his citadel.

Within its thick walls he soon hoped to discover the way to achieve the total mind control, which so far had eluded every other doctor on the payroll of the CIA and other Western intelligence organizations.

8

Ultimate
Weapons

Madeleine lay in the narrow, rubber-sheeted bed, watching
the first gleam of daybreak bringing into focus the furniture
and her dressing gown hanging from the hook behind the
door on South-Two. She had lost count of how many times
the machine had been wheeled to her bedside, each time to
shock her into unconsciousness. When she awoke, her head
always throbbed with the most strange and inconceivable
pain and her mind felt like a blurred, pounding emptiness.
Yet, while her memory had been affected, the treatment had
not banished the Wise Men and the creature on the floor by
the door, the one she called the Sloth.

He had become a part of her life, like telling Eddie she still
loved him when she didn't, like saying to Dr. Cameron she
wanted to live when she didn't, like promising the Wise Men
she would take them away from South-Two if only they would
first drive out the Sloth, knowing she couldn't leave.

She was certain the room had been the creature's and that
Dr. Cameron had assigned it to her as one of his punish-
ments, like his latest decision to restrict her privileges by not
allowing her outside the building because she had been caught
trying to steal a knife from the dining room.

The Sloth appeared, without fail, every night after the
nurse watched her swallow her bedtime medication and
switched off the light. The tablets would only have started to
dull her racing thoughts when she saw the black mass on the
carpet in front of the wardrobe. It was about the size of the
beach ball her father used to throw into the frame at the back
of the house. As she watched, always too horrified to scream,

her mouth dry from the drugs, it unraveled and slithered over the carpet to settle itself on the floor by the door, blocking any escape, cutting off any help. In the darkness it gave off a pale glow—and Madeleine imagined it smelled of the sour earth of the cemetery where her father was buried.

She looked toward the window. It was daylight. She looked at the door. The Sloth had gone. Soon a nurse would come with the machine and one of the residents to work it.

Over the past three years Madeleine had been hospitalized five times—forty-four weeks in all, almost a year of her life spent on South-Two. In that time hundreds of syringes had been emptied into her arms and she had swallowed thousands of pills, and enough electricity to light scores of bulbs had passed through her brain.

On three occasions after being discharged she had virtually wrecked the apartment searching for capsules, not believing Eddie when he had said that, on Dr. Cameron's order, he always carried her medication with him. Twice she had attempted to kill herself by other means. Once the Wise Men led her to the bathroom and watched approvingly while she used one of Eddie's razor blades to cut her wrists. Leaving a trail of red spots across the carpet, she had sat on the bed and telephoned him. She had begged for forgiveness, unaware the connection had been broken, when Eddie, followed by an ambulance crew, burst in; her wrists were quickly bandaged and she was bundled into the ambulance and returned to South-Two.

Three months later, when she had come home, Eddie had learned to shave with an electric razor and there was nothing sharp in the apartment. That only made the Wise Men more inventive. One Sunday morning, while Eddie slept, they urged her to slide out of bed and go to the kitchen. Opening the cutlery drawer she removed a silver-plated cake knife and used its blunt tip to open the wrist scars. She had watched herself bleeding, not feeling anything, except the tears rolling down her cheeks and mingling with her blood. Her sobbing finally awoke Eddie and once more she had been rushed to the old mansion on Mount Royal.

Each time a doctor ran through a checklist. Had she heard voices? Had she really wanted to kill herself? Did she sometimes think people were plotting against her? She had refused to answer. Afterward a nurse would unpack her case, the one Eddie called her "going-away-coming-home bag." When he visited he sat on the bed and she clung to him, oblivious of everything, especially of her mother, who on those first occasions had insisted on coming with Eddie and had stood, silent and brooding, inside the door. Dr. Cameron told her it was best if she stayed away and not upset herself at seeing her daughter in this situation. Madeleine had been grateful for that. That was also the moment she had been most conscious of the dreadful pain on Eddie's face. She had wanted to comfort him but could not.

Gradually, over those past three years, her feelings had receded so that most of the time she felt nothing but a deadening, broken only by another sudden overwhelming desire to try and kill herself so she could be with her father. Realizing she had no means of doing so, she would once more feel totally incapable of any emotional responses. At those times she was no longer a person. She would emerge from dreams more frightening than anything Dr. Cameron ordered to be done to her while she was awake, and would lie in bed, her body wracked with tears that would not come and her scarred wrists throbbing. She felt the world around her had somehow altered, that it had become even more alien and unreal.

Recently, on his morning rounds, Dr. Cameron had turned to a new doctor and sketched in the events of her past three years. The younger physician then asked her a number of questions in an articulate, even, controlled voice. He said to Dr. Cameron she seemed to have symptoms of depersonalization. She had looked at him, wondering what he was talking about, even though Dr. Cameron clearly understood, nodding quickly and not looking at her. From that day the electroshock machine had been brought to her room more frequently. It blotted out many memories and left her feeling increasingly dull and unable to express any coherent thoughts through the fog shrouding her mind.

In the corridor she heard the first sound of a new day, the trolley bringing medication. She had come to know all the noises of a place she had once told Eddie "was a fancy dumping ground for well-to-do misfits." That had been when she was an outpatient. Inside, in the day hospital, the illusion persisted: that part was art deco. South-Two looked more like she imagined a mental hospital should: doors, some closed, some partially open, cheerful but always watchful nurses and doctors who came and went at all hours through the door marked THERAPY UNIT. There was an occupation-therapy room where grown men and women were encouraged to finger paint, cook, use the laundry machines, or improve their ironing skills.

At South-Two no one looked crazy, at least in the way Madeleine imagined crazy people should look and behave. There were no mad shrieks, no wide-eyed Medusas strapped to their beds howling obscenities. But patients seemed as drugged as she felt, shuffling along from meal table to play room or being taken away for treatment. One would return asleep on a stretcher. Another would reappear in South-Two wearing a football helmet. There were a large number of patients who wore those helmets all day. She had wondered why—just as she was puzzled over what happened behind the door marked SLEEP ROOM. Why did some of the nurses dislike going in there? She tried to ask the head nurse, Peggy Mielke—who managed to be both firm and empathetic—but was told she was not to concern herself with such matters.

Shortly afterwards she tried to sneak out the knife from the dining room. Dr. Cameron addressed her, his face as grave as his voice, on the need to help her manage her suicidal feelings and how she must not see her treatment as punishment. From then on she had all her meals in her room, watched by a nurse who carefully checked that no cutlery was missing from the tray. The machine had been wheeled in twice a day, early morning and late afternoon, five days a week.

She sensed the familiar panic nibbling at her mind. Her nightdress and bedclothes were damp from perspiration. So was her hair. She still feared the Sloth would emerge from his hiding place and absorb her into its mucous-covered body. All she could do was to react the way she did every morning: Her stomach heaved and she was sick on the coverlet. She was still staring at the mess when the door opened.

A nurse wheeled in the trolley with the black box and, beside it, a tube of lubricating jelly and two wooden spatulae covered with cotton to form a mouth gag. The nurse removed the soiled bedding and pillow, talking cheerfully all the time, trying to engage Madeleine's attention. She continued to stare at the black box, with its dials, knobs, and switches. The nurse unplugged the lamp above the bed and connected the cable from the machine to the power supply. She watched the dials flicker when she adjusted some of the controls.

Madeleine begged the nurse to give her an injection to help her relax. She was told she must wait for the doctor. When he arrived he explained that Dr. Cameron had said a sedative was not necessary in her case. Every time Madeleine received the same reply.

The doctor fiddled with settings and adjusted the automatic timer. He rubbed some of the jelly on her temples, told her to blow her nose, to breathe deeply, and to keep her mouth open. He next placed the gag between her teeth, checking that it was in contact with her lower jaw to prevent her tongue from protruding. He asked her to close her mouth as tightly as she could, adding that if she wished she could also shut her eyes. She felt something colder than the jelly on her skin, hard and pressing against the sides of her head, icy iron squeezing her brain. They were electrodes saturated with saline, which the doctor held in position. The nurse checked a dial and announced that it was on.

As she always did at this point, Madeleine began to struggle. She could not help herself.

The doctor held the paddles a little more firmly against her skin, ordered her to relax and not be afraid, said she would feel nothing. Over his shoulder he called to the nurse, "Ready here. Go!"

The nurse touched a button.

Madeline could never be certain—because Dr. Cameron himself said it was physiologically impossible for her to feel the treatments—but she had the idea that her brain was sizzled in her skull and that her body leapt from the bed. In that moment between the doctor saying "Go!" and the nurse pressing the button, she perhaps only imagined the great searing flash of pain that passed through her brain. In actual time, it lasted only for a second. In electrical measurement it was 150 volts—the power needed to light a 100-watt bulb. The electricity made her body twitch uncontrollably and she began to dribble spittle. After a four-second delay, the machine's automatic timing device repeated the electroshock. It did so four further times—six separate shocks in all.

The doctor removed the electrodes when the nurse pulled out the plug and reconnected the lamp. The nurse then wiped off the jelly and removed the gag. Finally, she placed a linen square over Madeleine's lips to absorb the saliva. The doctor checked her pulse and then preceded the nurse out of the room. From her arrival to departing with the trolley the procedure had taken ten minutes.

In the corridor they checked the list of others scheduled for early-morning electroshock treatment. Jeannine Huard was next.

Dr. Morrow opened the patient's file to make sure there was a signed consent form for treatment, then began to read the history of the sedated middle-aged woman lying on the table. Dr. Morrow had spent another morning working in the white-tiled and sterile room on the ground floor, close to Dr. Cameron's private office. Among the junior doctors the room was known as the shock shop. Her morning had been spent either anesthetizing non-fee-paying patients or acting as Dr. Cameron's button pusher at the electroshock machine after he had administered sodium amytal to those private patients he decided should have premedication.

Usually there was no time between patients for Dr. Morrow to more than glance at a case file; as long as the consent form was signed she was satisfied, even though privately she wondered whether shock treatment would be a benefit in all cases. But among the many things she had learned during her six months at the Allan Memorial Institute was never to challenge the treatment methods of Dr. Cameron. As was often the case, he was late—though not even the most senior doctor would have dared to question his punctuality.

The woman on the table was the last case of the morning to be wheeled into the brilliantly lit room, smelling faintly of chemicals and urine.

Working with senior doctors, Dr. Morrow had learned a great deal, including paying the closest attention to how a patient recounted a history. Her father had explained to her that taking a careful history was time well spent. He had also said that what could be learned not only depended on the doctor's skill in putting the questions, but a patient's willingness and capacity to cooperate. Her father had added that no medical history could reproduce precisely what had occurred in nature. To even begin to do so required a doctor to put aside any preconceived notions; otherwise all that would be produced was a history that included everything and revealed nothing.

Yet sometimes Dr. Cameron would be satisfied with only reading the case notes before starting treatment. In all Dr. Morrow's previous experience, a senior doctor *always* made his own clinical assessment, no matter how detailed a case history had already been obtained.

When she had been assigned by Dr. Cameron to work on Dr. Cleghorn's service, Dr. Cleghorn had explained that one of psychiatry's greatest contributions to medicine was the introduction of what he termed a patient's scientific-human biography—that, just as Koch's law had become the Magna Carta of medical research, so did the taking of a new kind of medical history pave the way for modern dynamic psychiatry. Then, with that infectious smile that contrasted with Dr. Cameron's invariably severe face, Dr. Cleghorn added that the case-taking method had been perfected at this hospital.

Dr. Morrow continued to read the clinical assessment of the patient on the trolley. Nothing in the notes indicated further electroshock treatment would benefit the woman—let alone the radical method Dr. Cameron used. It was based on a technique developed in 1948 by two English surgeons, L. G. M. Page and R. J. Russell, at the Three Counties Hospital, Arlesey in Bedfordshire. The Page-Russell technique used powerful multiple shocks—but no more than five in one treatment.

Dr. Morrow had often been asked by Dr. Cameron to set the timer to give *six* jolting shocks to a patient, with the settings twenty times more powerful than she had ever seen used elsewhere. "They would go from one shock into another with apnea. That means their breathing would stop. And it was the most terrifying thing I've ever seen in my life before or since," she would say later.

Dr. Cameron insisted this form of convulsive treatment should be used whenever possible, though it was clear to Dr. Morrow that like everyone else, he knew very little about how the Page-Russell method achieved any result. The caring and sensitive Dr. Morrow had been often upset to see that the only immediate effect of repeatedly sending a current of very low amperage through a patient's brain was to create confusion and loss of memory.

Her own clinical experience showed that in extreme cases of tension and anxiety, small doses of insulin had proven to be beneficial—and produced no distressing side effects. Dr.

Morrow began to think that Dr. Cameron, despite his exalted position, did not really bother to use insight and understanding in dealing with the suffering of his patients. That, she knew, only came when a doctor had a caring relationship.

She was glad to be on Dr. Cleghorn's service. In everything he said or did, the tall, gentle-voiced psychiatrist exemplified the rational being brought to bear on the irrational. When he was not seeing patients, Dr. Cleghorn spent long hours in his laboratory, working on such complex mysteries as the stimulating effect of electroshock on the adrenal cortex, or encouraging his equally dedicated research team to continue investigating the chemicals excreted by the pituitary gland and hypothalamus—which he correctly predicted would one day win a Nobel Prize. Because of his own reputation as a researcher, he had attracted some of the most prestigious names in medicine to work with him. Among them was the vivacious Marian Birmingham, engaged on a biochemical study of the adrenal function of the brain, and Paula Ward and Edward Schonbaum, painstakingly moving toward their triumph of isolating a new steroid from the adrenal tissue. There were half a dozen scientists in Dr. Cleghorn's laboratory seeking answers to various affective disorders.

Dr. Morrow enjoyed the privilege of being associated with such distinguished figures. She had been all that more shattered to learn that Dr. Cameron had introduced into Dr. Cleghorn's team a rogue scientist, a fast-talking, persuasive clinician who almost wrecked the carefully constructed reputation Dr. Cleghorn's leadership in applied research had given the institute. The clinician had conducted an investigation into whether the color of a patient's eyes could help identify the presence of schizophrenia. Many of the institute's researchers—not least an outraged Dr. Cleghorn—thought the project was something left over from the unfinished work on Jewish women and children of Dr. Joseph Mengele at Auschwitz. Dr. Cleghorn's anger had deepened when he discovered that Dr. Cameron had allowed the clinician to seek funds from a thoroughly disreputable financier; the man was suspected of having links with the Mafia—though why the Cosa Nostra would wish to finance such a piece of nonsense was beyond Dr. Morrow.

What finally brought the matter to a head was Dr. Cameron approving publication of a paper in a Canadian medical journal, listing Dr. Cleghorn as co-author of the study. The deputy medical director's fury boiled over; no one could remember anything like it. Dr. Cleghorn insisted that the clinician be fired on the spot, and that the journal remove his name from what he castigated as "the worst piece of research I have ever seen in all my life." Dr. Cameron, on the editorial board of the journal, shrugged off the protests. The paper was published—though the clinician, in the face of Dr. Cleghorn's unabated anger, left the institute. But the senior psychiatrist made no secret that he ultimately held Dr. Cameron responsible, and that his superior had "a serious personality flaw in not being able to spot a phony."

Dr. Cameron strode into the room, and Dr. Morrow thought, "He really is a self-serving megalomaniac; he really doesn't care very much about anyone except himself."

He plunged the needle into the patient's arm, watching the clear liquid flowing into a vein, and told her to count backward from ten. When she reached five her jaw slackened and she breathed noisily. He placed the gag between her teeth, pressing his hand under her chin to force her jaw closed. He told Dr. Morrow to hit the button. When the patient had received six jolting shots of electricity, Dr. Cameron marched from the room without saying a word, and Dr. Morrow was even more convinced he had "thrown away the wisdom of the ancients, the good of his patients."

Then she added fiercely to herself that she would never do that, though she also wished she was not such a perfectionist. Perhaps then she would not feel so anxious.

He was on tenterhooks, waiting to know whether the Society for the Investigation of Human Ecology would approve his grant to begin brainwashing, among others, Madeleine Smith and Jeannine Huard.

The application had arrived at the society's elegant headquarters on East 78th Street in New York on January 23, 1957. Dr. Monroe immediately sent a copy to Dr. Gottlieb in Washington, who forwarded it to the director's office.

Dulles's ties with Dr. Cameron had gone well beyond invitations to Clover's parties, or her consulting the psychiatrist over the mental anguish her husband's infidelities had caused her. They had extended back to the war years, back to the days when spymaster and clinician had formed a common alliance to help destroy Nazism.

While Allen Dulles brilliantly manipulated first the German generals and then Admiral Canaris's Abwehr from his office in Switzerland, he had received invaluable insights into the enemy's mentality from Dr. Cameron and other psychiatrists who were members of an ultrasecret committee meeting regularly in the offices of the American Psychiatric Association in Washington to assess the changing attitudes of Germany and its leaders. Dr. Cameron's insights into the German mentality made it easier for Dulles to have manipulated Himmler's Gestapo toward overthrowing Hitler, and helped him to use German liberals to spread hysteria among the population. Dr. Cameron had synthesized the techniques in documents like "Mass hysteria in a war situation" and "The mechanics of civilian morale and wartime pressure." Some of Dr. Cameron's suggestions had struck Dulles as original and far-reaching—such as his proposal that after the war each surviving German over the age of twelve should receive a short course of electroshock treatment to burn out any remaining vestige of Nazism.

In victory, Dr. Cameron had been a logical choice for the U.S. government to send to Nuremberg to establish the state of mind of Rudolf Hess. In May 1941, the deputy führer had flown to Scotland with the avowed aim of convincing Winston Churchill to surrender. Hess had languished in an English prison and had been brought to Nuremberg to stand trial with other Nazi leaders, having been pronounced sane by a British psychiatrist. The Americans, like the Russians—both were coprosecutors in the war crimes trial—insisted on their own psychiatric assessments.

Dr. Cameron had arrived on a late autumn day in 1945 in the city that had been the nursery of Nazism. He had met Dulles for the first time and an immediate rapport developed; both found they had a suspicion of the English and a hatred of the Germans equaled only by what they felt about the Russians. Over dinner in the cavernous dining room of the Grand Hotel, Dulles first swore Dr. Cameron to secrecy, then told him an astounding story. He had reason to believe that the man Dr. Cameron was to examine was not Rudolf Hess, but an impostor—that the real deputy führer had been secretly executed on Churchill's orders. Dulles had explained that Dr. Cameron could prove the point by a simple physical examination of the man's torso. If he was the genuine Hess, there should be scar tissue over his left lung, a legacy from the day the young Hess had been wounded in World War I. Dr. Cameron had agreed to try and physically examine the prisoner.

Next day he had been taken to the prison where the Nazi leaders were held. A white-helmeted British military policeman had brought a handcuffed figure to an interview room and had formally introduced him as "Hess, Rudolf, prisoner awaiting trial."

The deep sockets of Hess's blue eyes gave his pallid face the appearance of a skull. He wore an old tweed jacket and baggy trousers. He had on neither collar nor tie nor a belt around his waist—precautions against suicide attempts. His feet were encased in the Luftwaffe flying boots in which Hess had flown to Scotland. Prisoner and escort remained handcuffed to each other while Dr. Cameron questioned Hess for several hours. But when he had asked the policeman to remove the handcuffs so that Hess could be physically examined, the escort had refused, explaining he had no authority to do so. Dr. Cameron had not pressed the matter, reporting to Dulles what had happened. If the spymaster was disappointed, he kept it from the psychiatrist, who had indicated he was willing to act in an unorthodox way. No one would ever know whether Dulles's story about Hess was true or what he called one of "my little tests." When they went their separate ways—Dr. Cameron having pronounced Hess to be clinically not insane—both had agreed they must do everything possible to protect the world from communism.

Now, twelve years later, they were once more united in confronting that enemy.

Dr. Cameron's proposal had arrived at a time of mounting frustration for Dulles. The Society for the Investigation of Human Ecology had turned out to be a costly flop. It was not the $1,200-a-month rent on the townhouse or the $180,000 annually spent on salaries and running costs, or even the $5 million of CIA money that had been channeled in the past three years through the society's books—Dulles could live with those kinds of losses. What he could not accept was that there was almost nothing positive to show for all this expenditure of secret funds, except endless promises and finally acute embarrassment.

This was particularly galling because elsewhere the Agency, under his stewardship, had achieved spectacular successes. It had dug a tunnel under the West Berlin border into the eastern sector to tap the main Soviet communications network carrying top-secret messages between Moscow and its satellites. Dulles had personally masterminded the overthrowing of the fanatical Mohammad Mossadeq in Iran and restored the shah to the throne. He had supervised the toppling of the Socialist dictator of Guatemala, Jacobo Arbenz, who had overreached himself by trying to expropriate land in Guatemala owned by the United Fruit Company, an American corporation that had used John Foster Dulles as legal counsel and still had Allen Dulles as a substantial shareholder. Dulles had encircled the globe with secret bases for covert operations in Japan, Greece, Germany, and England. Each was staffed with a cadre of CIA officers trained in all kinds of guerrilla warfare and ready to lead hired mercenaries into battle. One of the officers was the up-and-coming William Buckley, operating in Southeast Asia.

The past four years, in so many ways, had been good ones for Allen Dulles, not least because he was certain the multitude of operations were hastening the end of the dying lion that had once been the British Empire. In all parts of the world—particularly in Africa, India, and Asia, areas where Britain's writ once ran unchallenged—Dulles had infiltrated agents. He had also extended the Agency's control of the stratosphere. Obsessed with the idea of Soviet treachery, he had persuaded his fellow members on the U.S. Intelligence Board (USIB) to set up a subcommittee, under the chairmanship of Edwin Land, the driving force behind the Polaroid Corporation. Land had concluded that the only way to monitor military activities was to build a very high altitude reconnaissance aircraft equipped with special photographic equipment, capable of identifying a man's face from six miles above the earth. The USIB agreed to finance the project and to hand it over to the Agency.

At nights, in the spacious mansion on Highlands Avenue in Washington that Clover Dulles had rented on the advice of her Jungian therapist—who had told her she would never rid herself of the memories of infidelities while she continued to live in the Q Street house—Allen Dulles had mulled over the blueprints of the U-2 project. He was convinced that with the spy plane he would at last know what the enemy was doing. But he still had to know how the Russians and Chinese controlled minds.

The answer remained as unfathomable in some ways as what went on in his son's head. His physical scars had healed, but the Chinese bullet had left the younger Dulles forever mentally among the walking wounded. At times, Clover would recall, their son would look with "such distaste at his father that Allen would shudder as if he'd gotten a sudden chill. Afterwards, he'd say, 'I don't know what we're going to do with him.' "

Dr. Cameron's proposal had reached the director's desk in an office that had doors with two combination locks and yet was furnished simply—no ostentation, no self-serving photographs of handshakes with world leaders, only a few prints on loan from the National Gallery. In his office Dulles had stuffed flakes of tobacco into the bowl of his briar pipe and, reading, had known that, four years later, even he could no longer be certain when the rot had set in over the research into mind control.

Had it already been there, incompetence masked by overconfidence, even in the first high days of that fine summer in 1953 when the Society for the Investigation of Human Ecology had received so many requests for funding from respected researchers that Dulles had happily persuaded two existing philanthropic organizations to act as conduits for a further $5 million in grants? They were the prestigious Geschichter Fund for Medical Research and the Josiah Macy Foundation, close-knit family trusts whose heads were old friends of the director. That summer had looked so promising. Stalin was dead; both John Foster and Eleanor had agreed with him that the balance of power had tilted a little more from the old to the new world. All Allen had to do was to find out how the Communists bent those minds.

Dr. Gottlieb had convinced Dulles that Communist brainwashing techniques were, after all, rooted in the use of drugs—it could be LSD, mescaline, cocaine, or even nicotine. Dr. Gottlieb didn't yet know, "but it had to be something like that," he said. Dulles's own gut feeling supported the idea. So, all over the United States, at the great research centers like Boston Psychopathic, the University of Illinois Medical School, Mount Sinai, Columbia University, the University of Oklahoma, the Addiction Research Center at Lexington, Kentucky, the University of Chicago, and the University of Rochester, and still other centers, researchers had begun projects funded by the Agency through intermediaries.

Within the Agency Dr. Gottlieb—between supervising the production of more effective poisons for field officers like William Buckley—found time to lead the chemists of Technical Services Staff on a series of increasingly daring experiments with LSD. They spiked each other's coffee and liquor; they spread it on their tuna fish salads and hamburgers and french fries; they sprinkled it on their chocolate malts. They tripped out in their offices and in safe houses in Washington and beyond, in the Maryland countryside. They were stoned for days at a time.

There were moments of black comedy: an hallucinating scientist suddenly decided he was Fred Astaire and grabbed the nearest secretary, convinced she was Ginger Rogers. The typist had also eaten a doctored sandwich and the pair had spent an entire afternoon dancing on a conference room table before they were led away by anxious colleagues who had sat with them throughout the night until the couple returned to normal. More disturbing was the behavior of a TSS doctor who drank a spiked coffee in a safe house near the Potomac and suddenly ran from the building shouting he was going to throw himself into the river. He was overpowered by his fellow physicians when he was about to jump off a parapet.

Dr. Gottlieb regarded such incidents as the usual hiccups in searching for the magic technique he was convinced the Communists were using. Years of hard-won experience had shown the scientist that, just as there were no shortcuts to learning an intricate folk dance step, so there were none in harnessing science to counterintelligence. Both required a willingness to spend long hours in practicing and a readiness, at the end of it all, to accept pitfalls. But his sixth sense—that deductive reasoning that made him such a respected figure among his peers—convinced Dr. Gottlieb that there might be no quick answers. The only certain way to arrive at the one successful one that mattered was to continue experimenting.

In that summer in 1953, he encouraged his staff to seek how to take possession of a man's mind. He was no longer only the Beast to Richard Helms's Beauty, but also became known as Merlin, the Great Wizard. Watching his colleagues expanding their conception of reality under the influence of LSD, he would sometimes dance a jig. Those were among some of his happiest hours at the Agency, equaled only by rising at dawn to milk his goats.

Late that summer he had gone to Dulles and said that the only way to decide about the drug's potential would be to hold a full-scale trial—trying out LSD on somebody totally outside the Agency. Dulles, to Dr. Gottlieb's surprise, had hesitated; the politician never far from the surface in the director warned of the danger if something went wrong. He told Dr. Gottlieb to continue with experimenting only upon TSS staff.

There was also a more attractive option, one that carried less of a risk factor. Morse Allen had once more moved close to center stage in his bid to be first within the Agency to solve the riddle of mind control.

Morse Allen's many talents included being able to gut even the most complex or boring of texts to its essentials. He had also mastered the technique of hypnotism. In his early days with the Agency he had often asked to be given a chance to try out his skills, but no one had taken him seriously. During that madcap adventure of Dr. Wendt's, Allen had momentarily calmed his fury by spending his nights in the safe house in Frankfurt reading the definitive work on fungi, Gordon and Valentina Wasson's *Mushrooms, Russia and History*. He discovered unsuspected details not only of the subtle differences between the many varieties of mushrooms, but how, even before Christ, they had been used in covert operations by the Egyptians, Greeks, and Phoenicians to poison their enemies. The Roman Empress Agrippina had terminated her husband, Claudius, by lovingly feeding him a platter of deadly fungi so that her son, Nero, could rule. Morse Allen had been particularly struck by an observation of the Wassons that the fungi Agrippina had selected, the *amanita phalloides* mushroom, would, in a modified form, leave a person no longer in control of himself. It was as good as any previous description Allen had heard of for mind control. In his typical cautious way, he had spent months preparing the groundwork for a memo to Dulles. What it lacked in style, it compensated for in research, including details of Allen's own meetings with many of the leading mushroom growers in America, who had told him that the most exciting fungi grew in Mexico. The memo urged that the Agency should go in search of the magic mushroom the Indians used. Strictly speaking it was not a fungi, but the seeds of the piule plant which left the natives strangely intoxicated.

Dulles immediately accepted the suggestion that the seeds could contain a possible truth drug. An Agency scientist was sent south of the border to look for the special seeds that the Aztec priests called "teonanactl," God's flesh. The project was given another of the director's endless list of appropriate code names—Operation Flesh Hunt. The scientist returned with carefully labeled sachets of piule seeds, identifying where they had been picked and details of the surrounding vegetation and soil conditions.

Word reached Dr. Gottlieb of what seemed a promising discovery. He quickly persuaded Dulles that Morse Allen's Office of Security did not have the expertise to fully investigate the potential in the seeds. That was a job for the chemists of Technical Services Staff. Dulles, just as he could be overawed by Dr. Wolff, with an equally deferential respect for Dr. Gottlieb had agreed. Morse Allen was shunted aside, another victim of the machinations that ruled the Agency, and that were discreetly encouraged by its director on the premise that divided he ruled, united his staff could conquer him.

Once Dr. Gottlieb had landed God's flesh, he realized his laboratories, despite being the best equipped within the Agency, were still too limited. What began as a modestly budgeted trip of $5,000 to Mexico now began to grow with alarming speed. Another $100,000 was drawn from the Agency's coffers to contract work to, among others, the chemists at Parke-Davis in Detroit and a number of researchers in universities. Mycologists in a dozen cities began to happily work long hours for the Agency, who kept them supplied with any amount of God's flesh, the result of harvesting expeditions to Mexico. In a memo to Dulles, shortly after he had been asked to hold over field testing LSD on non-Agency personnel, Dr. Gottlieb had enthused, "We are on the fringe of a completely new chemical agent which will, of course, remain an Agency secret."

Now, four years later, in February 1957, with Dr. Cameron's proposal before him, the director knew that Dr. Gottlieb's promise, like so many others, had not been kept.

Dulles's old wartime ally, Albert Hofmann, the chemist who had discovered LSD, with the help of a French mycologist, Roger Heim, at the Sorbonne, had managed to isolate the active chemical ingredients in God's flesh. He had named it psilocybin.

It was a bitter blow, and for someone less resilient than Dr. Gottlieb, it could have been a final one. Instead, when he recovered from his disappointment, he shifted the focus of Operation Flesh Hunt from research to field trials. He purchased a large quantity of psilocybin and farmed it out to his medical friends in the prison service. The first batch of ampoules went to Dr. Harris Isbell at the Addiction Center in Lexington, Kentucky. Dr. Isbell injected nine black inmates and then measured their psychological responses. He noted that

after thirty minutes anxiety became quite definite and was expressed as fear that something evil was going to happen; fear of insanity, or of death. At times patients had the sensation that they could see the blood and bones in their own bodies and in that of another person. They reported many fantasies in which they seemed to be elsewhere, such as taking trips to the moon or living in gorgeous castles. Two of the nine patients felt their experiences were caused by the experimenters controlling their minds.

It was not conclusive. But Dr. Isbell's own conclusion— that some of the prisoners believed their minds were being controlled—finally persuaded Dulles to accede to Dr. Gottlieb's repeated requests to perform a full field test with LSD.

Even now, long after the dust had settled, the director supposed he would never know the full truth about what happened. Only the handful of Agency operatives who were present knew all the details of what followed when Dr. Frank Olson, a distinguished biochemist, joined Dr. Gottlieb and his colleagues for a seminar in a log cabin deep within the woods of western Maryland. Dr. Olson worked at Fort Detrick—his speciality, the airborne distribution of biological germs. Since 1943, Dr. Olson had developed a range of lethal aerosols in handy-sized containers, disguised as deodorants and shaving cream and insect repellents. They contained, among other agents: staph enteroxin, a crippling food poison;

the even more virulent Venezuelan equine encephalomyelitis; and, most deadly of all, anthrax. He had been asked to Dr. Gottlieb's soiree in the woods to describe further weapons he was working on—including a cigarette lighter that gave off an almost instant lethal gas, lipstick that would kill on contact with skin, and a neat pocket spray for asthma sufferers that induced pneumonia. The first three days of the seminar had passed uneventfully, with Dr. Olson explaining and demonstrating, and Richard Helms, Dr. Gottlieb, and his assistant, Dr. Richard Lashbrook, listening attentively.

On Thursday evening, November 19, 1953, the group sat down for dinner, discussing, among other matters, that day's editorial in the *Washington Post,* which robustly attacked the use of chemical warfare. The general consensus was that the *Post* was pinko, and that Senator McCarthy should investigate its staff. After dinner Dr. Gottlieb, ever the attentive host, poured Dr. Olson a glass of Cointreau. He did not reveal that the drink had been spiked with LSD.

Within an hour the biochemist began to behave strangely. The Agency men observed him carefully, noting how Dr. Olson first laughed and then became depressed. Finally, there were clear signs of psychotic behavior. Dr. Olson's intelligence became impaired, and so did his comprehension and memory. His sense of time and place grew vague and his level of concentration altered from one minute to the next. Like a small child, Dr. Olson could not pay attention for long. His emotions became unstable and changeable, with abrupt swings from pointless euphoria to equally inappropriate anger or weeping. His behavior continued to deteriorate, becoming more childlike. That night Dr. Olson slept fitfully. Next morning, Dr. Gottlieb and his companions continued their observations. Dr. Olson was still clearly acutely disoriented and hallucinating, in the grip of a deepening psychosis. It was decided to take him home.

Mrs. Alice Olson, a calm, mature woman used to living on the edge of the gray world of intelligence, had long come to terms with what her husband did for a living. Nevertheless, she was stunned by his appearance when he arrived home late on Saturday afternoon, November 21. "He was uncharacteristically moody and depressed," she said. "He was in great distress and in obvious need of help. My husband was a remarkably stable man. He had never had any psychiatric problems."

Yet it was obvious to Mrs. Olson that her husband needed to see a psychiatrist. "But instead of being taken to one in Washington or Maryland, Dr. Gottlieb and Dr. Lashbrook took Frank to an allergist in New York, Dr. Harold Abramson."

Dr. Abramson had no formal training in psychiatry, but was a physician interested in probing the responses of the mind. He was involved with, among other Agency operations, Project M-K-Ultra. Dr. Abramson quickly diagnosed that the biochemist was in a chronic confused state, unaware of his own identity, sometimes repeatedly examining some part of his body as if it did not belong to him. Dr. Abramson prescribed a sedative, Nembutal, and a glass of bourbon—a treatment not found in any textbook on psychosis. During his days in New York, Dr. Olson also visited the famous conjuror, John Mulholland, whom Dr. Gottlieb had recently signed on as an Agency consultant. Mulholland's brief was to write a manual on how the magician's art could be adapted to covert activities such as delivering various materials to unwitting subjects. The biochemist became agitated when he thought Mulholland was going to make him vanish like one of the magician's rabbits.

Dr. Olson was taken back to Dr. Abramson. This time the allergist did not prescribe whiskey and a sleeping tablet, but a plane ticket. He told Dr. Olson he should go home to his wife and family for Thanksgiving and forget about his recent experiences. That night, while his Agency escort slept, Dr. Olson crept out of the hotel, convinced he was on a secret mission and that the first step was to destroy any evidence of his identity. He tore up the contents of his wallet in a subway and then returned to the hotel, skulking in the lobby. When the Agency men found him he insisted he was being watched and followed, talked about, and plotted against by unspecified enemies. His minders decided the sooner they returned Dr. Olson to his family, the better. They all flew to Washington.

Alice Olson would remember her husband telephoned saying "he was afraid to return home because he might do something wrong in front of the children." Dr. Lashbrook took him back to New York for a further consultation with Dr. Abramson. Even the allergist realized his patient was in a psychotic state with delusions of persecution. Dr. Olson had begun to hear voices, hostile and reviling. A qualified psychiatrist would have wondered whether this was the onset of paraphrenia, one of the subgroups of paranoid schizophrenia, a highly destructive mental illness.

That night Dr. Olson and Dr. Lashbrook shared a twin-bedded room on the tenth floor of the Statler Hotel. After dinner Dr. Olson telephoned his wife. She was to recall that he said he felt much better and "everything is going to be fine." At midnight Dr. Lashbrook switched off his reading light, satisfied Dr. Olson was asleep. Two hours later the Agency physician awoke in time to see Dr. Olson running across the room and plunging through the drawn blinds out the window and down to the sidewalk.

It had taken Dulles all his considerable persuasive skills to cover up Dr. Olson's death. People outside the magic circle would never understand why Dr. Olson had died. No one, after all, had wanted to kill him; there was no malignant purpose in what had happened. It was a professional mistake, no more than overzealousness on the part of Dr. Gottlieb. And, in the end, the damage sustained in the whole misadventure was truly negligible. The director had been at his dissembling best.

Dr. Gottlieb received no reprimand. The Olson family would have to wait until 1976 when some of the truth surfaced and Congress passed a bill authorizing Dr. Olson's widow $750,000 in compensation.

But late in February 1957, Dulles faced a difficult choice. No real progress had been made in any area of mind control. Dr. Cameron's proposal suggested how a breakthrough could be achieved. Yet there was a risk attached. Patients could die. There would be questions—and a foreign government, even a friendly one like Canada's, would not be as malleable as the administration in Washington. For days the director had deliberated on what to do, weighing the risks against the range of delicate information about the enemy's strengths that only he knew. He had always said the final way to resolve doubt was to deny its legitimacy.

On February 25, he approved Dr. Cameron's application. It would be administered by Dr. Monroe. He would work directly with Dr. Gottlieb.

Next day, Dr. Monroe, in a memorandum, laid down how the Society for the Investigation of Human Ecology

. . . will act in the capacity of a cover organization. The

(revised) cost of the program for a period of two years will be $38,186.00. Charges should be made against Allotment 7-2502-10-001. The Society will request the return of any unexpended funds received under the grant from the Society. Requirements for a six-month informal accounting on the part of the principal investigator is waived.

Dr. Monroe had concluded with a note on security.

No Agency staff personnel will contact, visit, or discuss the project with Dr. Cameron or his staff except under extreme circumstances. If it is necessary for Agency personnel to contact Dr. Cameron or his staff, the matter will be discussed with the Office of Security and the desk involved for evaluation and advice as to the proper procedures to be taken.

It was another chance for Morse Allen to become involved in mind control. In the society's office Dr. Cameron's proposal was entered into the M-K-Ultra program as subproject-68. It was classified top secret. The Agency noted, without comment, that one of the drugs Dr. Cameron would use "in an attempt to develop better methods of inactivating the patient" was the one that had driven Dr. Olson to his death —LSD-25.

On February 26, Dr. Allen telephoned Dr. Cameron with the news that "you have a green light."

9

The
Mind-Bender

No one would remember March 18, 1957, as different than any other day at the Allan Memorial Institute. There was continued speculation at what was happening in the basement, part of it having recently been declared off limits by Dr. Cameron to everyone except Rubenstein and Zielinski. For the past few weeks there had been the sound of their hammering late into the evening and the sight of both men moving in equipment. No one was willing to go to the basement and find out what was going on and risk Dr. Cameron's wrath; he had fired people for less.

Coincidentally that same day, Dr. Monroe had also issued contracts to two sociologists at Rutgers University, Richard Stephenson and Jay Schulman, to start an investigation into the sociology of the Communist system. It was also the day the society issued another check to doctors employed at Iona State Hospital in Michigan to continue probing the minds of sexual perverts. Dr. Gottlieb had concluded that rapists and child molesters may have developed the same skills at repressing healthy, normal thoughts as Soviet spies would need. It was just an idea—but it ensured that the prison doctors would receive a further $50,000 in funding. The projects were intended to be adjuncts to Dr. Cameron's work.

At the institute, Dr. Cleghorn arrived early to measure the corticoid output in the urine of a number of his patients; it was one way to assess stress. Other scientists prepared for another day of testing and evaluating, exploring the extent to which emotional distress produced cardiac pain in some patients, and whether this was caused by a diminished blood supply to the heart through vasoconstriction or a sudden demand for oxygen because of an anxiety attack. In one corner of the laboratory complex a team studied phobic reactions—intense emotional experiences that led to severe psychological crippling. One clinician correlated the links between the obsessions some of his patients displayed and their uneven sleep patterns. Another tabulated the remarkable coincidence between raised blood pressure and anxiety; he was looking for evidence of pressure fluctuations when patients were asked about matters intended to agitate them—questions about their sex lives, families, and relationships. The researcher was trying to quantify the different pressure readings between when a patient was emotionally disturbed and calm.

Dr. Charles Shagass continued to probe the quantity of barbiturate needed to induce sleep in various categories of mental illness; it would eventually receive worldwide recognition as the sedative threshold test. Dr. Hassam Azima, rumored to be a blood relative of the shah of Persia, would spend his day preparing another application for funds to pursue his research into a battery of psychological tests designed to make occupational therapy more specific to individual psychiatric conditions. Tall and darkly handsome, the Iranian sometimes reminded Dr. Cleghorn of the skipper of an Arab dhow running before the wind, rather than a scientist whose capability was only limited by the amount of money that could be charmed out of a sponsor.

Much of the research would take years to produce results; some of it would be abandoned. All of it ultimately depended on the whim of Dr. Cameron. He was the final arbiter of which projects needed his fund-raising skills. Dr. Cleghorn was not entirely convinced that this was an ideal situation, if only because the institute's chief doctor usually allowed himself little time to fully assess the merits of each proposed investigation. Sometimes Dr. Cameron made a snap judgment, often on the move between going from ward to treatment room, after pausing to listen briefly to a researcher waiting in a corridor. Once he had ruled, he could not be budged. Anyone who persisted was moved to the outer reaches of the empire Dr. Cameron had created. Known as the McGill Psychiatric Training Network, it embraced eight Montreal hospitals, had its own diploma course in psychiatry, and gave its founder more power than any other doctor in the city. That, too, worried Dr. Cleghorn.

Dr. Eve Lester, soon to become one of the youngest professors on the McGill faculty, was beginning another long day of working with disturbed adolescent patients; Dr. Cleghorn sensed she was one of his colleagues on the verge of international recognition. Dr. Ken Adam, one of the team of psychoanalysts, was another. Ruggedly good-looking, his skill at drawing therapeutic conclusions from carefully observed symptoms had already assured him a future among Canada's leading analysts.

Increasingly, Dr. Cleghorn had noticed a growing rift between the psychoanalysts and the clinical psychiatrists who sought cures with a syringe or electroshock, and had little patience with analytical colleagues whose methods had been arrived at empirically and depended almost totally on observation. While the psychiatrists grudgingly admitted psychoanalysts had the structure of a science, they saw it essentially as no more than a philosophy of life—and of little value in supporting their drug-oriented treatments. The analysts doggedly clung to their belief that patients could be helped by being encouraged to reveal themselves to an attentive, patient, and sympathetic physician; they spoke of the danger of chemicals and electroshock destroying that special region of the mind—not, of course, anatomically located—where thoughts, feelings, impulses, wishes, and instinctual drives existed, blind and inarticulate, awaiting to surface and be properly motivated under analysis. There were sudden, sharp exchanges between both factions over such matters as transference neurosis. The psychiatrists sometimes doubted if it really existed; the analysts said its comprehension was vital, adding that often the extent of physical treatment—especially electroshock—ruined any chance they had of a successful follow-up.

Dr. Cameron encouraged the dissension; he thought the squabbling made for better doctors. And, like his old friend, Allen Dulles, he had long known the advantages of ruling over a divided house. Bickering between the factions had increased with the opening of still more research units. Doctors eminent in their field found themselves cramped together, fighting for space, for money, and above all for the predominance of their theories.

That had heightened speculation over what was going on in the basement. The consensus was that Dr. Cameron was setting up one of his projects. He had sometimes said he would like nothing better than the chance to pursue all his theories free of the responsibility of administering what amounted to a sizable corporation; ultimately hundreds of people answered to him all over Montreal.

No one, least of all Dr. Cleghorn, believed for a moment that Dr. Cameron would ever willingly relinquish his unique position. At times his deputy wondered what drove Dr. Cameron. It could not be money; he was wealthy enough. Power? But what further power could he want? There was not a door closed to him in the medical world and he was probably more powerful than many Canadian politicians; he could reach the highest in the land and make or break a physician's career with a single phone call—just as he could drum up money in a way few professional fund-raisers could match. So what was it? That question increasingly bothered Dr. Cleghorn. Nor did he like the way Dr. Cameron cajoled, maneuvered, and— where need be—exploited them all in a dazzling display of medical politicking, supporting one group against another and then, just as quickly, switching sides. He was promoter and concert master of an orchestra that often played brilliantly but rarely in complete harmony.

Doctors came and went. Dr. Mary Morrow had gone to another hospital in Montreal and Dr. Cleghorn was hopeful she would find a niche for herself once she learned to handle her anxiousness. If he had taught her nothing else, he was certain he had impressed her with the belief that psychiatry was no place for the nervous-dispositioned, the bungler, or the uncaring doctor.

The senior psychiatrist in his mind had begun to level the latter charge against Dr. Cameron. Like Dr. Morrow, Dr. Cleghorn felt that he had lost sight of caring for the patient. Too often, Dr. Cameron referred to a case by the symptoms— "the lassie in North-Two is a catatonic"—seeming to forget that no patient is simply a question of melancholia, manic-depressive psychosis, or obsessional neurosis. Those were only labels: abstractions, hypotheses, a mere pointer toward reality. And that reality, for Dr. Cleghorn, was always the suffering individual. Nowadays, Dr. Cameron would only lend an impatient, if tolerant, ear to such sentiments; somewhere along the way he seemed to have abandoned Dr. Cleghorn's own spiritual guide through the medical world, Goethe's "one understands only what one loves."

At nights, when he had visited his last patients, Dr. Cleghorn returned to his office and reread Dr. Cameron's papers on measuring the body heat of schizophrenics; the effect of physical pain on depressives; the change of electrical brain waves during insulin treatment; the effect of small doses of Adrenalin on certain of the higher mental functions; studies in senile nocturnal delirium in which patients had been blindfolded, resulting in a rise of blood pressure and a marked inability to remember what they had been told; the speech patterns of psychotics; and behavioral changes in chronically tense people.

There were a score more of such papers with catchy titles like "Remembering," "Research and Society," and "Psychiatry and Citizenship." There was no stiffness in the writing, nor the cant that marred so many such papers. Instead, there was the certainty of the evangelist: Dr. Cameron was right and what he had set down was to be followed by lesser mortals. Such certainty and self-importance sat uneasily with the self-effacing Dr. Cleghorn.

Yet after studying it all carefully, Dr. Cleghorn had decided that Dr. Cameron's work "lacked a profound scholarly acquaintance with the field under study." He also realized that as Dr. Cameron had climbed the hierarchy, a veritable medical Jack and the Beanstalk, depositing publications to mark every step upward, he avoided crediting others who had often done the crucial preliminary work that enabled him to conduct his research. No matter how exalted, whether it was Freud or Jung or one of the other founding figures of modern psychiatry, Dr. Cameron would, whenever possible, ignore their contributions to his own findings. Dr. Cleghorn not only found that a revealing insight into Dr. Cameron's personality, but to a scientist, it was troubling; it was tantamount to cheating.

Most disturbing of all for the deputy medical director was Dr. Cameron's obsession with psychic driving. Because there was nothing in the literature, Dr. Cameron had created his own language to describe the treatment. Long ago, Dr. Cleghorn had learned that medical language had a peculiarly affective quality. Just as he knew that phrases like coronary thrombosis, tumor, and psychoneurosis caused high anxiety in patients, so he felt a similar response to the words Dr. Cameron used for psychic driving. They worried Dr. Cleghorn because they formed a nonsense language to describe a treatment that had been cobbled together from numerous sources: the Linguaphone Company and the improvisations of the medically unqualified Leonard Rubenstein.

Something else concerned Dr. Cleghorn. Two years earlier, at the annual conference of the American Psychiatric Association, Dr. Cameron had promoted psychic driving through the columns of *Weekend Magazine*, a mass circulation tabloid normally preoccupied with the lives of movie stars and household hints. He had referred to the technique as "beneficial brainwashing." Accompanying the interview was a photograph of a young woman wearing headphones and the caption described her listening to her repeated confession. Dr. Cameron was credited with inventing "a daring idea designed to help neurotic patients by using a modified form of brainwashing." He had added he was confronted with "the same problems as professional brainwashers" because his patients, "like prisoners of the Communists, tended to resist and had to be broken down."

Dr. Cleghorn and many of his colleagues were horrified at such sensational statements. But was that, Dr. Cleghorn had since wondered, really how Dr. Cameron viewed his treatment—as beneficial brainwashing? It was indeed troubling if that was the case.

He had begun to feel equally concerned about his superior's multiple and massive electroshocks, for which Dr. Cameron had also created a special word—depatterning. Dr. Cleghorn saw no long-term benefit for a treatment in which a patient was first put to sleep for three days and then, still comatose, given between thirty to sixty electroshocks over a short period and, in between, doses of 1,000 milligrams of Largactil, a powerful tranquilizer, to combat anxiety. What especially disturbed Dr. Cleghorn's sense of medical propriety was that when he finally queried the total amnesia the treatment produced, Dr. Cameron had simply said the patients' families would have to "help them build a scaffold of normal events."

Those sentiments had not improved the cooling relationship between the two most senior doctors in the hospital.

* * *

The head nurse on South-Two, Peggy Mielke, a trim, vivacious twenty-four-year-old who had circumvented Madeleine's
questions about why patients wore football helmets, sometimes wondered if her reluctance to discuss with anybody
what went on in the Sleep Room—the dormitory of twenty
beds, always filled and kept in continual semidarkness, and
situated at one end of the wing—was her own concern at
being unable to find an answer to a nagging question. Had
she spent her years of training to end up working in this
strange twilight world supervising a treatment she had never
read about in her textbooks or seen in any of the other
psychiatric hospitals where she had nursed?

From beyond the closed door of the dormitory came the
sounds of the institute settling into its early morning routine.
The first of several hundred tablets were being dispensed and
swallowed; the contents of scores of ampoules were being
drawn up into syringes before being injected into veins and
muscles; gel was being smeared on temples; electroshocks
were being administered and the first patients of a new day
were being rendered unconscious by electricity. It was a
world Nurse Mielke understood.

But in the Sleep Room the tomorrows came and went,
each day indistinguishable from the last. Some of the nurses
called the place the Zombie Room.

Nurse Mielke stood inside the dormitory door, adjusting
her eyes to the gloom and her nose to the smell of chemicals
and human odors. The patients looked like aliens from another planet. Some lay inert, listening to instructions endlessly repeated from speakers under their pillows. Sometimes
they whimpered unintelligibly at the sound of their own
recorded voices or that of Dr. Cameron. Others had been
aroused by the night staff and shuffled around the dormitory
wearing the specially adapted football helmets. A few sat at
the table in the center of the room, being spoon-fed by
nurses and oblivious of anything except the tapes being played
through their helmets.

It was those helmets that had first given rise to Nurse
Mielke's doubts. What also concerned her was that Leonard
Rubenstein and Jan Zielinski were allowed to come and go as
they pleased, to replace tapes or fit a helmet on a patient.
When she had queried this arrangement, she was told that

the two men had special permission from Dr. Cameron—and were the only non-medical staff allowed in the Sleep Room. Nurse Mielke thought it a highly irregular arrangement. She had never before encountered a situation where patients were routinely handled by staff who had no formal medical or nursing training—let alone the special skills required to deal with the acutely disturbed.

What especially upset her was that neither man appeared to fully understand that this was a ward for the seriously ill. Rubenstein could never resist joshing with the nurses or delivering his latest joke and braying at his own wit. Nurse Mielke thought at times he was off the wall. Zielinski rarely spoke, but peered owlishly at patients and often shook his head; she thought he resembled a barn owl.

She sometimes thought the two men were role-playing and that in their white coats they perhaps imagined they were doctors. Certainly when she spoke to Rubenstein, his language was peppered with medical terms and he constantly spoke about his ongoing research in his behavioral laboratory. Many of the doctors referred to it as the workshop. It was housed in one of the converted stables at the back of the mansion. Years ago the Allan dynasty had kept some of the finest stallions in Canada, purchased from their profits as shipping magnates. In 1940 Sir Montagu Allan had bequeathed the family mansion to be converted into a hospital. Rubenstein and Zielinski worked in a horse trailer storing their tape-editing machines and football helmets against walls that still bore the imprint of horseshoes.

At first Nurse Mielke had put down Rubenstein's attitude as egocentricity and was mildly amused that he sounded so self-important, behaving at times as if he was not only the chief's right hand but also his closest confidant. But she had seen that Rubenstein was not above telling a nurse, or even a doctor, not to touch a pillow speaker or remove a helmet without him being present, insisting that was how he and the chief wanted the matter to be handled. She had considered raising this issue with Dr. Cameron, on that day when Madeleine Smith had somehow escaped from her room after her morning electroshock and out of the Institute, staggering in her nightdress, barefooted, down the drive and out into the street, dodging in and out of the traffic. Nurse Mielke spotted her from a window in South-Two and, after raising the alarm, ran in pursuit, sprinting so fast that her cap flew off. She caught up with Madeleine as she narrowly escaped falling under a van. They had struggled briefly in the snarl of the traffic before she led the exhausted and distressed woman back to the institute. Madeleine looked unbearably vulnerable, like a lost child.

Dr. Cameron had appeared with Rubenstein. The doctor ordered Madeleine to be taken to the Sleep Room. She had wept uncontrollably before crumpling up in a ball and beating her fists on the floor. Dr. Cameron had looked down at her and said firmly, "Lassie, stop that. You will not get better like this." Rubenstein lifted Madeleine to her feet. The psychiatrist placed an arm around Madeleine's shoulders and said, "Lassie, I want to help you." The men had led her to the Sleep Room, with Nurse Mielke tagging behind.

Madeleine had been kept in a chemically controlled sleep for thirty-six days and was awakened only to eat. In between her meals she received thirty more multiple shocks.

In the four months she had taken the drugs Dr. Cameron had prescribed, those same drugs had given Mrs. Velma Orlikow only problems. The large doses of desoyn and sodium amytal first drove her anxiety deeper within her, confining it in a chemically created cocoon she felt would never stop growing. The other drug, LSD-25, had burst the cocoon, leaving her badly frightened that her old self—the hopeful and desperate woman who had made an 1,800-mile train journey from her home in Winnipeg to find help—had been transformed into a confused person. Dr. Cameron repeatedly insisted she must challenge former values, such as her relationship with her mother and her love for her husband, David, and their daughter, Leslie. As well as being by profession a chemist, her husband was a long-standing member of Parliament and one of the country's most respected politicians.

She had come across Canada to tell Dr. Cameron her story because other doctors had said he was the only physician left who could help. She had told it, piece by piece, but all she saw on that first interview was his expressionless mask. She had stumbled on, knowing the tape machine on his desk was recording every word: that she was forty years old, that David was a chemist and Leslie eight years old, that her marriage had been happy, which was why she was all that more bewildered over her loss of sexual desire after her daughter was born. At first she thought it was no more than a passing phase, and David had been patient. But months later, when he had wanted to make love, she had felt vague pains in her abdomen and had refused him. Her loss of libido had increased and was accompanied by a growing feeling of fatigue and mood swings that made her feel she was on a roller coaster, hurtling out of control.

That feeling lasted sometimes for weeks at a time and was accompanied by splitting headaches and sleeplessness. David had given her Largactil. He had prescribed it without consulting a doctor. She had taken it for a year, even though it made her skin and hair feel as if they were on fire. She persevered because she wanted to be a good wife.

Finally, when Velma had told her family doctor about the side effect, he stopped her from taking the drug. The headaches had returned and she had turned to a tried and trusted remedy David sold over the counter to his lady customers—tablets made from acetylsalicylic acid and codeine, sold to relieve premenstrual tensions. Her frame of mind had not improved and she had entered the Mayo Clinic in Winnipeg where she was seen by a psychiatrist who said her symptoms were caused by frigidity. Velma had spent almost four years in psychotherapy, during which she became so desperate that she actually begged the doctor for electroshock treatment. She hoped it would short-circuit her time in analysis.

Velma told Dr. Cameron how she had talked over the idea of electroshock with David and how he suggested she should discuss the matter again with her therapist, who had finally agreed. She had no idea what the treatment entailed, and the doctor had not explained. Velma had shuddered in Dr. Cameron's office as she recalled her feeling of helplessness and fear as she was wheeled into the shock room at the Mayo Clinic and how, when she had regained consciousness, there followed even more blinding headaches. The foggy confusions and memory gaps had remained. Worst of all, she had not felt better. She had begun to think she was incurable. Somehow she had plucked up enough courage to make love with David and had become pregnant. Her Winnipeg therapist strongly urged she should have a therapeutic abortion, and the pregnancy was terminated; at the same time her fallopian tubes were ligated. The doctor also recommended she go to Montreal and become Dr. Cameron's patient. It was her only hope. She had looked across at Dr. Cameron, at last finished, waiting.

He had questioned her—not about her marriage or her present symptoms, but her childhood and parents. Not really understanding why he was interested in such matters, she had nevertheless answered him truthfully. Her father was "a very charming but irresponsible Irishman who carried on affairs of which my mother knew." He had deserted the family when she was seventeen. Her mother was very possessive.

When Dr. Cameron had finished with his questions Velma was taken back to her room, thinking she had never felt more lonely. She had pulled the sheets over her head, to hide the misery that welled from a continuously renewing source deep within her. She had cried and slept, slept and cried.

Finally, a young man arrived carrying a tape recorder, similar to the one Dr. Cameron had on his desk. He placed it on the bedside locker and plugged it in, smiling all the time. He had a strange accent. He had explained: "I'm Rubenstein. I'm English." In his white coat she had assumed he was a doctor.

Dr. Cameron arrived carrying a kidney bowl and a syringe. He said he was going to give her an injection. She had asked what it was for. He replied, "Just trust me," and slipped the needle into a vein in her arm. He patted her on the shoulder, turned on the recorder, and walked out of the room, telling her to say or write whatever came into her mind. Rubenstein handed her a tablet of paper and pencil and settled in the armchair, urging her to take no notice of him.

She looked at the paper. She had no idea what to write. She stared at Rubenstein. He smiled back. She looked around the room. It somehow seemed different. Then she realized the washbasin had moved. It was on the ceiling, upside down, the faucets reaching toward her, coming ever closer. She turned to the paper, thinking she must record what she could see. But her hands were trembling so badly that she couldn't grip the pencil. She shook her head to clear it, thinking it was not possible. Washbasins did not move. She looked again at Rubenstein. He sat unperturbed in the chair, smiling. The faucets were coming closer. There was no doubt about it. Suddenly from both faucets came fiery jets and she felt "a terrifying panic. I had absolutely no control over me.

And I felt that all my bones were melting." She felt she was locked in a room that was shrinking, that the walls and ceilings were coming closer and would eventually crush her. That must be why she experienced a sudden urge to "go zigging and zagging." The whirling in her mind grew. Her body ached from the huge black bubble of fear. Then: "I was a squirrel, in a cage. I couldn't get out. I tried to climb the walls. And I felt if I was to lie down I'd never get up."

Velma had wept—but had no clear further recall of what she had said or felt.

The turmoil had continued for hours until, exhausted, she fell asleep. When she awoke Rubenstein and the tape recorder were gone.

Days passed during which she had slept, waking suddenly from her nightmares, then, once more exhausted, had fallen asleep.

When Velma telephoned David, the connection to Winnipeg was poor; but through the static her husband was reassuring. However dreadful it had been, there must be a good reason for the treatment. He told her over and again, "Sometimes you have to feel worse before you feel better."

Dr. Cameron questioned her further about her parents. What did her mother symbolize to her? Her younger sister? She had struggled to give meaningful answers. He had examined her feelings when her sister was born. Had she felt rejected and overshadowed by her arrival? Was that when her shyness started?

When the questioning was finished he had walked Velma back to her room, accompanied by Rubenstein carrying a tape recorder. Dr. Cameron had once more switched on the machine. Her own voice came through the speaker. She hardly recognized the words through the tears. One minute she spoke about the death of a young cousin and how, when she saw him in the coffin, she had only felt resentment "because they all paid great attention to him." Next she spoke of her mother driving her to achieve still better results at school. Then she rambled on about her father being charming and fun, and how much she had missed him, and how her mother always seemed burdened through being breadwinner and housekeeper. Finally, she remembered she had said all those things during an earlier interview with Dr. Cameron.

Velma had pleaded with Dr. Cameron to switch off the

tape. Instead, he had once more given her an injection. When it took effect, she was again gripped with the fear that the walls had turned into a cage and she was a squirrel.

A few days later Dr. Cameron questioned her again. When her father had left home, how had she felt? Sad? Guilty? Had she drawn closer to her mother? Did her mother always regard her as a child, even when she was an adolescent? Even when she had married David?

She had been taken back to her room and given another injection and once more began to hallucinate.

She had finally learned what was in the syringe when she saw her name on a card in the nurse's office: "Mrs. Orlikow, lysergic acid diethylamide-25." She did not know what it meant—and no one would tell her. She had called David. He was equally mystified. There was nothing about LSD in the literature the drug salesman left with him on his calls.

Finally she had come to a decision. No matter what Dr. Cameron said, she would refuse any more injections. Her mind made up, she waited resolutely in her bed. When Rubenstein arrived with the tape recorder she ordered him to take it away. He looked at her in surprise.

Dr. Cameron arrived and Rubenstein explained what had happened. Dr. Cameron spoke to Mrs. Orlikow.

"Lassie, don't you want to get better?"

She heard a tiny, distant voice saying what she had said many times before—that, just as the hallucinations filled her with fear, so she could not cope with listening to her voice remembering things she thought she had long forgotten.

He told her to stand up. "Come on, we'll walk down the hall."

Outside in the corridor he put an arm around her shoulder and said, "Come on, lassie, you're going to take the injection for me. You know you are."

She begged him to understand. He ignored her pleas. "You're going to take the injection. You are."

She looked at him, feeling the strength in his arm. The warmth of his body was calming. What would she do if he sent her away? What had David said—that no doctor would want to harm her? What if she didn't do as Dr. Cameron asked? Would the rest of her life be filled with that awful void and pain that filled her abdomen and made her fail David as a wife?

Dr. Cameron spoke again. "Lassie, just the injection. But you must have the injection."

She nodded.

Velma had become Dr. Cameron's first patient to be used in the M-K-Ultra subproject-68.

Dr. Cameron had spent every available free moment since Dr. Monroe's telephone call reviewing the case files of the one hundred patients under his care to select those most susceptible to having their minds restructured by chemical agents, psychic driving, and even more radical courses of electroshock. He had drawn up a list of those with something significant to hide in their pasts—memories they were ashamed of, and which made them feel guilty—just as he believed the Chinese, in particular, had chosen their prisoners with care, selecting only those who could be reduced to a state of infantile dependency and subsequently would accept their interrogators' views as their own.

Dr. Cameron intended his treatment to strip his patients of their selfhood and introduce into their minds what he wanted them to believe. That they were already mentally ill was all the greater a challenge: the Chinese had only dealt with healthy fighting men; he would have the infinitely harder task of brainwashing those who were disturbed. By successfully manipulating the psychological mechanisms of denial and repression in his patients, he was certain he would have solved the mystery of mind control.

He had been encouraged by his old friend Dr. William Sargant. Many of Dr. Sargant's own observations had been applied by English police interrogators and those employed by M15, Britain's counterintelligence service. Dr. Sargant had sent Dr. Cameron a proof of his forthcoming book, *Battle for the Mind*, urging him to read the chapters on brainwashing techniques. Dr. Cameron carefully noted that one method was, having found a sore spot, to keep touching it. Dr. Sargant wrote that it was also important to make a person fill in long questionnaires "to fatigue him further, rather than exact any new information of value. When his memory begins to fail him, the difficulty in keeping to the same story makes him more anxious than ever. Finally, unless some accident brings the examination to a premature end, his brain will be too disorganized to respond normally; it can become trans-marginally inhibited, vulnerable to suggestions, paradoxical and ultra-paradoxical phases may supervene and the fortress finally surrenders unconditionally."

Dr. Cameron thanked Dr. Sargant for his advice and the English psychiatrist had responded in typical fashion, scribbling a note from his hospital desk in London saying, "Whatever you manage in this field, I thought of it first!"

Velma's history had singled her out because Dr. Cameron had concluded that her real problem—the one she still could not speak about even under LSD—was that "she might have an unconscious incestuous relationship with her mother which prevented her from having sexual relationships with her husband."

Dr. Cameron had decided that the second patient to be used in the secret project would be Madeleine Smith.

In their converted horse trailer, Leonard Rubenstein and Jan Zielinski spun through the spools of tape containing Madeleine's innermost secrets—searching for the segment Dr. Cameron wanted turned into a loop. Her voice had become familiar to the technicians as they spun the tapes, looking for the key statement.

Surrounded by tape recorders, editing machines, and shelves stacked with pillow speakers and football helmets, microphones, cables, and boxes of new tapes, Zielinski felt the place was "more like a Radio Shack than a science lab." But he also had to admit the pay was good and the work always fascinating; he could think of no other job, outside of actually being a psychiatrist, or perhaps a priest, that allowed him to have such access to human frailties. Where else, he had often reminded himself when he had to work late, could a Polish emigre with limited English and no medical training have ended up as one of the assistants to the most powerful psychiatrist in North America, if not the Western world?

Wandering through the rooms of the sick, Zielinski had often looked at a patient and tried to match what was said on tape with his or her appearance.

Much of what Zielinski saw he did not fully understand. Why were patients kept asleep for so long? Some of those in the Sleep Room had been there for two months. Why were patients so frightened of the shock room? He'd seen grown men and women struggling desperately with nurses who were trying to hold them on the trolley as it was pushed into the treatment room. Why was there so much tension between the doctors? And why did many of them make it clear they disliked Rubenstein and himself? That had hurt Zielinski. After all, he was only trying to help patients.

In the months Zielinski had worked at the institute, the backstabbing had increased. When they thought he had not been able to overhear, physicians and nurses had ridiculed the idea of making patients listen to their own voices. Rubenstein had told him they did not understand the wealth of important psychological data that could be spotted by repeated replaying of the tapes: the shifts in cadence, the tiny mental blocks, the change in speed and emphasis, the hesitations and silences. They were all stored on the tapes and provided Dr. Cameron with invaluable information. Rubenstein had called it "a whole universe of nonverbal communication carried on below the perceptual level."

Descriptions like that made Zielinski believe that Rubenstein was serious when he said that Dr. Cameron and himself would one day become the world's authorities on continuous radio telemetry of human activity. The lanky twenty-eight-year-old ex-Army signalman envisioned the time would come when "there would be no secrets of the mind that we cannot probe electrically." Zielinski had been fascinated as Rubenstein had breezily told Dr. Cameron how this would be achieved. All the psychiatrist had to do was ensure a continuous supply of patients and the wisecracking Cockney would create the electronic equipment that "would enter the deepest corners of their minds."

Dr. Cameron had accepted the technician's claim without quibble. Yet Rubenstein, for all his banter and horseplay, remained a puzzling figure for Zielinski. The Englishman discouraged questions about his background. Despite his lack of formal medical training, he was one of the very few staff who could approach Dr. Cameron at any time, the psychiatrist never showing the impatience he frequently displayed to others. The pair often spent hours alone in the doctor's office, usually late in the evening. Rubenstein had never mentioned what they discussed.

Early in March, Rubenstein had told Zielinski that Dr. Cameron had finally given the go-ahead for part of the institute's basement to be turned into a radio telemetry laboratory. Rubenstein enthused that its purpose would be not only to measure behavioral activity of patients more closely, but would also provide the groundwork for a system that could be used to monitor human activity at a point remote from the subject under study. In other words, Rubenstein had added, "we'll develop a system that will keep tabs on people without their knowing what we're getting from them."

When the work of editing and splicing tapes ended each day, the two men worked in the basement building a Grid Room and an Isolation Chamber.

The Grid Room had lines drawn across one wall and a hard-backed chair in front of them. At the opposite end of the room a carefully concealed hole had been made in the wall, only big enough for the lens of a movie camera mounted on a platform on the other side. Anyone sitting in the chair would be unaware he or she was being secretly filmed. Rubenstein had explained to Dr. Cameron that the Grid Room was meant to measure in a patient "the angle of the trunk axis when sitting down," and to record on film how much energy output was used by a patient when moving. Each patient would be fitted with electrodes, which Rubenstein called potentiometers, and which would convert an analog signal and telemeter it to a receiving station—a cubbyhole in a corner of the basement packed with electronic equipment. Most of it was purpose-built by Rubenstein. It included a large machine with dials and switches, which he called the body movement transducer. He predicted it would provide "up to ten thousand bits of information per second" from each patient. The Grid Room had also been fitted with concealed microphones to record any verbal sounds a patient made. Zielinski had been impressed but nevertheless was still unclear how Dr. Cameron would use such a vast amount of data.

The purpose of the Isolation Chamber was much clearer to Zielinski. It not only looked like a prison cell, with its heavy double-thickness door and cladded walls, but was intended to perform a similar function. The chamber was designed to test an old theory of Dr. Cameron's that certain mental illnesses were caused by disharmony between a patient and his or her environment, and the only answer was to remove the patient from his distressing surroundings. Zielinski had overheard Dr. Cameron telling Rubenstein that the problem he faced in treating such cases was not very different from the one that faced the interrogators of the Communist world. Both he and they were concerned with putting their subjects back in harmony with their environment—either by curing a neurosis or ideological dissent. Dr. Cameron had asked Rubenstein to build the Isolation Chamber because it would help his patients if they could be first isolated and then disoriented before he tried to restructure their attitudes. Even spending a short while in the chamber gave Zielinski a bad feeling. Yet Rubenstein had said that patients would remain incarcerated for weeks, months, and if need be, years—until they were ready to listen to what Dr. Cameron wanted them to hear.

Madeleine's voice had uttered the words Dr. Cameron wanted.

". . . I used to stay out late just to get him going. I wanted to arouse him. I wanted him to love me so I could love him the way my mother never had. I wanted him . . ."

Rubenstein isolated the statement, fashioned it into a loop that could be played continuously back to Madeleine by Dr. Cameron in the hope it would help him find the answer to mind control for the CIA. A seriously disturbed young woman's sexual fantasies were being used by her doctor in yet a further violation of his sacred oath to do a patient no harm. He believed he was entitled to do so to protect the United States and its allies from what many of its leaders were convinced were the perils of communist medical manipulation.

10

Dilemmas

Though Dr. Cameron had not spoken a word, the atmosphere crackled with hostility. He sat, arms folded, shirt cuffs visible in all their starched whiteness, one ankle crossed over the other, socks held in place by suspenders, each shoelace identically tied with a reefer knot. His face white and still, the blue eyes fixed on some point over their heads, he was forbidding, intimidating, and ominous.

Dr. Peter Roper thought there was something more that gave Dr. Cameron the ability, without saying a word, to instill fear. In all his thirty-five years, the English-born psychiatrist had not encountered anyone who could do so in quite the same way. Some of the senior medical staff stirred uneasily in the small lecture room where Dr. Cameron sometimes presented the institute's more unusual or resistant cases. Rubenstein stood guard over a tape recorder, solemn-faced for once.

Dr. Roper had wondered briefly why the technician was present, just as he had given a passing thought to the weatherman being so accurate over the forecast. Overnight the snow had turned the landscape into a windswept blur. That morning, January 17, 1958, as he drove to work, the car skidding on the wet slush, he used the sort of skills he had needed in the cockpit of a Spitfire. But his children, Christopher, Mark, Gordon, and Jane, loved the climate: it was all part of their new life of spinning Frisbees over the snow, learning French at school, and eating steaks the size they had never seen in England. Only Agnes, Scottish and Calvinistic, worried him. His wife would not learn French and disliked the piety of their Catholic neighbors. Instead, she clung fiercely to being British. In many ways she reminded her husband of Dr. Cameron.

After six months on Dr. Cameron's service as his senior resident, Dr. Roper had frequently encountered the intimidating stare and silence, usually when a patient asked questions or a doctor had not answered quickly enough. Dr. Cameron's reaction conveyed his anger more clearly than any words. It reminded Dr. Roper of Agnes; she also knew how to manipulate a situation.

Dr. Roper now knew religion was at the root of their marriage problems. He was Catholic, Agnes devoutly Protestant. In England he had tried to be understanding when she opposed the children being baptized into the Roman Catholic Church or going to a Catholic school. He hoped she would grow out of her attitudes—and, in the meantime, had plunged himself into peacetime work, first as a medical student at Dr. Cameron's old university, Glasgow, and then as a doctor in the RAF's medical aviation branch. He had been sufficiently promising to be sent for further training at one of the world's leading psychiatric teaching hospitals, the Maudsley in London. There, a few years before, Dr. Sargant, already a rising star in the medical firmament, had formulated his first ideas on how the Russians brainwashed subjects for their postwar show trials.

On a head-hunting visit to the Maudsley, Dr. Cameron was so impressed by Dr. Roper that he offered him the post as his resident, and the promise afterward of a good career within the network. The question of Dr. Roper uprooting himself and his family had been settled in a few minutes. Since arriving in Montreal the cracks in their marriage that he had tried to paper over with patience and understanding had widened, until their relationship was as troubled as those of many of his patients.

Once more, Dr. Roper sought refuge in work, spending longer hours at the institute than any other psychiatrist except Dr. Cameron. It gave the resident further insights into his superior's methods of treatment. Dr. Cameron often gave electroshocks late in the evening, and afterward went from bed to bed in the Sleep Room, bending over a drugged patient to listen for a moment to the words coming from the pillow speaker or a football helmet. He would invariably murmur, "Take it all in. All of it. It's your only way to get better. You want to get better because I am telling you." After giving further orders about medication to the nurses or duty doctor, he would then veer away, striding unsmiling through the corridors, his brooding presence everywhere. Those were the times, in particular, when Dr. Roper wondered about the compulsive forces that consumed Dr. Cameron, and which no doubt had played their part in creating the cold, silent anger that now once more enveloped him in the lecture room.

Now, Dr. Cameron nodded to Rubenstein, who started the recorder. A voice said what they were about to hear was not only Top Secret, but any violation of secrecy would lead to prosecution by the U.S. government. Rubenstein stopped the tape. Several of the doctors looked quickly at each other, mystified. No one, not even Dr. Cleghorn, asked the question that Dr. Roper wanted to put. Why were they going to listen to a tape that, for some reason, was sensitive enough to carry such a warning? Dr. Roper was not prepared to seek the answer if his senior colleagues thought it imprudent to do so.

At times Dr. Cameron gave a passable impersonation of being a personality not unlike Captain Queeg in *The Caine Mutiny*, appearing unexpectedly in a treatment room, at a sick bed, or behind a researcher working in a laboratory, and after moments turn on his heels. To Dr. Roper, "he seemed to be always checking up. Making sure that no one was doing anything he didn't know about. But he didn't reciprocate. No one knew what went on behind the doors of his office." Dr. Roper could not help wondering if the tape was somehow connected with Dr. Cameron's sudden trips to Washington and why he always kept his office locked when he was away.

Dr. Cameron ordered Rubenstein to restart the tape.

We, all prisoners, solemnly appeal to you as follows. The armed intervention in Korean internal affairs is a barbaric aggressive action to protect the benefit of the capitalist monopoly of the United States. Let us fight for right against wrong, bravely opposing those of our leaders who would lead us into a war against Russia.

To Dr. Roper the recorded voice sounded young, but he

had not lived long enough in Canada to tell whether the accent was American or Canadian. The tall and good-looking former RAF fighter pilot, an authentic hero of the Battle of Britain, was riveted by the extraordinary statements on the tape.

. . . Dachau, Auschwitz, Hiroshima, Nagasaki. What extreme ferocity capitalist regimes can unleash. The Second World War made that so clear. Anguished humanity cried out in unison. Never should such cries be allowed to happen again. But they have. The highest technological achievements of the United States and all the resources of its capitalist industry have been used to bring new horror. We, all prisoners, appeal to an international body to impose the respect for law on the capitalist and reactionary forces. Let moral condemnation of such actions be clearly expressed . . .

Despite all he had experienced—first as a pilot in daily combat over wartime Britain, which had taught him how to give and execute orders with speed and efficiency, and then dealing with the psychological traumas of others—Dr. Roper had never heard anything so bizarre as that voice calmly attacking the Western way of life.

. . . re-education and not punishment—that is the fundamental difference between our system and that of other countries. Thanks to the system of re-education, it has been possible for me to be integrated into a new world. Please be aware that this re-education has not meant preventive detention, as happened to the Japanese in the United States during the Second World War . . .

If Dr. Roper shared anything with Dr. Cameron, it was a belief that communism was an even greater threat than Nazism. Yet, there was a simplistic attitude to such matters among his colleagues, which the battle-hardened flier found hard to accept.

Nor did Roper always find it easy to understand his colleagues on a clinical level. He had been approached by an analyst to see a patient who had been in therapy for months with a recurring dream about a small alligator that vomited blood all over the keyboard of a piano. The case file contained a history of how the patient, as a child, had a pet alligator she used to dress up in doll's clothes and wheel about in a baby carriage. She had done so until the age of twelve. The analyst had suggested that the blood the alligator spewed was associated with the probable onset of menses—"an example of the displacement of one organ by another." The rest of the woman's history contained similar interpretations. Her mother had been a concert pianist and often was away from home. The analyst thought that vomiting blood over the keyboard was a sign of the deep-seated resentment of the patient at feeling abandoned at such a young age. But such analysis had not produced a satisfactory solution to her problems. She had grown increasingly depressed. Dr. Roper suggested a course of electroshocks. After a dozen convulsions the woman's dream, and depression, had disappeared.

Yet behind Dr. Roper's breezy and somewhat no-nonsense approach to psychiatry was a sensitivity he concealed by steely control, and underneath his flamboyant manner a shy and cultured man who had suffered. It gave him a sneaking regard for Dr. Cameron, whom Dr. Roper suspected had also weathered his share of storms.

The voice continued describing life in a Chinese re-education camp.

. . . we ran our own lives. We held weekly meetings to discuss how we were all doing and every month we would hold a more formal meeting at which it was decided who would get commendations, rewards, and then release. We all worked very hard to develop a new consciousness . . .

Dr. Cameron told Rubenstein to stop the tape.

Once more he sat staring into space. Dr. Cleghorn noisily cleared his throat and some of the other doctors fidgeted. Dr. Roper was increasingly puzzled. Dr. Cameron had almost certainly brought back the tape from one of his Washington visits. But for what purpose? There was nothing Dr. Roper had heard that suggested anything secret was on the recording; over the years the newspapers had been filled with similar accounts of confessions by soldiers brainwashed in Korea.

Dr. Cameron began to speak, his voice low, the burr more

pronounced than usual, a sign Dr. Roper had come to recognize as another way to measure Dr. Cameron's level of anger. "When he was aroused, the Scot in him surfaced. Then he sounded like a clan chief psyching himself up to go to war."

The chief psychiatrist started to review the tape, saying the important thing to remember was that the American had been brainwashed, because the Chinese had succeeded in creating in the prisoner's mind a sense of participation, convincing him they were deeply in earnest about their thought reform.

Dr. Roper sensed the bewilderment mounting around him. Dr. Cameron continued to expound the theories of brainwashing. Abruptly, with a ferocity that stunned them, he changed direction. It had come to his attention there had been gossip over what was happening to patients on his service—especially those undergoing treatment in the basement. He had been surprised to learn that some of his more senior colleagues were at the forefront of such criticism. He paused and searched each face in turn, then continued, his voice thicker, the accent still more pronounced. What he found especially distressing was that not one of them had asked for an explanation. Once more he fixed them with a steely gaze.

No one spoke.

Dr. Cameron told Rubenstein to rewind the tape.

Dr. Roper remained nonplussed. It was true there had been considerable discussion, largely because no one knew what was going on in the basement. Patients were brought from the Sleep Room, still heavily drugged, by nurses who were met at the door of the Radio Telemetry Laboratory by one of the technicians or Dr. Cameron himself. Dr. Cameron had posted a memo saying the laboratory was out of bounds to all unauthorized personnel. While there was nothing unusual in a research project being declared off limits, his decision to do so had inevitably increased further speculation. But the connection between what had happened to a captive in North Korea and the treatment of institute patients still escaped Dr. Roper.

As the recording was replayed, Dr. Cameron told Rubenstein to stop it from time to time while he drew their attention to how effectively the prisoner's mind had been remotivated. Yet, he added, they could be certain that the man's new attitudes were not entirely divorced from his former self. What had happened was that he had himself refilled the inner voice his captors had carefully carved out of his mind—though it had also been done under the broad moral guidance of his interrogators. Dr. Cameron looked at the psychoanalysts and addressed them. Did not their success depend upon unraveling the unconscious so that the hidden traumas of their patients became known to them, and they could then be liberated for more productive living? He turned to the clinical psychiatrists. Would they not acknowledge that the therapeutic challenges their patients presented were greater than ever before—simply because their own knowledge as doctors was continually expanding?

There was murmured agreement around Dr. Roper. For his part, he would not quarrel with such sentiments. The gap between the science of medicine and the art of healing was narrowing, the gap between what is mind and what is body was being bridged, and a growing understanding was developing of how mind and body influenced each other. It was no longer enough to say that the mind was the output of the functioning brain, but that perhaps all mendation—emotion, volition, and perception—was muscular activity and that there was no separating the psychic from the somatic. But what, he asked himself again, had the tape to do with all that?

Once more Dr. Cameron stared at his doctors. Surely they could see what he was driving at? He stared over their heads for a moment. He reminded them that they all pursued their work with the appropriate technique—and always strove to establish correlation. They knew they must not be unduly influenced by causality, as they were not dealing with invariable relationships, because mental illness was not an immutable effect, but rather the outcome of a process of development in which innumerable factors came into play. They must now realize what he was driving at?

He paused, gathering himself together, the way Dr. Roper had seen him moving toward the climax of a fund-raising speech. Dr. Cameron reminded them he, too, was primarily interested in mental motivations and discovering the laws that governed them. So, it appeared from the tape, were the Chinese. They also had studied suppression and repression, projection and displacement, to achieve conversion. *Now* could they see what he was leading to?

Not waiting for an answer, he provided his own. What he was intent on achieving in the basement was essentially no different from what the Chinese had done to the prisoner on that tape—with one significant difference. Their techniques were designed to harm. His methods were meant to be only beneficial. Did they understand—*beneficial?* Therefore he wanted an end to the rumors. What was happening in the basement was positive treatment.

Dr. Roper would never forget how the words fell upon them, "like a whiplash. Crack-crack. Positive treatment. We had better all understand that."

Dr. Cameron looked unblinkingly at them. He finished, "Now. Here and now."

He rose to his feet and walked from the silent room.

The idea to play the tape had been suggested by Dr. Monroe when he had visited the institute earlier that month. No one had paid him any special attention; there was a steady stream of doctors from foundations walking the corridors, seeing how grants were being used. After his tour, Dr. Monroe had suggested it would be a good idea to defuse any curiosity over the true purpose of the basement facilities, and had proposed that the best way to do so was by suggesting to the medical staff that it was no more than an extension of Dr. Cameron's well-publicized beneficial brainwashing. Dr. Monroe's ploy reflected a Dulles maxim that the most effective way to disguise a secret was to pretend to share it with others.

Six months later, Dr. Monroe could reflect that if Dr. Cameron had still not achieved a total breakthrough in his quest for a successful method of mind control, his latest report was more promising. In previous papers he had concentrated upon attempts to use increased electroshocks to depattern patients. The approach had proved singularly unsuccessful—though Dr. Cameron indicated he would still continue to explore multiple shocks over a prolonged period to obtain results.

The new report at the end of July 1958 was devoted to psychic driving. It was accompanied by Dr. Cameron's receipt for $4,775, the quarterly payment he received for M-K-Ultra subproject 68. Dr. Cameron had described his experience with twenty patients who had each been driven over a period of two months.

In an attempt to explore the ramifications, a variety of
possible applications were introduced. Among the variations
in driving techniques which have been explored are the use
of ceiling microphones and how to present the driving in a
multiplicity of ways, such as the playing of a supportive
mother role or of that of a youthful peer in terms of intona-
tion and in terms of choice of words.

Dr. Monroe perfectly understood the use of microphones
concealed in ceiling light fittings—the Russians did that to
condition their subjects, with the disembodied voice of a
Soviet interrogator suddenly booming out from nowhere. He
was, however, bemused at the idea of Dr. Cameron portray-
ing a patient's mother or a younger brother. Of more immediate interest was the statement that since the last report on
psychic driving Dr. Cameron had increased the length of
time a patient was driven to up to twenty hours a day. Using
only a four-hour break from the voices coming through the
pillow speakers or football helmets, Dr. Cameron was close
to the optimum daily level of driving. He had himself said
that nonstop, twenty-four-hour driving could be harmful.

There followed a detailed case history of a woman, code-
named "Mary." She suffered from what Dr. Cameron had
diagnosed as marked feelings of inadequacy and ambivalence
toward her husband, much of which he believed was derived
from an earlier relationship with her mother.

He described what happened when Mary was forced to
listen repeatedly to her own account of being beaten by her
mother—who had also told Mary she had tried to have an
abortion when she was carrying her. He had then played a
tape in which Mary described very different feelings toward
her father. She had broken down and, as Dr. Cameron had
hoped, confessed her sexual longings for her father. Mary was
Madeleine Smith.

His account of breaking through into her secret world was
indeed encouraging for Dr. Monroe. It came at a time once
more of mixed fortunes for the Agency.

The U-2 flights were a spectacular success and the intelligence data they provided allowed Dulles to puff contentedly
on his pipe as he studied vividly clear photographs taken
from 65,000 feet above the earth not only of Russian installa-

tions, but also of those in China, Manchuria, and Tibet. On the ground, his station chief in Taiwan, Ray S. Cline, had agents in place in Peking and Shanghai. But a carefully prepared Agency plan to overthrow the pro-Communist President Sukarno of Indonesia—an operation budgeted at $10 million—had failed, and one of the pilots, Alan Pope, who took part in the first bombing raid, had been shot down. Dulles was concerned that Pope had somehow been brainwashed: How else to explain the pilot's abject admissions that he worked for the CIA? To try and ward off further damage, Dulles persuaded his brother, John Foster, to authorize 37,000 tons of rice and $1 million worth of arms to be sent to Indonesia, as a gesture of American friendship. Attached to the gift was a polite request from the Secretary of State for Pope's safe and immediate return. Sukarno had accepted the offerings—but the pilot still languished in a Djakarta jail (and would remain there until 1962).

Allen Dulles's preoccupation with learning the secrets of mind control had, if anything, increased with the news that Cornell University had finally severed its ties with the Agency. Dr. Harold Wolff, however, remained closely connected with the M-K-Ultra brainwashing project. As president of the society, he had also used his connections to fill its board of directors with some of the most prestigious names in North American medicine. They included the energetic Carl Rogers, professor of psychology and psychiatry at the University of Wisconsin; the urbane John Whitehorn, chairman of the department of psychiatry at Johns Hopkins University; the professorial Dr. Joseph Hinsey, president of the New York Hospital–Cornell Medical Center. Dr. Lawrence Hinkle, who had worked on that first study of brainwashing techniques, was the society's vice-president. Soon to serve on the board would be Leonard Carmichael, head of the Smithsonian Institution; George Kelly, professor of psychiatry at Ohio State University; and Professor Barnaby Keeney, president of Brown University.

Dr. Wolff, who was making slow but sure progress in treating Dulles's son for his head wound, had made it clear that, in serving the society, he also expected to be reimbursed —in his case with grants to finance his own research on the brain and spinal cord. The director well understood such a trade-off and allocated a $300,000 contribution. It was, after all, small enough when compared to what Dulles paid for a transcript of a speech Nikita Khrushchev made to a closed session of the Politburo denouncing Stalin ($750,000); for the blueprint of a new Soviet tank ($1.5 million); and for a Soviet technical report on a space rocket capable of encircling the world ($42 million), which was the Sputnik.

But, while Cameron regularly brought to the director's office new gadgets—a hunting knife that had a powerful radio transmitter in its handle, a paper clip that was an incendiary device, a golf ball that was a bomb, and an innocent-looking tube of toothpaste that could cause gums to rot—there was no news of a real breakthrough from Montreal.

Now, at last, Dr. Monroe could let Dulles know that things looked promising.

Dr. Cameron continued to visit Washington regularly, officially in his capacity as president of the American Psychiatric Association. Velma Orlikow had sat in his office listening to him making travel arrangements—and it had struck her as curious that her doctor had so much business in the American capital. But even if she had thought of a way to do so, she would never have dared broach the subject. It might have meant another period of Dr. Cameron ignoring her; several times he had walked past her in the corridor and refused to see her in his office because she had dared to question why she must spend hours writing reactions to what she heard herself say on the tapes. "I had to write papers every morning, every afternoon, and every evening. Over and over and over again. And over and over and over again. Till I just wanted to tear them up."

Sometimes he would ignore her for days, leaving her feeling in pieces; she thought it was the most cruel thing he could do to her, knowing how much she needed his support. But he remained oblivious to her tearful pleas.

Finally, when he decided to resume seeing her, he would always begin by saying, "Lassie. You must do exactly what I say." She would try—only God knew how hard she tried. But the hours and hours of writing would weary and distress her. Then, once more, she would be banished from his presence. She felt he was like a medical Svengali and she was his puppet. But there was nothing she could do. She needed him—and he knew it.

She was fragile from having to cope with all the memories he had stirred up and impressions he had planted. He wanted her to accept things that she could not—that she felt sexual urges for her mother and that perhaps she didn't love David. It seemed to her, she had thought through her tears, he wanted her mind to be in a mess.

Dr. Cameron had suddenly decided she should become a day patient, ordering her to take a room in Montreal and report daily to the hospital. "I had to go each day to this little room that had a bed, a chair, with a recorder, and me, and write my tapes. And then have my lunch and write my tapes. And then I got my sleeping pills for the night and I went home. And I had to do my tapes. And they had to be in his office or I was not given my sleeping medication."

Velma's responses featured in Dr. Cameron's reports to the society. Long ago, in Brandon, he had used work therapy as a treatment; patients who refused to perform tasks he gave them were denied food or restricted to their wards. His operant condition approach to Velma contained the same underlying assumption that she could be motivated to write her reports. The purists at the Agency, led by Dr. Gottlieb, might object that Dr. Cameron's approach fell short of their methods of behavior control—he had not troubled himself with schedules or reinforcement techniques to eliminate undesirable personality traits. But they had to admit that his technique worked. If a person like Velma could be brainwashed—even if the method was difficult to separate from torture—then so could others.

Among the few people Dr. Cameron had discussed his approach with had been Dr. Sargant. They continued to meet at medical conferences where they had each read papers to respectful colleagues. At night, over a bottle of vintage wine, they spoke about Dr. Cameron's project. Neither mentioned the CIA, though Dr. Sargant was certain "who was behind his work. But you don't raise that sort of thing with a colleague."

In Washington, when the day's medical business was over, Dr. Cameron sometimes met Dulles. One of those who recalled seeing them together was the up-and-coming William Buckley, back on leave from one of his forays to the Far East. To the intelligence officer, "Dr. Cameron was one of the few non-Agency men who turned up regularly at the parties. He and the director got on famously. No one, of course, knew exactly what the doctor did for the Agency. But we all just knew it had to be important."

11

The Chamber of Horrors

After four frustrating years of what William Buckley—at that time deskbound in Washington waiting for reassignment—called "pussyfooting around the cream bowl," his superiors no doubt felt highly pleased that, by early 1960, they had in Dr. Cameron a psychiatrist ready to pursue experiments in sensory deprivation to their ultimate conclusion—the irreversible scrambling of a patient's mind. Further, Dr. Cameron did not require the Agency to provide expendables because he used his own patients.

Those around Dulles, as well as the director himself, deeply respected and admired such determination and dedication in a man who had steadfastly refused to give up his American citizenship and become a Canadian, and who had never failed to vote Republican, traveling south every four years to do so, and who used his high offices—he was now the president of the World Association of Psychiatrists as well as president of the American and Canadian psychiatric associations—to publicly lecture on the perils of communism. Dulles called him a true patriot; there was no higher accolade the director could bestow. More pragmatically, he and his staff never forgot that Dr. Cameron's secret research was happening on foreign soil, beyond the laws of the United States, and the Agency could relax; even if by remote chance someone in authority in Canada began to question what was happening at the institute, there was virtually no chance of it being traced back to the CIA.

That was welcome news after what had been a period of strain and personal tragedy for Allen Dulles. It had begun on

Sunday morning, May 24, 1959, when he had stood at the foot of his brother's bed, surrounded by all the family, and watched John Foster die from the pneumonia that followed an operation for hernia. A few days later Allen had railed at the ailing President Eisenhower for ordering that his former Secretary of State must have a full state funeral. In a rare outburst, Dulles had said, "We're Presbyterians and we've always gone to the Presbyterian church here. Why can't we have a small, simple funeral?"

The president and the family overruled him. Marching behind the coffin through the great crowds of silent people, tears dampening his cheeks, Allen Dulles may well have pondered the fickleness of public opinion. Only a few weeks ago, John Foster had still divided the nation with his intransigence, rigidity, and inflexibility. In death, everyone seemed to be united in mourning him. After the funeral Allen had said to Eleanor and Clover that he also hoped to die in office. His wife had looked at him curiously and walked away. Eleanor had smiled; she understood. Not only was she a Dulles but she had a shrewd idea that what she called "Allen's spider's web" was in danger—even if her brother would not accept it.

She was proven right. The new Secretary of State, Christian Herter, had begun to tighten the reins, ordering his deputy assistant secretaries and senior Foreign Service officers to challenge position papers sent over by the Agency. Richard Helms was not alone in sensing the subtle differences, a feeling that the old days had gone.

In the end Eleanor was the one to be toppled. Eleanor was moved by Herter from her key post at the Berlin desk to a far less important one with State Department intelligence. Everyone said it was because the president wanted her to take it easy after a gallstone operation. No one within the Dulles clan was fooled. They warned Allen to take care. It was "Brutus time," Clover would remember, though she knew little of the machinations swirling around Allen's head. Her role had been long fixed: party-giver and devoted mother to Allen Macy, still recuperating from his head wound. Dr. Wolff had said it could take years before any further significant progress could be expected.

Over at State the new regime had started to pick at the Agency's failure to deal with Fidel Castro. Less than a year before, Castro had seized power from the dictator Fulgencio Batista. The United States had promptly sealed off its vast military, naval, and air base at Guantánamo, which had been a U.S. post since the Spanish-American War. Even before his coup, Castro had been a thorn in the side of Washington. Among his more annoying escapades had been taking a group of Marines hostage and holding them captive in his Sierra Maestara mountain redoubt until the State Department arranged discreet payment of a ransom. Castro had promised the people that when he took control he would drive out the Yankees and effectively end Cuba's position as an American offshore playground, filled with brothels and gambling dens. Nor had he stopped there: Legitimate U.S. businesses on the island were nationalized and the United States found the threat of first socialism and then communism had moved into its backyard.

Dulles had dusted off his well-tried formula for staging a countercoup. It had worked in Iran and Guatemala and other troublesome places; he saw no reason why it should not do so in Cuba. But with John Foster dead, neither the president nor his new secretary were prepared to sanction turning loose the Agency once more. There had, after all, been some close shaves in the past, where only sheer luck had saved the CIA from heaping embarrassment upon the White House. Besides, the perception of Castro at the State Department was very different to the view Dulles held. The director still saw Castro as yet another rebel who should, he now conceded, have been snuffed out when he started kicking up a ruckus a couple of years earlier. There was still time to rectify the mistake.

Herter regarded Castro not only as a sound tactician but also as a highly charismatic figure who had swept his people along, very like Nasser had done in Egypt when Britain's nose had been rubbed in the mud of the Suez Canal. The secretary had convinced Eisenhower that any move made against Cuba required the most careful thought—and certainly there was no room for the derring-do scenario the Agency proposed.

Dulles had suggested training and then infiltrating into Cuba a couple hundred dissident Cubans who would link up with what anti-Castro factions remained. The United States would covertly supply them, once more using the Agency's private air force. In a position paper Dulles had spoken of "creating a true underground network within the island." Herter had scribbled a margin note: "Dangerous. Could invite Moscow to join the party."

Elsewhere in the Agency's sphere of influence, yet other matters had run a rough course. The Russians had picked up several CIA agents in East Germany and Poland, and Dulles had needed no convincing that their brains had been picked clean. There had been incidents in West Berlin. The Agency had failed to predict them—just as the Tokyo station had underestimated the new Japanese animosity toward the United States. In Paris the Agency's traditional working ties with the French security service were strained because the French government believed the CIA was interfering in what remained of France's colonial interests. On the domestic front the presidential election was shaping up into a classic duel. Both nominees—John F. Kennedy and Richard Nixon—had only entered public life at the end of World War II and were vigorous men, barely into their forties. It was another sign that the United States was no longer the same nation Dulles had once effectively ruled as a member of a triumvirate. Both candidates had made it plain that if they reached the Oval Office the Agency could expect further changes, and they had wondered aloud about the CIA's omniscience.

But Allen Dulles refused to learn new ways, let alone heed the danger signals. He still had what he called his "lucky talisman in the skies"—the U-2 planes. An improved version had been developed, capable of cruising at 90,000 feet and silently gathering up priceless intelligence through its cameras. Yet, within the Agency, men like William Buckley worried how long it would be before the Soviets pressed a button and launched a missile from a pad in Siberia that would end the spying missions. Why they had not already done so, when the Agency had proof that Soviet radar was tracking the flights, was one of the many imponderable questions discussed.

If Dulles heard these questions, he gave no sign. Instead, in between refining his plans to remove Castro, he studied the reports Dr. Monroe sent from New York on Dr. Cameron's work. It must have been all that more satisfying to the director that the Agency was achieving such promising results not only through his old friend, but from the same campus that had rebuffed the CIA. The Agency had tried to persuade Dr. Donald Hebb, the head of the psychology department at McGill, to pursue still further his own pioneer work in extra-sensory deprivation. Dulles, encouraged by Dr. Gottlieb, believed the technique was perhaps the source of mind control.

Dr. Hebb had received grants from the Rockefeller Foundation —which had provided the initial finance for the creation of the Allan Memorial Institute—and the Canadian Department of Defense, and had used the money to convert a room in his laboratory into an isolation box into which volunteers were placed, fully briefed as to what was involved. They were encased in high-altitude flying suits and wore goggles and earmuffs. The air in the box was filtered to remove smells, and from time to time the subjects were exposed to a constant bleeping sound. Each volunteer was told he would be released as soon as he pressed a panic button. No one, whether he wished to or not, had been allowed to remain in the box for more than six days. The Agency, working through Dr. Monroe, had tried to persuade Dr. Hebb to go further, to keep volunteers for lengthier periods in isolation and to give them drugs. Dr. Hebb had flatly refused to entertain such proposals.

Morse Allen had persuaded Dr. Maitland Baldwin at the National Institutes of Health to try his hand at what Allen's report to Dulles suggested could be terminal type experiments. Dr. Baldwin had come to the Agency's attention after he had himself kept an Army volunteer in an isolator for forty hours. The soldier had broken out and in Dr. Baldwin's account, "He began to cry and sob in the most heartbreaking way."

Dr. Baldwin had agreed to cooperate with the Agency on certain conditions. The CIA would provide expendables, and must fully understand and accept that after a week in isolation, there would be "almost certainly irreparable brain damage." Allen had chaired a number of meetings within the Agency to see how best to fund Dr. Baldwin. The Society for Human Ecology would not be a suitable conduit in the circumstances, in view of the potential terminal nature of the research. Even a dead expendable on American soil could lead to awkward questions and would expose the carefully nurtured cover the society had built up to protect, among others, Dr. Cameron. But before a satisfactory way of funding was agreed, Dulles had ordered the project abandoned as too risky to perform within the borders of the United States. Once more the director's attention focused upon Dr. Cameron.

The reports on Madeleine had been a vindication of what Dulles had always maintained: that the human mind was far more resistant than people realized. That, of course, made it all that more baffling as to how the enemy—the director had come to lump together both the Russians and the Chinese in such matters—had been so successful. There was a point at which the strongest of wills could be broken; Dulles had discovered as much from reading *Battle for the Mind*. Clearly, the skill depended on knowing just how far to take a subject. The enemy had discovered the secret, so why couldn't the Agency? From all he had read, Dr. Cameron was getting close, and Dulles could feel a growing confidence that the final answer to mind control could emerge in time for him to place it before a new president. That would be a fitting introduction to the skills of the Agency and its director.

On April 13, 1960, Dulles was summoned to the White House to discuss yet another U-2 mission over the Soviet Union.

It was the same day that Dr. Cameron finally decided what he must do about a new patient—Dr. Mary Morrow.

Dr. Morrow so much wanted to believe what Dr. Cameron had said: that when she was well again he would consider taking her back on his staff so that she could complete her fellowship in psychiatry. But first he would have to treat her.

She had tried to put out of her mind her previous impression of him being cold, humorless, and indifferent, and convinced herself that he would treat her with compassion and care. If she had been unable to believe that, she would have been even more upset—almost as much as she was at not being able to cure herself. Her only comfort was that her own father often said physicians rarely managed to treat themselves successfully. Besides, she wanted to believe so much in the *doctorness* of Dr. Cameron. As a man he might still lack many of the qualities she admired, but having reached his high position, he must have medical judgment and insight that she did not possess, and would know what had made her so frightened and desperate. She had to trust him and put aside all her earlier feelings. It was the only way, she had kept saying to herself, her only way back, her only hope of going forward.

She had wanted to speak to Dr. Cameron, doctor to doctor, about her symptoms, to explore them together, colleagues joined in the common cause of healing her. She was willing to listen and to bow to his vastly superior knowledge. She would do anything to get better. All she wanted from him was an assurance that when she did, she would return to medicine and help others. But she had not been able to say any of that. Instead, she had sat there, feeling somehow on the defensive, unable to begin to share such thoughts with a stranger. Dr. Cameron had made no attempt to help her, except to say he was a doctor and she could tell him anything, without fear, and that he would neither judge or condemn. On that first afternoon he had ended his visit by saying, "I want to help you." She had watched him run his tongue over his lips after he spoke, before finally adding the word "doctor." At least, she had thought, he had not called her "lassie." He had ended each visit with the same words. He never explained how he would help.

But it was true, she had endlessly told herself. With his great knowledge he had to know she was curable. It was, as she had so often said to her own patients, only a matter of finding the correct treatment, perhaps in her case no more than the right combination of drugs. Certainly nothing else. After all, she reminded herself, she was a doctor and knew what was wrong. She had a reactive depression complicated by an amphetamine psychosis brought about by swallowing uppers and downers.

Looking back, she felt she should have spotted the signs; after all she was so good at picking up on the hidden symptoms in her patients. There had been that first nervous quiver in the stomach, the first skipped meal, the first gulped Dexedrine to keep going just a little longer, the first phenobarbital capsule to snatch a few hours' sleep, the first outburst of tears, the growing tiredness. The symptoms had fed off each other, creating the crisis that had grown inside her and finally taken over her life.

When she had left Dr. Cleghorn's service things had at first gone well. She worked hard with a challenging caseload and felt "in seventh heaven," even if the pace was more frenetic than usual because she was studying for her higher qualifications in neurology. Within weeks of the examinations she developed pansinusitis and was admitted to the Royal Victoria for surgery. As soon as she was discharged she had plunged back into work. Then she developed otitis media in both ears, a painful condition. Determined to obtain the coveted Royal College certification, she pushed herself even harder and had passed her written paper. But at the oral test, with her ears still troubling her, she had been presented with a patient suffering from a bruit, difficult to diagnose at the best of times. With her impaired hearing she failed to recognize the symptoms through her stethoscope and failed the test. "That was the end of my life," she said. "I went into a deep, deep depression. It was loss of face. I was just in a bottomless pit. I was just in a hole."

The dream of running her own department at St. Mary's was shattered. The first tears of helplessness had welled up behind her eyes. She had worked so hard and come so far; it was so unfair. "I couldn't talk to anybody, look at anybody, not even my own family."

Further harsh realities crowded in upon her. Without the higher qualification, her career prospects had dramatically altered. Her stipend at the epilepsy clinic was given to a colleague who had passed the Royal College Board. She felt suddenly an outsider, shrinking away like a wounded deer, back where it was dark and she was alone, with only the sound of her own heartbeat in her ears. She took more pep pills in the day and sleeping tablets at night, to try and cope with her work as a junior doctor at the Montreal Neurological Institute. One day, to her horror, she had suddenly burst out in tears during ward rounds. She knew the Dexedrine was responsible, just as she knew she could only "hold my head up" by continuing to take amphetamines. "I would weep copiously or be irritable and cranky with everybody. And I just went from bad to worse."

Pain persisted and deepened, filling her with a continual despair. She began to ask herself why she should go on pretending she had any worthwhile future. Increasingly she felt no strength to resist the pain. It shook her body and pounded in her ears and filled her mind with a furious blackness. At times it seemed to envelop everything around her. Day and night she took her tablets. She hated the demeaning ritual. But it was the only way she could cope. She had no one to talk to, to explain the tensions and abrasiveness that filled her, the drug-dependent loneliness and the feeling that her very mind was atrophying. There was really nothing to live for.

She knew death could not possibly be more horrifying than the way she felt. Finally, she chose the day that would be her last. She went through it all in a daze, seeing patients, encouraging them to believe in a future she had herself decided did not exist. She was going to commit suicide. That night she went back to her apartment and swallowed the sleeping pills—not bothering to count them, just taking what she had thought would be sufficient—and lay down on the bed. It was done. Soon there would be nothing. She had fallen asleep. Next day she had opened her eyes.

At first she could not believe it. There was a roaring noise in her ears and her vision was blurred. Her first conscious reaction was to say out loud, "I am alive." But the words would not pass her dry lips. She would not remember how long she lay there or what else she had thought, or if she thought anything at all. But gradually her mind cleared and she began to concentrate. She was alive. Whatever had been her intention, she still had no solution to the torment that returned as soon as she was capable of thinking clearly. The days dragged on like a sleepless night.

By late September 1959, her last formal ties with doctoring were severed with both St. Mary's and the Montreal Neurological Institute. She was almost on the breadline when she spotted a position for a nurse in a convalescent home on the other side of the city. She took the job even though it meant traveling two hours a day by bus to work her shift. A combination of taking drugs and not eating or sleeping continued to steadily take its toll. By early December she had started to ask herself what she was doing, realizing that this existence was not living, but a living nightmare. But this time her thoughts had not turned to suicide.

The only way out of her crisis was to do what she had done when she was well—confront it head-on. Whatever were the mysterious and potent forces that occupied her mind, they were not going to tie her down to a life of bus rides and bed-pan changing. It was not all over! She would fight her way back! And the way to do so was obvious: Dr. Cameron. He had never complained about her work. And, though she had not always approved of his methods, she had done as bidden. She would willingly do so again. All she wanted was a chance to be a doctor. She would do anything legal to once more practice medicine, to help the sick, and in doing so to cure her own illness. Finally, close to Christmas, she had called Dr. Cameron's secretary for an appointment.

The day before the interview she had been on night shift. With her breakfast coffee, she swallowed still more pills and walked to the institute. "I had no money and I must have seemed an awful mess." But, filled with chemical hope, she believed she could persuade Dr. Cameron. She had arrived early and sat in the waiting room, trying to control her anxiety, clenching and unclenching her hands, pursing her lips, and having to swallow to keep down the anxiety that surged from her stomach into her throat; it was a tangible thing, like a ball that threatened to choke her.

His door opened and Dr. Cameron asked her in. He led her to the solitary chair placed at an angle to the massive walnut-brown desk. He motioned for her to sit and went behind the desk to his high-backed brown leather padded chair. On the wall behind him was a recorder.

He wore a dark suit and his long fingers were laced across his stomach. He didn't say a word but stared at her appraisingly. She had felt small and insignificant. When he spoke his voice was soft and confident. What had she been doing since they last met? Whom had she worked with? What had it been like? The questions were banal. He would know about what she had done. But she had tried to answer. He had made no comment and the gaps between her last answer and his next question lengthened.

From the depths of his chair he had told her she was nervous.

She had leaned forward, anxious to reassure him.

He had insisted, "You are nervous. I can see it."

Sensing his annoyance, she had blinked and shrunk back into her chair.

"Why are you nervous, doctor?" His voice was soft, but he was pinning her down. "Tell me why?"

"It's just . . . it's a bit difficult . . ." She stopped, looking down at her hands. "I just want . . ." The sentence had hung in the air.

He had asked her for the third time to tell him why she was nervous. "You have something troubling you. Tell me."

She had tried again. Yes, she was nervous, but that was only because she hoped to convince him to give her a job. That was all she wanted—a job.

He had studied her for a long time. Then, raising his voice a little, he had said that before he would ever consider taking her back he wanted her medically examined. He had stood up and walked her to the door.

She had returned home, deflated. She could not understand why she should be medically examined for work she was absolutely certain she could do.

Christmas came and went and she continued to ride the bus to work as a nurse. She felt her life still crumbling around her. She was helpless and in despair. She had no real friends and an existence that was worthless. Her only hope was to become a doctor. Without that she felt condemned to a future of endless work as a nurse, living forever close to financial insolvency and on the brink of emotional destruction. She went on taking the pills, telling herself again that once she was back in medicine, she would give them up and lead a more sensible life.

She had telephoned Dr. Cameron twice asking for a job. He had listened politely, but each time he said she must first agree to be medically examined. Finally she had admitted herself to the Royal Victoria, forming her own diagnosis that she was suffering from a nervous reactive depression caused by amphetamine psychosis.

In the four weeks she had been in the hospital, apart from a thorough physical checkup, she had received little in the way of treatment except bed rest. On Dr. Cameron's visits she had told him nothing at all of what had happened to her in the past year and he had not probed. Nevertheless, on his last visit he had abruptly said he wanted her transferred to the institute. She felt the old knot of pain coursing through her body and wanted to cry.

Dr. Cameron had sat staring at her impressively and said again, "I want to help you." Too depressed to speak, she had nodded. He had left without saying another word.

Now, a few days later—at about the time Allen Dulles was being driven to the White House to see President Eisenhower about the next U-2 mission—Dr. Mary Morrow entered the institute as a patient.

12

Unquiet
Minds

Resembling an invincible phalanx, with Dr. Cameron at its head and, matching him stride for stride, the equally commanding Dr. William Sargant, the morning medical round proceeded through the institute. Doctors and nurses strove to keep pace with the two senior psychiatrists.

Dr. Roper thought it must have been the classic attraction of opposites that had originally drawn both men to each other. Dr. Cameron was his usual taciturn self. He rarely used a round to teach or place a case in the wider confines of medicine, but confined himself to observations like "a good example of reactive depression" or "a textbook case of hypomania."

It reminded Dr. Roper of his days in London when he had trailed behind a distinguished teaching professor at the Maudsley. He supposed it was probably inevitable that, with his renowned reputation as a mass communicator, Dr. Sargant would want to share his ideas, however familiar they may be. And, even without his accent, there would be no mistaking him as anything but English-trained and London-based: He had the commanding, incisive, all-knowing presence that somehow only the great professors of London possessed. It marked him as much as his Savile Row suit, silk tie, and burnished shoes. He was Harley Street and St. Thomas's Hospital to his last declension. Listening to him, Dr. Roper felt a twinge of nostalgia. He would, however, not mention such a thought to Agnes: It could be enough to trigger another of her rages at having to live in such an alien culture and see her family exposed to religious influences she increasingly resented.

What saddened him was that she was blind to the fact that the children were integrated into Canadian life, and in every way had a better future to look forward to than in England.

In these past months his wife's mental condition had worsened. Yet she refused to seek help. A colleague of Dr. Roper's had suggested that, for the sake of the children, he should divorce her. At first he rejected the step as unthinkable. But with the tensions at home often unbearable, he had begun to seriously consider the matter. What stopped him was the hope that Agnes would herself realize she needed treatment; he dared not raise the matter. It often took hours for Agnes's agitation to subside. Then, for a while, there were periods of almost complete normality. He knew that those temporary recoveries meant she might still recover totally from her illness—if she would accept help. There were doctors on the institute staff who would treat her.

Dr. Sargant's presence was a courtesy Dr. Cameron rarely extended to a visiting physician. The English psychiatrist was in Montreal to deliver yet another lecture on the proven success of physical treatments such as Largactil, electroshock, the antidepressant drugs, and modified leucotomy. He said again that in the next decade the bold use of these treatments could ensure the end of the traditional mental institution, and that the day was fast approaching when psychiatric illness would be routinely treated in general hospitals and only the most chronic would need to be confined in what were still called, in Britain and Canada, asylums.

As the round wheeled in and out of wards and the fee-paying patients' private rooms, Dr. Sargant reminded the residents, walking a respectful pace behind Dr. Cameron and himself, how great were the changes since his first visit to the institute in the mid-fifties. Then, only about a third of depressives and schizophrenics—still by far the commonest types of mental illness—recovered sufficiently to be sent back into the world. The remainder, he said, were "human refuse to be consigned to the great mental dustbins that scar the countryside."

Walking past the row of stretcher patients outside the shock room, Dr. Sargant had enthused that "nowadays we may only need to prescribe four or five electrical shock treatments and the patient is himself again without any need for elaborate case history or social investigation and all that jaw-jaw of the Freudians."

That was perfectly true, Dr. Roper reminded himself. All around him he saw evidence of what physical treatment had achieved and he wholeheartedly agreed with Dr. Sargant's maxim that "we should never be content in either psychiatry or general medicine with only a single treatment approach." That was one of the many lessons he had learned from Dr. Cameron: Anything could be tried. Dr. Roper had himself been experimenting with various deconditioning treatments to help sexual deviants—using a combination of electroshocks and drugs to try and break their abnormal patterns of behavior. He was also treating alcoholics and other social misfits, and had tackled another problem that for years had been very much the prerogative of the analysts: the menopausal flushing that left many a middle-aged woman patient frustrated and bewildered. An analyst was prepared to often spend years trying to get a woman to cope with her decreased sexual desires. Dr. Roper had used a simple physical treatment, prescribing one of the female sex hormones, which dramatically reduced flushing while the patient's body adjusted to the glandular changes.

Dr. Roper felt a real sense of pride that he was part of the ongoing revolution. Yet it had become increasingly difficult to push back the frontiers. The psychoanalysts continued to resist the advance of physical treatments. Their opposition had grown that much more noticeable after a patient had received her 1,300th separate shock and had become completely moribund. Dr. Cleghorn had raised the implications of the case with Dr. Cameron, who had agreed that a committee should be set up to decide which patients were most suitable for depatterning, and how many electroshocks they should receive. Its members were drawn equally from among the clinical psychiatrists and psychotherapists, and they met weekly in Dr. Cameron's office. He tape-recorded the discussions, and in a deadlocked situation made the casting decision. Sometimes he sided with the analysts. Dr. Roper saw that as a shrewd move to defuse the groundswell of opposition. Yet opposition was growing all the time, not all of it purely clinical. French-speaking doctors were upset about Dr. Cameron's Americanism and the way he ridiculed French-Canadian aspirations for their language and culture.

A more serious criticism from some of the analysts was that he had no real understanding of the ethnic background of many of his patients—something they felt was essential to grasp for successful treatment. They argued that cultural factors could throw light on psychoses and morality. Just as in other societies, culture varied considerably in the social strata of Canada. There was, for instance, a marked difference between the ideas and attitudes of a Montrealer and a patient who came from the Rockies. The debate had swirled around the doctor's common room until Dr. Cameron finally said he would provide funds for a research project that explored the matter. For the past three months researchers in one of the converted stables had been examining the role social criteria played in creating symptoms. Dr. Roper dismissed it as esoteric.

Yet, Roper thought, it was typical of Dr. Cameron that money had been found for a project that probably held no real interest for him. He also felt it was very much in keeping for the analysts that, having gained another toe-hold, they continued to criticize the director. They spoke of him behind his back as a labeler, one of those doctors who often did not look for the deeper cause of an illness, who did not recognize, as they did, that while disturbances could indeed be seen in the physical awkwardness and strange contortions of some patients, those postures did not really explain how they felt. Unlike Dr. Cameron, they murmured to each other, they were less willing, for instance, to rely solely upon the six main symptoms of schizophrenia—the disturbances of emotions, thought, the will, delusions, hallucinations, and body movements. Instead, they spoke of "the various shades of the shallowness of emotionality" and "the degrees between thought disorder."

Dr. Roper was delighted when Dr. Sargant said that psychiatry was only just emerging from the kind of era in which general medicine had once been confined, and that it was not that long since physical illness was portrayed philosophically as a struggle between external and internal humors, vapors, and innate heats. Now, in all but a few places, doctors had ceased speaking of mental illness in similar metaphysical terms.

On that optimistic note the round swept into South-Two.

Head Nurse Mielke realized that though she worked closely with him, Dr. Cameron remained an enigma to her. She always obeyed him unquestioningly, though he could be unpredictable toward the nursing staff, one moment showing himself as friend and companion, the next behaving as condescending as any junior doctor. She had learned to live with that. What she found harder to cope with was his attitude toward the patients. When they were in the blackest desolation he could be at his most distant. She found that puzzling because she believed a psychiatrist must always try and bring not only insight and understanding but compassion to suffering people. That quality, she told her nurses, did not result merely from clinical knowledge of a patient; it came from building a trusting and secure relationship with those they cared for.

Many times in these past three years she had held a patient in her arms. By being visibly supportive, she had wanted that person to know the struggle for recovery was a shared one. The most important thing in dealing with the sick, she always said, was to make herself available. But Dr. Cameron almost never seemed to do that.

After a visit from Cameron she had returned to a patient and often found him or her distressed over the doctor's coldness. She sat on their bedside listening to their fears, understanding perfectly well that their anxieties were usually the result of some conflict in their lives. The rooms of South-Two were filled with men and women who had succumbed to the struggle between a powerful instinctive urge and an equally strong prohibition of conscience, and the resulting friction had led to almost unbearable tension. Yet Dr. Cameron took no account of such matters.

Dr. Sargant had observed that in his own hospital he had found that traumatic events must be relived by a patient in the present tense. "It's not a bit of good if a patient just describes what has happened to him or her in a dull recital of events," he said. "We always try and get them to go right back into the situation which has caused their mental problems. We make them live through the crisis once more, only this time they have all their feelings and rememberings noted down."

By itself, Nurse Mielke thought, there was nothing very remarkable in that. Yet, in his own personal relationships with patients, Dr. Cameron was unable to show any warmth; it was almost as if he thought that, too, unimportant; all that mattered, his manner increasingly suggested, was that patients were there to be treated.

As usual, she saw, he seemed oblivious to the sights and sounds of South-Two. A mental unit was very different from a surgical or medical ward. Patients could erupt into violence or turn their anger upon themselves. That required swift and sure judgment on her part. Physical outbursts must always be restrained, but sometimes anger could be therapeutic for someone whose mind had only recently broken down under the stress and strain of illness. Releasing pent-up fury helped return the nervous system to its more normal functioning. Inducing laughter was also another way of helping patients; it stopped them from becoming emotionally overwrought.

Ultimately, such methods had helped scores recover—if only for a while. Velma Orlikow had become sufficiently well to make the long train journey back to Winnipeg. Jeannine Huard had also been among those who had walked down the drive and out into Pine Avenue to begin a new life. Nurse Mielke still enjoyed great satisfaction from such results.

Nurse Mielke nowadays felt so many of Dr. Cameron's treatments still seemed to be empirical. Nor could they be used on some of the most difficult cases. For instance, no amount of electroshock worked in many cases of obsessive compulsive illness, and, in spite of Dr. Roper's efforts, in few of those with severe sexual deviations. Almost without exception, no physical treatment had succeeded in helping a patient with a chronically inadequate personality.

What had increasingly come to concern the head nurse was the decision-making process behind the treatments. When and how did Dr. Cameron decide to send someone to the Sleep Room? What made him increase electroshocks or a drug dosage? He never explained. Yet he must have known, and she had certainly always believed, that successful psychiatric therapy was a cooperative enterprise between doctor and nurse—and, of course, the patients. It was not like going to the dentist or having an appendix removed. She saw psychiatric treatment almost in a poetic sense—"a journey of exploration through partly familiar, partly uncharted country, in which the more experienced travelers, the doctor and nurse, acted as guides and if their companion, the patient, refused, or was unable to open his or her eyes, they would all come out of the journey without benefit."

Not one of the patients sent to the Radio Telemetry Laboratory showed any signs of improvement afterward. Most were returned to the Sleep Room; a few had been suddenly transferred to one of the city asylums. She regarded psychic driving as at best unproven, and in many cases she saw it clearly heightened distress.

It seemed to Nurse Mielke that some patients' trauma had been brought on by psychic driving—and could have been avoided if Dr. Cameron had recognized that all the patients were engaged in a constant battle with their anxieties—and that their fears could not be alleviated by simply allowing Rubenstein or Zielinski to plonk helmets on their heads, which forced them to listen to either the voice of Dr. Cameron or their own abject recorded confessions.

Yet he insisted that people must undergo such treatments, just as he routinely prescribed electroshocks on a massive scale and held patients for weeks at a time in chemically controlled sleep. He also supported research projects that were even more bizarre than trying to establish that schizophrenia was related to the color of a person's eyes. Recently, another researcher had spent months trying to prove that mental disturbances could sometimes be helped by contact with soil. He had sown grain seeds in horticultural trays and ordered patients to sit before them for hours at a time, passing their hands back and forth over the earth. The intention was to discover whether the soil acted as a conduit for body heat and if, somehow, tensions could be transferred into the earth, perhaps even poisoning it. The proof, he had said, would be if the seeds did not germinate, or sprouted in a mutated way. They had grown normally.

Nurse Mielke had never understood how a scientifically trained doctor came to be involved with such claptrap. Now, she would never have the answer. In a few days the institute and its director would be behind her. She was leaving to get married and begin a new life in Toronto. Dr. Cameron had given her a glowing reference. In the end, that was how she would prefer to remember him—"as someone who had some strange ideas, but showed me every courtesy."

Dr. Sargant's visit to the institute had greatly disturbed him. He could find no scientific rationale for much of what he had seen. Always prepared to accept that it was difficult to be certain whether a particular treatment—such as electroshock or drugs or their use in combination—helped patients to recover, he was quite sure of one thing: "What was being done to patients was wrong, wrong, wrong."

In the privacy of Dr. Cameron's office, Dr. Sargant had

continued to forcefully express himself. In previous visits he had already expressed his reservations about the excessive use of electroshocks. But now, in May 1960, he was "frankly horrified. And I suspect I hadn't seen everything. For instance, I never went into the Sleep Room or down to the basement."

When he shook hands with Dr. Cameron on the steps of the institute, he had made a conscious decision "not to have any part of this. It had a bad taste to it." Equally, out of professional respect for an old colleague and friend, he would keep his views to himself. After all, he rationalized, it was a matter for the Quebec medical authorities, or even the Canadian government, to act. He certainly was not going to blow the whistle. But he would never again visit the institute.

Shortly after Dr. Sargant departed, Dr. Cameron received an urgent telephone call from Dr. Monroe asking him to go to Washington to help with the gravest crisis the CIA and the Eisenhower administration had ever faced in relations with Russia.

The previous day, Thursday, May 5, 1960, Nikita Khrushchev had addressed the Supreme Soviet for almost four hours. His concluding remarks had caused pandemonium in Washington. With a crucial summit conference in Paris only eleven days away—an event intended to climax Eisenhower's presidency, when he, Khrushchev, President de Gaulle, and Prime Minister Harold Macmillan were due to sit down in the Elysée Palace and try and resolve the world's problems—the Soviet leader had announced that a U.S. aircraft had been shot down over Russia. He had branded the flight as one of aggressive provocation aimed at wrecking the summit.

Dulles had swiftly arranged for NASA to announce that one of its weather observation planes was missing over Turkey after its pilot reported oxygen trouble. The pilot may have strayed over the Russian-Turkish border. Next, Lincoln White, the State Department spokesman, had read a prepared statement insisting "there was absolutely no—N-O—deliberate intention to violate Soviet air space, and there never has been." NASA named the weather pilot as Francis Gary Powers.

Within hours Khrushchev had informed the Supreme Soviet that Powers had been captured alive after a Soviet missile had shot down his plane from an altitude of 65,000 feet. The black-painted aircraft, powered by a single turbojet, had been 1,300 miles inside Russian airspace. It was no weather flight that had strayed off course, Khrushchev had thundered; it was a spy mission—another of the U-2 flights the Russians had been monitoring for some time. Then the Soviet premier had delivered another bombshell. "The pilot had made a full and detailed confession about his mission and previous ones."

That revelation had plunged Dr. Cameron into the escalating crisis. From all the hundreds of questions the fiasco begged, one had been isolated by Dulles for Dr. Cameron. Could the Russians have managed in the space of forty-eight hours—the interval between Khrushchev's first announcement on May 5 and his May 7 revelation of Powers's confession—to have brainwashed the pilot? All else—how the United States would respond to Khrushchev's threat to launch his rockets against any country that had harbored the U-2 planes, the fury of America's allies, and the summit—depended on Dr. Cameron's answer.

Dr. Cameron had studied the Agency's medical file on Powers. His last physical showed no abnormality. His psychological profile identified his diligence, reliability, and lack of imagination. The description had served as a starting point for the psychiatrist's own attempt to assess the pilot's personality and likely responses to his captors.

Powers was a high-tech mercenary; it was not so much love of country but of money that motivated him. He had signed on with the CIA at $30,000 a year—three times his salary as an Air Force first lieutenant. That was an important factor in arriving at any judgment.

Then there was another in one of hundreds of top-secret messages transmitted to Washington from the U-2 base in Peshawar, Pakistan. Shortly after the mission, Powers had asked the base's senior CIA officer a number of questions. "What if something happens and one of us goes down over Russia? That's an awfully big country and it could be a hell of a long walk to a border. Is there anyone there we can contact? Can you give us any names and addresses?"

The intelligence officer, reporting the conversation verbatim, had replied, "No, we can't."

Powers had insisted. "All right, say the worst happens. A plane goes down and the pilot is captured. What story does he use? Exactly how much should he tell?"

The only suggestion he had been given was that if he found

he was running low on fuel over the Soviet Union, he should take a shortcut in the Murmansk region for a designated emergency landing field in either Finland or Sweden.

Dr. Cameron had pondered over Powers's questions. Again, they did not fit the Agency's psycho-profile. The queries showed a degree of self-concern that should have immediately aroused the suspicion of the CIA officer at Peshawar; there was also a dangerous naïveté about them. Powers did not seem to have been at all a suitable choice for such a hazardous mission.

It was the longest mission yet of the U-2 program. For nine hours, after lifting off from Peshawar, Powers had been scheduled to fly over Afghanistan and the Hindu Kush, before entering Russian air space near Stalinabad. Crossing high above the Aral Sea, he would shortly afterward have switched on the infrared cameras located in seven portholes under the fuselage as he flew over Russia's Tyurantam Cosmodrome where Soviet missiles were positioned. His course called for him to pass over the military and industrial complexes at Chelyabinsk, Sverdlovsk, Kirov, Archangel, Kandalaksha, and Murmansk. From there he should have flown over the Barents Sea and landed at Bodö in Norway. Four-fifths of the 2,900-mile journey was inside the Soviet Union. After takeoff, Powers had broken radio contact with the Peshawar base.

While Dulles wrestled with the aftermath of the mission, Dr. Cameron carefully studied the preflight preparations for further clues as to Powers's mental state. From the time the pilot arrived in Pakistan, things had gone badly. The spy plane that had been reserved for his flight was the most sophisticated U-2 yet built. Among other gadgets, it was fitted with a granger, a device capable of deflecting ground radar as the plane cruised at 100,000 feet. But on the very day he had inspected the long, sleek, high-tailed aircraft, it had developed an engine problem. Powers was assigned the only serviceable U-2, listed on the Agency books as No. 360. It had been the pilot's reaction to the switch that interested Dr. Cameron. Powers had told the briefing officer for the mission that 360 "was a dog." It could only fly to 80,000 feet, and had a long history of malfunctions: engine cut-outs and blockages in the fuel tank leads. He had repeatedly informed other pilots that he was unhappy "at flying a dog on such a mission."

Powers's words further confirmed Dr. Cameron's fears. The pilot was not only very different from the laconic, solid man presented in the Agency files, but he was someone who was increasingly jittery and overly concerned with his own safety.

For three days the pilot's departure had been delayed while President Eisenhower hesitated over whether the mission should go ahead in view of the imminence of the summit. Dr. Cameron had asked whether Powers had been informed of the reason for the delay. He was told that the pilot had been "fully briefed and knew of the president's interest."

Finally, on May 1, 1960, Powers was ordered to prepare for takeoff. Once more he had behaved out of character with his Agency file. On each mission a U-2 pilot carried the suicide lucky silver dollar impregnated with curare or cyanide. Powers had first refused to carry the coin, arguing it was pointless. Then he suddenly changed his mind, saying the device would make an effective weapon. He had slipped the dollar into a pocket of his outer flight suit. On his body he had also stashed a shaving kit, a packet of filter cigarettes, photographs of his wife, deutschmarks, Turkish liras, Russian rubles, and gold coins, watches, and rings—all to be used for barter or bribery. He also had a billfold of U.S. dollars, some American postage stamps, a Defense Department I.D. card, a NASA certificate of employment, a Selective Service card, his social security card, and an American flag emblem, with a legend printed in fourteen languages, including Russian: I AM AN AMERICAN.

Putting aside the obvious question of why Powers had been allowed to go on such an ultrasecret mission with so many pointers to his identity, Dr. Cameron focused on the pilot's change of mind over carrying the lethal silver dollar. The Agency's file suggested he would not have hesitated to use it, to commit what psychiatry labeled altruistic suicide, the kind of self-sacrifice that, for instance, Captain Oates had shown at the end of Scott's ill-fated expedition to the South Pole, and the hari-kiri Japanese officers had performed in World War II. But in assuming that Powers would have followed their examples, the Agency, in Dr. Cameron's view, had made a fundamental mistake.

The pilot's behavior in the days before his mission suggested he was a man who would do anything to stay alive. There had been his strongly expressed anxiety over crashing in Russia and his reaction to having to accept an inferior plane. Both instances indicated a powerful desire to survive. That would have been compounded by the knowledge that the president had personally authorized the mission; it could only have been a further boost to Powers's ego, driving the strength to commit suicide further from his mind. His decision to take the silver dollar not as a means of killing himself but as a weapon was another confirmation of his wish to remain alive. Again, in carrying all that identification—whether he had really been authorized to do so or not was beside the point—Powers had displayed a desire to carry with him ties to his home. A personality like that would not require the Russians to exercise undue coercion. He would have accepted his fate, knowing that in the end he would not spend the rest of his life in captivity. To that extent he would have almost certainly made the confession Khrushchev had described.

Dr. Cameron's assessment was one of several Dulles had commissioned from psychiatrists and psychologists both within and outside the Agency. How much attention he paid to them would remain a matter of conjecture.

But William Buckley was one of those who felt that "the director was running on three cylinders instead of four. There were just so many things going on in the Agency that he could not properly have kept a full rein on all the details. Things were just beginning to get out of control." Buckley himself was once more off to Southeast Asia, where the Agency had started to run heroin to finance covert operations in Vientiane, Phnom Penh, and Saigon. A smell of decay was attaching itself to the CIA's reputation. Buckley sensed a growing mood in the Agency that the director was looking to make a comeback, show the world he was still top dog after the U-2 shambles.

In spite of that most discouraging report on Powers, Dr. Cameron's own research into mind control remained, in the view of many Agency stalwarts, among the most promising ways to achieve the success the director so urgently needed.

13

Edge of
Darkness

Madeleine Smith had been transferred by Dr. Cameron
from the institute to a Montreal neurosurgical unit to undergo a prefrontal lobotomy, and the night before a nurse had
shorn her hair with shears and lathered her scalp with a
shaving brush before using a barber's cutthroat razor to leave
her head shiny and bald.

After forty days in the isolator followed by a further period
in the Sleep Room, her chronic schizophrenia was to be
treated by a surgical procedure Dr. Cameron still called the
new psychiatry, a description coined by the *New England
Journal of Medicine* in 1949. His decision came at a time
when many psychiatrists had concluded that such operations
did not alleviate the illness. Despite some apparent immediate improvements, patients usually relapsed. Further brain
surgery resulted in them becoming more confused and incontinent, alternating between inertia and stubbornness. Many
developed alarming symptoms: overeating and childlike emotional crushes on nurses and doctors, rolling on the floor, and
alternately weeping and laughing for no good reason. Lobotomized patients generally lived out their lives in asylums.

Medical experts had increasingly turned away in horror
from what many saw as a surgical treatment of last resort. But
there had been one exception, Walter Jackson Freeman, the
most radical neurosurgeon in the United States. A goateed,
flamboyant antiestablishmentarian, he was also a genuine ec-
centric. As professor of neurology at George Washington
University his demonstrations of anatomy had included on-
the-spot dissection of one of the human brains he always

carried around in a pickling jar. He used a sharp-pointed wooden stiletto—which he kept in his breast pocket—to expose centers of brain cells and nerve pathways. He also wrote simultaneously with both hands to illustrate the anatomy of the nervous system. He had fathered four children in forty months of marriage and, when the youngest was four, Dr. Freeman had made them climb with him to the top of Mount Washington, the highest point in the eastern United States.

His fascination with nature in the raw was something he shared with Dr. Cameron. On occasions they disappeared into the wilds to pit themselves against the elements, telling no one what they did or spoke about. At medical conferences the two men—each normally so acerbic and opinionated—listened respectfully as, in turn, they presented papers in a dramatic, self-assured, and well-organized way.

Dr. Freeman had long been the acknowledged expert in North America on leucotomy. He perfected his technique by practicing on formalin-fixed brains from the morgue. He had promised his first human patient, a woman with a fine head of hair, that he would preserve her curls. At the last moment he had shaved her head. But, as he told Dr. Cameron, afterward she no longer cared.

Since then Dr. Freeman had performed over 4,000 further lobotomies, using the technique to destroy the brains of those suffering from apprehension, anxiety, depression, compulsions, obsessions, as well as drug addicts, sexual deviants, and of course schizophrenics. He was convinced the frontal lobes of the brain were somehow responsible for aggression or, ultimately, a patient's refusal to cooperate in what he termed an acceptable way.

Dr. Freeman most probably would have found Madeleine fit that criteria. In her drugged condition she had made sounds in the isolator that the voice analyzer in the Radio Telemetry Laboratory had identified as "father," "want baby," and "father." Transferred back to the Sleep Room, she had somehow found the strength to use her helmet to butt a nurse. Such behavior came well within Dr. Freeman's guidelines for those who could benefit from psychosurgery.

Madeleine would undergo what Dr. Freeman had defined, with a high sense of medical and social mission, as "the appropriate destruction of brain tissue to disconnect one part of the brain from another with the intent of altering behavior."

In the halcyon period between 1944—when the first patient from the institute had been referred for psychosurgery—and 1960, over 100,000 such operations had been performed in North America. The figure for Europe was similar. Tens of thousands of lobotomies had also been carried out in the Pacific Basin, mostly in Japan and India. The technique used there was more primitive than even Dr. Freeman recommended. Patients were generally wheeled fully conscious into the operating room and given an electroshock to render them unconscious; it was cheaper and quicker than using an anesthetic. A trocar, a gradated instrument rather like a miniature ice pick, was driven through the bony orbit behind the eye socket and tapped gently with a surgeon's mallet to destroy brain cells and nerve fibers. Three or four patients could be handled in an hour. It was a bloodless but horrific experience that left them deprived of a significant part of their intellectual capacity.

Despite a growing hesitation among his peers, Dr. Cameron regularly still sent patients to be lobotomized. There were even more theories than methods and, like electroshock, no one knew exactly how psychosurgery worked. Dr. Cameron had once told Dr. Roper that it didn't really matter how the result was achieved.

A theater porter wheeled in Madeleine and he and the nurse transferred her from the trolley onto the operating table. Madeleine wore only a surgical gown. She stared, fully conscious, into the powerful overhead light.

The radical lobotomy would be performed under a local anesthetic so that the surgeon could immediately judge her disorientation, indicating how successful was his severing of her frontal lobes. Until he observed the required signs, he would continue to destroy that portion of Madeleine's brain.

Dr. Cameron arrived in the theater and began to scrub alongside the surgeon and his assistant. The psychiatrist frequently attended the lobotomy of what he called his more interesting cases.

The surgeon fitted an eye shield over Madeleine's brow to protect her eyes while he swabbed her scalp with antiseptic. The skin gleamed under the powerful light. The surgeon called for a scalpel and, using the blunt end, drew a scratch mark around the area to be incised.

The resident handed the surgeon a syringe filled with a

local anesthetic. He injected around the circle. The surgeon was handed a second syringe of anesthetic and injected this in the same area. It would act as a hemostat, reducing bleeding when the cutting started.

"Do you feel anything, lassie?" Dr. Cameron always asked. Madeleine mumbled.

Blood marked the knife's progress. The resident used a curved forceps to hold back the skin flap. The only sound was of a discarded instrument being dropped into the bucket.

The nurse had laid her instruments out in a preordained pattern. Dominating the trolley was the steel brace for drilling through Madeleine's skull. The surgeon continued to use a retractor to peel another portion of scalp from the bone.

"All right, lassie?"

The surgeon turned to the metal basin and dipped his gloved hands in an antiseptic solution. He found it easier to work with damp gloves; they clung better to his hands and gave more sensitivity to his fingers.

The resident sluiced the operative area with an antiseptic solution. The nurse handed the surgeon the brace with its bit already in place.

He drilled for a few moments and a fine spray of bone shavings spumed into the air. The surgeon asked for a dural hook, an instrument very similar to the one dentists use to locate tooth cavities, and probed the hole. If he detected a crack he knew he had gone through the skull. There was no crack. Madeleine had a thickish skull. The drilling continued through the bone. After he finally retracted the brace, the resident collected the skull shavings from Madeleine's head and placed them in a small gallipot. The dust would be used to fill up the burr hole at the end of the operation. The surgeon used a syringe to wash the cavity clean.

Next he asked for a tenotome. The nurse handed him the small scalpel with its finely honed blade. He snipped a corner of the dura mater, the tough membranous covering of the brain. Then, using a dural scissors, he began to cut away the skin, fraction by fraction.

Madeleine's brain was exposed, milky pink in color.

The surgeon asked for a long steel spatula that had replaced the wire stylet Dr. Moniz had used as a leucotome in his first operations; the stylet had proven not to be stiff enough, and the wire had a tendency to bend in a patient's brain, traversing through blood vessels and tissue not meant to be destroyed. The journals had been filled with accounts of patients who had started to have epileptic seizures and other serious complications caused by the wire. The spatula was an altogether more sturdy weapon.

"Lassie, count to ten."

A series of grunts came from Madeleine.

The surgeon inserted the spatula into the burr hole. He worked to a definite routine: down a few centimeters, then a pause to move the instrument a few centimeters laterally. Each move destroyed more of Madeleine's brain.

"Can you sing your favorite song?"

A strange moaning came from Madeleine.

The surgeon drove the spatula further into her brain, extending and widening the wound, from which blood oozed. The resident wiped the area clean. The surgeon asked for a suction tube to go even deeper into her brain. Every few centimeters he wiggled it around to widen the path of destruction.

"Lassie, count to ten."

There was a grunt from Madeleine.

The surgeon continued to destroy her brain.

"Do you feel sleepy?"

She gave the same response.

The surgeon withdrew the tube and asked for a cannula, a heavy-gauge hypodermic needle. He inserted it in the hole and, using steady pressure, drove it down to the spheroidal, the bony ridge at the base of her skull. The cannula was then withdrawn. Once more he inserted the spatula, and swung its handle upward, so that the blade could be drawn along the base of her skull and a cut made as far to the side as possible in her brain. The spatula was pulled out and the burr hole rinsed of the oozing fluid. In all, four cuts were made, two to each side of the hole.

Dr. Cameron continued to ask questions. They were part of what he termed the disorientation yardstick—his means of knowing how much brain destruction was being achieved. The surgeon continued his work, poking and cutting.

"Lassie, speak to me."

A further grunt.

The surgeon continued, crushing forever Madeleine's prime areas of emotional responses. Finally, she made no more sounds, closed her eyes, and fell into a stupor.

The surgeon started to close up. Dr. Cameron bent over Madeleine. Removing the eye shield, he lifted one and then another of her eyelids. She stared vacuously back at him.

"Lassie, it's all over, no more pain."

He left the theater to return to the institute for his morning ward round.

Later that day Madeleine was transferred to St. Jean de Dieu Hospital, to enter the custodial care of the religious sisters who maintained a number of zombies like her.

Her visions of the Wise Men and the Sloth may have continued to appear to her in spite of her irrevocably destroyed brain. She might still have incestuous thoughts about her dead father. No one would ever know. The surgeon's instruments had affected her speech. She could babble incoherently; usually she gave only simian grunts. She had lost the ability to read and write.

Her husband, Eddie, like everyone else, would never know when Madeleine might have stopped hoping to be cured, or if she ever did. He had remarried and lived in Detroit. He sent Madeleine a Christmas card every year. Her family had long given up visiting her at the institute after Dr. Cameron told them it was pointless, as she was an incurable schizophrenic and would remain all her life in an institution. They did not know she had been lobotomized, nor was it legally required that they should be told. Her consent form covered all treatment eventualities. After the operation her case no longer appeared in Dr. Cameron's reports to the Society for the Investigation of Human Ecology. No one there asked what had happened to her.

President Eisenhower returned to Washington from Paris publicly humiliated. Khrushchev had roundly abused him at the summit before striding from the Elysée Palace, having canceled Eisenhower's invitation to visit Russia. The summit had ended in unprecedented disarray among the Allies, with de Gaulle making plain his rage over the U-2 flights.

Lesser men would have wilted under the crisis. Dulles met it head-on. Eisenhower had barely recovered from jet lag before the director was closeted in the Oval Office. After quickly dismissing what had happened in Paris and Tokyo as Soviet mischief, Dulles warned the president that the Russians were moving into Africa, working through the most hotheaded black politician on the continent, Patrice Lumumba.

He had become the country's first leader during the transition of the Belgian Congo from a white colony into a black African republic.

Dulles painted a graphic picture of the "whole of Africa coming under the hammer and sickle. Our supply lines around the cape would be threatened. It is a situation every bit as grave as Korea." The director told the president that Lumumba should be terminated.

Eisenhower, old and tired, agreed; he only had a few weeks left as leader of the most powerful nation in the world and he longed to be free of his responsibilities. Retirement would be a welcome relief from the burdens of office that required he approve the murder of another head of state.

Dulles assigned the task of preparing the assassination to Richard Helms. Dr. Gottlieb had come up with a perfume that could be sprinkled on pillows and sheets which, upon inhalation, was instantly lethal. Lumumba's food could be poisoned with the latest toxins. His car could be blown up by one of the new line in miniature limpet mines the Agency had developed. There were endless possibilities.

Dulles had been sufficiently impressed with Dr. Cameron's evaluation of Gary Powers to ask him to assess Lumumba's personality. William Buckley was assigned to take the Agency's file on Lumumba to Montreal.

Buckley was back at Langley for reassignment, and he had spent his time reading reports from stations around the Far East. It was routine intelligence, what he called the "nuts and bolts for securing together an analysis." The pieces, however, all fit—not neatly as in a spy novel, but they came together to create a mosaic that only made sense when placed alongside other completed puzzles. There were no blinding revelations and it was hardly exciting work.

The boredom had been partly relieved for Buckley by attending parties given by Dulles and his wife. Clover seemed more relaxed and calm, and confided to Buckley that she had returned to God. Jeanie Houston, the tall, lissome blond wife of the Agency's general counsel, Lawrence Reid Houston, was instrumental in Clover's religious awakening. Herself a devout churchgoer, Jeanie had urged Clover "to pray and God will do the rest. Make your son better and stop Allen from straying." Clover had taken the advice and, to her astonishment, her son had improved and her husband, as far

as she knew, had given up womanizing. Certainly the stud
squad was no longer on duty at their parties.

A staunch Catholic, Buckley had been impressed at his
hostess's testimony—just as he was by the strong Christian
commitment among many of the Agency's older generation.
They spoke of God being on the side of America, and that the
Agency had been chosen by Him to fight the forces of evil.
Those men often openly said it was God who had ensured
they had survived.

Buckley had come to know some of them well, and admired the way they made it clear they would still walk
through fire for Dulles. One was William Casey, though
Buckley found it hard to accept that the bulky, bumbling
lawyer had once ran thirty teams of agents actually inside
Hitler's Berlin in the last weeks of the war in Europe. Recalling that time to his guests, Dulles had spoken affectionately
of Casey's skill in recruiting German prisoners-of-war to form
those teams—though doing so was in direct violation of the
Geneva accord. Casey had lowered his head and half-closed
his eyes, mumbling that war was war, and that really he had
done very little.

Casey had questioned Buckley on various matters: U.S.
foreign policy, the relationship between the State Department and the White House, and whether there was a feeling
nowadays within the Agency of being gripped in a vice. It
had all been very casual but, Buckley decided, shrewd; Casey
clearly knew a lot about the inner workings of government.
Buckley had afterward wondered whether the former OSS
man simply kept abreast of events because he missed the
excitement of intelligence work, or whether his visits to Washington were preparation for something else—perhaps a post
in a future administration.

Between parties, Buckley had traveled to Montreal. His
cover was one he had used before, that of a science journalist
come to interview Dr. Cameron. Buckley would remember how
"I just sat in his office after he locked the door and told his
secretary no one was to disturb him. He went through the file
very quickly and then dictated his observations on tape. He
handed it to me, together with the file. I don't think we had a
dozen words of social conversation in the whole afternoon."

Dr. Cameron concluded that Lumumba possessed a vain
personality, paid particular attention to his dress and looks,

and seemed to especially cherish his teeth. He displayed
them, Dr. Cameron saw from the photographs in the file,
whenever he could.

Helms decided the obvious way to kill Lumumba was to
ensure his toothpaste was impregnated with one of the deadly
strains of germs Dr. Gottlieb always had on hand. Tubes of
paste were prepared and shipped to Leopoldville, the
Congolese capital.

Dulles had promised Eisenhower there would be no slip-up
this time. And, he had hinted to the woebegone President,
he might have important news shortly about a subject that
had fascinated Eisenhower since he had read *The Manchurian
Candidate,* the best-selling novel by Richard Condon about a
Soviet-Chinese plot to use an American soldier captured in
Korea and condition him at a special brainwashing center in
Manchuria to become a remote-controlled assassin. Dulles
had, of course, not added that Condon's fictional camp in
many ways had been actually reproduced in Montreal.

Worst of all was her sense of powerlessness. It left Dr.
Morrow in a state of panic. She had screamed for hours that
she had not consented to electroshock treatment. When she
no longer had the strength to shout, she repeatedly sobbed.
Every morning she heard Dr. Cameron striding past her
room. She thought he was "cruel, savage, inhumane."

Waiting was as bad as not knowing what to do. Increasingly, she felt weak and exhausted, finally not even having
the energy to get out of bed. She was left with a sense of
nothingness. The numbing apathy was as agonizing as any
pain. The fear seemed to squeeze her heart. Outside, in the
corridor, she heard nurses occasionally laughing as they passed.

One morning Dr. Cameron appeared with a junior doctor.
He carried a tray covered with a surgical towel. She knew
what was underneath and repeated she had not given her
consent for electroshock.

Dr. Cameron didn't answer, only stood towering above
her. She couldn't stop the rush of words. "I don't want it. It's
wrong for me. I don't want to be zapped like that. I don't
want electroshock. You can't force me. You can't make a
patient have treatment she doesn't want. I'm a doctor. I know
what I'm talking about. Do you understand? I know what I'm
talking about."

Somehow she had to make him understand.

"Lassie, listen to me." Dr. Cameron spoke precisely. "We're going to put you to sleep. And we're going to give you shock treatment when you're asleep."

"No!"

She tried to form distinguishable words but she seemed to be choking.

Dr. Cameron removed the cover from the tray and picked up a syringe, already filled with clear liquid. He removed the sheath from the needle.

She thought: *My God, he can't do this. He can't!* A great band seemed to be stretched around her chest and cutting off the words.

"Give me your arm, lassie."

"No! Please! No!" Somehow the words escaped.

"You've seen it help others. Don't you want it to help you? What are you afraid of?"

She shook her head. Once more she couldn't speak. It was terrifying. She knew what she must say, but no sound came from her lips.

"Your arm, lassie!"

She hated him. He had lied to her; it had all been a trick on his part to get her to come in voluntarily. There was no such thing as *voluntary.* He stood over her with the needle poised.

"No shocks! Please!" She screamed, all control gone. "No shocks!"

He injected her.

Through the door came a nurse wheeling the electroshock trolley.

"No . . . Nooooooo . . ."

Darkness.

Dr. Cleghorn increasingly felt Dr. Cameron's methods were lacking in validity, and concluded this was probably due to "his deficiency of training in a basic science where he might have acquired an attitude of scientific appraisal and caution."

Observations like that ran through the notebooks he was filling with an account of life at the institute. It served as a matter of record of what he privately thought of his superior's methods.

Psychiatry, like other branches of medicine, was changing, often dramatically. Diagnosis was becoming more sophisticated. Various forms of schizophrenia were being identified.

At the same time the methods of treating an illness were more specific. Every few months a new antidepressant appeared: minor tranquilizers and the more powerful phenothiazines helped to control the physiological function of almost every organ system in the body. "The age of the blunderbuss approach, when a patient was shot full of everything in the hope some of it would work, is almost over." Such conclusions enlivened his notes.

There were also the first indications of public awareness of the dangers of overmedication, the first stories in the press about the first lawsuits brought by patients in the United States who claimed they had been maltreated, the first calls for government regulation. It was a time, Dr. Cleghorn reminded his own staff, for the utmost care never to overdose or prescribe drugs indiscriminately, and never to do so without the most thorough physical examination.

Dr. Cleghorn felt all these developments had bypassed Dr. Cameron. He appeared still rooted in another era, living off a transcendent belief that, with his methods, any patient could be "reconstructed." Dr. Cleghorn felt the word itself had an antediluvian ring to it.

Also disturbing to the fastidious Dr. Cleghorn, whose own scientific publications had placed him at the forefront of medical research in North America, Dr. Cameron continued to support "bootleg research. He still had a blind spot for psychopaths. His failure to identify deviants and possibly a reckless acceptance of such characters in his entourage, was deeply worrying."

Those private judgments presented an insight into the increasingly strained working relationship between the institute's two most senior doctors.

Publicly, Dr. Cleghorn, however, still felt a sense of loyalty to the chief psychiatrist. He studiously avoided voicing any open criticism about Dr. Cameron's treatments and detested the personal gossip about his senior. Junior doctors had spread the story that Dr. Cameron was having an affair with a patient he saw in his office twice a week late in the evening. The doctors claimed they had heard giggling coming from the office. One of the nurses on South-Two insisted she had seen Dr. Cameron embracing the woman. Working late one evening, Dr. Cleghorn had passed Dr. Cameron in a corridor and had been astonished to see what looked like a lipstick smudge on his collar.

Dr. Cleghorn now realized that Dr. Cameron had even manipulated evidence. In his latest paper on psychic driving Dr. Cameron claimed a total success in all patients treated. Yet Dr. Cleghorn knew that the treatment—one which he steadfastly refused to use on his service—was anything but effective. Nearly half of the several hundred who had received psychic driving in the past five years and then had been discharged had to be readmitted to the hospital within a year. Depatterning had also proven to be equally ineffective for curing schizophrenia; it often only replaced one confusion with another. Yet again Dr. Cameron boldly claimed a high success rate for that method by using a "mumbo-jumbo of statistics which were dressed up in fancy tabulations."

Dr. Cleghorn had come to see that what was essentially wrong with Dr. Cameron's approach was that it lacked a properly organized system. "There were too many assumptions and inconsistencies; Dr. Cameron seemed primarily concerned with pacification, sedation, and repression. He was too quick to label, to fall back on jargon, to behave at times with the moral stricture of a judge or schoolmaster rather than a physician."

He had begun to ask himself how long the situation could continue. Just as medicine was changing, so was the relationship between senior doctors and their juniors. There was more open discussion. Yet, a resident who had queried a diagnosis had been sent packing; a nurse who had refused to work in the Sleep Room was dismissed. Such behavior had only encouraged enmity. Clinicians on the staff who had been at most indifferent to Dr. Cameron were now implacable opponents.

Dr. Morrow awoke with a blinding headache. She felt she was "in a deep, dark, pitch-black hole with no sense of appendages, like a worm. There was no sense of solidity, like I was not on ground and I was not on water. It was like being suspended in an eerie black hole."

Next morning she received another series of multiple shocks. That night she dreamed she was being electrocuted. Two mornings later, Dr. Cameron, a junior doctor, and the nurse with the trolley came again. And three more times the following week. She wondered when the ritual burnings would end and how much longer she could endure the searing pain in her head.

On the eleventh day, a Saturday, Dr. Cameron gave Dr. Morrow twelve consecutive electroshocks; no other patient had received so many in one session. He then went home for the weekend. She was unconscious for most of the day.

That evening her sister, Margy, came to the institute. She had traveled from New York after receiving a phone call from their mother. Mrs. Morrow had suffered a recent stroke and, because of that, had been unable to visit the institute. But her daily calls to her daughter's bedside had alarmed her. Mary, she had told Margy, sounded more and more strange.

At the institute, Margy was refused permission to see her sister. Already emotionally overwrought, Margy threatened to call the police and was reluctantly allowed to visit. The sight of Mary deeply upset her. She rushed from the hospital to their mother. In spite of her infirmity, Mrs. Morrow was a calm and resourceful woman. Having listened to Margy's tearful report, she telephoned Dr. Cleghorn. He was sympathetic but said that, as Dr. Morrow was not his patient, there was no way he could intervene. He recommended she call Dr. Cameron.

It was Saturday evening when she contacted Dr. Cameron at home at Lake Placid. He was politely distant and interrupted her. "The best you can hope for is that your daughter will go into a home. She'll never again practice medicine." He hung up.

Mrs. Morrow called the institute and told several nurses and doctors that under no circumstances was her daughter to receive any further treatment. The senior doctor on duty telephoned Dr. Cameron. He ordered that Dr. Morrow be given 300 milligrams of Largactil.

For the next two days she was maintained in a drugged stupor, as the dosage of Largactil was stepped up to 600 milligrams. She developed a rash.

Back at work after the weekend, Dr. Cameron did not visit her. His absence struck an instant of cold fear in Dr. Morrow. Dr. Cameron was probably preparing something else for her. That terrifying possibility gave her strength she thought she never possessed. The first glimmer of anger took root and quickly grew, wild and raw and therapeutic. He had been like a seducer, sitting in her room in the Royal Victoria and dangling the prospect of taking her back as a doctor, all the while "scheming to use me like a pink mouse in a laboratory experiment."

The anger grew, surfacing through the Largactyl, nourished by the way he had treated her. She began to feel truly alive for the first time in a year—perhaps in several years. She reminded herself that she had been sick, and was not well now. But she was not helpless—and he was not going to make her dependent on him. He had treated her as if she were a schizophrenic. Well, she wasn't—and she would show him. The anger continued to surge through her, powerful and invigorating. He had not once asked her how she felt as a person, and never discussed her feelings as a human being. Yet he had gone ahead and blasted electricity through her brain. My God, how he had duped her! Looking back on her whole relationship with him, she realized he had not even bothered about her as a patient; she had just been someone else on whom to try out his theories.

Dr. Morrow used her bedside telephone to call a doctor she trusted at the Royal Victoria. When she explained her symptoms he promised to come at once.

Waiting, she continued to fuel her fury, knowing it was one way to keep her mind alert. She had always wanted to believe Dr. Cameron cared for his patients. "But he didn't," she realized now. "They were just symptoms, to be injected, shocked, and put to sleep." He never related to a patient but remained behind his own line of demarcation: He was healthy; a patient was sick. He had actually made her feel guilty for daring to resist his methods. There was, she decided, something about him that was mad and evil.

The doctor she had called arrived. He examined Dr. Morrow's throat and arranged for her immediate transfer to the Royal Victoria Hospital. As she left the institute she again thanked God that she had escaped whatever fate Dr. Cameron had planned for her.

But what of the others? That question filled her mind as the taxi drove her to the Royal Victoria. What about the hundreds of patients who, over the years, had come into his hands? What had happened to them? She felt a sense of kinship with them. If what had happened to her was typical, and she increasingly believed it was, then he had also treated them as less than human. They needed to be helped—and the sooner she found a way back into medicine, the better she could offer it.

*   *   *

The toothpaste plot to kill Lumumba failed. The CIA agent in Leopoldville was unable to find a means of introducing the poisoned tubes into his bathroom. Lumumba was finally deposed by a rival and shot dead trying to escape from captivity on January 17, 1961. Three days later, John F. Kennedy was sworn into office and found himself grappling with his first foreign crisis: Throughout Africa the rumor spread that the CIA had crudely butchered Lumumba. In Washington, the file on the matter was included in Dulles's briefing for the new president. No one, of course, blamed Dr. Cameron for how the matter had become such an embarrassment. But once more his name was associated with an unsatisfactory Agency operation.

At that first meeting in the Oval Office Dulles raised a matter of far more import to Kennedy: Fidel Castro. Kennedy had campaigned vigorously for the Cuban vote in Miami and promised American aid to overthrow Castro. He needed no convincing from Dulles that Castro was not a mere maverick like Lumumba, but a serious threat to U.S. interests in the Caribbean. He avidly read the CIA's psycho-profile on Castro, which included such clinical clichés as "irrational," "unpredictable," "psychoneurotic," "manipulative," and "motivated by inferiority." The evaluation sounded impressive but it had been prepared by Agency psychiatrists working for the most part from news clips. It was an inauspicious start for a plan that became a great debacle for the Kennedy administration.

The sorry enterprise ended in Cuba's Bay of Pigs. Kennedy shouldered the blame publicly. In private he and his brother Robert, the attorney general, castigated Dulles, who offered to resign. Recognizing that would cause his fledgling administration further humiliation, Kennedy compromised. Dulles must go—but only after a decent interval. He could remain until the CIA's new complex at Langley, Virginia, was officially opened.

On September 28, 1961, Kennedy announced that he had nominated John A. McCone to become the next head of the Agency. It was the end of a dynasty; only two years earlier John Foster, Allen, and Eleanor Dulles had stage-managed the foreign policy of the United States; now, only Eleanor remained in government—and she would not last long, dismissed like a temporary secretary, on Robert Kennedy's order. In the meantime, McCone had begun to dip into the Agency's files. By November he reached Project M-K-Ultra.

Dr. Cameron's formal links to the program had ended on August 26, 1960, when he received a cashier's check for $4,777, the final payment on his grant. However, he continued to send copies of his research papers to the Society for the Investigation of Human Ecology. These had been passed to Washington and were read by, among others, Albert Wheelon, a Californian who, like McCone, had been recruited from the aerospace industry. Wheelon was head of a new Agency department, Science and Technology, into which Dr. Gottlieb and the other TSS scientists were amalgamated. Wheelon was no match for the folk-dancing Dr. Gottlieb; hopping from one foot to the other, his eyes darting and hands waving to make his points, the diminutive scientist persuaded Wheelon to let him remain in charge of M-K-Ultra.

In more horse-trading, McCone approved the appointment of the tall, debonair Richard Helms to run Clandestine Services, soon to be itself renamed as the Directorate of Operations. The status quo was maintained. The Agency may have acquired new heads, but the body politic remained as intact as it had been under Dulles. Dr. Gottlieb had convinced Wheelon and McCone that, among other work in progress, the Agency was really on the verge of cracking the secret of mind control; further, he implied that Soviet techniques had become so sophisticated that they could have been used on Castro to make him more malleable as Moscow's surrogate in the Caribbean. It was a move designed to head off Robert Kennedy. McCone was sufficiently impressed by what Dr. Gottlieb had said to urge the attorney general to allow M-K-Ultra to continue. The attorney general agreed that the search should be intensified to not only discover but surpass the Communists at mind bending.

That Christmas of 1961, for the first time in years, Dr. Cameron's bottle of malt whiskey from Dulles came gift wrapped through the mail—not by diplomatic pouch.

14

Madness, Madness

Jan Zielinski increasingly dreaded going to the Sleep Room. The groaning and moaning was too upsetting. He had come to compare what he was ordered to do with the way the Nazis, and later the Russians, behaved in his own country. He knew he was not alone in feeling horrified at what was happening. Some of the institute's doctors had expressed shock that Dr. Cameron now gave patients curare to paralyze them so there was no way they could physically stop or remove the tapes used in psychic driving.

When Zielinski tried to discuss matters with Rubenstein, the senior technician sharply reminded him how much they both owed Dr. Cameron, that in years to come people would look upon him as a great benefactor. What other hospital in North America, Rubenstein had asked, allowed so many foreigners on its staff—and not only Europeans like they were, but doctors from Asia and Africa? As he spliced tapes, Rubenstein never tired of discussing a vision in which the "medical sons of Dr. Cameron" would one day occupy all the important posts in psychiatry throughout the free world.

A glimpse of that future was in a paper Rubenstein coauthored with Dr. Cameron and published in the prestigious *Journal of Mental Science*. The technician conceded that that only came about because of the reputation of his collaborator. Dr. Cameron had also encouraged Rubenstein to write an account of a system to measure objectively the continuous behavioral activity of patients hospitalized in a psychiatric institution. It had appeared in *Nature* in March 1962, under his byline. The respected journal had published a paper by an author who had no formal clinical credentials. Rubenstein had ordered a stack of reprints.

All around Zielinski were indications the institute was no longer the place he first came to work in. Then, it had been a close-knit community. Now, new faces regularly appeared and every square foot of the mansion was utilized, with laboratories crammed into the basement and even up in the watchtower. Where once the staff had been only English- or French-speaking, the dialects of Africa, Asia, and the Middle East rang through the wards and corridors. Zielinski had no trouble understanding the Irish and European doctors. But some of the Arabs and Iranians did not even know how to read the settings on the electroshock machines.

With Dr. Cameron once more abroad, his patients were the temporary responsibility of Dr. Cleghorn.

Dr. Cleghorn was increasingly uncomfortable with Dr. Roper. For the past few weeks Dr. Cleghorn had been treating Agnes Roper as a patient. She had come into therapy on the strict condition that her husband must not know, because it would embarrass him. Dr. Cleghorn had reluctantly agreed, though he knew it would only be a short time before Dr. Roper discovered the truth.

As a couple, he liked them both. Agnes Roper still showed glimpses of what she had been like when well, a witty and vivacious woman. Her husband was one of the most dedicated and insightful physicians on the staff, who willingly took on cases that were labeled as no-hopers and final referrals.

Dr. Cleghorn's concern was that the senior resident drove himself too hard and, having begun to treat Agnes's fears and frustrations, he sympathized with why her husband did so. She had turned their home into a battleground with her manic-depressive illness, with its headaches, sleeplessness, and her racing thoughts, which at times took Agnes across the border of sanity. Dr. Cleghorn realized that her symptoms were well advanced, and he could not be certain that any treatment would more than partially help. Being happily married himself, he did not like telling a colleague that at the root of her illness was Mrs. Roper's conviction that her marriage was doomed.

Dr. Cleghorn's morning round was an altogether more leisurely one than Dr. Cameron conducted. Dr. Cleghorn spent considerable time with each patient, discussing with them their progress when they were able to respond. He invited junior doctors to pose supplementary questions and used the answers to help him to judge the overall clinical picture.

On August 26, 1963, three years to the day since the Society for the Investigation of Human Ecology had paid its last check on behalf of the CIA to Dr. Cameron, a meeting was held in Dr. Gottlieb's office at Langley to consider whether the Agency should once again finance Dr. Cameron's research. He had approved of the society seeking further funding for psychic driving and sensory deprivation research. Those present included Dr. Harold Wolff, Dr. James Monroe, Dr. John Gittinger, and Dr. Walter Pasternak, two Agency staff psychologists.

Previously Dr. Gottlieb would have come to a decision without consultation; a telephone call to Dr. Monroe would have sufficed to decide whether or not to reactivate subproject 68. But that easygoing time was over. Director McCone and Albert Wheelon, for all their lack of experience in espionage, believed that the CIA should be run like any other company. Along with that decision had come accountability. While McCone and Wheelon, the head of Science and Technology, wouldn't interfere with Dr. Gottlieb's projects—currently including searching for new ways to murder Fidel Castro and plant listening bugs in the Kremlin—they wanted to know the cost. Dr. Gottlieb realized that Dr. Cameron's previous grant had produced little of tangible value to the Agency. He could not be certain what further funding could achieve. That was why he had asked those present in his office to advise him.

Dr. Gottlieb was himself also once more embroiled in a time-consuming inquest, every bit as embarrassing as the Olson affair. With Allen Dulles nowadays busily writing articles for *Fortune* and the *Encyclopaedia Britannica* on intelligence matters, Dr. Gottlieb had no one to head off the questions from the inspector general's office over M-K-Ultra subproject 3.

It had started off as a serious inquiry to assess the use of sexual entrapment in covert operations. Dr. Gittinger, Dr. Pasternak, and another Agency psychologist, Dr. David Rhodes, had organized what unofficially was known as Operation Climax.

An apartment was rented by the Agency in San Francisco; the city had been chosen because a memo on the project described it as sexually open. The apartment became a brothel, the first the Agency had directly financed and set up. Dr. Gottlieb had approved bills such as $300 for photographs of naked women in bondage and Gay Paree posters to give the bordello what another memo described as the authentic French feel. Prostitutes were hired from the city's Tenderloin district. They were paid between $500 and $1,000 a week, depending on the hours they worked. In between they had been patiently questioned by the three psychologists about why they got into the business, how they felt about selling their bodies, and what they spoke about to their clients, especially in the postcoitus, shared-cigarette period. The psychologists had learned that most men talked about their families and work. It was hardly an earth-moving discovery.

More money had been spent: $44.04 on a telescope for the Agency men to better observe the girls at work through peepholes in the apartment's bedrooms; $1,000 on liquor to increase that authentic French feel and to encourage the whores to help answer more questions about sadism and torture. One Agency man, who acted as the apartment's barman, would recall that everyone had a wonderful time on taxpayers' money. Clients had been surreptitiously slipped itchy and smelling powders, had endured stink bombs planted under the beds (the intention of that experiment was to evaluate what effect the stench had on their sexual activity), and given drinks spiked with powerful diuretics.

The psychologists had compared their observations, and seriously pondered whether it could be possible to actually train prostitutes to become intelligence officers. Not only did the spirit of Mata Hari permeate the apartment but so, too, did the vision of George Orwell, who in 1984 had predicted the day when the government sponsored prostitution.

The doctors had decided to test another of their theories: that it was perfectly feasible to infiltrate a public gathering, such as a cocktail party, and spray the unsuspecting guests with LSD, sending them on a collective trip.

Dr. Gittinger flew to Washington to get the scientists at Technical Staff Services to fill aerosols with LSD. They were variously labeled as insect repellent, deodorant, and perfume. Meanwhile, Dr. Pasternak and Dr. Rhodes had spent a week visiting most of the bars in downtown San Francisco issuing invitations to selected strangers to come to a party. They sought a cross section of personality types.

The chosen day was a Bay Area broiler—sultry and humid. The psychologists made sure no detail was forgotten. The girls looked their best. The canapés had been catered in at a cost of $195, and there was beer and wine on ice. The windows were closed so that the sprayed LSD would not escape. Guests who did not know each other or their hosts arrived and, as with all such parties, there were a number of gate-crashers. The apartment was soon overflowing. The psychologists decided to wait until everyone was at "second-drink level" before beginning spraying.

But while the guests happily swallowed CIA booze and pawed CIA-paid tarts, they also began to open the windows. In vain had the Agency men rushed around closing them. Soon every window in the apartment was wide open to let in the first evening breeze. The doctors, somewhat desperate, had begun to spray, going from room to room, mumbling that they wanted to freshen up the place or kill off the roaches. No matter how diligently they worked, the LSD mist drifted out the windows. Finally Dr. Gittinger went to the bathroom and doused himself from a can, hoping to trip out for a few hours to forget the farce, while Dr. Pasternak and Dr. Rhodes ushered the tipsy guests out of the apartment.

Operation Climax had come to an inglorious halt. The San Francisco episode was under investigation by the Agency's internal watchdog, the inspector general's office. Dr. Gottlieb hoped that in the end nothing much would come of the investigation. He would be proven correct. But it had made him that much more cautious about involving the Agency once more with risky projects such as Dr. Cameron's.

An operation on foreign soil was nowadays increasingly a risk when the Agency did not have full and direct control. The Canadian government, as Dr. Gottlieb knew from the Agency's regular meetings with members of the Royal Canadian Mounted Police and the Department of Defense in Ottawa, was becoming ever more sensitive about their country's position as a collaborator with the CIA in intelligence work after the Bay of Pigs fiasco and the deepening crisis in Vietnam. Yet the temptation to once more use Dr. Cameron was very great. He remained the most powerful single figure in psychiatry in North America—if not the Western world. He held more titles than any of his peers; he had unparalleled access to any clinical research institute. In every way he remained the ideal cover for the Agency's quest for mind control. He had also clearly shown he needed no prompting to take a subject to the terminal stage.

The presence in Dr. Gottlieb's office of two of the perpetrators of the San Francisco fiasco was intentional. Dr. Pasternak had, some years before, visited Dr. Cameron to assess his work. He concluded it was difficult to say whether the research would ever achieve what the Agency required. Dr. Gittinger was present for an altogether different reason. He was looking for a new place to further test the method he had invented for assessing personality and predicting future behavior. It was called the Personality Assessment System, and was seen by many, including Dr. Gottlieb, as also a potential key to mind control.

Over $1 million had been spent to develop the system, which had involved testing no fewer than 29,000 unsuspecting subjects across the Untied States who, upon consulting their physicians, found themselves answering Dr. Gittinger's questionnaires. He fed the responses into a computer. It separated personalities into two broad categories: Regulated, R-type; and Flexible, F-type. By placing a personality into either category, a number of important judgments could be applied to his or her behavior. It was possible, for example, to predict whether a person would remain faithful, would become a drunk or a sexual deviant, and of course whether the person had the qualities to make a good intelligence officer—a tight control on imagination, a thorough grasp of detail, a high boredom tolerance. It could also help predict whether someone was a potential double agent—what the system defined as the flashy, unstable, and overindulgent type of personality.

Dr. Gittinger had refined his system so that it could make an astonishingly accurate estimate of how anyone fitted into society. It allowed for ethnic variables and could be applied equally successfully to a North American, a Russian, or a Chinese. For the Agency it was an invaluable tool for case officers to use when handling agents or interrogating suspected spies.

Research into this system had been funded by the Human

Ecology Foundation, which a few months earlier had provided Dr. Gittinger with the cash to open a splendid new office in Washington called the Psychological Assessment Associates. It now had suboffices in Tokyo and Hong Kong to test potential employees for commercial firms; it was one way to recoup some of the Agency's huge investment in the Personality Assessment System.

Dr. Gittinger was now interested in testing out the system on schizophrenics, so that he could compare their assessments with those of more normal types of personality. By using a checklist of forty personality pattern trends he hoped to focus on the psychological differences between a healthy and chronically sick personality and to uncover at a still earlier stage concealed schizoid symptoms in a supposedly normal person. But first he needed a readily available supply of schizophrenics. Dr. Cameron's Institute, he was told, was a good source for human guinea pigs.

Dr. Wolff was present because, he, too, had made the journey to Montreal to review Dr. Cameron's work. Like Dr. Pasternak, he had not been overly impressed, and some of the research, in his view, was bizarre. But he had also reminded himself that Einstein had been considered crazy.

Besides, as they all saw from the reprints before them, Dr. Cameron had continued to publish in some of the world's leading journals results that clearly suggested he could be at last on the verge of the long-awaited breakthrough. From the *American Journal of Psychiatry* there was a paper, "Repetition of Verbal Signals: Behavioral and Psychological Changes." It claimed that attitudes and interpersonal relationships and self-concepts had been dramatically changed under psychic driving. Rubenstein was the paper's coauthor. In the same journal, Dr. Cameron had published another paper, "Images of Tomorrow," which envisioned a future where the restructuring of personality would be routinely achieved with suggestion and extrasensory perception. He had returned to the theme in such journals as *Comprehensive Psychiatry*, the *British Journal of Psychiatry*, and a half-dozen others. In all his conclusions Dr. Cameron claimed a remarkably high degree of success.

The question Dr. Gottlieb wanted answered was: Did all this published evidence indicate that Dr. Cameron had, in the past three years, made significant progress that was of potential benefit to the Agency? He could have added a rider that they should bear in mind the singular lack of success the Agency had still experienced elsewhere in seeking answers to mind control.

Concurrent with the madcap venture in brothel keeping, there had been some other experiments that had set Dr. Gottlieb jigging from one foot to another—always a sign he was upset. Dr. Wolff had set off a bout of foot-tapping as a result of what happened when he tried to convert one hundred Chinese—all of whom had been young students in the United States when the Communists took over their country in 1949—into agents who would return home, and, if need be, act as the Agency's version of *The Manchurian Candidate*, killing China's new leaders.

Dr. Wolff had worked hard to instill in them the will to withstand what he imagined could be the vilest form of interrogation methods the Red Chinese practiced. A sizable team of psychiatrists, psychologists, and transculturalists had devised all kinds of stressful situations; some were based on watching movies from Hong Kong. It had all been to no avail. Not one of the Americanized Chinese had shown he would really survive the rigors of a Peking interrogation center. The project had cost over $90,000 and there had been uncomfortable questions about such freewheeling expenditure.

Undeterred by Dr. Wolff's failure, Dr. Gittinger brought his considerable intellect to bear on the mystery of mind control and concluded that a combination of drugs and hypnosis would work. A few weeks earlier, in June 1963, his theory had been tried out in Mexico City. An Agency counterintelligence officer and a hypnotist—code-named Mindbender—had flown south across the border. Two adjoining rooms had been booked in a hotel. In one was a Mexican, a low-level CIA agent who was suspected of working for the KGB. With him were the chief of the Mexico City station and his deputy, William Buckley, newly arrived from Asia. The three men were seated around a table playing cards when Mindbender and his companion arrived at the hotel.

At a predetermined moment Buckley and his superior grabbed the Mexican and wrestled him to the floor. The noise of the scuffle was to be the signal for Mindbender to appear and immediately hypnotize the luckless agent into becoming an assassin, primed to murder the Soviet KGB resident in Mexico—a touch that Dr. Gottlieb had rather liked. Once he had hypnotized his subject, Mindbender was to inject him with a syringe full of a drug that was supposed to ensure that the instruction remained in the man's subconscious. Instead of appearing, needle in hand, Mindbender had remained rooted to the spot. At the last moment, the prospect of using his skills to try and create a murderer had proved too much.

Buckley and his colleagues hoisted the bewildered Mexican off the carpet, explaining that they had merely been practicing their unarmed combat technique. With air fares, hotel charges, and Mindbender's half of his fee—the Agency flatly refused to pay him the balance—the incident cost M-K-Ultra $6,480.90.

After such esoteric attempts to solve the riddle of mind control, it could only have been a relief for Dr. Gottlieb that the men in his office agreed Dr. Monroe and Dr. Wolff should once more travel to Montreal to reevaluate Dr. Cameron's work and to discover whether he had a sufficient number of suitable schizophrenics for Dr. Gittinger.

Walking up the drive, Velma Orlikow thought again what a spooky place the institute was. For the past three years she had traveled at regular intervals, a week at a time, to Montreal. Each day, as an outpatient, she had sat in a room with a tape recorder and a notebook, listening and writing. Rubenstein regularly came and replaced a spool or took away her full notebook. He often made some inane remark that set her teeth on edge. Dr. Cameron still gave her injections of LSD, and her mind would fill with gothic images of cages and creatures, coffins and bodies. When she came out of the nightmares, her symptoms remained: the depression and the feeling that life was not worth living. Yet there were also times when she believed herself cured—and her distress was all that greater when the depression returned.

Entering the institute, Velma wondered again why Dr. Cameron's treatment had not worked after all these years. Indeed, it might even be making her worse. David had raised the possibility.

But walking into Dr. Cameron's office she once more had the strange feeling she described as being "in a web and you can't even countenance doing anything else."

She wanted so much to talk to Dr. Cameron, to tell him about her feeling of hopelessness and of not being able to control it, not even for David, who was so loving and patient. Instead, she had spent her time sitting silent and distraught while he watched her, saying nothing. Today, though, she was determined to speak.

"I . . . I don't want to . . . come anymore."

He stared at her, looking through the tent of his fingers at some point over her head. He reached forward and switched on the tape recorder on the desk and asked her to repeat what she had said.

"I-I-I don't want to come. David says it isn't working."

"Yes?" He let the question hang.

She looked guiltily at her fingertips.

"Why don't you want to be helped?"

She wondered why he sounded so self-assured and decided it must be because of the total power he had over her. She was once more frightened.

Yet there was nothing understanding or compassionate about the man across the desk. That was enough reason for her reticence to confide in him. And how she hated being made to listen to her own voice going over and over the same awful memories—as much as she hated having to write down her comments. Or experiencing the terrifying nightmares that followed the injections. How could she have begun to discuss anything with him? She wished she had never come.

He rose to his feet. "Lassie, go to your room and write it all down. It's the only way I can help you. Write it all down. What your husband said. Everything. Everything that comes into your head. What you feel like when you make love. What you think about your husband. Everything."

She thought of David and of lying in his arms while he had tried to soothe her mind and body. She thought of Leslie and the way she was growing up. She looked at Dr. Cameron.

"I want to go home. I want to try and get better myself. I'm upsetting everybody I love, being like this. Please try and understand. Please."

The words tumbled from her lips, and even as they did so, they sounded trivial. She knew he would never understand.

"Lassie! Stop this!"

Dr. Cameron got up and walked past Velma, opening the door of his office, waiting for her to leave. She gathered her pocketbook, conscious that he was watching her every awkward movement.

"Thank you for seeing me."

She knew, after all, that she was desperate not to incur his displeasure. "Then, he could be a very cold and austere man," she remembered. "If you didn't say what he wanted you to say, he would not speak to you. And he would say, 'Until you're ready to tell me what I want to know, don't come back.' "

This time Dr. Cameron had a different message.

"Lassie, you'd better think about coming back in. Never mind what your husband says. It's what I say that matters here."

She ran from the office to her room. There, behind its closed door, the flood of tears finally wracked her body. Will it ever end? Ever?

But the pain and blackness remained imprisoned inside her.

In the end, due to Dr. Cameron's other commitments as well as Dr. Wolff's own busy schedule, Dr. Monroe and the Cornell neurologist did not visit the institute until Thursday, November 21, 1963. They took the morning flight from Washington, arriving in Montreal early in the afternoon. The newspapers they read on the plane were filled with accounts of President Kennedy's triumphant progress into deepest Texas and how he appeared to be healing the factionalism between the governor, John Connolly, and Senator Ralph Yarborough, which at one time had threatened to disintegrate the state's Democratic party.

Dr. Cameron greeted his visitors and led them on a tour of the wards. At each bed Dr. Wolff flicked through a case file before questioning those patients who were conscious. Some merely lay there, eyes open, staring fixedly. Others were too regressed to communicate.

Both visiting physicians did not bother to disguise their dissatisfaction. Dr. Wolff, in particular, asked time and again one question: "Are these typical of your successes?"

Dr. Cameron repeated that the patients were good examples of positive treatment, either from depatterning or psychic driving.

Dr. Monroe had the feeling that "we were distinctively living in two worlds. His and the real one."

They had reached South-Two when a nurse ran from the patients' day room shouting, "He's been shot! Someone's shot the president!"

Dr. Wolff pushed past them to the day room. There, on the television screen, an announcer continued to interrupt the afternoon soap opera with the news from Dallas that President Kennedy had been assassinated.

Dr. Monroe, abandoning any thought of completing the visit, asked to use the telephone in Dr. Cameron's office to call Washington.

Thirty minutes later, with both his visitors heading for the airport, Dr. Cameron sat alone behind his desk, knowing that not only his president had died. As Dr. Monroe left, he had said he would not be recommending that the Society for the Investigation of Human Ecology support any new grant application.

The Agency's decision had a sudden and growing effect on Dr. Cameron. Almost overnight he had aged and become even more withdrawn: He would often only break his silence to complain that the French-speaking members of the McGill faculty were trying to railroad him out of the institute in the wake of a highly critical report on the state of Quebec's mental hospitals, which had singled out the institute as using more electroshocks than any other hospital in the province. In 1961, twelve thousand electrical treatments—on the Page-Russell system they amounted to 60,000 separate shocks—had been given to a thousand patients in the institute. The report had also criticized the disproportionate amount of funding the institute received when compared to French-speaking hospitals. Dr. Cameron saw this as a further sign of the rise of French nationalism. He told Dr. Roper that "they are out to get us."

No one suspected—because he kept such matters strictly between himself and the finance office—that the institute's fiscal position had become grave. Dr. Cameron had routinely hired top staff and had expected the overworked finance office to somehow find the money to pay for them. That had worked, barely, when research grants flowed in. For instance, the Society for the Investigation of Human Ecology paid Rubenstein's entire salary for two years. But with the failure of the society to come forth once more, there began a general withdrawal of research funds from other American foundations. Dr. Cameron would remain forever convinced, in Dr. Roper's words, "that someone had done the dirty on him."

Dr. Cameron was reduced to making cap-in-hand fund-raising trips to Quebec City, dealing with French-speaking administrators who often matched him for arrogance. Hardest of all to bear, for a man who relished being at the seat of power, must have been that his relationship with the secret intelligence world—which had begun in World War II, flourished at Nuremberg, and continued throughout the Dulles years—was finally over. As casually as he had himself often fired an intern or a nurse, Dr. Cameron's services had been dispensed with by the CIA.

Having ascertained from Dr. Cameron's secretary that he was not seeing a patient, Dr. Roper knocked on the chief psychiatrist's door and, without waiting for a response, pushed it open, barely able to control his fury. That July morning in 1964 he had come from a divorce court in Montreal where his marriage had been annulled. He had finally accepted divorce as the "best possible option for us both. I couldn't live with her; Agnes couldn't live with herself."

His compassion for Agnes had turned to disbelief, and then anger when, toward the end of her testimony, she revealed that, as well as consulting Dr. Cleghorn, she had also seen Dr. Cameron. A dumbfounded Dr. Roper listened as Agnes recounted how Dr. Cameron said her husband possessed "this character fault which was showing in his work and, as far as he was concerned, my husband was to get no further in his work and that he had been pushy and aggressive."

Standing before his desk, Dr. Roper confronted Dr. Cameron. Had he said any of that?

Dr. Cameron sat bolt upright, staring at him and saying nothing.

The senior resident felt suddenly sorry for the gaunt-faced man seated behind his vast expanse of desk with a tape recorder before him. Dr. Roper's anger evaporated as quickly as it had surfaced. What did it matter now what Dr. Cameron had said to Agnes? That part of his life was over. Dr. Cameron seemed not only old, but like "a man staring into defeat. There was no confidence about him."

Dr. Cameron broke his silence. "It's the French. They ruin everything. Your lassie. Everything."

He slumped back in his chair, staring at some point over Dr. Roper's head.

The resident turned and walked from the office wondering if Dr. Cameron was ill.

Two days later, on a Thursday morning, Dr. Cameron summoned the entire medical staff to his office at the hour he should have been conducting his rounds. When they were all assembled he stood behind his desk.

"As of this moment I am resigning."

He walked across the room to the door, turned, and surveyed the stunned faces.

"I don't want a party."

It was the last order he gave. By nightfall, Dr. Cleghorn had been appointed to replace Dr. Cameron. His first instruction to the staff was, "Okay. No party. But no wake either. We've all got plenty to do."

The more people pondered what had happened, the less they understood. Dr. Cleghorn confided in his notebook that the resignation was unfathomable. "It was too big, too sudden, too overwhelming, and it meant too much."

Those who had detested Dr. Cameron, and the few who still wholeheartedly admired him on the staff, were united by the surge of emotion that followed his departure. They spoke of the gap he had left, and how his drive and fund-raising skills had made the institute what Dr. Roper called the most exciting frontier post in medicine. Psychiatrists and psychologists who well understood the phenomenon that when a leader departs, myths emerge, nevertheless remembered Dr. Cameron the way they had wanted him to be; there developed a determination among them to dismiss any belittling of what he had done as at best an imperfect understanding of the truth.

Within twenty-four hours Dr. Cleghorn had ordered a halt in all depatterning and psychic driving. The Radio Telemetry Laboratory was closed and the Isolator Chamber dismantled. Rubenstein was among the first of the staff Dr. Cleghorn dismissed. The technician returned to London as mysterious a figure as when he had arrived. Zielinski left soon afterward. Among the doctors who were sacked was Dr. Ataturk, who returned to Ankara to work in a Turkish prison.

No one wondered, on that first evening of his resignation, why Dr. Cameron loaded into his car several box files. They contained all his paperwork relating to M-K-Ultra subproject 68. Nobody remotely suspected that what he had done to his patients had been in the name of the CIA and, ultimately, the government of the United States.

Watching him drive away, filled with her own sadness, Dorothy Trainor felt "the magic was gone."

So was the sorcery.

Dr. Cameron's resignation caused consternation within the Agency. There were several meetings chaired by Dr. Gottlieb to decide what should be done.

William Buckley, who was currently at Langley being briefed for his return to Vietnam, felt the reaction verified that intelligence work was very fragile, complex and above all uncertain. "The resignation created a chess game played against the clock. Everyone knew there were a great number of moves to be made—and only very little time in which to make them. One small mistake could lead to gigantic repercussions."

To avert that possibility meant that Dr. Cameron had to be, in Agency terms, urgently secured.

Dr. Gottlieb decided that none of the Agency's doctors should make any further contact with Dr. Cameron. Instead, Buckley was sent to Lake Placid.

He arrived in the early evening. Buckley was astonished at the physical changes in the psychiatrist. He appeared not only to have shrunk physically, but looked gaunt. Instead of the well-cut suit he had worn when Buckley had brought the Lumumba file to his office, Dr. Cameron wore baggy trousers and a cardigan.

After a preliminary greeting, Buckley was taken to Dr. Cameron's den. After getting their drinks they sat facing each other in armchairs.

Buckley explained he had come for the box files.

Dr. Cameron stared at him for a while before silently rising to his feet and leaving the room. He returned with the files and handed them over. He gave no explanation as to why he had taken them from the institute or where he had kept them. Buckley sensed it would be pointless asking.

He moved to the next part of his assignment, reminding Dr. Cameron he must never reveal his links to the Agency.

Dr. Cameron nodded.

Buckley pressed on, asking why he had resigned.

"Look," said Dr. Cameron, breaking his silence, "what has that to do with the Agency?" The irritation was clear.

Buckley explained that the speculation continued, that Montreal was full of rumors.

Dr. Cameron had shrugged and said he didn't listen to rumors.

Buckley had the distinct impression that part of Dr. Cameron's life was closed.

Suddenly, rattling the ice in his glass, Dr. Cameron had said that it was the French who had forced his hand. "They squeezed my funding. And when you guys pulled out, so did the others this side of the border."

Abruptly rising to his feet, he said there was nothing else to say on the matter.

Buckley pressed. Was that really the only reason?

Dr. Cameron had stared at the agent, flint-eyed and silent, making it plain it was time for Buckley to leave.

On August 15, 1964, Buckley submitted a report marked MOST SECRET to Dr. Gottlieb. It concluded it had been "part ego and part fighting the French" that drove Dr. Cameron to resign. Buckley was, however, certain that the psychiatrist would make no disclosure about his connections with the Agency.

Dr. Gottlieb recommended that no further action be taken. Above all, absolutely no inquiries were to be made of any of Dr. Cameron's patients. That would be looking for trouble.

The feeling at Langley was that a potentially difficult situation had been successfully contained.

Throughout the remainder of 1964 and 1965 Dr. Gottlieb authorized that over a dozen M-K-Ultra subprojects related to the work of Dr. Cameron be placed under a new acronym, M-K-Search. Many of the investigations dealt with means to exploit human weaknesses and destabilize personalities.

Over $30,000 was set aside to maintain a number of safe houses in Washington, New York, Chicago, and Los Angeles. Buckley was among several Agency employees who knew the intention was to use them as places where expendables could be tested under full medical supervision. There was talk of secretly flying in captured Vietcong for terminal experiments.

Dr. Gottlieb approved a $150,000-a-year payment to a Baltimore laboratory to research into microorganisms with the capability to kill. At the same time he signed a further $200,000 authorization for similar research to continue with the Army Biological Laboratory at Fort Detrick, taking care to be sure that the military scientists were unaware of the Baltimore contract. Obsessive secrecy had become another of Dr. Gottlieb's traits. The civilian researchers, according to an Agency document dated September 10, 1965, were to attempt to find a variety of psychochemicals that could induce anything from kinky sex to simulating death by carbon dioxide—in other words, to produce a weapon that could be used to fake a common means of suicide.

With CIA funding, Dr. Cameron's isolator was rebuilt at a laboratory of the National Institutes of Health. But instead of a human, like Madeleine Smith, being incarcerated, lobotomized apes were kept for months in total isolation. Rubenstein's radio telemetry techniques were adapted so that radio frequency energy was beamed into the brains of the already crazed animals. Several were then decapitated, and their heads transplanted on to the bodies of other headless simians, to see whether the energy from the radio frequency could somehow bring the animals back to life. The experiment was known around the Agency as Operation Resurrection.

Nearly $700,000 was spent supporting research on terminal cancer patients and mental defectives at the Georgetown University Hospital in Washington, which long had enjoyed close ties with the Agency. Patients were given a variety of stimulants, depressants, and stress-inducing drugs to see whether the results Dr. Cameron had claimed for psychic driving could be reproduced. They could not.

By early 1966 the lobotomized apes who had survived faced another experiment. They were bombarded with radar waves to the brain to render them unconscious. Autopsies revealed their brain tissue had been literally fried. What a scenario for a horror movie script had to do with intelligence gathering or countersurveillance would remain unexplained.

A new conduit for drug funding was created—the Amazon Natural Drug Company, with a registered office in Iquitos, Peru. It was run by John King, who had headed the Agency's

Western Hemisphere Division until the Bay of Pigs fiasco. He had left with Dulles. Dr. Gottlieb discreetly brought King back into the Agency fold, providing him with a budget of nearly $1 million. King used some of the money to buy a houseboat, stocking it with the best malt whiskey and sailing the backwaters of the Amazon with a small team of Agency botanists who gathered leaves, roots, and barks which, back at the TSS laboratories in Langley, were pulverized into dust and fed to still more apes to see if they were driven mad or killed each other. Many were, and did.

For one of King's voyages, Buckley, by then a seasoned Vietnam jungle operative, was assigned to provide protective firepower against unfriendly natives. He had a small arsenal of weapons, including grenades and a mortar gun. They were never called into play, and his abiding memory was of the slow-speaking King sitting in his canvas chair on the deck, sipping Scotch while the botanists hacked off pieces of the undergrowth. Buckley thought several of the crew were stoned most of the time on yage, a common hallucinogen plant in the jungle. He returned to Vietnam.

On June 30, 1966, Richard Helms became director of Central Intelligence. His arrival on the seventh floor at Langley was greeted with unbounded satisfaction by, among others, Dr. Gottlieb and Buckley.

For the scientist, Helms was the perfect patron, cut from the same unflinching mold as Dulles. Helms made fast decisions and did not hesitate about taking risks or cutting corners, always providing a fall-back position had been fully prepared. Behind his edginess was a genuine warmth for old hands like Dr. Gottlieb. The scientist was satisfied that Helms would head off the overzealous watchdogs in the inspector general's office. Dr. Gottlieb could continue unfettered and untroubled with what he was undoubtedly outstanding at doing—devising new and better ways to disorient and discredit, to maim and kill.

Buckley regarded Helms not only as a superb strategist and analyst, but as someone who still gave off that heady whiff of wartime OSS: swagger and arrogance mingled with well-judged profanity and rule-breaking. In addition, Helms had a lawyer's mind and a street hustler's savvy. Buckley was further impressed by how, at a large meeting to discuss increasing the Agency's involvement in Vietnam, the director had tuned in to a half-dozen conversations at once. Helms's other gift stemmed from his newspaper days. He was an avid reader.

Among his first reading as director was material to refresh his knowledge of the long and complex history of the Agency's search for mind control. While he had been directly involved in many early aspects, such as the covert use of chemical and biological weapons, in recent times he had remained distanced from the M-K-Search subprojects. It did not take Helms long to realize that Dr. Cameron may well have been close to a breakthrough—and that the subprojects could still achieve one.

With his blessing, M-K-Search went into overdrive. Abandoned projects were reactivated. Old ideas were dusted off. The safe houses were placed on full alert to expect Vietcong expendables. A mood of déjà vu excitement permeated TSS.

No one quite knew why, but the emphasis suddenly focused on hypnotism. Dr. Gottlieb had shown a long and strong personal interest in the technique. Largely under his encouragement, twelve years before, in January 1954, Morse Allen—then at his peak within the Agency, though now shunted aside, another victim of Dr. Gottlieb's power plays—had persuaded Dulles that it was possible to hypnotize a person into becoming a killer. After the fiasco in Mexico City, the idea had been written off.

Dr. Gottlieb gave the project a new code name, Operation Spellbinder, and assigned an initial $50,000 to try and actually create a sleeper killer—someone who could be turned loose upon receiving a key word planted in his mind under hypnosis.

A member of the American Society of Clinical and Experimental Hypnosis was recruited. The society was one of the many reputable outside organizations from which the Agency regularly drew experts. The hypnotist was known to the Agency team as "Dr. Fingers," because of the theatrical way he used his hands to put a patient into a trance. He had been selected because his file said he would have no qualms about conducting potentially terminal experiments.

It was explained to him that the intended victim, once more, was to be Fidel Castro. Dr. Fingers and several TSS psychologists had traveled to Miami and had begun to move through the city's large Cuban community, posing as potential employers of the largely jobless immigrants. Likely candidates for Dr. Fingers were invited to a motel room.

The hypnotist had sat the first unsuspecting Cuban before him. Then, with a display of hand waving, he sent the man into a trance. He spoke to him about the need to kill Castro, and that doing so was not a crime but the only way to liberate Cuba. The man nodded. Encouraged, Dr. Fingers then set about planting the key word. When the man heard it and he was in the presence of Castro, instructed the hypnotist, he must immediately kill him. The word was "cigar." To prove how effective he had been, Dr. Fingers ordered the man to imagine he was at Castro's side. Watched by the Agency psychologists, Dr. Fingers uttered the word. Nothing happened. He tried again. Nothing. Finally, perplexed, Dr. Fingers brought the man out of the trance, and once more said "cigar." The man looked at him blankly and said he didn't smoke.

The next man refused to awake on command, and the alarmed Agency men hurriedly drove him back to the Cuban quarter and dumped him on a street corner, still asleep. A third became violent under hypnosis when Castro's name was mentioned and started to smash up the motel room. He was quickly brought out of his trance.

The defeated Agency team returned to Langley.

By late 1966, the dozen M-K-Search projects had cost almost $2 million without any real results. Euphoria turned sour. There were bitter recriminations. Men spent days writing reports to justify failure.

That was undoubtedly a contributing factor to a growing number of resignations within the Agency's scientific community. The most common reason given was an offer of better pay from one of the drug houses the CIA had originally approached for help. Scientists who had worked on pain-inducing projects accepted fat salary increases to research for mass-market painkilling drugs; men who had been solely concerned with terminal work were financially induced to go into the business of discovering new cures for arthritis, lumbago, and heart disease.

Alarmed at what was happening, believing that the brain-drain would leave the Agency naked against its Soviet counterpart in the black art of scientific intelligence, Helms called in an old friend, William Casey. In the intervening years after the lawyer had been introduced to Clover Dulles as an investment expert, Casey had created for himself a formidable reputation, and fortune, through his astute handling of stocks and shares.

Casey traveled to Washington on a November day in 1966. Helms met him for lunch in a suite at the Jefferson Hotel, owned by a mutual friend, Edward Bennett Williams, one of the city's leading attorneys. Over the poached salmon and chablis, Helms outlined the problem. The government's pay structure did not allow him to compete with the salaries offered by the drug companies. What could be done? Casey's solution was simple. The Agency could create a foundation to help its staff with long-term, low-investment loans for such matters as house purchases and college education. He would not only be happy to structure such funding but would like to make a personal contribution of $50,000.

After almost a twenty-year gap, Casey was once more actively associated with the Agency. When he heard the news, Buckley predicted that it was only a matter of time before the big, ambling man would be a permanent sight at Langley.

15

The Oath Breakers

Buckley's reports from Saigon were among the most carefully read at Langley. After processing, they went on the BIGOT list, and often formed part of the National Intelligence Daily (NID), a précis of the Agency's trawl across the world. Only a hundred copies of NID were printed and sent to divisional chiefs in the Agency, the secretaries of State and Defense, and of course the president. The agent's work regularly appeared on an even more restricted position paper, President Johnson's daily intelligence brief, a single page on which appeared only the most important and exclusive items.

What made Buckley's intelligence so fresh and valuable was that, unlike other Agency men who contrived to rarely venture outside Saigon, Buckley repeatedly risked his life to move up the Ho Chi Minh Trail to talk directly to his assets. The Vietcong called his informers American puppets. If discovered or betrayed, Buckley's sources could expect only to be tortured and executed for helping him. Several had.

The sums he paid them were small, as were the favors he arranged on their behalf: a home in the United States for an elderly relative of a village chief, a foreign scholarship for the daughter of a local administrator.

His network was wide: Buddhist monks and Catholic nuns, doctors and nurses, farmers, politicians, and local journalists. They operated from Hanoi in the north all the way down through the towns and villages on either side of the trail. His assets placed listening devices in hundreds of spots in the jungle. These provided a rewarding harvest, such as the time a Vietcong cadre had camped beside a buried device. Their presence had activated the concealed tape recorder, designed to switch on at the sound of a human voice. When the tape was retrieved, it contained information that enabled B-29 bombers to pinpoint and destroy a North Vietnamese arms dump further up the trail. Buckley's human resources regularly produced information that enabled the CIA and the U.S. military to more accurately interpret their own non-clandestine operations of monitoring radio signals and high-level photography of Hanoi and other enemy cities.

On his field trips Buckley increasingly saw and heard a great deal that, on his return to Saigon, made him ask questions and study files. He began to worry more and more about the underlying reason for the American presence in Vietnam. The Johnson administration was paying a high domestic political price for remaining involved in the war. Yet Buckley realized that the growing antiwar demonstrations back home would boil over if the full truth of how the United States was behaving in Vietnam became known.

He had also come to understand that before the Americans there had been the French in a hundred years of occupancy, and before that the Chinese in a thousand years of slavery.

When the North Vietminh came, there had been a general rush of patriotic feeling. Everybody was going to be free. That mood had been everywhere—a great outpouring in all the farms, villages, and jungle towns.

Buckley had listened and understood. That was the way in—into their minds, into their trust.

Using the basic tools of the intelligence man, he had confirmed much. The war would only escalate—and no matter how deeply involved it became, the United States could not achieve a victory. Further, whatever the rhetoric in Washington, the U.S. commitment on the ground in Vietnam was half-hearted.

That could have explained, though in Buckley's eyes never condoned, the atrocities committed by American forces in Vietnam. They were on the increase and far greater than anyone in Washington, including President Lyndon Johnson, probably knew. It was not only the haphazard saturation bombing of civilian targets, or the use of chemicals to defoliate the land, but the senseless brutality of the ground forces that concerned Buckley. American soldiers were regularly raping and pillaging, almost certainly with the knowledge, if not the actual blessing, of their field commanders and, ultimately, their superiors in Saigon.

Even more shocking was that some military doctors were unprotesting witnesses to torture or, on occasion, actually performed torture themselves.

Buckley's professional concern was to establish what use the enemy made of such behavior. By May 1967, he had no doubts. He reported to Langley that American military behavior in Vietnam made it that much easier for the Vietcong to succeed in its widespread campaign of brainwashing the civilian population.

The emotive word—brainwashing—rang alarm bells in the Agency. The specter of the Korean War emerged from its closet. Dr. Gottlieb warned Helms that what the Vietcong succeeded in doing in Vietnam today, they would achieve elsewhere tomorrow. The scientist had stood in the director's office and envisaged a time, not far off, when the whole of Asia would be filled with brainwashed zombies controlled from Hanoi, Peking, or Moscow.

Buckley received a message encoded FLASH—the highest priority in the Agency's chain of communication—ordering him to send all available evidence of Vietcong brainwashing techniques.

The agent would never quite overcome his feeling of distaste at the way the original thrust of his report had been brushed aside and the crosshairs of the target realigned.

On May 15, 1967, he sent a lengthy report describing how the Vietcong used scientists of all disciplines to achieve political indoctrination and that, just as there had been in Korea, so there were camps deep in the Vietnam jungle where the process was carried out. Buckley explained there appeared to be little resistance to such methods among the civilian population. He warned again that U.S. military behavior was playing into the hands of the enemy.

When his report reached Langley it was decoded, and after Dr. Gottlieb had read and initialed it, it was sent to Helms, bearing the stamp: DCI EYES ONLY.

Years later, when everything Buckley had said, done, and written was under scrutiny, some savvy Agency hands said that report marked his fall from being a candidate for a top desk job to someone destined to spend the remainder of his days in the field. They claimed that Helms, encouraged by

Dr. Gottlieb, felt Buckley had gone soft on the Vietnamese. That, they added, would account for Buckley's sudden and unexpected recall to Langley for the role of Agency drudge, somebody to be sent to represent the Agency at military exercises, attend low-level security meetings, or accompany some minor fact-finding mission whose conclusions, like his report, would be pigeonholed.

Shortly after Buckley had sent that report, three physicians arrived in Saigon. Two were Agency doctors. The other was Dr. Lloyd Cotter, a psychiatrist from Pomona, California, and a teaching consultant at the Pacific State Hospital. They made their way to the Bien Hoa Hospital in the suburbs of Saigon. They had come to experiment on patients.

Dr. Cotter, as he later wrote in the *American Journal of Psychiatry*, had chosen to fly halfway across the world to "introduce the latest in the treatment of psychiatric hospital patients."

The hundreds of chronic schizophrenics at Bien Hoa, he had decided, would be suitable, and no doubt more malleable than his California patients, for what he had in mind.

The Agency psychiatrists proposed to conduct totally unethical tests on a number of Vietcong prisoners, who were held in a small, heavily guarded and high-walled compound at the rear of the main hospital.

All three doctors would use Dr. Cameron's trusted standby of massive electroshocks in their experiments.

Addressing the medical faculty on his first morning, Dr. Cotter proclaimed that "the longer a schizophrenic is allowed to remain regressed, the less recovery one can expect."

Meanwhile, Dr. Cotter had set about his latest treatment. Selected patients were told that they could be discharged, but that they must first prove that when they returned home they would be able to support themselves and not become a burden on the hard-pressed economy. To provide that proof they must work, for a few cents a day, in the hospital: cleaning, slopping out, and washing up. Those who refused to work would receive three electroshocks a week until they changed their minds. Dr. Cameron had tried a similar approach in Brandon almost fifty years earlier.

That afternoon the first Vietcong soldier was taken to a treatment room in the compound and strapped to a table. Using a Page-Russell electroshock machine they had brought with them, the Agency doctors gave the man six separate electroshocks. Twelve hours later he received a further series of multiple shocks.

Within a week Dr. Cotter began to see "evident improvement in the behavior of the patients." He was convinced that this was "a result of their dislike or fear of ECT."

In the compound, the Agency psychiatrists continued their work. They were trying to establish whether Dr. Cameron had been correct when he said depatterning could dramatically change a person's ideological views. The Vietcong prisoners had been chosen because they were what the Agency doctors classified as typical cases of Communist indoctrination.

After seven days, when the first soldier had received a further sixty electroshocks, he died.

Meanwhile, Dr. Cotter continued with what would be a busy summer, administering the "several thousand shock treatments as we started about one new ward a week on the program."

After three weeks, the last Vietcong prisoner was dead. The Agency men packed away their machine and flew home. Their complete failure was a further proof that psychiatric technology would still not bend itself totally—at least not to the will of the CIA. More difficult to separate was the dividing line between treatment and torture in what Dr. Cotter did.

One evening in September 1967, the telephone rang in Dr. Cameron's home at Lake Placid. It was Allen Dulles calling from Mississippi. He had been brought out of retirement by President Johnson, first to be a member of the Warren Commission, which had investigated the assassination of President Kennedy, and now to act as a one-man presidential mission to investigate racism in the Deep South.

For the old spymaster, who had once ruled over the murky world of intelligence, where plots involving the murder of heads of state had been commonplace, inquiring into the deaths of a handful of Civil Rights workers was a long step down. Hobbling through the enervating heat of a southern summer, his left leg throbbing once more with gout, a residue of the childhood operation on his club foot, Dulles was also troubled by a failing memory. He just couldn't remember things; he had to write everything down on a little pad he carried in his pocket. The problem was, he sighed on the phone to Dr. Cameron, he couldn't now always read what he'd written.

"Lord, Ewen," he added, "what shall I do? I seem to remember you were pretty good in the memory field."

It was an old friend seeking, perhaps, no more than advice.

William Buckley, who was seconded by the Agency to accompany Dulles on his trip, would remember how the former director put down the telephone in the hotel and repeated, in a slightly puzzled voice, what Dr. Cameron had said.

"He told me to go and get a good doctor. Lord, that's a strange thing for a doctor to say, isn't it, Bill?"

Agency physicians became increasingly desperate in their search for mind control, driven in large measure by what Director Helms had described as "Yuri's credibility factor."

KGB Colonel Yuri Nosenko had defected to the United States in February 1964. He had provided the Agency with mind-boggling information, revealing, for instance, the precise way the KGB had bugged the U.S. Embassy in Moscow. A DDO team had flown to the Soviet capital and reported that Nosenko's revelations were only too true.

In the meantime, the defector gave the Agency a list of over twenty Soviet sleeper agents in the West. The names were passed on to M15 in Britain and other European counterintelligence services, as well as the FBI. Once again, Nosenko proved to be a totally credible source.

The Agency interrogators had questioned him about Lee Harvey Oswald, who had himself been murdered shortly after assassinating President Kennedy.

Nosenko was just as stunningly forthcoming. He said he had inspected the file the KGB had on Oswald—and discovered there was no Soviet involvement with the death of Kennedy. However, what the dossier did strongly suggest was that Oswald could have been a hit man for a consortium of right-wing American millionaires who wanted an increasingly liberal president permanently silenced.

That possibility had caused consternation on the seventh floor at Langley. It begged a thousand questions that, in the end, came down to one: Was Nosenko telling the truth—or was he, after all, a KGB plant?

And that one question had sparked off others. Had Nosenko been allowed to deliberately sacrifice Soviet intelligence assets—to reveal the blueprint of the embassy bugging, to offer so much genuine new information about the KGB's penetration of the West—because he was himself the most daring of all Soviet intelligence ploys? Was he a modern-day human version of the Trojan Horse, sent to wreak havoc within the U.S. intelligence community and government?

Certainly, if what he claimed was true about the Oswald file, then there existed within the United States a secret group so rich and powerful that it had the president killed.

Yet if Nosenko was not a plant, he could be a dupe—a carefully prepared victim of the KGB's own undoubtedly brilliant and Machiavellian machinations. Had Soviet psychiatrists spent years, perhaps, preparing Nosenko to unwittingly become a traitor, while at the same time his superiors deliberately allowed him to have access to material of vital interest to Russia's enemies? Was he the joker in the classical espionage game? Was he real or fake?

The questions came to obsess Helms. He had ample grounds to fear and respect his counterparts in Moscow. They possessed not only a brute cunning, but also a reputation for never repeating a ruse. And there was nothing in the Agency's files to show precedent for such a breathtaking operation by the Soviets. So Nosenko could well be the trump card in the KGB's intelligence deck—played with all the KGB's aplomb.

On March 16, 1964, Helms assigned a special unit of psychiatrists, psychologists, and interrogators to discover the truth. They had spent weeks preparing their ground. Among much else they had read up on Dr. Cameron's work. The files Buckley had recovered from Lake Placid were carefully perused. Then, building on what they had learned, the Agency doctors prepared a program of medical torture to try and establish if Nosenko was lying.

He was driven to an Agency safe house in the western Maryland countryside—coincidentally near the lodge where Frank Olson had been given LSD. Nosenko's new quarters contained two rooms which he was undoubtedly familiar with from his days in the KGB. The first was covered with heavy padded material designed to absorb electrical emissions. Against one wall was a tape recorder and a polygraph machine sophis-

ticated enough to measure minute involuntary responses—
body temperature, the electrical conductivity of the skin, and
pulse rate. It could also calibrate and analyze variations in the
pitch and delivery of words. It was the latest refinement of
the equipment that Jan Zielinski had monitored in the institute basement.

Over a period of hours Nosenko was polygraphed. The
conclusion was that Nosenko could be using sheer willpower
to defeat the lie detector.

Once more he was strapped about the chest. One of the
Agency psychiatrists told Nosenko to breathe deeply—and
the pens had, for a moment, careened quickly over the
paper. The variations were noted. They were a bench mark
for the interrogators.

That night Nosenko had been taken to the second specially
prepared room, which would have reminded him of Russian
interrogation methods. It was almost an exact replica of Dr.
Cameron's isolator—a free-standing cell-like structure in the
basement of the safe house.

After twelve hours Nosenko was brought out of isolation
and again polygraphed. The same questions were put to him
as those Dr. Cameron had asked Madeleine Smith. At exactly
the same point as before in his interrogation, Nosenko was
asked to breathe deeply. The graph measurement was compared with the earlier one—to see if solitary confinement had
affected him. It had not. The Agency team decided that, if
Nosenko was lying, he was doing so superbly.

For a whole month the questions had droned on, alternating with periods of ever-lengthening isolation. The very techniques Dr. Wolff and Dr. Hinkle had posited for Dulles as
those used by the Communists to obtain their confessions
were being used to try and break the defector.

The unfolding strip of sensitized paper was endlessly evaluated. Every night one of the team summarized the spiked
chart and reported personally to Helms.

The director spent many hours sitting in his office—the
only light coming from a lamp—staring at the findings.

Alternately, Helms was convinced that Nosenko was telling
the truth about the Oswald file—a prospect which made the
lines around the director's jaw tighten—or that the KGB man
was a plant. The uncertainty grew more troubling.

After three months, Helms gave an order to increase the

psychological pressure on the Russian. Nosenko was moved to a new cell. A powerful light bulb burned continuously and CIA officers stood guard over him around the clock, removing his last vestige of privacy. He was allowed nothing to read. The labels from his clothes were cut out, and the writing on his toothpaste tube was obliterated. When he tried to occupy his mind by making a chess set from threads he pulled from his sweater, the CIA men dressed him in a nylon running suit.

The polygraphing continued—a relentless charting of Nosenko's steadfast refusal to confess. Instead, the greater the pressure, the more insistent he was that he had only told the truth.

After five hundred days he was placed in a specially built vault, twelve feet square and made of steel. It cost $8,500 to manufacture. On his seven hundredth day in captivity Nosenko finally broke down, weeping and pleading to be believed. The electrodes strapped to his skin confirmed he was not lying. But Helms refused to accept the evidence. The interrogations continued.

New Agency psychiatrists were brought in. They proposed even harsher methods. Nosenko was starved, in the belief that, physically weakened, he would lose his mental strength to resist. He did not. Earphones were strapped to his head and a cacophony of sounds played for up to twenty-three hours at a time—Dr. Cameron's optimum level for psychic driving. Nosenko still insisted he was telling the truth.

Still further techniques, which had so horrified Dr. Monroe and Dr. Wolff on their last visit to Montreal, were brought to bear against Nosenko. He was given LSD, in the same doses that Velma Orlikow had received. He was given drugs that plunged him from manic elation to the depths of depression.

For more than three and a half years—1,277 days—he continued to be medically tortured by the Agency's physicians and interrogators.

Reluctantly, they had come to regard him with awe. If he was lying, he was simply the best liar they had encountered.

Now, in the autumn of 1967, an increasingly angry and divisive debate had erupted within the team—and spread throughout the Agency.

Men like Buckley felt that the CIA physicians had overstepped every ethical boundary. Others, notably in TSS, urged Helms to continue; here was a rare opportunity to solve the wider issue of brainwashing.

In his director's suite, Helms listened for hours to the tapes of Nosenko's interrogations. Over the years the Russian's voice had lost its strong vibrant quality and had become reedy and more animal than human.

But was it the voice of truth—if no longer completely lucid reason—or of deceit?

Helms had begun to look as haunted as Nosenko sounded. On September 21, 1967, the director called another case conference. Throughout the day he listened to argument and counterargument. Finally, Helms ordered that Nosenko be set free. The director went home for dinner—drowning the last vestige of doubt in his brandy.

Out of his converted slave cabin, Dr. Gottlieb sipped a glass of warmed goat's milk. For almost fourteen years he had spearheaded the search for answers to mind control. Finally, the hunt had come full circle in that safe house. Against the backdrop of the Appalachian Mountains, in many ways such a typical American scene, everything that the Communists were reported to have done had been tried out on Nosenko—without success.

After weeks of rehabilitation, during which Buckley was among his minders, Nosenko was given a new identity and settled into American society.

Throughout 1968 Dr. Gottlieb continued to preside over his empire of scientists who still prowled the backwaters of the world seeking new roots and leaves that could be crushed and mixed in the search for lethal ways to kill. In their behavior laboratories the psychiatrists and psychologists continued experimenting.

Once more they had turned back on an earlier line of research—implanting electrodes in the brain. They had done that with animals in the early 1960s, using radio signals to manipulate the chimpanzees into fighting and even killing each other. But no one had then been prepared to go further. Vietnam, with its almost endless supply of expendables, made it possible to see whether such control could be reproduced in humans.

An Agency team flew to Saigon in July 1968. Among them was a neurosurgeon and a neurologist. Their basic research had been conducted on animals at another CIA front organization, the Scientific Engineering Institute near Boston. It had been founded in 1956 under the presidency of Polaroid's Dr. Edwin Land.

In a closed-off compound at Bien Hoa Hospital, the Agency team set to work with three Vietcong prisoners who had been selected by the local station. Each man was anesthetized and the neurosurgeon, after he had hinged back a flap in their skulls, implanted tiny electrodes in each brain.

When the prisoners regained consciousness, the behaviorists set to work. The prisoners were placed in a room and given knives. Pressing the control buttons on their handsets, the behaviorists tried to arouse their subjects to violence.

Nothing happened.

For a whole week the doctors tried to make the men attack each other. Baffled at their lack of success, the team flew back to Washington. As previously arranged in the case of failure, while the physicians were still in the air the prisoners were shot by Green Beret troopers and their bodies burned.

On September 9, 1968, the telephone rang in the office of Dr. Sargant in London, bringing him the news that the day before, Dr. Cameron had died from a heart attack while climbing a mountain near his home. The caller, an editor on the *British Medical Journal* staff, asked Dr. Sargant to write an obituary.

On September 23, 1968, the journal carried his fulsome tribute:

Cameron had great organizing abilities, but he remained a clinician till the end. He always insisted on treating a number of his patients himself personally, rather than sitting too much in his professorial chair, which also carried so many administrative and teaching responsibilities. By this means he always remained aware of the individual patient's problems and was also able to discuss treatment matters from personal experience. He did not always tolerate fools gladly, but supported with all his energies those he felt were doing all they could to improve the treatment of the mentally ill. He refused to follow the craze for psychoanalyses which swept American medical schools after the Second World War. Cameron died as he would have wished, in full and active harness still planning his future research program. Ewen Cameron by his work and example, helped not only many psychiatrists to become much better doctors but directly and indirectly helped hundreds and hundreds of patients, both personally and through those he had inspired and taught.

In Langley, a copy of the obituary was placed in one of the M-K-Ultra/M-K-Search files.

On her fiftieth birthday, September 13, 1967, five days after Dr. Cameron died, Dr. Morrow formally launched a legal action against his estate and the Allan Memorial Institute. She claimed $100,000 damages for unethical treatment. Preparation for the proceedings had consumed her for the past six years. One lawyer after another had listened with mounting disbelief as she described her seventeen days in the institute. At times she had had to remind herself that she had indeed not imagined some of it.

Part of the problem, she realized, was that when she had first consulted a lawyer, there had been considerable gaps in her memory as a result of the electroshocks.

She had obtained a post as a teaching neurologist at the University of Louisville in Kentucky. Between classes, she saw patients in six of the state's mental institutions. She spoke to more lawyers. One after another they had shaken their heads and asked the same question: Where was the proof for all she said had happened? Still she refused to give up—even when her mother and sister looked defeated.

At long last, she found a lawyer prepared to take her case. But he had said that her only hope of winning was to find expert medical witnesses who would testify that she had been the victim of gross malpractice.

It had gradually become clear that her prospect of finding psychiatrists willing to stand up in court and denounce what Dr. Cameron had done would be increasingly difficult. She felt the power of the McGill network had spread far and wide. "If somebody in psychiatry had not been a member, then they knew someone who was. It was a classical brick wall. Cameron had erected it and nobody was going to dismantle it."

She sat in one doctor's office after another, patiently ex-

plaining what had happened, remembering, with the passage
of time, a little more on each occasion what Dr. Cameron had
done. She no longer had to close her eyes to imagine how he
had stood there, needle in hand, ignoring her protests, injecting her, and then electroshocking her. She told her story
quietly and matter-of-factly, the way her lawyer said she
should. But still no doctor in Canada had been prepared to
pit his or her reputation against Dr. Cameron's.

She refused to give up. Finally, through the Law Medicine
Institute at Harvard, she found three American psychiatrists
prepared to describe how standard treatment in a case like
hers was totally different from what Dr. Cameron had done.

When Velma Orlikow learned about Dr. Cameron's death,
she fit it all into what she was continuing to discover from her
own suffering. Her mentor was a Winnipeg psychiatrist, Dr.
Gordon Lambard. She and David had moved back to the
prairie city so that Leslie could attend the University of
Manitoba. Though her husband commuted every week for his
parliamentary duties in Ottawa, she felt her marriage was
loving and secure.

Dr. Lambard, with warmth and gentleness, had helped her
unlock some of the mystery of her own pain and see that
ultimately the experiences that had driven her to seek help
were not unique. The only aspect of her story that singled
her out, he had said, was what had happened to her during
treatment, and Dr. Lambard made no secret of his own anger
over the way Dr. Cameron had mishandled her.

Velma now felt Dr. Cameron was evil. Nothing he had
done, in the end, had helped. The nightmares and the endless hours spent listening to tape recordings that Rubenstein
fetched and carried away—smiling that inane smile and making his foolish jokes—had all been part of a horrendous psychiatric torment, wrapped up in that one sentence: "I only
want to help you, lassie."

For so many wasted years she had believed him. Now, if
not exactly free of mental torment, she could live with it that
much better.

Dr. Roper had also learned to become philosophical. Dismissed by Dr. Cleghorn, he had fought a spirited and long-
running battle for reinstatement. Finally, he and Dr. Cleghorn

attended a meeting of the staff relations committee of the senate of McGill University. Dr. Roper had submitted extensive documentation to show he had been unfairly fired. The whole issue, he argued, revolved around personal conflict between himself and Dr. Cleghorn, a charge that Dr. Cleghorn readily conceded. He had told the committee that "either Dr. Roper or I had to go."

The committee delivered judgment. Though Dr. Roper still held an academic appointment to the university, it had become an empty shell since the termination of his hospital appointment. Dr. Cleghorn had erred in not stating in writing why he did not wish Dr. Roper to be on the institute staff, especially as Dr. Roper's career "was on the line and he was entitled to a fair opportunity to defend it." However, it was not "necessary to conduct a legal trial. Any procedure that satisfies the substantial spirit of fair play is acceptable."

Dr. Roper had shrugged. He had expected no more—or less.

He had opened a private practice close to the institute, and from time to time sent patients there. When he visited the institute to see them, he often found another member on the medical staff had departed—usually among the foreign-born doctors. Dr. Roper sometimes wondered what use they had made of their experience now that all of Dr. Cameron's methods were banned at the institute.

16

The Devil Seekers

Buckley was surprised and delighted to receive an invitation to the Dulleses' 1968 Christmas Eve party. Like everyone else in Washington, he knew that since the trip to the Deep South, the former director had suffered several strokes that had affected his sight and speech. Dulles had been in and out of hospitals. When Buckley had called to inquire how he was, Clover had chattered on that her husband was just fine, and that she was filling his bedroom with fresh flowers every day.

After parking his car under the watchful eyes of young Agency officers who had driven senior CIA men to the party, Buckley was greeted at the door of the Georgetown townhouse by Clover. Sensing his surprise, she said that Allen was in bed with a cold but had insisted that was no reason to cancel the party.

Buckley was struck at Clover's appearance. Close to her seventieth birthday, she was dressed for a woman half her age in a sheath dress and seasonal glitter on her blue-rinse.

Yet, despite her vivaciousness, Buckley sensed a tension among many of the guests.

It was present in the group of aging SIS veterans, standing beside the decorated tree. They kept glancing toward the door, as if they expected Dulles to appear. It was there in the face of Helms, and the Agency's current general counsel, the curt-mannered Lawrence Reid Houston. Both men frequently looked toward the ceiling, to the room above them where Dulles lay in bed.

Though almost six years had passed since President Kennedy had fired Dulles, his reputation still ensured that the cream of the capital's intelligence community had turned up. There were, Buckley guessed, probably more than fifty active spies and counterintelligence men sipping drinks and making polite conversation. A Dulles party, he thought, was still the place to be seen—and a chance to plant or exchange the tidbits of information that made their secret world go round.

Natalie, the Dulleses' cook, had once more provided an exquisite buffet. The theme was Christmas in the sun. There were salads created from exotic African plants, and wines from Australia.

By the fireplace a group had formed and were singing carols.

Finally, Jeanie Houston asked their hostess whether there was too much noise for Allen.

"No. He's fine," Clover replied, moving quickly to the door to greet still more guests.

Jeanie Houston turned to her husband. "Larry, I'm concerned. I think you should go upstairs and see how Allen is."

Houston nodded.

Helms, pleading he had to attend several more parties, including one at the White House, made his farewell.

Buckley thought that nowadays the director looked increasingly grim. Perhaps this time the Washington rumor mill was telling the truth—that President-Elect Richard Nixon had already made it clear to Helms that he wanted better results from the Agency's intelligence-gathering operations in Vietnam. Watching Helms depart, Buckley was reminded that Washington could be the meanest and loneliest town in the world for those whose careers stood or fell during a change in the Oval Office. But Helms was tough; he had adapted with the changes in intelligence business. He knew all about harnessing technology; as he had once said to Buckley, "We can spy, not by just looking up their assholes, but by peering down on their heads."

Houston returned to the living room and, ignoring Clover, cut a path through the guests to Jim Hunt. He was one of Dulles's oldest friends, as well as a long-serving case officer with the Agency.

Houston whispered urgently to Hunt. The two men went upstairs.

Several guests looked pointedly at Clover. Smiling fixedly, followed by Jeanie Houston, she left the room. Buckley thought how old and vulnerable Clover suddenly looked. Standing in the hall at the foot of the stairs, he heard raised voices from Dulles's bedroom.

"God Almighty, Allen's sick, Clover." Houston sounded exasperated.

"It's just a cold, Larry. Really it is."

"Nonsense! He's sick as a dog. Maybe dying." Hunt's concerned rumble carried clearly from above.

Buckley heard Clover's pleading reply. "Don't be so dramatic. He saw the doctor only this morning. He's only got the flu. Stop worrying me like this. He's been getting these spells after his last stroke."

"Jesus, Clover! This is not just a spell! Can't you see how ill he is?" Hunt was almost shouting.

From the living room, the carol singing was at full bellow.

Hunt appeared at the top of the stairs. Pointing at Buckley, he shouted, "Shut those goddamn people up. And call an ambulance. Tell them it's urgent."

Senior Agency men looked at him. One of the SIS veterans called out, "What the hell's happening? We gotta right to know."

"Allen's sick. We're moving him to the hospital." Houston came bounding down the stairs, his voice adding authority, his manner brooking no argument.

The guests started to drink up and head for the street.

Clover stood in the hallway, endlessly repeating, "Thank you for coming. Allen will be sorry to have missed you."

Jeanie Houston led her back upstairs.

The last guests were driving away when an ambulance arrived. Two male attendants ran up the stairs with a stretcher. Buckley followed them.

They found their way into the bedroom, blocked by a now suddenly resolute Clover. "No stretcher," she repeated firmly. "Absolutely no stretcher!"

Buckley remembered that Clover had once explained that the Dulles family detested stretchers—they represented a degree of helplessness that, for a Dulles, was unthinkable.

Motioning the attendants to stand back, Buckley went into the bedroom.

Dulles had somehow found the strength to push back the bedclothes and sit on the edge of the mattress. He tried to stand, failed, and made a second attempt, once more falling back on the sheet, gripping the bedhead with one hand to support himself.

Between them Houston and Hunt helped Dulles to his feet and half-carried him out of the bedroom and down the stairs. In the hallway the ambulance men took over. Draping Dulles's arms around their shoulders, they hurried him to the ambulance.

Clover followed, once more helpless and uncertain.

"You'd better go with him," said Hunt brusquely.

"But what about Natalie?" Clover began.

"The hell with her. Get in the ambulance!" Houston said gruffly.

Clover did as the lawyer bid.

Jeanie Houston came running out of the house with a hat and coat for Clover. She was too late. The ambulance, siren wailing, was already down the street.

Five weeks later, on January 29, 1969, Allen Welsh Dulles died. Buckley was unable to attend the funeral. He was on another low-level chore.

Beginning in 1969, a team of Agency scientists from the Office of Research and Development (ORD) ran a number of bizarre and potentially far-reaching experiments in mind control. ORD had replaced TSS as the Agency's flagship for the unorthodox. The most innovative and daring doctors had been transferred to ORD, and a number of young consultants from civilian medical research laboratories had been recruited. They were attracted to the Agency by the fringe benefits William Casey had designed to stop the flow of talent from Langley. The ORD team included chemists, biologists, and general physicians from the Army Chemical Corps.

Dr. Gottlieb had persuaded Helms to authorize $150,000 as an initial grant. Asked to think up a suitable acronym behind which to hide the funding and its purpose, the senior scientist had not hesitated. It would be called Operation Often. Operation Often's roots could be traced back to the research Dr. Cameron had approved in trying to establish links between eye coloring, soil conditions, and mental illness. Working his way through the files Buckley had brought back from Lake Placid, Dr. Gottlieb came across the uncompleted research, and was again struck that, as in so many areas of interest to the Agency, Dr. Cameron could have been on the verge of a breakthrough in exploring the paranormal. Operation Often was intended to take over the unfinished work, and go beyond—to explore the world of black magic and the supernatural.

The ORD team first tried to create a super virus by exposing a range of already deadly bacteria to ultraviolet light—a logical extension of the soil experiments conducted at the Allan Memorial Institute. While that work continued—and looked promising—ORD psychiatrists and behaviorists had set out across the country, visiting palmist parlors, fairground fortune-teller booths, and in the larger cities the well-appointed offices of the psychics who served the rich and powerful.

The Agency men generally introduced themselves as researchers from the Scientific Engineering Institute. A number of clairvoyants were persuaded to become consultants to a vaguely defined educational research program.

It became a common sight around the institute to see long-bearded men or gypsy-garbed women talking earnestly to preppy, gray-suited behaviorists about how to identify and interpret lifelines and distinguish the different bumps on a person's head. An astrologer from San Francisco who specialized in delineating character through the color of a subject's eyes was brought to the institute and carefully questioned before he was unmasked as a fraud. However, he still received his travel expenses and fee. Undaunted, the CIA continued to search for ways to use the paranormal in spying and counterintelligence.

In October 1970, the possibility of stationing psychics at strategic points around the Soviet Bloc was considered. The intention was to use their powers to tune in to places like East Berlin, Warsaw, and Moscow, and see what vibrations were picked up. The proposal was abandoned because it was discovered it would take years for the psychics to become fluent in Russian.

A medium was taken to the United Nations building in New York and asked to wander through its public areas accompanied by an Agency operative equipped with a concealed camera. Whenever the clairvoyant felt himself in the presence of an evil type of personality, he was to inform the operative. In the weeks that particular experiment ran, not a single evil type was discovered.

The Agency went to considerable efforts to get the palm prints of that old bogeyman, Fidel Castro. These were studied by the palmists who were not told to whom the prints belonged. Castro was variously described as a born leader, a deeply religious man, perhaps a person high in the church, possibly a future Pope, and a male with strong homosexual leanings. The latter tidbit was passed along to the Political Psychological Division and incorporated into the Cuban's psycho-profile.

By May 1971, Operation Often had on its payroll three professional astrologers. Each received $350 a week plus expenses, to cover what they claimed would be their loss of regular earnings. Their task was to predict the future.

The astrologers sat for hours in soundproof booths in the Scientific Engineering Institute and read a wide selection of newspapers and magazines. They extrapolated items that psychically alerted them. They taped what came into their minds about how some particular event or happening would develop.

There were interesting predictions. One astrologer forecast that President Richard Nixon would win a second term, but would experience severe political damage during it—though the seer had not mentioned Watergate. Another foresaw that the Vietnam War would end in disaster for the United States— not a difficult piece of forecasting for a conflict that was now costing $25 billion a year, and with American dead approaching 40,000. Nearer to home, the astrologers all saw an increase in serious crime, while internationally the highjacking of airplanes would become the single greatest threat to travelers.

Asked by the behaviorists to produce a psycho-profile of a typical skyjacker, the palmists settled for a young, dispossessed Cuban type of personality—apparently a youth who was impetuous and disillusioned enough with the United States to be prepared to risk his life to hijack a plane to the island.

The psychics were asked for suggestions to combat the hijackers. Among the more memorable ones were that airline stewardesses should be trained to seduce hijackers; passengers should be made to travel in their undergarments, with an airline cloak to allow them their modesty; and before each flight the pilot should play through the aircraft public address system the Cuban national anthem and arrest anyone who stood up. The only suggestion the Agency passed on to the airline industry was that every pilot should carry approach maps for José Marti Airport in Havana.

By early 1972, Operation Often had taken on two more palmists, both Chinese-Americans, to probe still further how hand-reading could be adapted to intelligence work.

The Agency behaviorists already knew that different cultures produced varying personalities. Each society had a particular vision of masculinity and femininity, of rights and obligations. The question the palmists were asked to answer was how much of this could be discerned from palm lines.

The hand-readers set to work. Posing as educational psychologists, they visited a number of ethnically variable communities, traveling north to Alaska to study Eskimos and south to New Mexico to look at the hands of Indians.

While they were about their business, Operation Often went deeper, into demonology. In April 1972, an oblique approach was made to the monsignor in charge of exorcisms for the Catholic archdiocese of New York. He flatly refused to cooperate. Undaunted, the Agency behaviorists approached Sybil Leek, a Houston sorceress, who cast spells with the help of a pet jackdaw called Hotfoot Jackson. With the bird perched on her shoulders, Mrs. Leek gave the "two very nice gen'l'men" from Washington a fast course on the current state of black magic in the United States: four hundred regular covens operated by five thousand initiated witches and warlocks, who formed the low-profile apex of a prediction industry that supported 10,000 full-time fortune-tellers and 200,000 part-timers, as well as a growing publishing business in tarot cards and factories that produced a widening range of anti-Christian tokens. Satan was not only alive, but thriving in the United States.

To corner him for the Agency, it was recognized at Langley that the Devil must be made respectable. Working through conduits, the Scientific Engineering Institute helped fund a course in sorcery at the University of South Carolina. Two hundred and fifty students enrolled. The scientists of Operation Often studied carefully the results of classes devoted to fertility and initiation rites and raising the dead.

Concurrent with those investigations, ORD had taken up the challenge of brain implants. The failure at the Bien Hoa Hospital in Saigon was rationalized: the team had been in too much of a hurry, and had worked under far from ideal conditions; the proximity of a full-scale war was not the place for such delicate experiments.

Before setting up their own program, the ORD scientists evaluated the results achieved by Dr. Jose Delgado, a Yale psychologist. He had faced a charging bull, fitted with electrodes in its brain, and with no other protection save the small black box in his hands, Dr. Delgado had deliberately goaded the bull by activating the implant that provoked the animal to become further enraged. Then, with the bull almost upon him, the psychologist had pressed another button. The animal promptly stopped in its tracks, the result of a signal transmitted to the electrode implanted in the part of the bull's brain that calmed it.

Dr. Delgado freely admitted that his method of remote mind control was still crude and not always predictable. But Dr. Gottlieb and the behaviorists of ORD shared the psychologist's vision that the day must come when the technique would be perfected for making not only animals, but humans respond to electrically transmitted commands.

Dr. Robert G. Heath, a neurosurgeon at Tulane University, had brought that prospect closer through his experiments with electrical stimulation of the brain (ESB) to arouse his patients sexually. Dr. Heath had actually implanted 125 electrodes in the brain and body of a single patient—for which he claimed a world record—and had spent hours stimulating the man's pleasure centers.

Like Dr. Delgado, the neurosurgeon concluded that ESB could control memory, impulses, feelings, and could evoke hallucinations as well as fear and pleasure. It could literally manipulate the human will—at will.

Late in June 1972, Dr. Gottlieb had jigged back and forth on the carpet of the director's office, and his carefully controlled stammer had surfaced as he enthused that at long, long last, here was the answer to mind control, that ESB was the key to creating not only a psychocivilized person but an entire psychocivilized society—a world where every human thought, emotion, sensation, and desire could be actually controlled by electrical stimulation of the brain.

The possibilities, said Dr. Gottlieb, were far beyond the neurological masturbation of the pleasure centers. Not only could a rampaging bull be stopped in full charge, but humans could finally be programmed to attack and kill on command.

Another step forward was about to be taken in the Agency's search for the "Manchurian Candidate."

Helms agreed that research into ESB should come under the direct control of Dr. Stephen Aldrich. A former medical director of the Agency's Office of Scientific Intelligence, Dr. Aldrich was widely regarded among his ORD colleagues as a pathfinder. From dawn to dusk he spent his time speculating, theorizing, and experimenting with the possibilities of harnessing ESB for intelligence work. Using the latest computer technology, he developed Rubenstein's earlier work on radio telemetry, and the unfulfilled dream the English technician had shared with Dr. Cameron of a world of electrically monitored people became that much more of a reality.

In the safe house where Yuri Nosenko had been brutalized, Dr. Aldrich supervised infinitely more sophisticated research. Included in the equipment he used was a piece not even Orwell had dared invent for his *1984*. Called the Schwitzgebel Machine, the boxlike construction had been developed by Ralph K. Schwitzgebel in the Laboratory of Community Psychiatry at Harvard Medical School. His brother, Robert, had subsequently modified the prototype so that the final product was something Rubenstein would have taken pride in; indeed, in many ways it resembled a smaller version of the cumbersome transducer the technician had built in the Montreal basement.

The Schwitzgebel Machine consisted of a Behavior Transmitter-Reinforcer (BT-R) fitted to a body belt that received from and transmitted signals to a radio module. In the official description of the machine the module was "linked to a modified missile-tracking device which graphs the wearer's location and displays it on a screen."

The Schwitzgebel Machine—its very name suggested something designed to make people enjoy their servitude—was able to record all physical and neurological signs in a subject from up to a quarter of a mile—an impressive improvement over the distance between the Grid Room and the cubbyhole where Dr. Cameron had monitored Madeleine Smith and other patients.

By August 1972 other proponents of the Schwitzgebel Machine were voicing their enthusiasm. They were led by Professor Barton L. Ingraham, a criminologist at the University of Maryland, and Gerald W. Smith, professor of criminal studies at the University of Utah.

In a joint paper, Ingraham and Smith painted a vivid scenario of how the machine could be used to keep track of known criminals. He or she would be fitted with a brain implant and would be tracked, with the psychological data being transmitted from the implant to the machine. The machine, using probabilities, would come to a decision and alert the police if necessary.

Adapting that frightening vision of tomorrow's world formed part of ORD's concept of the New Jerusalem of intelligence.

On September 20, 1972, the station chief in the U.S. Embassy in Ottawa reported to the directorate of operations in Langley that Dr. Morrow was still actively pursuing her legal action against the Allan Memorial Institute and Dr. Cameron's estate. The intelligence officer regularly reviewed what, if any, progress Dr. Morrow had made. Previously his reports on the matter had gone unremarked. For some reason— Buckley thought it the surprise of one of the keen young officers who regularly passed through the DDO that after so long and so many setbacks Dr. Morrow was still pursuing her claims—the Ottawa report had been sent to the seventh floor.

Within hours the order came winging back to the DDO that a full check should be run on the status of every patient known to have been used in Dr. Cameron's research. Was there any way—any way at all—that what had been done to them could be traced back to the Agency? Six weeks later, on November 15, the DDO reported to the director that, as far as it could establish, there was no way the Agency could be implicated—except through the material in its own archives.

On December 10, 1972, Helms ordered Operation Often— all of it—cancelled. The probe into the occult, Dr. Aldrich's work, almost a score of active subprojects, were halted forthwith. In a terse, one-line memo—marked READ. DESTROY— the director offered Dr. Gottlieb no explanation. The senior scientist was mortified. He made several trips to the seventh floor to argue, and finally plead. Helms remained unmoved.

Buckley—once more back in the field, this time working in Cambodia—would recall that, on one of his visits to Langley around that time, "there was just a very unhappy air about ORD. Like everyone was in mourning."

Early in January 1973, Dr. Gottlieb resigned from the Agency. No effort was made by Helms to persuade him to stay. In the days before his departure, and acting on the director's order, Dr. Gottlieb shredded records of M-K-Ultra/M-K-Search.

On February 2, 1973—again without an explanation—President Nixon replaced Helms as director. In a farewell luncheon with his successor, James R. Schlesinger, Helms was asked if there was anything in the Agency's recent history that could cause problems.

Helms replied, "Nope. Not a thing."

Several floors below where the two men sat in the executive dining room were one hundred and thirty boxes in the archives, which contained incriminating material that Dr. Gottlieb, inexplicably, had failed to destroy.

Schlesinger soon realized he had inherited an Agency that had been on the rampage, riding roughshod over the Constitution and virtually acting as President Nixon's private security force. Since May 12, 1969—when members of Division D, the specialized unit that burgled and placed listening bugs, had planted seventeen wiretaps in the offices and homes of White House aides and newsmen following publication of the secret bombing of Cambodia—the Agency had routinely operated outside the law.

It had become involved in domestic intelligence-gathering, spying against Americans opposed to the Vietnam War. After *The New York Times* published the Pentagon Papers in 1971, fed to it by Daniel Ellsberg, the Agency provided backup support for a team of burglars, supervised by Howard Hunt and G. Gordon Liddy, to break into the offices of Ellsberg's psychiatrist looking for evidence that could discredit the newspaper's informant.

Time and again the Agency had carried out other break-ins—what were called surreptitious entries in the files marked TOP SECRET that Schlesinger had found in his office safe. It interfered with the mail and, after five men were arrested for breaking into the Democratic headquarters in the Watergate Building in Washington, the Agency did everything it could to hamper the FBI's investigation.

Schlesinger realized why Helms had been consigned to the other end of the world as U.S. ambassador to Iran. Removing him was part of a containment operation that the new director suspected had the full knowledge of the President.

Coming into office, the director had been presented by John D. Ehrlichman, assistant to the president for domestic affairs, with a thick file on the latest supposed Communist infiltration in the United States. The Communists were accused, among other things, of being behind a grave-diggers strike in New York, a walkout by air traffic controllers, and an attempt to undermine the morals of young Americans by getting teachers to introduce a more realistic sex education program. The trail of all this led back to Moscow, charged the White House document. Who else but the KGB would have encouraged the foundation of the Women's International Terrorist Conspiracy For Hell (WITCH), an aggressive feminist movement? Who else but the Soviet Union was behind the campaign for abortion on demand? Who else was behind the thousand bomb threats New York received every week? Who else stood to benefit from the call to revolution by Angela Davis, a daughter of the black middle class, and the Soledad brothers, three black militants not actually related to each other, but who were the torchbearers for violent action against the police? Who else but Moscow?

Schlesinger asked the Directorate of Operations to investigate what, if any, evidence existed to substantiate the White House allegations.

The file also contained claims that the Russian doctors had tortured captured Americans in North Vietnam and that the Patrice Lumumba Friendship University in Moscow had begun an even more intensive training of Third World physicians in the art of medical torture. There were allegations that the KGB had created what were described as torture centers in Bulgaria and East Germany, where opponents of communism were subjected to a wide range of medical torture.

Alarmed by the accusations of medical malpractice, Schlesinger ordered urgent checks to be made, only to discover that, while the charges were almost certainly true, they were hardly new. Station chiefs had reported them on several previous occasions.

Ironically, the White House file focused the director's attention on the Agency's own past record.

On February 27, 1973, Schlesinger sent an order to all Agency employees. The mimeographed memo—marked CON-

FIDENTIAL, the CIA's lowest form of classification—requested that the director's office should be informed at once about any instances where Agency officials had performed improper or illegal acts.

Career officers, who already regarded Schlesinger as a meddling outsider, were outraged. Some felt they were being asked to inform and spy on each other, to behave as if they worked for some banana republic security force rather than still the most powerful intelligence organization in the world.

A scientist with ORD sent the director a copy of one of Dr. Gottlieb's memos on Operation Often. "Our operation officers, particularly the emerging group of new senior officers, have shown a discerning care and realize that, in addition to moral and ethical considerations, there are extremely sensitive security considerations."

The message to Schlesinger was clear: Back off.

The scientist was promptly fired. There would be no backing off, and anyone who refused to comply with the director's command could also expect to be dismissed.

Within days, Schlesinger's desk was covered with piles of paperwork that extended back to the death of Frank Olson and Operation Artichoke. The catalogue of misdeeds ran from Korea to Vietnam. The paperwork mounted daily, keeping pace with the unraveling Watergate crisis.

Schlesinger grew increasingly stunned at the scope of the Agency's previous misbehavior. Nothing had been too great or small, too risky or vile to try. Blackmail, bribery, sexual harassment, and violence of all kinds, often ending in murder, had been commonplace. It was genuinely horrific. Yet somehow, in all the disinterring, not a word emerged about what had happened in Montreal.

Schlesinger knew there was absolutely no way that what had become known around the seventh floor as "the family jewels"—the ever-mounting evidence covering years of illegal and unethical behavior by Agency employees—could remain undiscovered. Who knew what else was squirreled away? What other incriminating paperwork was buried in some university campus office or stashed in a filing cabinet in one of the drug houses the Agency had used? The whole job had become a nightmare for Schlesinger.

On May 22, 1973, the DDO reported that it had been unable to establish any of the items in the White House file about Russian involvement in U.S. domestic problems. That night the President delivered a 4,000-word statement on national television flatly denying any knowledge of the Watergate burglary or cover-up. But he did admit that he had approved the CIA wiretap of reporters and his own aides. That, he added solemnly, had been done solely on the grounds of national security.

Schlesinger was stupefied. He had been given no warning that the president intended to publicly implicate the Agency. The director began to feel he should resign.

Instead, on July 2, after only five months in the job, President Nixon suddenly appointed Schlesinger as Secretary of Defense, a post where he would have his hands full fighting with Secretary of State Henry Kissinger. There would be no time for the ex-director to ask any more awkward questions of his staff about the Agency's past that could only further embarrass the administration.

For two months the president hesitated before appointing William Colby as director of Central Intelligence. The move was welcomed in the increasingly dispirited Agency. Behind his deferential smile, the tiny and trim Colby was hard-nosed and realistic.

It took him a week to appraise the situation. Seated primly at his desk, his World War II military-issue spectacles perched on the bridge of his nose, he did what he excelled at doing— digesting vast quantities of information with speed, the way he had done to become Phi Beta Kappa in his Princeton class of '40 and to obtain a Columbia Law degree in 1947. Then, with the ruthlessness that had allowed him to kill Germans in wartime France, Colby set about his work.

He decided that his priorities and loyalties lay with the *office* of the president—not necessarily the current incumbent. After that came the Agency. No one, or nothing else, ultimately mattered. There was, he also realized, no way of diverting the pack beginning to howl along the trail to Langley. But he was not going to make it easy for them. Omerta, the old code of silence that Dulles had operated, still meant a great deal to Colby.

He let it be known that if there were any more leaks, those responsible would answer personally to him—and that included former Agency employees. He was polite and never raised his voice. But the menace he conveyed was very clear.

He continued to prepare the Agency's defenses. Box after box of files were reviewed and explanations prepared.

In the meantime, Watergate bought Colby time. On October 10, 1973, Vice-President Agnew resigned. Ten days later, there was a further spate of resignations and firings from the Nixon administration.

Colby worked hard to distance the Agency from what, by July 27, 1974, had become inevitable. And soon after, the president told the nation he was resigning. The next day, Vice-President Gerald R. Ford became president.

That night he sent for Colby and asked to be fully briefed on the problems ahead.

Colby spelled it out. All of it—including what had happened in Montreal.

President Ford shook his head. "My God," he muttered. "Oh, my God."

The trigger, when it was pulled, was done so by an old Washington nemesis, *The New York Times*. On a December morning in 1974, Colby was among those who awoke to find that the *Times* carried a broad account of the Agency's illegal activities during the Johnson and Nixon administrations. There was a hint that the rot went even further back. To curb the national outcry, President Ford appointed a commission, chaired by Vice-President Nelson A. Rockefeller, to investigate the allegations. Its eight members included the governor of California, Ronald Reagan.

The commission's brief included examining CIA biomedical research and suggesting ways of ensuring any proven malpractice could never happen again.

In California, between his visits to Washington—he would attend only ten of the commission's twenty-six hearings—Governor Reagan was using his considerable charm to try and maneuver the Legislature to secretly finance a scheme that, when he had first heard of it, impressed him.

The governor, like most Americans, was obsessed with the violence that permeated the nation. Serious crime had reached unprecedented levels.

The answer, at least for California, its governor believed, was the one proposal by one of the state's most eminent psychiatrists, Dr. Louis Jolyon West, chairman of the department of psychiatry at the University of California at Los Angeles and director of its Neuropsychiatric Institute. In the early 1960s, when he had been at the University of Oklahoma, Dr. West had run an LSD research program financed by the CIA.

He had proposed to the governor the creation of a financially well-endowed multidisciplinary Center for the Study and Reduction of Violence. Within its confines, doctors would explore all types of violent behavior, what caused it, and how it could be detected, prevented, and treated.

It was planned to site the Center on a converted missile site in the Santa Monica Mountains. The psychiatrist proposed that the Center deal with persons who displayed antisocial and impulsive aggression. Its laboratories would be devoted to genetic, biochemical, and neurophysiological studies of "violent individuals, including prisoners and hyperkinetic children."

Other research would concentrate upon the "pharmacology of violence" and the best way to use "anti-violence inhibiting drugs."

One of the tried, though far from proven, techniques of the CIA that Ronald Reagan was helping to investigate in Washington was, in California, being given a warm welcome by him. He eagerly shared Dr. West's conviction that one day the behavior of all persons with violent tendencies—no one had yet decided the criteria for measuring the degree of violence—would be monitored by the staff at central control stations presiding over screens producing signals from the implants. The first indication of an abnormal impulse could indicate the onset of violence. Attendants would rush with suitable psychotropic drugs to overpower the person. The system would be expensive to operate, but Governor Reagan visualized the day when thousands of his fellow Californians would be permanently monitored in this way.

Among those who was considered to work at the Center was Leonard Rubenstein. Two South American doctors who had worked at the institute under Dr. Cameron had also been targeted, one to run the center's shock room—which would operate on a twenty-four-hour basis, seven days a week—and the other to assist in the center's psychosurgical operating suite, where the very latest techniques in lobotomy would be used. The doctors were currently employed in detention centers in Paraguay and Chile.

Despite his considerable persuasive techniques, Governor

Reagan failed to convince the California legislature to go ahead with Dr. West's proposal.

However, when the Rockefeller Commission report was issued, the governor provided a clear dissenting voice to the damning conclusion that the CIA had conducted a highly unethical program to "study possible means for controlling human behavior by irresponsibly exploring the effects of electroshock, psychiatry, psychology, sociology, and harassment techniques."

Governor Reagan, in defending the Agency, claimed that "in any bureaucracy of about sixteen thousand people there are going to be individuals who make mistakes and do things they shouldn't do."

Later, over dinner with William Casey, the governor had vowed that if he was ever elected to the presidency, he would make sure that the CIA would never have to fight with one hand tied behind its back. Instead, he would give the Agency its freedom to carry the war to the enemy—wherever it was, and whoever it might be, and by any means the Agency chose.

Book Three

———

BEYOND
THIS TIME

Forty years after Nuremberg, torture with no pretense of research has become, in many countries, a common instrument of government. Modern medical knowledge and technology, and occasionally medical practitioners, are implicated in this "epidemic" of torture. Because torture is applied to the body and ravages the physical and psychological constitution of its victims, people with special skills in affecting the body and mind may become accomplices in the spread of this malignancy. There are many levels of cooperation in torture: the unwilling participant can be duped or coerced to join in torture; the willing participant engages in torture quite deliberately.

> —Albert R. Jonsen, professor of ethics in medicine at the University of California, San Francisco, and Leonard A. Sagan, former head of the Medical Committee of Amnesty International (USA), in "The Breaking of Bodies and Minds: Torture, Psychiatric Abuse and the Health Professions," a report by the American Association for the Advancement of Science, 1985.

There are people who will never understand why intelligence services ask doctors to help. They are the people who do not understand there is a gap between what is done in the name of lawful government and what is committed in the name of terrorism. It's really very complicated and unless you are in the business, the distinction is not easy to grasp.

> —William Buckley, then an officer in the Directorate of Operations of the Central Intelligence Agency, in conversation with the author; Rome, November 12, 1983.

17

Onward, Ever Onward

That promise of a free hand formed part of the continuous debate William Casey conducted since President-Elect Ronald Reagan offered him the post of director of Central Intelligence on Tuesday, November 18, 1980. There were several reasons for Casey's hesitation.

First, the offer came late in the day, when most of the plum jobs in the new administration were already filled. Caspar Weinberger was the nominee for Secretary of Defense; Alexander M. Haig, Jr., was down for Secretary of State. Casey had wanted the State post. He believed he possessed the experience and background to leave his mark on either foreign or military affairs. After running a model election campaign for Reagan—all the more spectacular because he had been the outsider among the Californians—Casey had expected no less in return than a top seat in the Cabinet.

Now, in the midst of the Iran hostage crisis, the only exception in a sorry debacle had been the CIA. It had managed to get a handful of agents into Tehran to prepare the ground for a rescue. The knowledge that the Agency had behaved with courage and honor had stirred deepseated memories in Casey of those days in World War II when he had run OSS teams into the very heart of Hitler's Berlin.

Casey knew that Colby had lasted until January 30, 1976, grimly obeying the orders of congressional committees to hand over secrets about his predecessor's involvement with Watergate. For reasons that were never made absolutely clear, least of all by Colby, he had given the Justice Department information that had led to Richard Helms facing a perjury charge for not testifying fully and completely about CIA covert action in Chile while he was director. Helms had been fined $2,000 and drew a two-year jail sentence—suspended.

Colby had become the leper of Langley—shunned and avoided for turning in Helms, who had lived by the old Dulles code: "We are the silent service and silence begins here."

After Colby had come George Bush, arriving on January 31, 1976, and departing three hundred and fifty-six days later, on January 20, 1977, to become Reagan's running mate.

Bush was followed, on March 9, 1977, by Stansfield Turner. A retired four-star admiral, a Rhodes Scholar, and one of the Navy's brightest strategists, he saw his role as steering the Agency away from a jagged coastline of compounded irresponsibilities stretching all the way from Korea to Vietnam and Watergate.

What happened in Montreal and elsewhere in Agency-sponsored gross medical malpractice had genuinely shocked Turner. It was a horror story, he said repeatedly, a godawful horror story, with Dr. Frankenstein cavorting in and outside the Agency. That must never happen again.

As director, he made his decisions as he had done for many years, after reading the weekly Christian Science lesson. The faith of his mother had carried him through almost as many personal tragedies as Dulles had endured. Turner's father had committed suicide in the wake of the 1929 stock market crash. His only brother had died in a car accident in the Depression. Only God could have begun to explain why he had been given so much pain, and since then the Almighty had guided his every decision. God was very much in Turner's mind when he started to deal with his inheritance at Langley.

Turner had taken a long and careful look at all the evidence Colby had stockpiled in his office—including some that it was a relief to see had not leaked into the committee rooms of Congress.

The vast treasure trove of past misdeeds was sealed and secured as anything could be in Langley and consigned to the depths of the archives. Each file was marked TO BE OPENED ONLY ON AUTHORITY OF DCI.

Turner had ordered the code of omerta to be urgently reactivated. What had been done could not be undone, but it would no longer be made public. That holy writ ran throughout the corridors of Langley. But forgiveness could only be bought at a price. Over a hundred men lost their jobs in what became known as Turner's Halloween Massacre of 1977.

The days of cowboy operations were over, Turner told William Buckley on the agent's return from Angola. Buckley had been sent to lend covert support to Jonas Savimbi, who was fighting Angola's Marxist regime in the bush of southwest Africa. Congress had ordered the Agency to cease its involvement as part of the general post-Watergate cleanup. But the director had reminded Buckley they could still do their work without "behaving like crazies."

Casey thought along the same lines and if he accepted Reagan's offer, Turner would have to go. That was the way of things. But did he want the job?

The matter continued to preoccupy Casey from the time he rose—usually around three in the morning—until he went to bed, around ten o'clock. He was long used to nineteen-hour days, breaking them up with rounds of golf and leisurely lunches and dinners.

Gradually, as he knew it would, the decision focused on a key question. He would have to become a visible and accountable figure to, among others, the Senate Select Committee on Intelligence; the National Security Council (NSC); the National Foreign Intelligence Board (NFIB); and the President's Foreign Intelligence Advisory Board (PFIAB), a jury of fourteen carefully chosen citizens who monitored intelligence activities for the president.

Casey hated watchdogs; even though he had himself been one, as one-time head of Nixon's Securities and Exchange Commission. His spell at the SEC had led to a perjury accusation—a spinoff from the endless investigations into the ramifications of Watergate. He had been accused of misusing his office to help the cover-up. In the end, as Casey had always predicted, it came to nothing. But the scar tissue never fully healed, any more than the public humiliation which had followed his one decision to actually run for elected office, seeking the 1968 Republican congressional nomination for his district on Long Island, New York. It had ended in disaster.

Yet running Reagan's campaign had not only been a bravura performance admired by the Californians, it had rekindled in Casey a feeling that public office, after all, was where he belonged. He knew he had learned from his previous mistakes in Washington: He was politically craftier, more cautious, even slower on a mumbled response than in his previous days there. He saw himself not only the master puppeteer who had ensured that Reagan had spoken faultlessly, but as the wise old man who would listen to the debate before giving the president the final nod. State or Defense were where he had thought to display those skills.

When he heard Weinberger and Haig had been given the posts, Casey had commented to his wife, Sophia, that that was to be expected: He had come late to the Reagan fold.

Then, early on that Tuesday evening in late November, the president-elect had called Casey, who was in his law office at 200 Park Avenue in New York. Reagan had been affable. How was Sophia? He still remembered how much he and Nancy had enjoyed meeting her. They must all get together again soon, and Bernie—how was the acting business going? Bernadette Casey was an aspiring movie actress in her early thirties. So far she had made a few TV commercials. The president-elect said what a fine job Casey had done as campaign manager, and how he and Nancy would never forget their debt, and how much they missed having him around.

Casey had sensed the old actor in Reagan surfacing. A pause, then the next words had been delivered in a measured tone. Maybe he would like to come to Washington? There was still a job to be done. Casey had listened—waited and listened, the way he had always done when an opposing lawyer was going to make his move.

The offer had come. DCI? Casey had mumbled his thanks, but, buying time, he had asked Reagan for a chance to consult his wife.

The president-elect had said that was also absolutely fine. In the meantime he would still like Casey to be present when Turner gave his briefing for the new administration. Casey had promised to be there. Privately, he was a little miffed that Reagan had sounded as if discussing the offer with Sophia was just a formality.

It was not. For over half a century Casey had made no move—in business or over a friendship—without consulting his wife. It was, he believed, what helped to make their marriage so different from what, for instance, the Dulleses' had been. Yet, in other ways, Casey was strikingly similar to the old spymaster. They shared the same ability to see a situation from all sides; the same logical process of step-by-step deduction; the same willingness to strike suddenly and ruthlessly; the same gift of being able to sleep soundly no matter what they had done when awake. Above all, Casey knew Dulles had shared his pride in being in at the beginning of modern American espionage and counterintelligence.

Casey talked over the offer with Sophia at Mayknoll, the magnificent Victorian mansion on the North Shore of Long Island. She had listened carefully, a trim, pert woman, her white hair held in place with spray. Finally she looked at him squarely, her eyes as trusting as they were on the day they were married during World War II. If running the CIA was what he wanted, then she would support him. But he must promise never to sell Mayknoll. After they had gone, it would be Bernadette's. They would also keep their winter home in Florida, even if becoming director meant they would probably have little time to visit either place. Nor, she had continued, if he took the job would he be able to find the time to finish his account of the OSS war in Europe against the Nazis. He had written some six hundred pages of manuscript. But it still needed polishing and revising.

Sophia delivered her final check-and-balance. Moving to Washington would virtually mean abandoning his favorite golf course, the Creek, close to Mayknoll. There he was a renowned double-bogey player, taking an average of two shots over par for each of its eighteen holes. That said, she had summed up, of course he must accept the job—if that is what he really wanted.

Although his domestic front was secured, in the two days before flying to Washington for Turner's briefing Casey continued ruminating.

His own research into the wartime activities of the OSS had involved talking to the handful of veterans still with the Agency. They had made it clear how great were the changes, particularly in field craft, since the time Casey had been operational. Remote controlled spying had often replaced human agents. Running networks of spies was an increasingly expensive and risky business. Vietnam had shown how easily such groups could be infiltrated. Both the Soviets and the Chinese regularly destroyed American cells that had taken years to nurture. Besides, one U.S. spy plane could collect more real information from a single flight than a score of agents could discover in months on the ground.

Casey reminded himself that no matter how sophisticated intelligence gathering became, it would still require the ultimate judgment to be human. All the gadgetry in the world could not take that away.

Casey, however, also saw that the enemy—his collective name for all those hostile to the United States—had expanded. The old faithfuls were still there, Russia and China, Cuba and North Vietnam. But, as he had discovered in preparing campaign issues, there were now a host of all-too-visible armies—the bands of terrorists who had introduced a harsh reality into everyday life.

It was no longer simply a matter of hijacks to Cuba. The Iran hostage crisis was a watershed. It showed clearly the brutal unpredictability of terrorist actions; how a group of revolutionary guards, run by an old mullah, Ruhollah Khomeini, who had the grand title of ayatollah, had made a mockery of established patterns of human behavior—and left the United States looking impotent to the world.

But Casey was convinced, not only from what he had read and heard, but from what he had gleaned in Washington during the election campaign, that little was really known about Khomeini and his underlying motives.

Clearly there was an urgent need to apply the CIA's resources to prepare not only a psycho-profile of the ayatollah, but also a proper evaluation of the thought processes of all terrorist groups. Dulles had shown the value of that when he had waged relentless psychological war against the minds of the Germans. He would also make it a priority to discover how terrorists were recruited, what were the criteria and differences for belonging to one group as opposed to another.

On one of the small file cards he carried with him, Casey made a note to look into these aspects, if he took the job of director.

In the remaining time before the Turner briefing, Casey made a number of calls to his intelligence contacts in the capital, trying to discover an answer to a matter that had deeply concerned him.

Running Reagan's campaign, he had been privy to a great deal of sensitive information about the Iran hostage situation. He had been told the CIA's agents in Tehran had learned that some of the Americans were being medically tortured— isolated, drugged, and coerced by doctors trained in such methods, to force them to make the nonsensical confessions that had become such a harrowing aspect of the nightly news shows.

The knowledge had not, as such, come as a surprise to Casey. He had read the Rockefeller Commission report and suspected that Dr. Cameron's work was being duplicated around the world. Soviet medical abuses of human rights had regularly come up during the campaign—and he had coached Reagan to take a hard line on Russian psychiatrists and the way they treated dissidents. He had encouraged speculation that Soviet physicians used Cuban prisoners for unethical experiments; and, indeed, wherever the United States had enemies—in Asia, Latin America, and Africa—Casey had deliberately dripped the poison that doctors there did unspeakable things to prisoners.

What disturbed him about the reports from Iran was not only that a commitment to terrorism was so strong that it could violate the traditional physician's oath to do no harm, but that the Agency appeared not to have followed up on those field reports. He would have put every available man into the area to establish the truth, and then would have had the evidence paraded at the United Nations. If nothing else, the embarrassment for Iran could only have helped to unseat the hostage takers.

Casey made another note on a file card. Pinning down the allegations of medical torture in Iran would be a priority if he took the job.

Still undecided, he flew to Washington Wednesday, November 19, 1980. That morning's newspapers had a story that the hostage crisis, in its 382nd day, would almost certainly remain unresolved until Reagan was in the Oval Office.

As usual when he came to Washington nowadays, he checked into a small suite in the Jefferson Hotel, where he continued to make calls and receive people until bedtime at ten. At three A.M. he was awake, padding around in his pajamas and robe, conducting a final review of all he had been told, sifting and sorting probability from possibility, rumor from fact. It all came down to one thing. Despite its good reputation prior to the actual rescue mission, the CIA's record in dealing with terrorism in Iran, and elsewhere, was patchy. In key areas of the Middle East, Central and South America, and part of Europe, the Agency possessed little hard intelligence on such groups as the Red Army faction in West Germany, the Red Brigade in Italy, ETA in Spain. Virtually nothing was known about the disparate Arab and Iranian groups.

That must be changed. Fast. He noted this on another file card.

Part of the reasons for this lack of crucial information, Casey had gathered, was Turner. He had been forced to spend too much time shoring up morale after Watergate and had only recently started serious intelligence-gathering operations. Casey hoped to learn more about those at the briefing. But overall, the picture seemed to be of a hard-pressed and hard-working director struggling to stay in front, metaphorically having to look over his shoulder all the time to see which watchdog was sniffing along the Langley trail.

It was no way to run an intelligence service. That would also have to change.

Yet Casey still did not know if he really should take on the job. It would mean living a Washington life: the endless embassy party circuit, endless meetings, endless lunches or dinners with boring congressmen and senators. It would be a long way from the peace and quiet of Mayknoll.

It would also mean reporting to Senator Barry M. Goldwater, the head of the most important of the intelligence watchdog committees, the Senate Select Committee on Intelligence.

It was not so much that Casey personally liked or disliked the senator; rather it was that he distrusted Goldwater's skills in assessing the overall intelligence picture. The senator saw everything too much in black-or-white terms. To be fair, though, Goldwater had put his career on the line when he had flatly refused to sign the report of the committee Senator Frank Church had chaired, which had investigated the Agency in 1975–76. In Casey's opinion, the inquiry had been a turkey shoot—he saw the Church hearings as simply feeding soft targets to a gullible media.

The idea of having Goldwater at his elbow became that much more disagreeable when Casey discovered that the senator was running a backstairs campaign to have his own nominee appointed as director. Goldwater's preference was for another sea-dog, Admiral Bobby Ray Inman, whose career in Naval intelligence had led to the top at the National Security Agency for Carter. By all accounts he had done a workmanlike job of commanding the most secret of U.S. intelligence agencies. From its nondescript headquarters at Fort George Meade out in the Washington suburbs, NSA electronically reached out into every corner of the world.

Goldwater argued that, with a new technological revolution about to burst upon the intelligence community, Inman was the ideal choice to run the CIA.

Casey still felt that, in the end, no matter how many spy satellites the United States eventually had orbiting the earth or geopositioned over key areas it would still come down to human judgment. He knew he could match, if not surpass, Inman on that.

At five o'clock Thursday morning, when he rang down for a room service breakfast, Casey found his bacon and eggs, toast, and coffee accompanied by a piece of news in the complementary copy of *The Washington Post* which placed him uncomfortably in the public eye. A headline pronounced he was in the running for the CIA job. The story made him sound like an antediluvian species who had emerged from the woodwork of World War II—and probably had no idea what modern intelligence work was about. It was too crude for Goldwater. Could it be the work of someone close to Reagan? Either it was a ploy to get him to come off the fence, or it was intended to test the opposition to his candidacy, to see what fire he might draw from Congress or the Senate. It was an old Washington game, running up a flag in the *Post* to see which way the wind blew.

Well, he still wasn't bucking for the job. If someone else wanted it that badly, he could have it. On the other hand, Casey reminded himself, the president-elect had offered it to him—and one thing Casey had come to know was that when Reagan made a decision he would have run it past Bush, the vice-president-elect, Meese, and the retinue of Californians who clung to Reagan like limpets on a Pacific Coast rock. And, of course, Reagan would have asked Nancy.

The *Post* story, equally, could be the work of Turner—trying to cling to his job by trashing a likely contender. That, too, was an old Washington game. Yet that didn't fit Turner's style. From all Casey had heard, he was a man of strong principles.

Whoever was behind the story, it probably, in the end, didn't matter a damn. Reagan *had* asked. In whose name also didn't ultimately matter—what mattered was that the president-elect was not going to change his mind once others had made it up for him. That was not his way.

Besides, if anyone wanted to play rough, Casey felt he could give them a run for their money.

In that rather bullish mood he took a cab to 716 Lafayette Park, across from the White House, and rang the front doorbell of the historic four-story, 113-year-old building.

An FBI agent, one of those helping to protect the president-elect, opened the door and showed Casey into a spacious living room. Bush, Meese, and several other members of the old California Kitchen Cabinet were already waiting for Turner to arrive.

Casey thought the briefing was masterly. Turner had clearly done his homework. It was reflected in the pages he steadily turned and read from, each one boldly stamped DCI EYES ONLY and GOALS: TURNOVER NOTES.

Much of it, Casey frankly conceded, was new and exciting. None of his discreet telephone calls had prepared him for the story of derring-do Turner unfolded, his eyes periodically lifting from the document to rake the president-elect and his aides, the director's brow furrowed in concentration beneath the shock of gray hair.

Turner sounded like a top executive presiding over his annual report to the board of management; his words carried the clear, if unspoken, reminder that their future success depended on keeping him at the helm.

Casey felt a twinge of sympathy for him. A few minutes before Turner had arrived in his chauffeured Oldsmobile, Casey had himself been warmly greeted by Reagan. Casually, as if it was a foregone conclusion, the president-elect had asked Casey one question. Had he talked over the offer with Sophia? Casey had nodded. Reagan had smiled and said that was fine. It had, in the end, been as simple as that for Casey to become the new director of Central Intelligence. Meese had suggested to Reagan that he should hold off passing along the word to the Carter White House until they had digested Turner's briefing.

Knowing the job was now his, Casey had settled down to absorb Turner's outline of his stewardship and the direction the Agency should be going. Turner was a careful speaker, clear and succinct. But his pace was even, with few highs and lows. He had to be listened to carefully.

Casey knew Reagan had a short attention span. He liked a topic reduced to a few sentences, a page at the most. It was the way he had learned his lines as an actor—a scene at a time.

Turner began with a lengthy preamble explaining the situation he had inherited—low morale, lack of coordination, the makings of an intelligence-gathering shambles. Casey saw that the president-elect was getting restless, glancing quickly at Meese, then at Bush.

Suddenly, Reagan was all attention. Turner was speaking of something that the president-elect could readily grasp—the Agency's policy on assassination; or, as Turner referred to it, termination.

It had been banned by an executive order President Ford had signed in 1976 and one President Carter had reaffirmed. Staring at Casey, Turner had said he agreed with the ban. Reagan asked in a bantering tone whether the KGB knew of the restriction. Casey thought the president-elect was trying to inject a little humor into the meeting—something he was prone to do when the most serious topics were under review. The California Kitchen Cabinet smiled. So did Turner. He knew a joke, and a joker, when confronted with one.

He continued. As they all knew, there had been a virtual clear-out of what he called the Watergate cowboys. But new blood had been found. There were some absolutely brilliant men now in the Directorate of Operations.

Once more Casey saw a glaze forming in Reagan's eyes. He was not interested in such details; he never had been. He wanted the stuff of headlines. It was not long in coming.

Turner unveiled the Directorate's list of targets, leaders the Agency was working on removing from office. It was headed by that perennial survivor, Castro. Next came Khomeini and then Muammer Qaddafi.

Casey had been mildly surprised to find the Libyan leader's name so high on the list. He had not, until then, thought of Qaddafi as a serious threat to the United States.

Turner developed his Qaddafi scenario. The colonel's recent military victory in Chad was bound to pose a new threat to U.S. and Western interests in Africa. Encouraged by that success, Qaddafi would try and plunder elsewhere. Perhaps he would even feel strong enough to make a grab for Tunisia, or head further south into one of the new African states. He might possibly even lend direct military support to the Marxist regime in Angola. He could even go as far south as supplying the African National Congress in its fight against white South Africa. While there were no definite signs where Qaddafi could strike next, the only certainty was that he would. Therefore, it was urgent that he should be toppled.

"If the guy's so strong, then who's gonna be able to knock him off his pot?"

The question came from an aide. Turner's reply was directed at Casey. Listening, Casey wondered whether Turner, after all, suspected the truth: that in a few weeks Qaddafi would no longer be his problem.

Turner conceded that the domestic and exiled opposition to Qaddafi was poorly organized and virtually ineffective. It needed funding, arms, and leadership.

"What sort of guy is Qaddafi?"

Reagan's question interrupted Turner's monologue. He reached down and produced a top-secret file from the briefcase at his feet.

Turner opened the file, explaining it contained the latest psycho-profile on Qaddafi. He began to read.

"Because of special circumstances in his childhood, Qaddafi absorbed, in exaggerated form, the bedouin characteristics of naive idealism, religious fanaticism, intense pride, austerity, xenophobia, and sensitivity to slight."

Reagan interrupted to say that the colonel sounded like a nut.

Turner read on. "As a result of the discriminatory treatment he received as a bedouin during his early schooling in Libya's cities, at the hands of urbanized Libyans as well as foreigners, Qaddafi developed an intense dislike for established elites, a rigid adherence to his Bedouin ways and a strong identification with the downtrodden. This has contributed to his own rebellion against authority and his total and indiscriminate support of rebel causes throughout the world. To defend himself psychologically, Qaddafi has developed an exalted, even grandiose sense of self-importance. His vision for Libya seeks to restore the purity that he supposes existed in earlier Arab history."

The president-elect repeated: A nut.

Turner closed the file and put it back in his briefcase. Then he resumed reading from the turnover notes. He said that Russian objectives were served by Qaddafi's behavior. He created mayhem and the Soviets endorsed it to the extent of selling him $1 billion a year of sophisticated weaponry. It was Russian firepower that had given Qaddafi the advantage in Chad. It would virtually make him unstoppable in Africa. Even the South Africans would find themselves with a real fight on their hands if Qaddafi made a serious move against them.

"The guy's worse than Castro," said one of the aides.

Turner shook his head. "As bad—but different. Qaddafi's not a Soviet pawn. Castro is—and has been for a long time."

Meese asked his first question. How much oil did the United States import from Libya?

Turner replied it amounted to almost ten percent. If the supply was cut off there would be a serious gasoline shortage in the United States, especially on the East Coast, where most of the Libyan oil was sold.

Reagan suggested that Turner should move on, making it clear he had heard enough, for the moment, about Qaddafi. The president-elect glanced at Casey. God Almighty, thought the director-designate, why does Reagan keep on signaling that Turner is out?

Casey made a note he would want Qaddafi's psycho-profile developed. There had to be more exploitable weaknesses in his character than simply pride, self-importance, and sensitivity to slight.

Turner waited until Casey had completed his jotting, then continued—selling himself and the Agency to a president-elect who had never before had a full-scale intelligence briefing. Turner explained about what he called the Navy Special. It was marked on the agenda paper before each of his listeners around the conference table as SNCP. It stood for Special Naval Control Program.

Smiling briefly at Reagan, Turner prefaced his remarks by saying that no Hollywood script writer would dared to have invented such a plot—a handful of brave American sailors risking their lives to carry the war to the very shores of America's enemies.

Casey felt even sorrier for Turner. He had tuned into Reagan's wavelength and was beginning to know how to reach him. Turner's efforts would make no difference.

But the president-elect was listening attentively as Turner painted a graphic portrait of SNCP's ultrasecret operations. They involved U.S. submarines regularly penetrating Soviet and Chinese territorial waters, and even sailing into their harbors. Turner explained that the purpose of these hazardous operations was not only to test the antidetection devices the submarines were equipped with against the best the Soviets and Chinese could produce, but also to sow pods. These were ultrasensitive electronic scanners that were attached to underwater communications cables. The pods could lift thousands of Russian and Chinese telephone conversations. When the scanners were retrieved they were fed through banks of NSA computers.

The information revealed an extensive range of hard intelligence about Communist operations. The pods had alerted the United States to Russian plans to support Guatemala's leftist-Marxist guerrillas, and had shown how the Chinese were trying to increase their hold over North Korea. Many hundreds of times the undersea intercepts had pinpointed the weaknesses and strengths of the opposition.

Reagan had grinned broadly at Turner when he finished. It would indeed make a great movie. "But I'll never get to play in it. No one will."

Even Casey smiled.

Turner said he would next like to explain the current list of SCE operations. Perhaps once more sensing he had lost Reagan's interest, Turner quickly described that SCE stood for Special Collection Elements—the elite CIA/NSA teams that bugged key offices in foreign capitals. They formed the Agency's Department D. Its members were presently operating in forty countries, including Syria, Iraq, and Iran.

Casey mumbled his first question. What had the SCEs gotten on the hostages?

Turner looked down the table to where Casey sat two chairs away from Reagan. Choosing his words carefully, Turner said that the latest SCE prediction was that the hostages could be out by Inauguration Day—Khomeini's final humiliation to Carter.

"On Inauguration Day would be perfect." Edwin Meese turned to Reagan. "It would be the best possible way to start your presidency. A clean sweep. A new start. Terrific."

Casey knew it would not be that simple. His own telephone calls—among them one to Helms, who had been U.S. ambassador to Iran from 1973 to 1976—had established that the ayatollah still smarted over the way the United States had extended the hand of friendship to the shah. The United States had created the shah's intelligence service, the SAVAK; it had trained his Imperial Army to subjugate his people. It had done everything wrong. Even when the warning signs were only too clear and nothing could stop the revolution from sweeping away the Peacock Throne, the United States had gone on regarding Khomeini as a decrepit, senile old cleric, someone to be politically patronized by Washington State Department Middle East gurus, patted on the head, and warned not to get any ideas of dealing with the Russians. The hostage crisis had shown the reality of the ayatollah: tough, pragmatic, and messianical in his crowd manipulation. A self-acclaimed prophet, to be sure, but all the more dangerous for that. Casey decided Khomeini was no pushover for a clean sweep.

Turner turned to some of the other key personalities under continuous surveillance by the Agency. Soviet Premier Leonid Brezhnev was sick, perhaps dying. His illness, according to SCE intercepts and confirmed by SNCP surveillance, suggested that there would be no immediate move forward on arms control talks until there was new leadership in the Kremlin.

Turner moved on. Crown Prince Fahd of Saudi Arabia was a heavy drinker. He was also a womanizer. The Agency had firm reports that several white girls were permanent members of his entourage, on hand to provide a variety of sexual services. It made the prince vulnerable to blackmail.

President Anwar Sadat of Egypt smoked marijuana in the belief it calmed his anxiety attacks.

The president-elect sat enthralled at the glimpses of the human weaknesses of other world leaders. He seemed less interested in following the story that Turner started to unfold on Poland, and the threat that country faced from Moscow's determination to crush the Solidarity trade union. Satellite surveillance photography showed Russian troops continuing to mass on the Polish border.

Reagan looked skeptical. He said he had heard that satellite surveillance had been crucial in Carter's plan to rescue the Iran hostages. And look where that had ended. Why did the Agency put such store on such things?

Turner hesitated. He had intended to deal with electronic surveillance, if only briefly, toward the end of his discourse. Now he saw he would have to immediately settle the president-elect's doubts.

He told his listeners about Project Indigo, explaining that it would be crucial when, as they all hoped, the day came when there would be agreement with the Soviets on arms control. Indigo was a multi-billion-dollar system of satellite surveillance that would use radar imagery to see through the thickest of clouds and at night. This would be a vital consideration over the Soviet Union and northern China, where in winter cloud cover lasted for weeks without a break. But to answer the president-elect's question: The satellite surveillance on the Russian-Polish border had produced photographs so clear that individual faces could be seen under computer enhancement, along with the insignias on their Soviet uniforms.

Reagan had made a long, low appreciative noise.

Turner explained that the Agency had deliberately leaked some of its information on the Polish crisis to the press, so that Moscow would realize that Washington was fully aware of the situation. It was a well-tried way to sound a warning.

"Good thinking," interjected Reagan.

Turner was clearly pleasantly surprised at the accolade. Poor son of a bitch, thought Casey; he's like a starving dog, grateful for a bone.

Turner had not finished with Poland. Once more surveying the room, he calmly announced that an SCE team had picked up some highly interesting telephone intercepts of conversations between Pope John Paul II and Solidarity leader Lech Walesa. The pontiff had urged his fellow Pole to stand firm.

The president-elect had not bothered to conceal his amazement. "You bug the Pope?"

Turner matter-of-factly explained that surveillance of the Vatican had been upgraded by the CIA with the election of Karol Wojtylah, the first Polish Pope, in October 1978.

What Turner did not explain, but which Casey had been told about in one of his telephone calls, was that the Agency, through some of its priest assets in the Vatican, had placed six bugging devices in the Secretariat of State, the Vatican bank, and the Apostolic Palace, where the Pope actually lived and worked. The devices were sufficiently powerful to enable conversations to be overheard within rooms with walls thick enough to withstand artillery fire. Working from safe houses in high-rise buildings overlooking the Leonine walls of the tiny city-state, CIA operatives had recorded often highly confidential discussions about papal plans.

The Agency's surveillance had increased since July 5, 1979, when Walesa telephoned the Pope asking whether John Paul would approve of the name Solidarity being used for the fledgling union. Walesa had explained he had selected the word from the pontiff's encyclical, Redemptor Homis. At its core had been an appeal for "acting together." The significance of Walesa's request was not lost on the pontiff—or the Department D electronic eavesdroppers.

The Pope had given his blessing. From that moment he had become the most powerful spiritual challenge not only to the Polish regime, but also to Moscow. Increasingly, John Paul had publicly involved himself in his homeland's domestic affairs, up to the brink of the crisis it now faced.

"Why don't the Russians snuff him out, like they did his predecessor?"

Turner stared at the Reagan aide. The story that the KGB had poisoned the first Pope John Paul after he had been in office for only thirty-three days continued to gain credence. There had already been hundreds of articles written on the matter and a book was in the pipeline. Yet, Turner explained, the story was a pure invention—conceived and circulated by the Agency's Political Psychological Division to embarrass the Soviets. The Agency was satisfied that the previous pontiff had died from a heart attack. His personal physician, Dr. Renata Buzonetti, who examined the body shortly after death, had been an asset for many years.

The poisoning story had not only embarrassed the KGB—the more the furious Russians tried to deny it, the less credible their protests sounded—but had furthered the CIA's own accepted position within the Vatican. Along with the Department D secret watch on the Pope, there was an altogether more formal link—one that Casey, a devout Catholic, had been able to easily confirm through his own position as a member of the military Order of Malta. His fellow member in Rome had told him that John Paul II had recently restored a custom of Pope Pius XII—to receive a weekly briefing from the CIA.

Friday was when the Agency's station chief in Rome delivered the weekly intelligence summary. Late in the afternoon he was driven from the U.S. Embassy on Via Veneto, past the Fountains of Trevi, and across the Tiber to the Vatican. There, the officer handed the report to a papal aide who carried the sealed envelope to the pontiff's private study adjoining his bedroom. The Pope usually studied the summary after dinner.

Turner chose not to share such details with the president-elect and his staff. Instead, as if he wanted to make one more grab for Reagan's undivided attention, Turner said that there was a very real possibility that the KGB, either directly or acting through a surrogate, might this time actually try to terminate the meddlesome pontiff.

"You mean, kill the Pope?" Reagan was genuinely bewildered. "That wouldn't do Moscow any good in image terms. If, as you say, the Russians are having a hard time living down something they didn't do, kill the last Pope, imagine what a bad time they would have if they were caught with their finger on a smoking gun like this one. They'd be isolated in the world. And all those Russian Orthodox folk. Think what they would do. There'd be a second revolution. Kill the Pope? Your people have gotta be kidding!"

There was murmured agreement around the table. Casey made a note to look further into what precisely the Agency knew about Soviet intentions toward John Paul II. He would also have a psycho-profile made of the present Pope.

In a somewhat strained atmosphere, Turner finished his survey of the trouble spots: South Africa, Central and South America, the Middle East, Asia. At each stopping point, he delivered a quick summary of what the Agency knew and how events were likely to shape up.

It made for grim listening. The United States didn't seem to have too many friends in the world.

When Turner had finished his two-hour lecture, the president-elect rose to his feet and said it had been quite an eye-opener, especially the bits about the submarines and the Pope.

Casey felt he had a great deal of studying to do before he moved into Langley.

18

Shaping the
Future

On Monday morning, January 26, 1981, the armored Oldsmobile that went with the job, along with an Agency armed guard beside the driver, chauffeured Casey from Langley. The Reagan administration was about to start its fifth day and Casey was on his way to the White House to give his first full presentation since accepting office. He had chosen for his theme the worldwide threat of terrorism and how it was being fermented by states like Libya, Iran, and Syria.

The master copy of the briefing paper was in the locked case on the seat beside him. Copies had been hand-couriered earlier that morning to all those attending the meeting. Each was marked TOP SECRET, followed by further restrictive letters, SCI—SENSITIVE COMPARTMENTED INFORMATION. Casey knew the document made frightening reading. He also intended it to signal his full authority in all intelligence matters.

Casey was still formally referred to as director-designate. But the confirmation from the Senate was a mere formality. At the hearing Senator Goldwater had made some throat-clearing noises about his high opinion of Admiral Inman. Goldwater had even carried his arguments all the way to the president. Reagan had been kind but firm with the old senator. He had given the job to Casey and there was nothing more to be said. If Casey wanted Inman as his deputy, however, that would be absolutely fine. Casey had said he hoped the NSA chief would accept the post. Goldwater had smiled, defeated, finally accepting he had been outmaneuvered.

Like everything else he had done in the weeks following the Turner briefing, Casey had explored the ground thor-

oughly over whom he wanted as DDCI. He had discussed
the matter with the present incumbent, Frank Carlucci, another of the great Langley survivors, cast from the Dulles
mold, ever upwardly mobile, and about to make another
career improvement by becoming Caspar Weinberger's deputy at Defense. Carlucci had no axe to grind and had pushed
hard Inman's candidacy, saying he was an outstanding
manager—responsible for over 40,000 people manning listening posts across the world and out at Fort George Meade.
Inman knew the Washington political scene as well as anybody, who to nudge in the continuous process of unlocking
still more government money for the secret world. Further,
the NSA chief was loyal and a renowned fighter for his
corner.

Casey had checked with Turner. His response had been
unenthusiastic. Inman, in Turner's view, was too strong a
personality to perform properly as a deputy director and,
with the NSA–CIA rivalry more intense and bitter after the
Iran hostage rescue debacle, the top careerists at Langley
would resent the intruder from Fort George Meade. Casey
had not commented after Turner delivered his judgment.
Privately, the director-designate saw it as evidence that his
predecessor had once more responded emotionally. During
various transition meetings—when Turner or one of the Agency's divisional heads had briefed Casey on Russia, Central
Europe, China, Asia, and Africa—Turner had not bothered to
conceal his hurt at the way he had been treated. He had kept
reminding Casey of the mess he had inherited and what a
task it had been to pull things together. The implication was
clear: Casey was inheriting a shipshape Agency that Turner,
if there was any justice in politics, should be still running.
Casey had avoided the pitfall of making any comment, not
even when Turner showed all the signs of someone who had
never gotten along well with Inman in the delicate matter of
live and let live in the inner world of American national
security.

Rejecting Turner's assessment, and at the same time put-
ting behind him the twinge of sympathy he had felt for him,
Casey continued checking. He talked to Bush, Colby, and
Helms. All agreed that Inman was ideal for the job. But still
Casey could not decide. The choice of deputy was crucial. He

was in a hurry to settle the matter, but he would not be rushed.

Finally, Casey saw Inman, driving out to the NSA headquarters and being escorted through the sprawl of buildings while Inman explained how his teams worked around the clock analyzing communications intercepts and breaking codes.

Casey was shown banks of computers which analyzed information from satellites on the edge of space, digital imagery that the computers enhanced to provide three-dimensional images of stunning clarity. Casey was shown bridges spanning the Volga and launching rigs at the Tyurantam Cosmodrome—over which the luckless Gary Powers had flown his U-2 plane, light years earlier in terms of aerial intelligence gathering. Continuing to use Powers's ill-fated flight plan as an illustration of how far technology had advanced, Inman had shown Casey a close-up of a smoking chimney stack in Chelyabinsk over which the pilot had flown. NSA computers had analyzed the smoke to decide what was making it. Inman displayed a satellite photograph of a military truck in the streets of Sverdlovsk and the actual faces of soldiers marching from a barracks in Kirov over which Powers had also flown. At approximately the point where the Russian rocket had ended the U-2 mission, an NSA satellite had photographed a mobile Soviet rocket launcher—one of hundreds, Inman explained, the Soviets regularly moved around the country.

Casey found Inman's enthusiasm infectious. The NSA chief was absolutely right when he said that electronic spying had an increasingly vital role to play. Yet Inman had been careful not to promulgate the virtual end of human intelligence-gathering. There was, he kept saying, a place for both.

Both men knew it was make-or-break time, when each would have to make up his mind if they could work together. Inman had explained that in the four years he had run the NSA he had concentrated on not only the Agency's prime targets—Russia and China, Cuba and Central Europe—but had begun to focus on new areas—Central America, the Middle East, and particularly Iran. What little was known about what was actually happening there—as opposed to what the desk men over at State posited—came from the NSA. Inman forecast the day was not far off when "we will be able to tell one mullah from another in Tehran by the size of their beards." Hyperbole, most certainly, but, thought Casey, forgivable after what he had seen.

He had asked Inman if there was any evidence of widespread torture in Iran, including doctors performing it. Inman said there was. NSA intercepts had positively identified four prisons where Iranian doctors observed or actually took part in acts of torture. Three of the jails were in Tehran—Evin, Qasr, and Komiteh. The other prison was at Salahabad, between the Iranian capital and the holy city of Qum. The NSA had established that in the jails doctors supervised whippings and the beating to pulp of the soles of a prisoner's feet. Doctors also performed electroshocks and carried out branding with red-hot scalpels.

Casey had asked about Libya. Inman had again been explicit. The NSA had pinpointed the old Ministry of Planning building in Tripoli as the country's main torture center. There, in the cavernous basement, physicians regularly supervised or performed electroshocks to the head and genitals and, what appeared a peculiarly local custom, doctors carefully cut an incision in a victim's stomach to allow a trickle of blood to emerge. A starving rat in a cage was strapped over the cut. The rodent swiftly gnawed open the wound. Other Libyan physicians were integral to the psychological tortures carried out in the basement. They included hooding and mock executions. Casey had asked for all the evidence to be sent over to Langley. Inman had immediately agreed. Both men realized it was a significant step—that Inman was signaling his willingness to work under Casey.

The meeting at the White House to which Casey was being driven would be the first public test of that relationship. The Iran hostage crisis had ended on its 444th day in a final public humiliation for President Carter—and a triumphant start for the Reagan presidency. The Iranians had waited until thirty minutes after Reagan was sworn in, watched by a doleful Carter, before allowing two planes with the hostages to leave from Tehran for the U.S. Air Force base at Wiesbaden in West Germany.

An Agency team of doctors were among the physicians who examined the freed Americans at the base hospital. The first conclusion of the CIA specialists was that not only had the men been severely tortured, but that only Iranian psychiatrists and psychologists would have had the expertise to have done so.

While the hostages were still in the air, Inman had formally accepted the president's plea that not only did Casey need him as his deputy, but that Reagan himself, as commander in chief, needed Inman there.

Riding to the Inauguration with Carter, Reagan spent the journey telling old Hollywood stories and saying how much he was looking forward to seeing Bob Hope and Frank Sinatra, while Carter tried to get information about the hostages.

Now, seated among the semicircle before the president in the Oval Office, Casey reflected how time can change a person. It seemed like only yesterday that the man on his far left, Secretary of State Haig, had presided over the last days of the Nixon White House. Then, he had fought a clever and devious battle to preserve the remnants of Nixon's presidency. Now, Haig sounded like a lifelong Reaganite.

Haig had turned up with Anthony Quainton, the State Department's resident expert on terrorism. At least the State official had not displayed the outwardly fierce ambition of the others who had attached their futures to Haig.

Casey's paper portrayed a chain of interrelated terrorist activity that stretched from Tehran into Damascus, and on across the eastern Mediterranean to Tripoli. From there Qaddafi exported it worldwide. Casey had used the updated psycho-profile he had requested from Dr. Post. The psychiatrist had added a new dimension to Turner's earlier version. Qaddafi, in Dr. Post's opinion, was now almost certainly affected with a severe personality disorder.

The president had interrupted to ask whether it would be possible for psychobiographies to be presented in video form, with footage of the person under review, and a look at the geography of his or her land, accompanied with a narrated explanation.

Casey remembered that the president liked nothing better than watching television. Usually after seven o'clock, if there was no formal engagement, he and the first lady sat in their pajamas before one of the White House sets eating a tray supper and watching a favorite movie. Reagan's request for future psycho-profiles to be in film form was, for the president, a logical extension of his new viewing habits.

When Casey finished his presentation on Qaddafi, Haig had asked Quainton to answer one question. Turning to his aide, the imperious Secretary of State delivered a thunderbolt that brought the president forward in his chair.

"How real is the threat of a terrorist group striking at our vital domestic resources? Our oil? Our nuclear facilities? At the very heart of government itself?"

Quainton said that the United States had never been so vulnerable. It was now absolutely possible for a terrorist group to strike directly at the country's vital resources. Terrorists had the capabilities with a single bomb to decimate New York's skyline or gouge out the heart of Washington.

As if on cue, Edwin Meese piped up that the administration would not be confronting such a doomsday scenario if Carter had not restricted his intelligence gathering, and if Turner had not behaved like an intelligence wimp. Terrorists, like spies, deserved to be shown no mercy. The administration had a solemn duty to protect the citizens of America.

Casey looked along the row of seated men to Inman, who shrugged his shoulder as if to say: Did you expect this? I certainly didn't.

The president glanced at his new FBI director. William H. Webster was the epitome of the clean-cut All-American boy. The sharp-eyed lawyer had become a federal judge before occupying the office of the legendary J. Edgar Hoover.

With a sense of relief Casey heard Webster say that he would not be stampeded into overinflating the gravity of the situation. It was serious. No doubt about that. But the FBI was also able to cope. Absolutely no doubt also about that. It had the men and the resources to keep track of all terrorist activities within the United States. The warnings his agency had issued about potential Iranian threats were just that—warnings. When the FBI had harder information, he would report it at once.

The president looked at Inman. He said that, as far as the NSA went, it was primarily a matter of money. The greater the investment, the better the job the Agency would do. It was as basic as that.

The president smiled. That kind of answer he understood.

When the meeting concluded and they had left the Oval Office, Haig told Casey that he had only been trying to help.

On Tuesday, January 27, 1981, Casey was confirmed as director by a Senate vote of 95–0. Next day he was sworn in. That night, the director paused in his reading of another pile of reports marked ACTION: DCI or EYES ONLY: DCI. He wanted to watch the early evening news, to see if Haig's performance really was as wild as Inman said. If anything, it was worse. The main story on all three channels showed Haig launching an all-out attack against the Soviet Union for funding, equipping, and training international terrorism.

Casey placed a call to Ronald Spiers, the head of State's intelligence department. Where had the secretary gotten his evidence on which to base such an attack? Spiers said, unhappily, he had no idea. Casey decided he really would have to watch Haig. He could ruin everything, blundering off like that.

Monday, March 30, 1981, the sixty-second day of the new administration, included for Casey an early morning meeting with Dr. Post and several other specialists from the Political Psychological Division. They had gathered in the director's office to preview the latest video psycho-profile before it was sent to the White House.

On to the television monitor came the warning: SENSITIVE INTELLIGENCE MATERIAL.

The caption faded. Then, growing steadily louder, came the plaintive sound of music: a recitative and restricted range of notes. The sound swelled, flutes and horns, tambourines and cymbals. The screen gradually turned blue, the hard, brilliant hue of a Near East sky. The film was a clip from the days when Iran had been on the holiday itinerary of more adventuresome Americans. Mountains filled the screen. The sorrowful wailing music accompanied a succession of panoramic views. Once more the sound faded, allowing Casey and the others to dwell upon the vista. The silence on the screen suggested Eternity.

Iran, intoned the narrator—a voice-over actor from television commercials—had always been a hard land. Suddenly, the picture changed to newsreel footage of Ayatollah Khomeini receiving the adulation of the Tehran mob. The narrator formally identified him. "Ruhollah Mussavi Khomeini. Known to his people as the Smasher of Idols, the Glorious Upholder of the Faith, the Sole Hope of the Downtrodden, the Vicar of Islam, His Holiness the Grand Ayatollah."

Such unrestrained worship, continued the narrator, could have created Khomeini's warped psychopathology. His functioning mental disease. It would account for his clear overestimation of self, his own sense of exaltation, dominance, and delusions of grandeur.

The camera zoomed in on Khomeini's distinctive dolichocephalic cranium, already a firm favorite with political cartoonists.

Born in 1903, Khomeini has never lost his longing for the land. There he feels safe from a world he perceives as hostile and contemptuous—one which he reacts against with a hatred and a readiness to put the very worst construction upon any mishap, however trivial or accidental it may be. All his life he has attributed misfortune to somebody else. His response is the classic example of the abnormal process of social behavior. In clinical terms this is more than merely a disturbance in the relationship between a person and society. It is an affliction of the brain. The memories of all he has imagined he has endured at the hands of others is photographed on his brain and remains as a constant reminder of suffering—and a need to obtain redress.

Over film of veiled women in the streets of Tehran, the narrator filled in Khomeini's domestic background.

For the first thirty years of his life, apart from his mother, he had no significant contact with women. Instead, from an early age, he had lived as a hermit-pupil in the ancient religious university of Qum. Finally, when he had graduated he had married, on his thirtieth birthday. His bride, Batal, was only ten. Their first child was born on her twelfth birthday.

He is old—but dangerous. Not quite clinically mad, but certainly far from sane. He is the textbook example that religious fanaticism often springs from the dissatisfaction with personal development in early life. He has cast himself in the role as God-instructor to his people. To maintain that myth he will need to act increasingly in a manner more dangerous to the United States, the Western world—and indeed the whole world.

The screen momentarily went blank. Then it was filled with that most endearing of Disney's creations, Mickey Mouse. With the gravity of a voice announcing a final significant revelation, the narrator said that the Ayatollah's favorite relaxation was watching cartoons of the fabled rodent. Did it indicate the onset of senility—or a desire to seek a lost childhood?

Increasingly, the director realized that the president had ample time on his hands. The troika who ran the White House arranged his working day so that Reagan was never in the Oval Office before nine-thirty and always left at five-thirty. The president rarely visited his workplace on weekends. His weekday schedule had lengthy gaps between appointments, during which he answered some of his sacks of fan mail.

His dependency on Nancy had, if anything, increased from that day in 1980 when, for the first time he took Holy Communion.

Casey's day, on the other hand, had been stretched to often twenty hours, seven days a week. He chaired interdepartmental meetings to unlock the impasse he had discovered on assuming office. Turner was right when he said there were good men in place both at Langley and out in the field. But they were inherently suspicious; they had learned from past experience that a new director meant mass firings or, as bad, languishing in an intelligence limbo. Casey had passed along the word to departmental heads that there would be neither. He wanted everybody to understand, down to the guards at the gates to Langley, that if not the ghost then the spirit of Allen Welsh Dulles once more walked the complex.

The director was always at his desk before the day shift arrived; he remained long after the night men came. At five A.M., if he was not already in his office, an Agency courier dropped a copy of the president's daily brief (PDB) off at the house Sophia had rented. Printed in the small hours at Langley, it was usually no more than ten pages long, and its distribution was restricted to Reagan, Haig, and Weinberger. Each PDB contained an update on Khomeini, Qaddafi, and the Soviet and Chinese leadership.

Casey's input was also noticeable in the National Intelligence Daily, now circulated to some two hundred key officials in the administration. The NID often contained summaries of what were still the director's most trusted means of intelligence gathering—spies in the field.

One was William Buckley, working in Chad, advising Defense Minister Hissen Habre in his war against Qaddafi. Buckley was also the Agency's conduit between Habre and the Sudanese leader, Jaafar Nimeri.

Casey had summoned Buckley to give him an on-the-spot report, something that even the most sophisticated satellite positioned over Central Africa could not do. Casey had asked, could Habre survive? Buckley had no doubt he could. Morocco, Egypt, Sudan, and most recently France had all provided Habre with covert support. All those countries feared that Qaddafi would target them—and that one way to contain him was to keep the Libyan fully occupied in Chad.

In Buckley's view, Chad had also pinpointed Qaddafi's weakness—his reckless way of overstretching his attack and supply lines. It left him politically vulnerable to a coup at home.

Casey posed another question. What would Buckley like the Agency to do? The officer had not hesitated. Nothing openly. Overt American action could turn Qaddafi into a Moslem martyr. Even moderate Arab governments would feel compelled to support him against another example of that blanket condemnation running through the streets of the Middle East and Africa—Imperialist aggression. But, argued Buckley, with France already doling out millions of francs to Habre, it was critically important for U.S. interests that the Reagan administration show it was prepared to discreetly support its friends. Habre needed arms and the men to train them. The Agency should provide both.

Buckley had returned to Chad while Casey had set about preparing his first major covert action. A few days earlier, the president had signed an order that released $8 million to support Habre. Buckley was ciphered the news at his mail drop, the U.S. Embassy in Khartoum, and told to shortly expect visitors—Agency officers to train Habre's men.

The news that the Agency was once more taking the war to the enemy was greeted with open satisfaction in Langley. Its staff felt they at last had a director who knew what a large portion of their work was all about—waging mayhem against the foes of the United States. After years of stagnation and pussyfooting, Casey showed he was ready to go where others had balked.

Casey's decision over Chad, like much else he did, was arrived at after a careful analysis. He had a knack—Buckley called it "intelligence green fingers"—of being able to decide with uncanny accuracy the precise evaluation to place upon a particular piece of information: to make finite judgments between electronic, satellite, and human-resource intelligence.

Often he asked for more information—the full copy of an electronic intercept, the complete set of satellite photographs, background files, previous position papers.

In that way he came across the Agency's operation against Patrice Lumumba and Dulles's cable of August 25, 1960, to the CIA station chief in what was then the Congo, and now Zaire, insisting that Lumumba's removal was of prime importance. In the same file was Dr. Cameron's psycho-profile of the African nationalist. Attached to it were cross references.

At nights, when he had momentarily cleared the workload from his desk, Casey had followed the trail of those cross references through the boxes Turner had marked EYES ONLY: DCI. Reading into the early hours, Casey, unlike Turner, had not been shocked by Dr. Cameron's exploits. Rather, he saw them as that of a courageous physician who had tried to keep his country at least abreast of its enemies.

Casey was certain he had been entrusted with a similar mission. He and Inman had settled in well together working in adjoining offices on the seventh floor. The DCI's desk was usually squared away, rarely a paper in sight; Casey's invariably overflowed with paperwork.

On that last Monday in March their prime intelligence targets not only included Libya and Iran and maintaining a close watch on Russia and China. A new one had been added—El Salvador. About the size and shape of the state of Massachusetts, the poverty-stricken country had been forced into the consciousness of Americans when Reagan had promised on the campaign trail that if he became president he would halt the growing Communist insurgency of the Sandinista rebels in "our front yard." The phrase had been Casey's. He had also fed some of the stories from the Reagan camp that the Sandinistas were committing acts of brutal torture—and that even the rebel forces doctors were engaged in such activities.

On becoming president, Reagan increased the number of American military advisors to the Salvadoran government. The decision ended the brief honeymoon between the White House and the media. The media were filled with foreboding that the United States was about to become embroiled in another Vietnam.

Casey could live with the headlines. What he planned to do, he would ensure, would never surface publicly. El Salvador offered the first opportunity to put into action his old belief that, just as he had successfully run those OSS teams into wartime Berlin, so he could once more organize a secret army to penetrate every corner of Central America to smoke out the threat of communism. There would be no holds barred to protect America's front yard.

As a first step, Casey asked Dr. Post and his team to prepare psycho-profiles of all the main Communist leaders in Central America.

Included in the flood of information cascading across Casey's desk were reports from Duane R. Clarrige, the middle-aged station chief in Rome who dressed like a playboy in natty cream suits, white shoes, and ties colorful enough to make the waiters still blink at the Hotel Excelsior, a few steps away from the Agency's offices on Via Veneto. Every week day Clarrige had a drink in the ground floor bar, greeting and being greeted by the parade of Italian nobility, movie stars, entrepreneurs, bankers and government officials. At least once a week he dined with one of his Vatican assets. The contacts helped Clarrige keep abreast of what was happening beneath the surface in Rome and beyond. The Italian capital was long a recognized crossroads for intelligence out of Africa and the Middle East, the Balkans, and southern Europe. A good officer like Clarrige often gathered more in a few hours than some field men gleaned in a week.

Normally, Casey only saw summaries of reports from station chiefs. But the Directorate of Operations had sent Clarrige's latest reports in full, deeming them of sufficient importance to be placed in a blue-border file, the recognized Langley way of alerting the director.

Clarrige's contacts in the Italian Secret Service had picked up a hint that Libya could be sponsoring a terrorist attack against an American target in Italy. The station chief had also received reliable information that Qaddafi was planning to have President Sadat of Egypt assassinated. The source for this was one of Clarrige's contacts in DIGOS, the Italian antiterrorist squad whose contacts within Libya were still strong.

Casey acted swiftly, alerting Haig and Weinberger over the threat to U.S. interests in Italy. The State Department sent a flash warning to all embassies in Europe to go on full alert.

The director ordered the Directorate of Operations to send Buckley at once to Cairo to review Sadat's security arrangements. With other Agency officers on the way to Chad, Buckley could be released for the task. With his background he was the best qualified officer on hand who had the necessary tactical expertise and diplomatic experience to deal with Egypt's president.

The orders were still being processed on March 30, 1981, when news reached the seventh floor that President Reagan had been shot on his way from a function in downtown Washington. The gunman, John Hinckley, had fired several rounds, seriously wounding Reagan, before being overpowered.

Even while he was deploying teams of officers to the case, Casey's reaction was to wonder whether Qaddafi was behind the attempted assassination. Had he financed Hinckley? Arranged for the youth to be trained? Had Hinckley been guided by a Libyan controller to the spot where the president made an easy target? Or, if not Libya, then the Soviets? Was Hinckley a KGB hit man? Had what Secretary of State Haig gone on predicting actually happened? Had Moscow effortlessly reached out and almost destroyed the very bastion of democracy?

After Haig's outburst on television, Casey had ordered the Agency's national intelligence officer for the Soviet Union— the key Russian analyst in U.S. intelligence—to prepare an in-depth study of Soviet links to international terrorism.

The director had discovered that Haig's information came almost word for word from a new book, *The Terror Network* by a Rome-based writer, Claire Sterling. Casey had read her work and was stunned to see the claim that massive proof already existed to link the Soviet Union and its surrogates in using terrorism to destabilize Western democracies. Sterling had identified a worldwide conspiracy in which the Cubans, Palestinians, ETA, the IRA, the Red Army faction of West

Germany, and the Red Brigade of Italy all met regularly in the Soviet Bloc under the chairmanship of the KGB.

Behind a vivid portrait of state-sponsored terrorism was the specter that somehow the Russians had brainwashed very disparate groups to wage war on a common front. But how? When had all that happened? Where had it occurred? And, most important of all, why had none of this surfaced in his trawl through the back-numbers—the files and boxes Casey had studied for hours, and which dealt with all kinds of hostile operations against the United States and its allies over the past quarter of a century?

Where had Hinckley learned to shoot so well? Was he another Lee Harvey Oswald, whose links with the KGB had never been completely resolved in Casey's mind? He had read the Nosenko file. Nosenko probably had not been a plant—but he could have been a dupe, just as Claire Sterling suggested the members of her "Guerrilla International" were pawns. What was going on?

The Agency's senior Soviet analyst refused to panic in the face of Casey's fusillade of mumbled questions.

The first results of a computer check on everything the Agency had on file about Soviet ties to terrorism simply refused to confirm Sterling's claims. Indeed, all the evidence pointed to the Russians treading warily when it came to using terrorists. Groups like the IRA and ETA, according to KGB defectors, were too unstable, their actions too likely to ricochet for the Russians to support their aims.

"Bullshit," mumbled Casey. "Absolute bullshit."

Inman agreed. Casey ordered another analyst to review the Agency's files. His brief was clear. He should not expect to find the kind of evidence that would stand up in a district court. That was not the KGB way. He must look for a pattern. Once he had established that, he would be able to make a judgment.

Clarrige sent another report, which was immediately routed to the director. Italian security sources had told the station chief that Claire Sterling had obtained most of her information from West Germany's BND, Mossad, and Turkish military intelligence, and that her allegations of links between the IRA and the KGB may have been part of a disinformation ploy by British Intelligence. Clarrige's informants had also told him that DIGOS was now certain that Libya was not involved in the attempt on the president's life, but that Qaddafi was still planning some covert action. An indication of this was that Frank Terpil had been recently spotted again in Tripoli.

Terpil, like Buckley, was an expert in counterterrorist methods and had been among the Agency's acknowledged experts on sabotage. Now he was a fugitive from American justice. A grand jury in Washington had indicted Terpil on supplying explosives to Libya, conspiring to assassinate one of Qaddafi's opponents in Libya, recruiting former American military pilots to fly Qaddafi's Russian-built planes, and employing retired Green Berets to run a terrorist training camp forty-five miles south of Tripoli City.

Casey's instincts—that old tingling feeling in his fingers that once had alerted him to danger in the last war—warned that something serious was afoot.

Whatever the truth about Hinckley the FBI had produced— that he was an unstable loner—Casey had an overpowering feeling that Hinckley had only been the beginning. The director could sniff the danger. If only he could begin to pinpoint where it might next surface.

When it did, on Wednesday, May 13, 1981, Casey was as momentarily stunned as everyone else. At 5:18 in the afternoon, Rome time, Pope John Paul was shot and critically wounded before almost a quarter of a million pilgrims in St. Peter's Square.

Buckley was among those in the crowd—drawn there, like almost everyone else, by the sheer charisma of the pontiff. The agent had been in Rome on a brief vacation from training Sadat's bodyguards. Within hours he was on his way back to Cairo. If someone could shoot the Pope, then clearly no leader was safe. All Buckley could do was drill his Egyptians until they could perform their duties as perfectly as humanly possible.

The news of the attempt on the Pope's life reached Casey as he was about to go to lunch with Air Force Lieutenant General Eugene Tighe. He was the silver-haired, kindly-faced head of the Defense Intelligence Agency, the DIA, which coordinated intelligence gathering between the Army, Navy, Marines, and Air Force. Tighe's prime responsibility was to use his widely spread resources to try and provide a warning of any Russian threat.

Casey liked and trusted Tighe. Behind his grandfatherly manner was steel, and a fast and sure analytical mind. Among the director's first telephone calls, when he had recovered from the news from Rome, was to Tighe. Was there anything, anything at all, that suggested the Russians were behind the shooting?

Tighe had nothing. Nor had the NSA. Nor had anyone in the Washington intelligence community.

Casey refused to accept that what had been done in St. Peter's Square was the action of another lone madman— Mehmet Ali Agca, the Turk who had been caught redhanded gunning down the pontiff. Mad? Possibly. But acting all on his own? How had he managed to get off so many shots before anyone had moved to stop him? It had all the stamp of a professional hit. Or at least somebody trained by professionals.

By early evening, Washington time—close to midnight in Rome—Clarrige had more news. The station chief had managed to get to one of the doctors who had examined Agca in Rome police headquarters. The gunman, when captured, appeared drugged. A physical examination revealed recent injection bruises on his body. Analysis of Agca's blood samples confirmed traces of amphetamines. Agca's first responses to interrogation suggested he had been medically helped for his mission. The Italian intelligence service physician had told Clarrige that Agca behaved like someone who had been brainwashed.

"Holy Christ!" exploded Casey.

Throughout the night Dr. Post and his specialists prepared a detailed study on the feasibility of programming a hit man to strike down one of the most revered figures in the Christian world.

The study formed part of Casey's briefing to the full National Foreign Intelligence Board at its headquarters on F Street near the White House. Inman, Tighe, Webster of the FBI, everyone was there who mattered in the intelligence community, on down to the heads of the intelligence units of the departments of Energy and the Treasury.

Like the specialists in the Political Psychological Division, the director had gone without sleep, reading, phoning, and thinking. He had spoken to Clarrige a dozen times, getting updates on what the Agency's assets were reporting from inside the Vatican. The consensus there was that the attack had been carefully planned. The Italian secret service said it increasingly bore the marks of being KGB-inspired.

The Paris station reported that Agca was already on an Interpol Red Alert for double murder in Turkey. From Tel Aviv came the news that Mossad had been trailing Agca for weeks until he had disappeared through Checkpoint Charlie into East Berlin. Casey had called Peter Mandy in Tel Aviv. The senior Israeli intelligence man was unusually forthcoming. On Good Friday, April 17, 1981, Mossad believed it had tracked Agca to the small university town of Perugia. The Italians had been alerted—but seemingly had not followed up the sighting. By the time a Mossad team had reached Perugia there was no sign of Agca.

Casey had asked Mandy one question: Why the interest in Agca? Mandy, his voice crackling over the 7,000-mile telephone link, had replied cryptically: a probable KGB link. Mandy added that Mossad had evidence Agca had been seen in not only East Germany, but also Bulgaria, each time in the company of Russian intelligence men.

Casey had called back Clarrige. What the hell had DIGOS been up to, letting Agca slip through their grasp like that?

The weary station chief, who by then had not been to bed for almost thirty hours, reminded Casey that relationships between DIGOS and the Italian secret service and the Mossad were far from ideal because the Israelis sent out too many fliers claiming that Rome was a hotbed of terrorism.

Casey told Clarrige to send a team to Perugia to see what pieces could be picked up.

The Bonn station had reported that a BND team had also been tracking Agca for the past three months as he had flitted in and out of West Germany and Switzerland, into Austria, and across various border points with West Germany, Hungary, and Czechoslovakia. The West German security service had been certain that Agca was an arms bagman, carrying large sums of money from clients to dealers. The BND had told its Turkish counterpart it would not allow Agca to be arrested on German soil, despite the Interpol warrant. The Germans feared it would provoke reprisals from one of the many Turkish terrorist groups that had based themselves in West Germany. Besides, the BND were more interested to see where Agca would eventually lead them. On his tour through Europe,

Agca had stayed in good hotels and appeared to be well funded.

Casey did not need reminding that only a very generous paymaster produced such large sums. It all indeed pointed to a KGB involvement.

"Holy Christ!" Casey swore again, this time to Inman. "Half the motherfuckers in European intelligence were on this guy's tail and yet nobody seems to know what he was really up to!" By the time he and his deputy sat down in the conference room on F Street, the director had formulated how he would run the meeting.

First he circulated copies of the psycho-profile Dr. Post had created of the Pope. It portrayed John Paul as physically and spiritually strong, the very symbol of righteous anticommunism. The

> committed, unswerving prelate is a man of indomitable courage, a figure to be feared by his enemies because of his immense skill at using words and his constant actions to reassure his flock. He has all the qualities of a great leader. A vision focused on set goals. A political maturity from dealing first with the Nazis and then the Communists.

For the past two years John Paul had increasingly challenged the Polish regime, and therefore the Kremlin, in his determination to have basic freedoms for his homeland.

> What almost certainly drives him is that all good and human happiness depend upon freely given, and allowed, personal relations and that evil and unhappiness spring from the inadequacy of these relations. In the Pope's case that would be his early realization of the evils of Nazism and communism.

It was basic textbook stuff; what it lacked in hard fact it made up with a picture of a man who had fought all his life for what he believed to be right.

Casey told his attentive audience that one incident could have finally triggered the Soviets to try to eliminate the pontiff.

The Agency's assets in the Vatican had confirmed that on August 4, 1980, John Paul had written a letter to Brezhnev. On a single handwritten sheet of stationery bearing the papal coat of arms, the Pope had expressed his utmost concern over the prospect of the Soviet Union invading Poland. He had added a final unprecedented sentence. If the Russians did so, he would give up the Throne of St. Peter and return to his homeland to lead the resistance of his people.

Casey reminded his listeners that the pontiff's calculated gamble had paid off. Russia had still not crossed the Polish border. The Agency's estimate was that the Soviet Union would not now do so.

But on the day that letter had been hand-delivered to Moscow by the Pope's diplomatic troubleshooter, Archbishop Luigi Poggi, John Paul became a target for the KGB.

Casey introduced the second document the specialists had prepared. He revealed there was a very real possibility that Agca could have undergone some form of brainwashing, his mind controlled by drugs or some other skilled medical intervention.

If not exactly *The Manchurian Candidate*, then what seemed a chilling look-alike had surfaced in Rome.

19

War on All Fronts

On Saturday, October 6, 1981, Buckley sat toward the back of the presidential stand in Cairo, watching the military parade pass in review. Below him, to his right, Anwar Sadat sat, dressed in the uniform of Egypt's commander in chief, watching his troops swing past. The parade was a further reminder of how totally dependent upon the United States Sadat had become since the Camp David Accord of 1978 and the peace treaty he had signed with Israel a year later. In return the Reagan administration continued to shower money and arms upon Egypt.

Yet behind the impressive display of precision marching and the columns of armor, the outward symbol that Sadat was the first Egyptian leader who believed he could always call for further military help from Washington, Buckley also knew, after his months in Cairo, that the Egyptian President found it increasingly hard to bear the isolation from his Arab neighbors.

Because of the peace pact with Israel, many Arab leaders wanted him killed. Syria's Hafez Assad had publicly said he would, given the opportunity, personally strangle Sadat, choke the life out of him for the promise he had made never again to allow Egypt to wage war against Israel. Despite his years of being the Agency's most distinguished asset in the Middle East, the constant supplier of invaluable nuggets of information, even King Hussein had told Washington that he would be unwilling to support Sadat should his enemies attack. A pariah beyond his borders, the president had also become a leper among his own people.

Buckley was certain that, apart from himself, no one in the review stand knew that not only the ambassador, but King Hassan of Morocco were also priceless Agency assets. His Majesty had been recruited by the Agency when he was a teenager. On becoming king in 1961, Hassan had asked the Agency to restructure and train his own security service. It had become one of the harshest in the Arab world, a rival in sheer cruelty to the shah's SAVAK. The Moroccan security service was fully staffed with doctors who supervised a wide range of tortures of political detainees at a purpose-built detention center near Tazmarent. It included isolation chambers virtually identical to the one in the basement of the Allan Memorial Institute. The center also had several Page-Russell electroshock machines, which were routinely used on prisoners. During the post-shock periods, Moroccan physicians questioned the detainees, seeking information about opponents to the king.

Sadat had allowed his country to become the most important listening post the United States had in North Africa. In the Atlas Mountains, NSA had set up the latest electrical technology beamed toward Libya. Other state-of-the-art equipment was targeted on Gibraltar, gathering up Britain's secret intelligence traffic in and out of the Rock. Still more American gadgetry swept the straits and reached far out into the Atlantic, collecting intercepts from Soviet ships. A Department D team was based in Marrakech, from where its members roamed the length of North Africa on bugging missions. Its targets included the homes of wealthy Arabs in Marbella and in Cyprus. Morocco's ambassador to Egypt contributed to the Agency's intelligence gathering operations in the Nile Delta.

In many ways the diplomat's input was not essential. In the past few months Buckley, through his unfettered access to the presidential palace while training Sadat's bodyguards, had placed a whole range of bugs in every conceivable outlet. He had systematically worked his way through every office planting them. One bug, the size of a pin, had been deftly placed on a notice board beside a military map. Another was sited in a bookshelf. He had stuck one under Sadat's own desk and, on the pretext of suddenly feeling unwell while briefing the president on the guards' progress, Buckley had been readily waved into Sadat's bathroom. The agent had bugged the room.

Department D operatives ran a constant surveillance on the palace, hearing everything Sadat said or did.

In his own conversations with the president, Buckley had found him often melancholic, saying he did not know how long the peace pact would last. The effects of his pot taking were very clear; at times Sadat seemed as spaced out as any Greenwich Village hippie. Those were the occasions when the president was most prone to say that it was Allah's will whether he lived or died—and that he felt God no longer favored him.

Buckley had repeatedly warned Sadat's bodyguards that they must never allow such fatalism to enter their work. They should only respond as they had now been taught. At the first sign of trouble they must form a solid phalanx around Sadat and shoot to kill. Time and again, in the endless practice sessions, with Buckley playing the role of the president, he had ordered the guards to first form that wall and then choose their target. He had shown them how to use night scopes and how to read the heat-activated sensors that surrounded the palace to alert them of intruders. He had made them watch hours of film of other attacks: the assassination of President Kennedy; the attempt on Pope Paul VI in Manila; and, more recently, film of the attack on John Paul. He had pointed out the lessons and the mistakes to be learned: how the Secret Service man with Kennedy in Dallas had thrown himself across the President's body while at the same time pulling Mrs. Kennedy to the floor; how the Filipino guards around Pope Paul had been momentarily paralyzed and had only acted when the pontiff's own personal bodyguard, Archbishop Paul Marcinkus, had disarmed the attacker; how, in St. Peter's Square, the lessons of Manila had been absorbed, with John Paul's aides shielding his stricken body from further attacks.

"Your life means nothing," Buckley had endlessly repeated. "The president means everything. To you. To Egypt. Never forget that."

He had taught them everything he had learned in Vietnam, Laos, and Angola.

The Saturday parade was the guards' first public chance to show off their skills. Some of them sat immediately behind

Sadat; others were positioned on either side of the stand. They were equipped with USI machine-pistols, the ideal close-range killing weapon.

An armored column, tanks and halftracks, trundled past. Suddenly, from behind the last tank, there was a break in the ranks. Soldiers were running. Instinctively, Buckley rose to his feet, feeling for the .38 police special in his shoulder holster. His shouted first commands to the bodyguards were drowned in a burst of gunfire. The oncoming men in soldiers' uniforms were raking the stand.

"Shoot! For Christ's sake, shoot!" Buckley shouted as he forced his way forward. The bodyguards stared dumbfounded at the oncoming gunmen.

"Shoot!"

A burst of ragged fire came from the first USI.

"Get him down! Cover the president!"

Buckley's order went unheeded.

The gunmen had paused and were kneeling, firing with deadly effect into the stand.

"Pick your targets! Christ's sake! Pick your targets!" Buckley was screaming.

The gunmen poured shots into the stampeding spectators and the president.

Hemmed in, there was no way Buckley could return the fire.

Sadat suddenly slumped in his seat.

Only then did the bodyguards form a protective shield. They began to pick off the gunmen. Bodies started to fall to the ground. From the parade itself soldiers broke ranks to help. The assassins were trapped between two fields of fire.

Buckley knew it was too late. One look at Sadat was enough to show him that the president was beyond help. Blood poured from his mouth, ears, nose, and chest. Buckley melted into the panic-stricken crowds, heading for the U.S. Embassy compound.

He arrived to find the place in uproar. A line had been opened to the State Department and a diplomat was yelling into the phone.

"He's still alive! The Egyptians are saying he's still alive!"

Buckley walked into the office, shaking his head, mouthing the word: dead.

The diplomat waved him away.

Buckley shrugged and walked to the Agency's offices at the rear of the building. The station chief was on the phone to the new DDO, John H. Stein, who had been in charge of Tripoli station when Qaddafi took power.

"The latest we have is that he's alive," said the station chief.

"He's dead," yelled Buckley. "As dead as a dodo!"

"Buckley says he's dead!" parroted the station chief into the mouthpiece. "But that's not what the Egyptians are saying."

Buckley motioned for the phone. He explained to Stein what he had seen, speaking slowly, knowing that the DDO was furiously writing it all down. That was Stein's style: No matter how great the crisis, keep a record, remain cool, ask few questions.

When Buckley finished, Stein said he should take the first plane to Washington.

Three weeks after Hosni Mubarak became Egypt's president, a comprehensive plan for a full-scale covert war in Central America had still to be agreed to by the White House—largely because Haig was pushing hard for President Reagan to have the CIA and NSA concentrate their efforts on Cuba, while Weinberger was not certain whether there should be any operation at all, because it could lead to a resuscitation of the two great bogeymen of Defense, overcommitment and escalation, the ghosts of Vietnam that never quite went away.

While all this and much else was in the intelligence melting pot, Casey was sidetracked with a pinprick from the past. Ottawa Station reported that Dr. Morrow and Velma Orlikow would soon be joined by other plaintiffs in their case against the CIA.

Velma had filed a lawsuit in Washington on December 11, 1980. She was asking for $1 million in damages. Her attorney was Joseph Rauh, America's most renowned civil rights lawyer. Shortly afterwards Dr. Morrow had become a coplaintiff.

Casey's response then had been to order the Agency's general counsel, Stanley Sporkin, to have his staff prepare to defend the action—and to legally delay a court hearing as long as possible. The director's strategy was that the plaintiffs were elderly, and when the last of them died, so would their legal action.

But Rauh had pushed his case along. He had been rummaging in the Agency's past, talking to Alice Olson about how

er husband had died; tracking down Dr. Gottlieb; talking to
ny number of doctors who had worked at the Allan Memo-
al Institute under Dr. Cameron; digging out all Dr. Cam-
ron's papers from the archives; having them evaluated by
Dr. Robert Lifton, who was conducting research into the
ehavior of Nazi doctors at Auschwitz and elsewhere; talking
) relatives of patients at the institute; and talking to senior
medical men who had known Dr. Cameron. Now Rauh wanted
) question Helms. He wanted the key to Pandora's Box.

In the midst of trying to deal with a hundred intelligence
sues that had a current bearing on the safety of the United
tates, Casey found himself dragged aside to discuss some-
ing that should have been long dead and buried.

But, insisted Sporkin, the matter could not be ignored.

Anxious to get back to the growing spate of reports from his
ations in Europe on Qaddafi's latest plans to kill Reagan—
ne London station said the Libyans planned to assemble and
unch a crude missile against the White House, using a
lueprint Qaddafi's men had reportedly given the IRA to use
Northern Ireland—Casey reluctantly agreed to deal with
ne residue of M-K-Ultra/M-K-Search.

On Monday, November 19, 1981, with Buckley kicking his
eels around the Directorate of Operations, Casey found a
ob for him. Buckley was dispatched to Canada to try and get
ackground on all the plaintiffs that the Ottawa station had
rovided. He was to concentrate upon their current medical
ate. Buckley realized it was drudge-work time again, the
nevitable aftermath of the failure of Sadat's bodyguards. But
was better than sitting around Langley.

While he was in Montreal he read a *New York Times*
eport that a five-man Libyan hit squad had somehow se-
retly entered the United States. Within forty-eight hours
ne reports had grown to a ten-man team—and that the
ibyans may have entered the United States by crossing the
anadian border.

Buckley telephoned Langley and asked if he should mo-
nentarily drop his inquiries to try and pick up the trail of
Qaddafi's men. He was told the matter was well in hand.

Next day the Libyan leader scored a major public relations
oup by appearing live on American network television to
eny he had sent any assassination squads to North America.

The day after, President Reagan publicly branded the colonel a liar. "We have the evidence and he knows it."

Buckley called a friend in the DDO. What was this evidence?

"It's White House evidence. Out of the basement."

Out of the basement was a common Agency dismissive description of the National Security Planning Group (NSPG) which operated in the bowels of the White House under the chairmanship of the President's National Security Adviser. The present holder of the office, Richard V. Allen, was on leave of absence, pending the outcome of the embarrassing allegation that he had accepted a $1,000 gift from a Japanese journalist to arrange an interview with the president. Among the newcomers to the NSPG was a young Marine, Lieutenant Colonel Oliver North. His immediate job was to liaise with Robert C. McFarlane, also a former Marine officer, now a State Department counselor directly responsible to Haig for coordinating a joint U.S. intelligence initiative against Libya.

On Monday, January 4, 1982, Buckley turned in a report to the DDO on the medical and mental conditions of Velma Orlikow, Dr. Morrow, and the other plaintiffs. They were all elderly and some were in poor physical health. But they were all united in a common determination to fight the CIA.

Casey had another job for Buckley. He was back in favor to be entrusted with an operation the director thought would not only put what he subsequently termed "the Montreal fuck-up" into perspective, but at the same time cause acute public embarrassment to America's enemies.

Buckley was given a list of countries and was told to use the DDO's resources to collect evidence of doctors torturing. Throughout the winter weeks of 1982 he put together a fearful picture of medical torture. From Ethiopia an asset sent details of experiments being conducted at the Central Revolutionary Headquarters in Addis Ababa. Physicians employed by the regime poured boiling oil and water on parts of prisoners' bodies and then tested various blood coagulants and serums to treat the massive blistering. The medicaments had been supplied by the Russians for the grisly trials in which many of the victims died in agony. From the tiny Marxist state of Djibouti he obtained proof that doctors in the *Brigade speciale de recherche de la gendarmerie* performed numerous tortures: injecting coma-inducing drugs, electro shock, amputations, and immersing victims in vats of brine

or weeks at a time, pickling their skin until it rotted from the
bone.

From Somalia came the report that physicians employed
by the National Security Service at its headquarters in
Mogadishu had created a noise room. In its confines prisoners were subjected for days at a time to increasingly amplified
sounds until they became permanently deaf.

An Agency asset in Kampala reported that, despite President Idi Amin being overthrown, torture was still widespread
under President Milton Obote. A dozen designated centers
throughout Uganda each had its doctors who supervised or
participated in such tortures as castration, the burning off of
breasts and genitalia, and surgical removal of tongues.

For the past thirty-five years the Agency had filed many
thousands of cases of medical torture in Russia. When required, these were fed to U.S. politicians to attack the Soviet
system, using the names of the doctors and the hospitals
where the abuses occurred. The files bulged with repeated
accounts of psychiatric abuses. Soviet physicians routinely
prescribed psychotropic disorientating and pain-inducing treatments for perfectly sane persons whose only illness was opposing the regime. Many of the drugs were given in massive
quantities and with a total disregard of contraindications.
Those who received them frequently became permanently
physically incapacitated or mentally deranged.

Inevitably Buckley found his research could not be neatly
compartmentalized. While medical torture was uniform within
the Soviet Bloc, it recognized no geographic boundaries.
What doctors did in Libya, he discovered, was virtually duplicated in adjoining Egypt. In the aftermath of Sadat's assassination, thousands of people had been arrested by the State
Security Investigation Service—itself virtually created and
trained by the Agency—and taken to one of several notorious
Cairo torture chambers: the Citadel, Tora Reception Prison,
and Al Marg Prison. In all those places doctors routinely
supervised or participated in torture that included determin-
ing the amount of whipping a suspect could survive and the
length of sensory deprivation he or she could endure in
stygian underground vaults.

In adding Iran and Iraq to his list of countries where
physicians formed an important part of state-sponsored torture, Buckley found—and it came as no great surprise—that

Israeli doctors employed by Shin Beth, the internal intelligence service, often determined how long a suspect could be hooded and repeatedly exposed to ice-cold showers and deprived of sleep and food.

Saudi Arabia, long deemed friendly by the Agency, was in terms of medical torture really no different from Syria. In both countries doctors supervised a wide range of torture during interrogation. It was a Syrian physician who had invented an instrument now commonly used in medical abuse in both countries. It was the *al-Abd as-Aswad*, the Black Slave. It consisted of a metal chair with a hole in its seat. A victim was strapped naked to the chair and then up through the hole came a heated metal skewer, which entered the anus, slowly mincing its way into the intestines. A doctor was often on hand to ensure the skewer was withdrawn before killing a person, though death generally came as a result of massive internal hemorrhaging resulting from repeated insertion of the spike.

In dealing with Central Europe, reviewing Soviet Bloc medical abuses, Buckley found it difficult to distinguish between them and what doctors did in adjoining Turkey, another friendly nation. Turkey provided the CIA and NSA with bases in the mountains on the Soviet-Iran border where both agencies ran operations similar to those in Morocco. Yet in at least two Turkish military prisons—at Mamat near Ankara and Metis in Istanbul—doctors supervised daily torture sessions, witnessing beatings, administering electroshocks, and deciding how long a victim should be hooded.

At Bien Hoa Hospital in Saigon, where Agency doctors had experimented upon Vietcong prisoners, Communist physicians now tortured those who refused to accept the new regime. Just as the American doctors had used massive electroshocks to try and restructure their prisoners, and Dr. Cameron had performed his work-or-be-shocked experiment, the Communist doctors used an identical approach.

In the Philippines, physicians in the employ of the National Security Service—yet another organization the Agency had helped train—authorized similar treatments for opponents of the Marcos regime.

From Africa to Asia, to Latin America, to the Middle East, in over eighty countries deemed to be unfriendly to the United States, Buckley gathered evidence of medical torture.

By June 1982 the horrific details had been sifted and sorted.
Then with the help of the specialists in the Political Psycho-
ogical Division—whose contacts reached into every corner of
he medical world—the material was carefully fed to human
ights workers: lawyers, doctors, and religious leaders. In
urn they passed on the evidence to organizations like Am-
esty International. Amnesty's own staff checked as far as
hey could: the facts matched what they had gleaned. Much
f the evidence Buckley had gathered was included in Am-
esty's regular reports on torture in the eighties.

There was no way that Amnesty International could have
uspected that the evidence it published was not only accu-
ate, but had originally been gathered by the Central Intelli-
ence Agency for a purpose very different from the aims of
he world's most celebrated human rights organization.

In early December 1983, Buckley was back in his favorite
ity, Rome, taking a few days leave from his new post—
tation chief in Beirut.

Lebanon had become the ultimate test for all he had learned.
Ie had sensed that from the day he arrived in the city the
revious April. His old friend Bob Ames had been right.
There was nothing quite like Beirut for testing all the accu-
nulated years of this business; everything that had gone
efore had only been preparation for this.

After completing his report on medical torture, Buckley
ad spent some time in San Salvador.

All he had heard was true—the Salvadoran regime sur-
ived through terror. Not even in Vietnam had he witnessed
uch a blatant disregard for basic human rights. In El Salva-
lor there were scores of detention centers where, he had
earned, vile tortures were carried out. Again doctors had
een identified committing them—using drugs to disorient
ictims, and that stand-by of all medical torture, their elec-
roshock machines.

On a visit to police headquarters in San Salvador Buckley
ad witnessed a physician, who was a regular visitor to the
J.S. Embassy, pouring sulfuric acid onto an already open
vound in an attempt to get a man to confess. What particu-
arly disgusted Buckley was the care the doctor took, admin-
stering a drop of acid at a time, so that its full burning effect
vould be maximized. But after Vietnam, Buckley had learned
o look the other way.

Buckley's role in El Salvador had been to help train the government forces in jungle warfare. The Sandinistas were expert at it. He had led patrols against them and had come to reluctantly admire their skills. They were genuinely motivated, to the point of being often foolhardy, while the government forces were inept and generally cowardly.

Then, returning from one patrol, he had been urgently recalled to Washington. Clair George, who had replaced Stein as DDO, had briefed him and then escorted him to the seventh floor.

Casey had spent a little while explaining the overall situation in the Middle East. He had seemed to mumble a little more, be that much more uncertain on his legs, puffing after shambling from behind his desk to show the DDO and his new station chief in Beirut out of the office.

Chuck Cogan, the Agency's head of the Near East desk, had delivered a final homily: *This is the big one. You're back in the driver's seat. Don't go off the road.*

Buckley had not needed to be told. The memory of what had led to his appointment would take a long time to erase. Ames had been among those who had died in the car bombing of the old U.S. Embassy on the Beirut sea front one day last April. With him had perished some of the Agency's best men in the region, a dozen officers from the Beirut station and Cairo and Athens. They had been friends with whom he had shared common aims and sometimes danger. He still missed them. Coming to Rome on leave was a respite from the constant knowledge that he could be the next to die.

In Rome Buckley stayed with a couple whose husband worked for the Agency. With Clarrige running operations in Central America, the Agency man had the enviable job of running the Vatican assets.

There were, he told Buckley, half a dozen priests who provided information. Some were paid cash; others took their fees in kind—expensive dinners and vacations. An Irish cleric regularly received his fare home and enough spending money to impress his friends around Dublin. A German prelate was given sufficient lire for him to shop at Gammarelli's, the Pope's tailor.

The informers provided a regular flow of information. The Vatican no longer believed that Libya had been directly involved in Agca's attempt on the Pope's life, but that it was the work of the KGB. But, pragmatic as always, the pontiff had recently sent Archbishop Luigi Poggi to Moscow to begin secret discussions in the Kremlin on the prospect of coming to a mutually acceptable accommodation over Poland: The pontiff would control Walesa if the Church was given more freedom.

Buckley found it interesting, but hardly earth-shattering. Returning to Beirut, he was plunged back into a volatile climate where many of the keys could be turned in the locks of doors that led to the deeper recesses of intelligence gathering.

Ames had been right when he said the city was unique. Mossad and Arab intelligence men operated in Beirut, turning assets against each other. Most European intelligence agencies had a strong presence in the city, sometimes working together, more often alone.

Buckley was running a network of informers that extended into the upper echelons of the shaky coalition government. Among them was Walid Jumblatt, the Druze leader, a warlord who survived by sleeping under a different roof every night in the Christian sector of the city. Jumblatt was the government's minister of tourism—a post that afforded him a chance to constantly visit the foreign embassies and encourage their staffs to think of ways to attract tourists to what had already become probably the most dangerous city on earth. In each of those embassies Jumblatt had his own man in place, gathering up tidbits of intelligence, which the Druze leader conveyed to Buckley.

Another asset was a PLO man who, at huge personal risk, met Buckley to brief him on Yasir Arafat's latest thinking. A third informer, a Syrian, supplied details of the latest groupings around President Assad in Damascus.

At times the sheer volume of raw intelligence was overwhelming. As well as keeping tabs on events in Lebanon, Buckley maintained a watch over Iran, using foreign businessmen who passed through Beirut from trading missions to Tehran. Like the Agency's Vatican assets, they briefed Buckley in return for often no more than a good meal.

On a daily basis Buckley handled up to a hundred separate items. Each one had to be assessed and sent on to Langley. Sometimes the station chief worked twenty-four stints for several days at a time before sleeping round the clock in his penthouse.

The intelligence from Beirut was slotted into the PDB that went over to the White House.

At the start of 1984, an election year, Libya continued to dominate Casey's immediate problems. Qaddafi was on the rampage. His hand was detected behind unrest in Egypt, Tunisia, and Algeria. His People's Bureaux were fermenting trouble in half a dozen European capitals.

In the White House basement a subgroup, created by the president's new National Security Adviser, Robert McFarlane, was preparing various options for covert operations against Qaddafi—or anyone else who threatened the United States. The most vocal voice was that of Oliver North.

Upstairs in the Oval Office, the president and his new Secretary of State, George P. Shultz, listened to Casey briefing them on the reality of Libya manufacturing a nuclear bomb. The director summed up.

"We believe Libya will not possess a nuclear explosion capability within the next ten years."

Casey had put a couple of questions. Why wait until then? Why not go in and get Qaddafi.

Get was a current Agency euphemism for terminate, which in plain language meant kill.

At three o'clock on the morning of Friday, March 16, 1984, Casey was for once still asleep when the bedside phone rang at his home, a tan brick house on what had been Nelson Rockefeller's estate in the northwestern suburbs of Washington. The caller was Clair George. The DDO had himself been rousted out of sleep by a shattering call from the senior night officer at Langley. A Flash had come in from Beirut that Buckley had been kidnapped.

Within an hour Casey was at his desk on the seventh floor, facing a growing group of stricken faces. George was there, manning an open line to the embassy in Beirut. He had been station chief in Lebanon for a year, 1975–6, when two U.S. government employees had been snatched and held hostage for four months before being released upon payment of a substantial ransom.

But the DDO sensed, from what he was hearing, that money would not so easily obtain Buckley's release.

McMahon arrived. His flabby face, normally suffused, was

white. Around the Agency he was known as "Smiling Jack," a nickname that had endured from his college days. His first question to George was one Casey had already asked.

"How the fuck does a savvy guy like Buckley go and get himself kidnapped?"

George shrugged. There were already too many unanswered questions.

Casey continued to give orders. He ordered a team to be put together—the best available—and be on their way to Beirut before breakfast.

The Rome and Athens stations should fly in men. Cairo should work its sources. The station chief in Ammān should get Hussein to mobilize his contacts in Lebanon. He wanted King Hassan of Morocco brought in. Casey wanted every available agent, asset, and contact throughout the length and breadth of the Mediterranean to drop whatever else they were doing and concentrate on finding Buckley.

Webster arrived. He offered the FBI's expertise on hostage taking.

Casey nodded. Webster went to an adjoining office to call his men.

Casey continued to give orders. Money was to be no problem. He would authorize payment—no matter how large—if it led to Buckley's return.

McMahon called the NSA. How soon could it get a satellite geopositioned over Beirut?

George groaned into the telephone. "Jesus Christ! Are you certain?" The DDO called to Casey. "They haven't found his burn bag. They think he had it with him."

"Oh, fuck," mumbled the director. "Of all the motherfucking luck!"

The burn bag would be a dead giveaway. Everyone in the office knew what that meant.

Dr. Post arrived. Casey told the psychiatrist to put together a team of specialists to prepare a full psychological evaluation of the kidnappers.

"Do you know who they are?"

"For a start, probably Moslems. Shiites. Have to be. When we get more, we'll get it to you."

Dr. Post hurried away.

Casey ordered an aide to get Peter Mandy to the phone in Tel Aviv.

George groaned again. "Jesus Christ!" The DDO relayed to the room that Buckley had told his driver/guard not to show that morning.

"Maybe he was running a sensitive contact. Someone who didn't want to be seen," suggested McMahon.

"Orders are fucking orders. I said a month ago that no one goes out alone in Beirut," mumbled Casey. "What the fuck was Buckley doing?"

The call from Tel Aviv came through. Casey told the Mossad deputy director what had happened. Mandy simply said okay, he would get his people onto it. He did not sound very hopeful.

Casey looked at McMahon. Some time ago they had agreed that one of them should pay a visit to Tel Aviv to let the Israelis know that the Agency was still a friend; Israel's own recent role in Lebanon had strained its relationship with the United States. McMahon began to make plans to fly to Tel Aviv.

The director called McFarlane. The White House security advisor asked if he should tell the president.

"You think Reagan's gonna ride into Beirut and rescue Buckley like in one of his old movies!" Casey's pent-up frustration and anger at the loss of his station chief had finally boiled over.

Throughout the spring of 1985, in Washington and elsewhere, the specialists had continued their work.

Case files on Nazi doctors were pored over in the search for further clues to Dr. al-Abub's personality. Questions were constantly asked. Was he like Josef Mengele, who had found complete self-expression through what he had done in Auschwitz? Was he like one of those Soviet psychiatrists who saw themselves as not so much acting on orders from the KGB, but performing the normal functions of a doctor? The whole gamut of behavioral technology was surveyed to see where the successes and failures had been. The results of the now standard procedure of hooding and isolation—crude forms of sensory deprivation—were examined as they were applied in places like Northern Ireland and in Chile by the security forces. What did hooding do to a man? How did, say, a hardened IRA man in a Belfast detention center respond differently to being hooded than an academic held in a Santi-

ago prison? There were differences, not surprisingly, but in
he words of one specialist, "They didn't help a goddamn in
assisting us to understand what Buckley was going through."
It was, he added, a measure of the desperation felt within the
division "to get answers to the seventh floor."

There, in an office suite whose windows looked out over
the treetops that gave the Agency's 210-acre site the appearance of being deep within a forest, Director Casey, wrestling
with a thousand other intelligence matters, unfailingly spent
a portion of each day reviewing the dossier on Buckley. He
had, he told McMahon and George, become obsessed with
getting the station chief back. And, he would sometimes add,
his voice more of a mumble than usual, he "wanted the heads
of every one of the motherfuckers who had hurt Bill. If it's
the last thing I do, I want those bastards brought to book."

Casey called the specialists regularly, asking sharp questions, noting the answers on one of the four-by-four cards he
carried around with him, using the gold Tiffany pen his wife,
Sophia, had given him one Christmas.

The use of drugs as a means of repression was endlessly
debated at breakfast meetings between the specialists before
they spent another long day slugging through the morass of
files.

The director reminded the specialists that money and resources were theirs for the calling. He arranged for DDO
George to provide them with reports from CIA stations in the
Middle East. NSA satellites were used to conduct constant
eavesdropping operations over Lebanon, electronically sweeping the streets of Beirut day and night and gathering up tens
of thousands of disparate conversations, in which NSA computers were programmed to search for key words or phrases.
These included "Buckley," "The American," "Dr. al-Abub,"
"doctor," and "Sheykh Fadlallah."

Deputy Director McMahon, a flabby-faced, high colored,
hard-driving man, daily badgered Dr. Post and his men for
progress reports. McMahon urged them on with words that
became a litany. McMahon would repeatedly emphasize that
President Reagan had personally taken an interest in the fate
of Buckley. At every meeting with Casey the president would
ask, "What's happening in that mess, Bill?" The director
would shake his head and mumble that "everyone was on top
of it."

The specialists questioned men who had known Buckley. Among them was Cogan, whose career, physical appearance, and mental attitudes were remarkably similar to Buckley's. Cogan had joined the Agency around the same time as Buckley. Slim and wiry, very like Buckley in build, he also had some of the station chief's mannerisms: a brief, no-nonsense handshake, a look that simply turned away questions, a soft voice that somehow never quite lost its steel. Cogan reckoned that Buckley was too steeped in that old Sicilian code of silence Agency veterans wore as a badge of pride to have talked.

Evaluating what he had said, the specialists were less certain. They knew from their studies that no one could ultimately withstand a skilled medical torturer, that the physiology of the human nervous system is the same for all people, regardless of race or culture—or, for that matter, profession. Nothing Buckley had been taught in the spy business would have made it any easier for his nervous system to better resist electroshocks, beatings, prolonged hanging by the arms or feet, drugging, isolation, and hooding. He was as vulnerable as anyone else—perhaps even more so, because the basic will to resist would be that much greater in him, and therefore, when it came, the collapse of that resistance all the more spectacular.

Casey could not quite bring himself to accept such reports. A fusillade of mumbled questions were invariably phoned through to Dr. Post and his team by the director. How could they be certain? Where was the proof? Was this really just psycho-guessing? How did this conclusion match what was on Buckley's personal file?

The specialists patiently fielded the questions. But the pressures grew. Many of them found themselves working at weekends. Those were the times when Casey was most likely to drop by their offices, coming to or from a golf course. In the early hours, any time from three A.M. onward, when Casey generally awoke to begin his day reading reports in his den at home, the specialists could expect a call from the director when a new thought struck him. How were the Shiite Moslems psychologically different from those in Iran? Were there any similarities between the Lebanese Muslims and those living in the Soviet Union? What about the Syrians— where could there be a psychological breaking point between them and the Hizballah?

The answers, perfectly typed and placed within folders marked FOR IMMEDIATE ATTENTION DCI, would be sent to his office. No one knew whether he read all the reports, let alone what he made of them, carefully couched as they were in what George called psycho-speak.

By mid-March, marking the passage of Buckley's first year in captivity, the specialists had ceased offering explanations about his responses. There was nothing new to work on: no further video, no message, only silence. Assuming he was still alive—an act of faith more than anything, they admitted—they added that any value he would have as a potential source of information had certainly ended: His captors must have long learned all he could have told them. The only hope they could offer Casey was that even by that stage Buckley was either totally unhinged or, preferably for him and the Agency, dead.

In the meantime, in the White House, Lieutenant Colonel North was busily concocting his own plan to solve what he had come to call "the Buckley screw-up."

He had been having a number of meetings with agents of the Drug Enforcement Agency (DEA) and one of their assets, a shadowy figure from Lebanon who had been a DEA informant for some years.

The asset told North that he had good connections in the Bekaa Valley—where the Hizballah, he added, produced heroin for export to the West to help finance their cause. Of more interest to North was the informer's claim that "a couple of hundred thousand U.S. dollars would be enough to spring Buckley."

The lieutenant colonel took the news to McFarlane, who carried it upstairs to the Oval Office. President Reagan—despite the administration's publicly stated position not to ever pay ransom—agreed that the money should be found to "buy back Buckley." But it must be done privately. McFarlane gave North the job of fund-raising. It was one that the Marine Corps officer knew exactly how to carry out. He flew to Texas to see one of the state's more colorful billionaires, H. Ross Perot. Six years earlier, while President Carter had still hesitated about direct intervention over the Tehran embassy hostages, Perot had hired a private task force to free two of his staff also held captive in Iran. The operation was a brilliant success. Once North had explained his plan, Perot handed over $200,000 in cash.

By early June, North refined his scheme into a four-page memo to McFarlane. Each page was marked: TOP SECRET EYES ONLY. SENSITIVE. ACTION. The gist of the memo was that the $200,000 was a down payment, that the "going price for springing a hostage" had risen to $1 million "and was non-negotiable." Buckley, the memo implied, might even cost more. But it would be money well spent. In the approve box at the end of the extraordinary document, McFarlane placed his initials. The $200,000 was handed over to the asset. He immediately disappeared—never to be heard of again until North subsequently and reluctantly revealed his existence to a closed session of the congressional hearings into Irangate.

While North had been preparing to bribe the Hizballah—and for his pains had been caught in a classic sting ploy, the first of many to befall the luckless Marine officer—more conventional specialists continued to develop their psycho-profiles of Dr. al-Abub.

They found little to disagree with. For example, in the view of Professor Anthony Storr, lecturer in psychiatry at Oxford University, a personality like Dr. al-Abub's was neither motivated by malice or sadism but by a fanatical self-righteousness; he could be classified as a man filled with moral certitude.

They accepted, too, he could well fit within the criteria outlined by Professor Robert Lifton, who had developed a psychological principle called doubling to try and explain the behavior of the Nazi doctors at Auschwitz and the other death camps. In Professor Lifton's theory, a personality successfully divided into two functioning wholes, so that a part self acted as an entire self. Using that approach, a Nazi doctor not only tortured and killed, but actually totally believed that what he did was not evil, but for the greater glory of the Third Reich. Those doctors had led successful double lives, on the one hand selecting those to die, and on the other going through the ordinary motions of everyday living, being good husbands and fathers and showing a proper respect for authority and a total belief in the prescription for the future they were helping to create.

The Nazi doctors, it had long been conceded among the specialists, had created the beginning of what Professor Lifton, among others, had defined as a psychology of torture. It had enabled them to embrace a wide range of evils, and in doing so it had made no difference to them whether or not they were totally aware of what those tortures were about. In Professor Lifton's view, "If there is any truth to the psychological and moral judgments we make about the specific characteristics of Nazi mass murder, we are bound to derive from the principles that apply . . . the extraordinary threat and potential for self-annihilation that now haunt mankind."

In all the specialists' cautious judgments about Dr. al-Abub, that reminder was always before them. Central to the Nazi doctors' ethos for what they had done was their claim to logic, rationality, and science. Assuming that almost certainly Dr. al-Abub was inculcated with the same monstrous belief, the psychiatrists believed it reinforced their conviction that he was in an advanced state of paranoia that had enabled him to logically systemize his behavior. That, agreed the behaviorists, would explain the underlying forces that had made him what he was and allowed him to operate as he did, just as it had enabled the Nazi doctors to function in the death camps. The Nazi doctors had finally shared a common sense of annihilation, believing that the system they had given themselves to could, after all, be destroyed, and the world as they knew it would be at an end. Yet, to the very last, to avert that unthinkable end, those doctors had striven ever harder to achieve what they saw as their sacred duty—the destruction of the Jewish evil. Very likely Dr. al-Abub was motivated by a similar kind of imagery, in which were mixed delusions and hallucinations and the most manic of absolute positivism.

Finally, to exist, the Nazi doctors had needed to virtually eliminate any capacity for normal human feelings; it was the only possible way for them to kill their victims. The specialists pondered whether Dr. al-Abub, in his mind, served the Hizballah in a similar way.

Just as the Nazi doctors could not be absolved from what Professor Lifton termed their Faustian bargain, neither, of course, could Dr. al-Abub. Nor, to be absolutely fair, were those Germans the first to be guilty of medical complicity in torture. In the Roman Empire, physicians were legally permitted to be present at, or take part in, the torture of those suspected of sorcery. During the Middle Ages, judges of the

Inquisition, regularly encouraged the use of priest-doctors to torture suspected heretics. Many of the ancient warlords of China and Japan included in their entourages a physician whose speciality was deciding which torture to use. The Spanish conquerors of Mexico and Peru took along their doctors who supervised the torture of Indians. The courts of England's Henry VIII, Edward VI, and Elizabeth I all had their physicians who attended torture sessions.

The experts knew that most certainly those doctors, like their Nazi successors and their Japanese counterparts in World War II, and all those who had followed—that all of them, despite the torture and murder they witnessed or actually committed, still had a strong belief in themselves as doctors. Indeed, it was often important for them to be formally addressed as Doctor; the title set them apart, gave them a special sense of identity, and enabled them to sustain their belief that they were the descendants of medical tradition and ethics and that what they were engaged in was ultimately no more than serving the greater cause of sovereign, state, or political cause above that of the individual. Those doctors had learned how to live in a very different reality, and the experts had no doubt that Dr. al-Abub did the same.

Like the Nazi doctors and their heirs central to that different reality was a combination of a feeling of total control over the fate of their prisoners and at the same time a strong sense of impotence—an overwhelming feeling of being a tiny part of an all-powerful and all-pervasive system controlled by others who were superior beings. The doctors thus felt far removed from direct involvement and therefore were able to adopt an overview. In Dr. al-Abub's case, the specialists knew that he accepted that his controllers, after Sheykh Fadlallah, were in Tehran. They were mullahs whose names he probably barely knew and whom he would most certainly not expect to meet unless he failed to carry out their instructions. Just as the Nazi doctors had once claimed they were only obeying orders enshrined in full legality, so would Dr. al-Abub very likely have said, should he ever be asked the question, that what he was doing fit a similar framework.

Many, too many, of his colleagues lived and worked by the same rationale. In the time Dr. al-Abub had studied medicine, elsewhere in the world hundreds of thousands of people had been tortured, often to the point of death, under political

ystems or in the name of political causes. Many had died
with a doctor actually present or close by. Those who sur-
ived bore forever the physical and mental scars of medically
ponsored gross ill-treatment.

The legacy of the great colonizers, the British, included
eriods when the physicians of the empire tortured in the
ame of their sovereign. For instance, between 1952 and
956 in Kenya, English doctors employed by the security
ervices were sometimes indistinguishable from the savages
f Mau-Mau. Those physicians had used a car battery with
opper wires attached to its terminals. They had watched
while interrogators had wrapped the wires around a Mau-
Mau suspect's testicles. The resulting shock rendered a vic-
m impotent. Previously the instrument had been used in
he closing days of the Raj in India; after Kenya it was
mported to Cyprus. Nowadays, within the electrically con-
rolled perimeter that helped to protect South Africa from its
lack neighbors, there are physicians who still swear by the
nstrument, using it on a regular basis on some of the more
ifficult prisoners in the jails of the republic.

In Algeria there were a number of survivors of French
medical torture during the 1960s. Then, physicians in the
rench Army regularly administered not only electroshocks
ut also the water torture, forcing the liquid into a victim's
ungs through a pipe, in almost precisely the way it had been
one during the Inquisition. The techniques of medieval
medically supervised torture also continued to be widely
sed throughout South America—much of it carried out in
hambers that resembled hospital operating rooms, each with
s bright overhead light and table to which victims were
trapped and then, among other tortures, wrapped in wet
loths to increase the effect of the electrical currents applied
o their bodies. Those atrocities were all too often done under
he supervision of doctors.

The specialists knew that those physicians had no difficulty,
o matter how crude their methods, in believing totally in
what they did. That was another important step in under-
tanding the mentality of Dr. al-Abub. He could have taken
efuge not only in the recent history of medical torture elsewhere, but could have drawn specific strength from the real-
zation that now, as never before, physicians in some of the
raditional bastions of medical torture, the Near and Far

East, very much a part of his culture, tortured on a scal
most certainly unequaled since the days Japanese doctors o
the Manchurian Plain had during World War II injecte
their prisoners with bubonic plague, cholera, syphilis, an
thrax, and other lethal germs to study the resistance of vari
ous nationalities and races to disease. More recently, doctor
of the Khmer Rouge had given similar injections to thei
prisoners. In Vietnam the use of medically supervised elec
troshock was commonplace in detention centers as part of
national re-education program. In Pakistan, doctors routinel
supervised a variety of tortures that included hanging prison
ers from the ceiling, often upside down, for hours on end
depriving them of sleep for periods of a week, and supervis
ing mock executions. In Sri Lanka, physicians used thei
skills to insert needles under finger- and toenails and int
sensitive parts of the bodies of Tamil prisoners. Taiwan doc
tors continued to supervise beatings, electroshocks, and th
fettering of prisoners with ball and chain. The list of medi
cally invoked atrocities was endless.

Just as the Nazi and Japanese doctors of World War II ha
operated within a legally recognized system that deliberatel
motivated them to first endorse, and then actually commi
acts of torture, so were their successors similarly precondi
tioned before they worked in the state-run torture centers o
Syria, Iraq, Iran, and, the most efficient of all, those of th
Soviet Union.

No other country had a comparable and more consisten
record in the development of medical abuse, especially in th
psychiatric field, than Russia. The first recorded inciden
where the due process of psychiatry was used in Russia t
suppress dissent was in 1836. The experts were certain tha
the case in which the philosopher Pyotr Chaadayev was de
clared clinically insane because he criticized the regime o
Czar Nicholas I formed part of the lectures Dr. al-Abub ha
received at Patrice Lumumba. In the century that followe
Chaadayev's incarceration, Soviet doctors had become an in
tegral part of systematically interning dissidents in menta
hospitals. Just as the fate of the hostages under the care o
Dr. al-Abub remained uncertain, so too did the future of al
those dissidents in Soviet hands.

Old files were worked and reworked at Langley. Inevita
bly, the specialists turned back to those dealing with the Naz

loctors. They had been the flag bearers, the trendsetters for
nedical torture. What they had done at Auschwitz, Buchenwald,
Dachau, and all the other camps had set the pace and led
ltimately to Dr. al-Abub. There was also another sobering
esson to be gleaned from those files.

Though only twenty-one German doctors had been charged
with medical crimes at Nuremberg, the Agency files on Nazi
nedical crimes clearly indicated that hundreds of physicians
participated in subsidiary roles in what were labeled clinical
rials, tests, and experiments on many thousands of prisoners.
Those unnumbered German doctors were the ones who had
valuated the results of medical torture in their hospitals,
universities, or drug company laboratories, far from the death
amps. Yet those doctors had only prided themselves at being
cientists whose research, in the words of one Nuremberg
lefendant, "was intended to benefit medicine."

The specialists felt that last fact offered an important clue
o understanding more about Dr. al-Abub. Clearly he, too,
lid not operate in a vacuum. For a start, he used drugs that
ltimately must have come from a manufacturer. Assuming
hat he was not Soviet-supplied, then the drug house was
nost likely either in Europe or the Middle or Far East. A
proposal was sent to DDO George: He should urgently assign
gents to try and trace the suppliers of a variety of drugs into
Beirut. It would take time and would be expensive, but it
ould be worth it. George took the suggestion to Casey. He
hrugged his massive hunched shoulders and said it could be
given a shot. Station chiefs in Europe and Asia were asked to
nake inquiries among local pharmaceutical industries.

Meanwhile, specialists continued to ponder how best to
lestabilize Dr. al-Abub's standing in his community. Among
he proposals discussed was planting a story that he was a
exual deviant. But lacking any real substance on which to
ang the smear, the idea petered out.

After a year of intensive work, all the specialists could say
or certain was that Dr. al-Abub was part of a growing num-
er of doctors who regularly committed acts of torture.

They realized that while it was true that the role of the
rained medical torturer could, in more recent history, be
pportioned to the Soviet Gulag and elsewhere, those places
ould not carry all the shame.

There was also a very different background—that of a North

American city. Because of what had happened there, it had become, the specialists knew, that much easier for the argument of clinical expediency to prevail. What had occurred in that city in the name of high-minded science, done by a doctor respected throughout an unsuspecting world, made it that much more possible for Dr. al-Abub to claim justification.

Confronted by their inevitably incomplete files on Dr al-Abub—which would not be closed until he was dead or disappeared beyond further inquiry—the specialists pondered. The contents of his physician's bag the very antithesis of his calling—always to heal, never to harm—did he ever try and justify the torture he continued to inflict upon William Buckley right to the very end?

For Buckley, release finally came during the evening of June 3, 1985, the four hundred and forty-fourth day of his incarceration. In Beirut the cells of Basta prison were crowded with hostages, foreign and Lebanese. The foreigners were grouped together, two and three in a cell. Buckley's companion was David Jacobson, director of the city's American University Hospital, who had been kidnapped weeks earlier. Buckley tried to describe to Jacobson what had happened to him. His thoughts were confused, his speech blurred. By that June day Jacobson was to recall—he would himself be released after seventeen months in captivity—that Buckley was "delirious. He was regurgitating. He obviously was running a very high fever. Then there was just a long, long silence. When you are in a small room there are certain noises associated with death." Jacobson did not see Buckley die because he was himself hooded. All he heard was his fellow American's body being dragged out. William Buckley had died, ultimately not only from what Dr. al-Abub had done to him, but from what the physician had failed to do—treat the peumonia that finally overcame Buckley's lung tissue, leaving him to choke on his own phlegm. His death was announced by the Hizballah on October 11, 1985. His body has never been recovered.

Casey called George. "I just want that motherfucker doctor. Dead or alive. I want him. And the rest of them. Fadlallah All of them."

The DDO said he would see how it could be done.

A few months earlier, on March 8, the Agency had all but

succeeded in killing Sheykh Fadlallah and the entire Hizballah leadership in Lebanon, as well as Dr. al-Abub, when they were gathered in the apartment-office of the spiritual leader of the movement.

Casey had authorized $500,000 for an English mercenary to arrange for a car bomb to be placed outside the apartment block in Bir Abed, a West Beirut suburb already smoke-blackened from years of war.

No one, apart from George or Casey, knew all the details. Shultz knew some. Weinberger had an idea. Not even the president had been given the full facts. He was simply told how close the Agency had come to succeeding. The car, primed with 2,000 pounds of explosive, had been driven across the Green Line and detonated outside Sheykh Fadlallah's home.

Incredibly, though several clerics were killed, Fadlallah and Dr. al-Abub escaped unhurt.

Casey wanted George to make sure they would not escape next time.

Once more an approach was made to the mercenary. There were meetings between him and middlemen. The Agency wanted to make sure it would not be directly linked to the new attempt to murder the Hizballah leader and its physician. Between November 1985 and February 1986, the discussions moved from London to Paris to Rome and back again to London. The mercenary asked for $1 million. The price was agreed—half on acceptance of the contract, the balance on completion. The mercenary traveled to Damascus and down by road to Beirut. He was back a week later for another meeting. There was no way he could carry out the mission. His own resources on the ground had just been killed in one of the street battles that were a daily occurrence in Beirut.

Early in March 1986, the NSA satellite permanently stationed over the city used its cameras to once more photograph Bir Abed. Outside Sheykh Fadlallah's ruined apartment block was a huge banner: DESTROYED BY THE GREAT SATAN.

Six weeks later, on Thursday, April 17, 1986, Casey received notification that Velma Orlikow, Dr. Mary Morrow, and seven other plaintiffs were still vigorously pressing their case against the CIA and that it now had a formal number: Civil Action No. 80–3163. A growing galaxy of doctors, led by

Professor Lifton, were being assembled to give evidence that the Montreal survivors had been medically tortured.

"They don't know what the word means," Casey would mumble. "Torture is what that motherfucker doctor did to Buckley. That's what torture is."

He had still failed to make the connection that what happened in that old mansion in Montreal had made it that much easier for all those who had followed to plead justification.

20

For the Moment

On May 6, 1987, William Casey died of pneumonia following brain surgery to remove a tumor. He had served his country for six years and a day.

On October 15, 1987, the Agency's Department D positioned several miniature scanners on the roofs of buildings in Christian Beirut, beaming the apparatus across the Green Line into the Moslem quarter. The surveillance was done with the blessing of the Syrian government—one of the results of a thaw between Damascus and Washington, itself brought about by a common realization that Qaddafi remained a dangerous threat to both countries.

Three days later, the scanners picked up the news that Dr. al-Abub was leaving Beirut for Tehran.

Behind, in the Moslem quarter, remained twenty foreign hostages.

At Christmas 1987, Amnesty International delivered its annual reminder for the world to pray for all the victims of torture.

On New Year's Day, 1988, the plaintiffs in the action against the Agency expressed for each other the hope they would live long enough to win their case.

On October 5, 1988, the CIA, represented by the U.S. Department of Justice, settled 750,000 dollars on the plaintiffs with the understanding they would never discuss the case in public again.

Notes

The story is not ended, it has not yet become history, and the secret life it holds can break out in you or in me.

—Gershom Scholom, quoted by
Professor Robert Jay Lifton in
The Nazi Doctors, 1987.

The vast volume of data available to writers of contemporary history usually makes that aspect of the research primarily a matter of knowing where to go, collecting and evaluating. The exception, I was to find, was dealing with a subject like medical torture, the more so when it is inextricably bound with the secret world of intelligence.

Many of the methods used by Dr. al-Abub are standard techniques among doctors who use behavior technology to achieve control either within other terrorist groups or inside the framework of state-sponsored terrorism. Hooding prisoners is as common in Beirut as it is in the jails of Santiago, Chile, and the prisons of Ho Chi Minh City in the Socialist Republic of Vietnam. This form of sensory deprivation is no more than a version of the isolator Dr. Cameron built.

The various psychological ploys of Dr. al-Abub were fundamentally no different from Dr. Cameron's techniques. The Iranian's use of drugs to reduce the willpower of hostages was only an extension of what Dr. Cameron did in the Sleep Room, or when he forced patients to listen to tapes endlessly played in their ears.

Both Dr. Cameron, who had supported the Nuremberg Code, specially designed to outlaw any medical maltreatment, and Dr.

l-Abub, who had effectively agreed to uphold the code's tenets
when he swore his physician's oath, were equally guilty of viola-
ions of basic principles of human rights.

Dr. Cameron was able to flourish partly because there is, in
pite of the Nuremberg Code, no total international agreement
hat forbids any government or organization from using doctors
o manipulate the mind. If there was, the Soviet Union would
nd it that much more difficult to still include classes on behav-
r control in its curriculum at Patrice Lumumba. Without the
nowledge he gained in Moscow, Dr. al-Abub would have found
much more difficult to achieve what he had done.

The emergence of doctors like him must be seen in the context
f broader historical development. The eighties have properly
een called the decade of terrorism. A relatively small group of
olitical extremists have repeatedly shown, in Beirut, Belfast,
nd elsewhere, that the crude use of terrorist tactics and rhetoric
an achieve its effect. They continue to attract unparalleled at-
ention to themselves and their causes, and are able to provoke
worldwide fear, create crises in governments, and increase inter-
ational tension. In Washington, London, Paris, Bonn, and Rome,
abinets are driven to devote increasing resources to the prob-
m of physician-terrorists like Dr. al-Abub.

Attempts to deal effectively with them began to accelerate in
988. While France continued to address the topic of terrorism
angentially, examining it within the field of pure criminology,
West Germany, Holland, the United Kingdom, and the United
tates increased the international network of scholars, scientists,
linicians, and government officials—usually professional intelli-
ence officers—who exchanged information on terrorism. The
West German government set aside DM2 million marks to re-
earch into the minds and motivations of men like Dr. al-Abub.
Data on him, along with many hundreds of other terrorists, was
ollected and stored on computers in Wiesbaden. German spe-
ialists continue their multivariate analyses, seeking common
ehavior patterns and evidence of progressive inhibition reduc-
on—the kind of emotional blunting that had made it possible
or Dr. Cameron to perform his experiments.

In Bonn, behaviorists are studying the complex mechanisms of
roup formation and processes that hold the clues to the leader-
hip requirements and the internal dynamics of such movements
s the Hizballah. Researchers analyze the social conditions that
ave led to the emergence of physicians like Dr. al-Abub.

Much of the research depends on multidisciplinary coopera
tion; inevitably, agreed-upon conclusions are slow in coming. A
clinical psychiatrist still often sees matters differently from
transcultural analyst, just as their predecessors did in Dr. Cam
eron's time.

In Italy, the specialists are concentrating upon the sociologica
aspects of terrorism, and the detailed life histories of terrorists
both leftist and rightist, are continually subjected to in-depth
analysis. Research in Britain and the United States reflects th
source of most of the funding—the government. Much of th
work is highly pragmatic and concentrates upon matters directl
related to the national security of both countries.

Israel leads the world in research into terrorism. A growin
number of scholars at various universities, who generally wor
closely with the Mossad and other intelligence services, ar
heavily engaged in collating and analyzing data. Many of thei
discoveries are classified MOST SECRET and shared only with thei
peers in Israeli intelligence.

Among the many conclusions the specialists have made is tha
terrorists "like a lot of people watching, not a lot of peopl
dead."

Yet hostage taking as a tactic has produced, in the end, ver
little apart from publicity. Governments—France excepted—hav
become more resistant to the demands of terrorists, even when
significant number of hostages, as in Lebanon, are involved
They are increasingly manipulated by doctors who supervise o
use both physical and psychological torture to force hostages t
make appeals designed to embarrass and manipulate governments

Yet, with a few notable examples, which I will refer to in
moment, medically sponsored terrorism is a subject that I found
to my surprise, has attracted little published interest among m
fellow investigators. I can now well understand why. Havin
come through the research mill, I do feel very definitely men
tally bruised and still not quite used to the realization of ho
close I was to being kidnapped in Beirut, or possibly killed i
Tehran and Damascus.

After over thirty years of trawling through some of the othe
genuinely horrific pivotal events of this century—when you hav
spent a good part of your life, as I have, examining the destruc
tion of Guernica in the Spanish Civil War, the first aerial wa
crime; the bombing of Hiroshima, without doubt the greates
war crime; as well as analyzing man's behavior in the aftermat

some of the great natural disasters of our age—I suppose I
ould be hardened.

I have reported half a dozen wars, from the Suez Crisis of 1956
Vietnam and, more recently, the conflict in the Gulf. I have
en Afghan rebels in 1987 use the head of a just-decapitated
oviet soldier for a polo chuck; the mutilated bodies of Israeli
y-soldiers in the hangar-sized mortuary in Basra, close to the
order with Iran; and the scarred corpses of Iranian children, the
ctims of Iraq's chemical weapons. I have observed more than
ough mutilation and death in the past three decades.

But nothing had quite prepared me for the horror that came
om spending every day for over two years, often twelve- and
urteen-hour days, dealing with the inescapable truth that doc-
rs have tortured—and still do. At the end of the research I
uld well understand why other investigators had shied from
e subject: it really is the stuff of nightmares. Therefore, my
dmiration is all the greater for the few who went before me.

No one can research the role of doctors in the intelligence field
ithout reading *The Search for the 'Manchurian Candidate'*
imes Books, 1979). The author is John Marks, a former Senate
de and State Department official. The book offered me a glimpse
f how the CIA under Allen Dulles used Dr. Cameron. Marks's
ork is a bench mark in writing about secret intelligence mat-
rs; he is among the first to lift such reporting out of the
otboiler genre and give it a veneer of real quality and authenticity.

Equally valuable is *The Breaking of Bodies and Minds*, a
eport published by the American Association for the Advance-
ent of Science in 1985. Primarily it is an account of medical
buse in the Soviet Union and Latin America, a learned and
areful assessment of why in repressive regimes some doctors
ave become willing or unwilling participants in malpractice,
specially punitive psychiatry. The importance of the book for
e was that it led me to some of those who have helped with
urney into Madness.

Amnesty International provided their detailed reports of tor-
re and ill-treatment in ninety countries, an authentic library of
orror. They are as harrowing to read as the transcripts of the
ar crimes trials at Nuremberg and Tokyo. Amnesty's reports
re the work of doctors who have had to investigate, judge, and
ften condemn their peers.

One essential focus of my investigations was the connection
etween Allen Dulles and Dr. Cameron.

In my own days as a foreign correspondent in the 1950s and 1960s, I ran into Dulles, among other places, at the State Department in Washington, at a party in the U.S. Embassy in Paris after the Suez Crisis, and in Delhi.

Like Casey, he was often forthcoming. One night in Rome over dinner at the Excelsior, he gave the rest of us at the table a brilliant analysis of the reasons behind the failure of Britain's Prime Minister, Sir Anthony Eden, to understand the mind of Egypt's President Gamal Nasser. "To Eden he was just a Nile wog. It cost Eden and Britain its place in the Middle East." On another occasion, in Vienna, Dulles gave me information that proved to be totally accurate about the ramifications of the defection to Russia of Burgess and Maclean, the British diplomats who were Soviet spies. "They're just the tip of the iceberg." All told we met about a dozen times, sometimes spending time together, on others merely exchanging pleasantries before Dulles would be off chasing some blond with a vacuous smile. But it gave me a feel for the man. That was reinforced by working through his papers at the University of Princeton and talking to his wife, Clover, and his colleagues.

Those interviews were fit in between my own field research: in Canada, the United States, Europe, and finally the Middle East—lengthy trips to Israel, Syria, Lebanon, Iran, Egypt, and Cyprus, journeys that can properly be said to have begun on that evening in Rome in December 1983 when Bill Buckley, a friend of his and myself dined in a restaurant in the old part of the city.

I had already known Buckley for several years. We first met in the closing stages of Vietnam and later in Washington where he had an apartment off Dupont Circle. For anyone who has worked any length of time in Washington, it was inevitable we would bump into each other on the embassy cocktail party circuit. We began by discussing common interests: Vietnam and the Middle East, where I had grown up, and which Buckley was fascinated by long before he went there. Rome was another bridge to our friendship. I had worked there as a correspondent in the late fifties; to Buckley, it was in every sense the Eternal City.

By the time he had invited me to dinner at his Washington apartment, I had a pretty good idea what he did. When I finally asked, he simply said, "Sure. I work for the Agency." He made it sound like a badge of honor. At first he spoke not so much about his own work, but on the broad philosophy of intelligence gathering. My late father-in-law had been an intelligence officer

unning a network out of Dresden in East Germany for M15 in
he hectic postwar period. He was caught by the Soviets in 1947
nd received a death sentence, commuted to fourteen years
mprisonment. When he came home to Berlin, the CIA sounded
im out on whether he would like to supplement his pension by
vorking for them. He was quite forceful in his refusal. Buckley
ad the same innate attitude to spying as my father-in-law:
overt action was an essential part of the decision-making process
f government.

As time went by, and I suppose Buckley came to trust me
nore, he spoke more freely about some of the Agency personali-
ies and filled me in on various intelligence operations of the
ecent past—on the strict understanding that it was background.
Ie said more than once, half-jokingly, that we should write a
ook together—one that would be an antidote to Philip Agee's
oured outpourings about the Agency. But we never seemed
ble to set a starting date. He would be off somewhere—it
urned out to be places like Angola, El Salvador, and Egypt—
vhile I would be researching a book in some other part of the
vorld: Japan, Australia, or South Africa.

Rome, by common consensus, became an agreed meeting
round. In 1983 I spent a year there completing a book on the
Catholic Church. During that time I made several trips to stay
vith Buckley in his Beirut apartment. He spoke feelingly of the
trains of being station chief and how he longed to get away to
ome for even a weekend.

Like anyone in my work, rubbing shoulders with professional
ntelligence men is part of the job. As a fellow investigator once
aid, "They have, we want." My own rule for dealing with spies
nd counterspies is a simple one: Listen—but beware, and
lways be slow to believe. It has stood me in good stead for three
ecades. Like my father-in-law and Buckley, the dozen or so
rofessionals I have met—or at least the ones I knew were in the
usiness—were very unlike the creation of Ian Fleming. More
ke le Carré or Deighton.

Buckley was middle-aged and a neat dresser, a good speaker
nd a better listener. He really believed in the Agency; he spoke
f it with the affection of family. When he talked about Dr.
Gottlieb and Dr. Cameron and the others from that time, he
eemed genuinely hurt at the way they had tarnished its image.

While we sipped coffee, at the end of that December 1983
inner, I told him I had finally decided to begin serious research

into Dr. Cameron and the whole business of the Agency's role in mind control.

"Did Dulles really think he could create the Manchurian Candidate?" I asked.

Buckley nodded. "And Casey. It's the dream of any intelligence chief. To have someone in his total control."

"Tell me," I said, "about Dr. Gottlieb."

As simply as that it had begun.

Buckley's own kidnapping and death came at a crucial stage in my research. The events in Montreal had been investigated; physicians and former patients of Dr. Cameron's had given their accounts. Listening to the doctors I kept asking myself, and finally them, why they had gone along with Dr. Cameron. They had looked at me blankly. Clearly the question had not seriously been asked before.

Absorbing the stories of the patients was an upsetting experience. Much of their testimony came from their affidavits, which Jim Turner made available to me. Turner had taken over the case when Rauh retired. This selfless and courageous young lawyer only asked that I tell the story of his clients as fairly as possible. It was a small price to ask for the thousands of pages of testimony and documentation he provided.

Much of it would have been virtually impossible for me to have unearthed; it had taken first Rauh's and then Turner's legal stratagems to uncover such nuggets as the original M-K-Ultra papers linking the Agency with Dr. Cameron through the Society for the Investigation of Human Ecology. Some of the documents will survive as revealing testimony for future historians. The affidavit of Richard Helms is among them. It is the stuff of a dozen spy novels.

In 1986–87 each of Jim Turner's clients who had been Dr. Cameron's patients were brought to Washington to be questioned by the CIA's lawyers. It was part of the myriad required legal maneuvers—the discovery, motions, declarations, and revised declarations, the answers to interrogators, more interrogations, and more answers. It was all part of the endless preliminary jousting before the main event—which, in 1988, still had no date set.

Reading the relentless questions the CIA lawyers put was an uncomfortable business; at times the probing seemed very close to harassment. But when all the Montreal story had been gathered together, I faced a question: What had happened was

orrific and should be put down on paper, but how could it be
made relevant to what was occurring in today's world—the world
where William Buckley pitted his skills?

His kidnapping provided the answer. Once I had overcome
my shock and dismay at what had happened to him, I began to
research how it had occurred and why. In a matter of weeks,
with help from some of Buckley's colleagues, I was on the trail of
Dr. al-Abub. The inescapable conclusion soon grew: He and Dr.
Cameron were essentially the same type of person. The focus of
my book became clear. In bearing witness to what had been
Buckley's fate, I would also chart the sequence of human actions
involved in a particularly unpleasant form of behavior—medical
killing, the kind that Dr. Cameron had done to Madeleine Smith
and who knows how many others. There was, I could see, a
direct progression from Montreal to Beirut. What Dr. Lifton had
described as the doubling of Nazi doctors had still been going on
with Dr. Cameron and later with Dr. al-Abub.

Much grew from that realization. Using it as a working tool, I
was able to understand more clearly the specialists whose work it
is to deal with a colleague like Dr. al-Abub. I was handed on
from one to another, a journey that took me back and forth from
Tel Aviv to Washington, to Bonn, Paris, and London, and back
to Tel Aviv and then on to Tokyo, Sydney, and back to Los
Angeles before once more beginning the long flight to Tel Aviv.
There were frequent sidebar trips to Toronto and Montreal,
Ottawa and Vancouver, to talk to patients and relatives of Dr.
Cameron, to put what I had learned into the context of what he
had done. Damascus, Tehran, and Baghdad were other points of
call.

Then there was Beirut itself. To go there is in every sense
foolhardy; to not go would have left an element in the story
unresearched. It is one thing to read about a place, another to
actually experience its sights and smells. As so often in the past,
I was helped by my friends in the newspaper world. Dennis
Hart, news manager of the London *Daily Express*, gave me
accreditation. David Staveley, news-features editor of the Press
Association in London, provided further cover. So did Gareth
Jenkins, features editor of the *Western Mail*, Cardiff, the flagship
of the Thomson Group of newspapers. Throughout my time in
the Middle East they published my reports from Beirut, Damascus, and Tehran. The editors of the *Toronto Globe and Mail*,
Toronto Star, and *Ottawa Citizen* also published my reports

from Beirut. Canadian newspapers still command respect in Lebanon, and the clips of the articles were carefully perused by the Syrians and the Shiite Moslems. I must also thank the tireless Joan Smith of Trans-Canada Features, who ensured my stories appeared throughout North America. As well as helping to fund a very expensive investigation, between them they made it that much easier for me to operate in a very inhospitable area.

There was Mark Barty-King. In thirty-five years of being an author, I have never known a better publisher or finer man. His enthusiasm is only matched by his total support coupled with fiercely protecting me from all the faceless predators who prowl multinational publishing nowadays. When the going got rough and it often did, Mark was always there.

My editor, again, was Kate Parkin. Lucky the author whose work she touches. She has that rare gift—unusual sensitivity and an unerring pencil.

Finally, but by no means last, there is my agent, quite simply the incomparable Jonathan Clowes. He has guided my career for almost twenty years. Without him—and this is a long-overdue tribute—I would never have had the courage to begin *Journey into Madness*. God only knows where he will send me next. All I do know is that he will have made sure the risks are acceptable. There is no one like Jonathan. There never will be.

Finally it was all done—or as far as I was able to take it. Further visits to Damascus, Beirut, and Tehran would, I suspected, produce little more and could, as had happened to several newspapermen, lead to my own kidnapping in the Lebanese capital.

On a cold winter's morning in 1988, the feeling of genuine fear in Beirut had, if possible, increased. The French-language newspaper, *L'Orient le Jour*, carried further columns of advertisements appealing for news of Lebanese who had been kidnapped. Since the civil war began twelve years earlier, an estimated ten thousand Lebanese have vanished. Little is heard of them in the West, where the focus is on the remaining foreign hostages. In the newspaper's property columns were scores of offers for "a ruined house" and "shopkeeper seeks quick sale for property in need of repair."

In Christian West Beirut the walls were covered with faded posters of Bachir Gemayel, killed by a bomb in September 1982. He had been a CIA informant as well as the Christian community's charismatic leader.

The Green Line, now six miles long and in places three
arters of a mile wide, was patrolled not only by the Syrian
my, but by units of the Lebanese Armed Forces. The Chris-
1 Eighth Brigade watched over the East side and, across on
: West side, the Moslem Eighth Brigade. The units are ner-
1s, trigger-happy, and almost daily staged little confrontations
h each other.

At Museum Crossing, the Hizballah checkpoints are immedi-
ly visible and more numerous. They are sited in the gutted
ional museum and among the ancient Roman ruins. The check-
nt I had negotiated in the past is still there—a permanent
ure in the ruined landscape.

Near the crossing is Buckley's old apartment block. From its
f flies a Hizballah pennant. Beyond lies the forbidding mass of
: Moslem quarter. Somewhere in its depths, say Buckley's
nds, lies his body, perhaps close to the hippodrome where,
ce more, races have started to be held; the track is the only
.ce where Moslems and Christians mingle.

Close by is the Movenpick Restaurant, where Buckley and I
I sometimes eaten—and where the first Israeli soldier was
ot dead during the occupation of 1982. The holes from the
lets that killed him are each neatly ringed in the wall—a
morial of sorts.

At the Spagghetteria Restaurant, where Buckley had met many
his contacts, the atmosphere was like that in any place where
ople felt the end was finally coming: too much loud laughter,
nking too fast, and the constant nervous glances at the passing
ffic. Diners were watching for what had become the arche-
al kidnap car—a Mercedes with smoked glass windows with a
rtain on the rear one. The kidnappers have gone up-market, at
st in their choice of transport, since snatching Bill Buckley in
it Renault.

The Hizballah presence is everywhere: posters extolling the
ned struggle, photographs of the fallen, portraits of the ayatollah.
Dominating the scene is the massive and ugly and still-unfinished
»sque where Sheykh Fadlallah preaches his hatred on Friday
;hts. Close by is Basta jail, where Buckley had been held.

The hatred in the air is tangible. It is there in the faces as
ople listen to the radio; in the broadcasts themselves, there
: repeated outpourings of hatred against the West. It is like
:ening to someone calling repeatedly for an end of the world.
leed, Armageddon seems that much closer in these streets.

It was not a comfortable feeling to be told, as I was by
emissary of Sheykh Fadlallah's, that I would not be welcome a
longer in Moslem Beirut.

In the end, I think that is what helped to spur me on
write—a feeling of genuine outrage that men like Sheykh Fadlall
could use their power to spawn and protect the likes of L
al-Abub. Just as Dr. Morrow will probably never forget th
image of Dr. Cameron standing over her bed with a syringe
his hand, so will I need a long time to no longer visualize L
al-Abub going about his unspeakable business.

Piecing together Dr. al-Abub's story was one of the harde
tasks in writing this book. So little was known about him; so litt
is known now. Members of Israeli intelligence provided many
the details. Another source was a member of the Druze Progre
sive Socialist Party of Walid Jumblatt; we met several times
the Sanaya Gardens in Beirut, just across the street from t
office of the prime minister. One of the intelligence officers wi
the Syrian Eighty-fifth Brigade filled in a few more details. The
were those mornings I spent at a Syrian checkpoint to the Gre
Line waiting to see Dr. al-Abub actually walking through t
Moslem quarter. It did help to locate him. Those sources,
Buckley would have said, are current and cannot be named. B
I thank them.

There are, to be sure, pleasant memories. The research
lowed me to renew my contacts with Dr. William Sargar
retired and, in 1988, cruelly afflicted with illness. Over dinner
his home near Salisbury, England, he recounted his memories
Dr. Cameron, providing hitherto unsuspected insights into
fellow psychiatrist.

Another enjoyable meeting was with Dr. Fred Allodi in T
ronto, a renowned campaigner on behalf of Amnesty Intern
tional, which itself was most supportive of my work. Dr. Allo
and I found we shared a common interest over the destruction
Guernica. From that admittedly unlikely starting point, we mov
into equally dark areas—the work of Dr. Cameron and his su
cessors. Dr. Allodi pointed me in many helpful directions.

On the other side of the world, in Tel Aviv, I was warm
received by Dr. Arial Merari at the Jaffee Center for Strateg
Studies. His insights were invaluable—as, of course, were tho
of his colleagues in Israeli intelligence. In return for guarante
of their anonymity, they spoke long and frankly in Tel Avi

rusalem, and south Lebanon. The book also owes much to
em.

Ellen Mercer at the American Psychiatric Association arranged
r me to have full access to Dr. Cameron's papers, which the
sociation has in its archives. They turned out to be a trove of
formation that enabled me to better grasp what he had been
out on his personal journey into madness.

A full list of primary interviewees must include Dr. Robert
eghorn. In March 1987, this sprightly eighty-two-year-old took
ne off from his still-busy daily schedule at Sunnybrook Hospital
Toronto to guide me through his own detailed, so-far-
published account of working with Dr. Cameron. It is, by any
andard, a truly remarkable document, filled with insight and
netrating analysis. Dr. Cleghorn recorded still further impres-
ons, updating his original ones, trying to put his old chief in
hat he hoped was "a fair light."

Mrs. Peggy Edwards (née Mielke) spent a long time recalling
er duties in the Sleep Room. Her testimony had the painful
nesty of a woman still deeply troubled that she had been a part
what she readily acknowledged was "a bad business." Dr.
dward Kingston, who had been one of Dr. Cameron's residents
d in 1987 was chairman of the department of psychiatry at
cMaster University near Toronto, produced a compelling over-
ew of his old chief. He always tried to balance his criticism
th understanding, constantly saying, "You have to try and see
in the context of the day," and "He wasn't all bad, but not all
od either; somewhere in between." Dr. Allen Mann, professor
clinical psychiatry at Montreal General Hospital, developed
e theme. Engaging and often witty, he made his points quickly
d without hesitation. The Dr. Cameron who emerges from his
ped reminiscences was altogether a kinder man than the per-
n David Orlikow described to me a few days later in his office
the Parliament Buildings in Ottawa. Mr. Orlikow was gener-
s with giving free access to his filing cabinets on his wife's
se. "Nobody wants to see their private lives washed in public,
t it is a small thing to bear for the truth to come out," he said.
ver dinner in the members dining room, Mr. Orlikow contin-
d to stress that he wanted only the truth to emerge—but
nceded it had many shades. "There's little point in talking to
elma or the other patients. They can't remember many things.
is one of the great tragedies of this case that their memories

were forever destroyed by Cameron." He didn't say it in ange
more in sadness.

From Ottawa I traveled to Detroit to speak with Eddie Smit
remarried and with a new family. At first he was reluctant
meet me. "It's over. Madeleine's gone. So what's the point?"
told him about Velma Orlikow not being able to remember. H
asked me to call him back in twenty-four hours. When I did, h
agreed to meet me. We sat and spoke from dinner until close
dawn, when he went off to work in an auto shop. Next evenin
he invited me home. There, in his den, he produced document
tion on Madeleine, including a copy of her case notes. In all
taped sixteen hours with Eddie. From them and his documents
fashioned the shocking story of Madeleine's life and death.

Once more in Montreal, I spoke to Alex Patterson, Q.C., wh
represents the institute in the legal proceedings brought by th
former patients. He proved to be not only an astute lawyer, but
man of considerable humor and charm. Where he could, h
helped; where he could not, he was not obstructive, mere
apologetic. The same could not be said of the public relation
department of the Royal Victoria Hospital, which has responsibi
ity for the Allan Memorial Institute. Their spokesperson refuse
to answer even the simplest of questions on the grounds th
"the whole episode is sub-judice." Not only was she a po
publicist, but also had an imperfect grasp of law. In the end
visited the institute. I could well understand what Velma Orliko
had meant when she called it spooky. It does look like a goth
house of horrors, at least from the outside. Inside, it had see
better days.

Behind the institute Dr. Peter Roper still had his practice, an
in his office over several days in March 1987 he dipped deepe
and deeper into his quite remarkable memory. Not only could h
recall minute details, but was able to explain how he felt they f
into the broad picture. His enthusiasm for telling the story wa
infectious, and meals were skipped as he talked on and on, and
kept on changing tapes. Spotting my difficulty with getting a ne
tape into my recorder, he grinned and said, "You could do wit
that bounder Rubenstein."

In many ways I realized that I had a choice to either set off
pursuit of Leonard Rubenstein or leave him out of the story. D
Roper convinced me. "You can't possibly tell the story withou
including him. Even if he doesn't speak to you, that's important

But first, interviewing Zielinski was one of the greater cha enges I have met as an investigator. Jan Zielinski went from I'm going to put the phone down now," to "Look, I'm only a Pole who doesn't want to make waves," to "No, it wasn't like that. I tried to help people. That's all. I tried to help." In between those seesaw statements, I kept questioning him. No, he would not meet me. Yet I could come to his home. No, I shouldn't do that. No, we could talk on the phone. Back and forth we went; gradually, I suppose I wore down his objections. Finally, for whatever reason, he began to talk. What he had to say was not only extraordinary but also of vital importance. Every word would end up in this book. I'm glad that he did finally agree to be so open and frank. I'm glad, too, that he also urged me to "go after Rubenstein."

I flew to London and did what any investigator does—tried to locate Mr. Rubenstein through the telephone company. He was not listed. I called in a number of favors from colleagues in the newspaper and television media. They tried their contacts. No luck. Defeated, and with time running out, I headed again for another session in Washington with Jim Turner. He had an address for Mr. Rubenstein in London. But he had moved. The woman at his old home remembered that somewhere she had a note of his new address. It took her a few minutes to locate it—and, manna for a tired researcher, she also had his unlisted telephone number.

I telephoned Mr. Rubenstein. I explained to him in detail what was the purpose of my call. He finally said he couldn't speak about what he had done. I asked him why. He said he was just about to leave the country. I asked where he was going and if I could come along. "I'm going to be away for a long time," he replied. Throwing caution to the wind, I asked him if he could even begin to justify what he had done to people like Madeleine. There was a lengthy pause, and then, to my utter surprise, he began to speak. "Yes, I can justify it. Dr. Cameron was a great man. . . ." For a good hour I scribbled furiously while he sought to explain himself. The voice in my ear was gentle and insistent. "Those were different times. Very different times." Then, as abruptly as he had begun, he stopped. "Got to go." He had put down the phone. A few days later, when I next called the number, the operator said it was a disconnected line.

One day, Mr. Rubenstein will perhaps feel it would be good to clear up the many mysteries about him.

Finally, there was Dorothy Trainor. I found her defensive.

Our interview was abruptly terminated in the gloomy surround
ings of the Montreal Press Club when she said she could be of n
further help. A pity: If she had given me the opportunity,
might have gleaned a little more about the "humanity" sh
repeatedly claimed imbued Dr. Cameron.

There were, inevitably, some refusals. Mrs. Cameron wa
unwilling to discuss her husband. Her son, Duncan, a Washing
ton lawyer, was sympathetic to my quest but felt he, too, coul
not help. I spoke to Dr. Morrow several times, running ove
with her various points in the lengthy deposition she had mad
to the CIA's lawyers and which Jim Turner had provided. Sh
was helpful, but explained she was writing her own account o
what had happened, and so could not provide me with all th
details I had hoped for. My impression was of a nice woman wh
had suffered a great deal.

In all, in various parts of the world, I spoke to over tw
hundred persons involved in the story. Buckley, of course, was
prime source for the CIA material. Casey was helpful.

I must finally thank Noel Walsh, professor of clinical psychia
try at St. Vincent's Hospital, Dublin, Ireland. More than anyon
else, this deeply caring and compassionate physician—who
coincidentally, had worked in Montreal, at St. Mary's, the hospi
tal where Dr. Morrow had once dreamed of having her ow
department—patiently answered my questions about psychiatr
and medical treatments in general. In writing this book, I fel
there was still hope when there are men like him in medicine.

Sources

Some time ago that most estimable of investigators, William Manchester, wrote that the only way to successfully approach our kind of work is to accept that no one can ever root out the truth, the whole truth, and nothing but the truth. That is a game lawyers play, and as Bill says, "There is something touching about their naive assumption that one gets the full story by putting a man under oath. In practice you get very little of it. Anxious not to perjure himself, the witness volunteers as little as possible. The author, with his tape recorder or shorthand notebook, gets a great deal more chaff; but in the long run, he harvests more wheat, too."

So it was for me.

I taped, all told, one hundred and twenty-four hours of recordings—raw material enough to fill a book twice this length. I also made use of the documentation that Jim Turner provided. This included:

DEPOSITIONS

Velma Orlikow. Before Patricia Gaffney, notary public, in the U.S. Attorney's Office, 555 4th Street, N.W., Washington, D.C., June 17, 1986. Appearances: Joseph Rauh, counsel for plaintiff; Scott T. Kragie, counsel for defendant, United States of America; Page Moffett, Office of General Counsel, Central Intelligence Agency, counsel for defendant. 155 pages, plus exhibits.

Mary Matilda Morrow, M.D. Before Judith F. Richard, notary public, at Judiciary Center, 555 4th Street, N.W., Washington, D.C., June 19, 1986. Appearances: James C. Turner, counsel for plaintiff; Scott T. Kragie, counsel for defendant, United States of America; Page Moffett and Barbara A. Rubino, Office of General Counsel, Central Intelligence Agency. 188 pages.

Jean Charles Page. Before the consul general of the United States in Montreal, June 24, 1986. Appearances: Scott T. Kragie, counsel for defendant, United States of America; Mrs. James C. Turner, counsel for plaintiff. 89 pages.

Moe Langleben. Before Patricia Mitchell, verbatim reporter, at 333 Constitution Avenue, N.W., Washington, D.C., May 6, 1986. Appearances: James C. Turner, counsel for deponent; Scott T. Kragie, counsel for defendant, United States of America. 103 pages, plus exhibits.

Rita Zimmerman. Before the consul general of the United States in Montreal, June 26, 1986. Appearances: James C. Turner, counsel for plaintiff. Scott T. Kragie and Ms. Rebecca Ross, counsels for defendant, United States of America. 34 pages.

Jeannine Huard. Before the consul general of the United States in Montreal, June 25, 1986. Appearances: James C. Turner, counsel for plaintiff. Scott T. Kragie and Ms. Rebecca Ross, counsels for defendant, United States of America. 114 pages.

Louis Weinstein. Before the consul general of the United States in Montreal, June 23, 1986. Appearances: James C. Turner, counsel for plaintiff; Scott T. Kragie and Ms. Rebecca Ross, counsels for defendant, United States of America. 112 pages.

Richard McGarrah Helms. Before Baleigh Milton, notary public, 1001 Connecticut Avenue, N.W., Washington, D.C., on March 14, 1983. Appearances: Joseph Rauh and James C. Turner for the plaintiffs; for Richard Helms, Robert M. LaPrade and Philip Kinsberg, counsel for Central Intelligence Agency; for the Central Intelligence Agency, Steven Hermes; for the United States of America, Les Strictland, assistant U.S. attorney. 268 pages.

AFFIDAVITS

Mrs. Alice W. Olson, widow of Frank Olson. October 6, 1986.

Robert Jay Lifton, M.D., Distinguished Professor of Psychiatry and Psychology, City University of New York, John Jay College of Criminal Justice. October 24, 1986.

Harvey M. Weinstein, M.D., clinical associate professor of psychiatry, Stanford University of Medicine. November 7, 1986.

eon Salzman, M.D., Professor of Psychiatry, Georgetown University Medical School. November 29, 1986.

Osmond M. Solandt, Ph.D., former Chairman, Canadian Defense Research Board. October 6, 1986.

ny Peterzell, Research Associate, Center for National Security Studies. November 5, 1986.

aul E. Termansen, M.D., F.R.C.P.(C), clinical associate professor, department of psychiatry, University of British Columbia. October 6, 1986.

loyd Hisey, M.D., former registrar and director, the Allan Memorial Institute. February 20, 1983.

David J. Rothman, Ph.D., and Bernard Shoenberg, professor of social medicine and director, Center for the Study of Society and Medicine, College of Physicians and Surgeons, Columbia University. October 15, 1986.

David I. Joseph, M.D., faculty member, Saint Elizabeth Hospital, and associate clinical professor of psychiatry and behavioral science, George Washington School of Medicine. November 7, 1986.

Brian B. Doyle, M.D., clinical professor of psychiatry and of family and community medicine, Georgetown University School of Medicine. November 3, 1986.

enator Allan J. MacEachen, former Canadian member of parliament and Secretary of State for External Affairs. October 29, 1986.

va H. Bothwell. November 4, 1986.

Vayne Langleben. August 26, 1986.

TRANSCRIPTIONS

Examination in chief by Maitre Alex Paterson; testimony of Dr. Allan Mann, taken May 5, 1981, before the Hon. Mr. Justice Marcel Belleville, Superior Court, District of Montreal, Province of Quebec; in Case No. 500–05–006872–788: Dame Velma Orlikow vs. Royal Victoria Hospital.

Direct examination of Dr. Peter Roper by Mr. Sullivan, taken on February 5, 1981, as expert testimony in the case of Dr. Mary Matilda Morrow vs. Royal Victoria Hospital.

DOCUMENTS

Plaintiffs' statement of genuine issues in Civil Action No. 80–3163
detailed in following separate exhibits:

a. The M-K-Ultra Program was established to explore cover
    brainwashing techniques for both offensive and defensive use
    by the CIA (Def. No. 6–9).

b. The central activity of the M-K-Ultra program was conduct
    ing and funding brainwashing experimentation with danger
    ous drugs and other techniques performed on persons who
    were not volunteers by CIA Technical Service Division em
    ployees, agents, and contractors (Def. No. 10–17).

c. CIA employees were negligent in killing Frank Olson in an
    M-K-Ultra experiment during November 1953, as related by
    his widow in her affidavit (Def. No. 18, 19).

d. The CIA negligently failed to implement appropriate mea
    sures to curb Gottlieb and Lashbrook (Def. No. 20–23).

e. The Society for the Investigation of Human Ecology (hereaf
    ter "Society") was established and operated by the CIA to
    conceal its role in conducting and financing brainwashing
    research (Def. No. 24–26).

f. In January 1956 an article by D. Ewen Cameron appeared in
    the *American Journal of Psychiatry* that described poten
    tially injurious experimental procedures similar to Commu
    nist brainwashing methods (Def. No. 27, 28).

g. John Gittinger and former Air Force brainwashing expert Col
    James Monroe recruited D. Ewen Cameron to perform experi
    ments with potentially injurious experimental procedures
    similar to Communist brainwashing methods (Def. No. 29–32)

h. The application submitted to the Society by D. Ewen Cam
    eron was a transparent proposal to conduct experiments with
    techniques extrapolated from the academic literature on brain
    washing, which deviated from the standard and customary
    psychiatric therapies during the 1950s and which ran the full
    gamut of brainwashing procedures, including depatterning,
    experimental drugs, psychic driving, partial sensory isola
    tion, and continuous sleep (Def. No. 33–38).

i. Without investigation of any kind, Gottlieb, Lashbrook,
    Gittinger, and their CIA colleagues approved M-K-Ultra
    subproject 68, which provided some $60,000 over four years
    for the brainwashing experiments described in the applica
    tion (Def. No. 39–48, 121–124, 127, 129).

. Gottlieb, Lashbrook, Gittinger, and their CIA associates failed to take any steps to ensure that only volunteers were used in M-K-Ultra subproject 68 or to protect the well-being of experimental subjects (Def. No. 39–48).

k. During the time CIA provided funds for M-K-Ultra subproject 68 Gottlieb, Lashbrook, Gittinger, and their associates failed to supervise the M-K-Ultra subproject 68 brainwashing experimentation in any way (Def. No. 39–48).

. Cameron was aware of CIA interest in the brainwashing experiments he conducted (Def. No. 29–31, 42–45, 48).

m. M-K-Ultra subproject 68 provided over $60,000 to support brainwashing experiments from 1956 through the early 1960s (Def. No. 39–48).

n. Plaintiffs never volunteered to participate in experiments (Def. No. 51, 68, 77, 92, 102).

o. Each plaintiff was subjected to one or more of the experimental brainwashing techniques (depatterning with intensive electroshock or LSD and other drugs, psychic driving, partial sensory, isolation, and continuous sleep experiments) described in the application and financed by M-K-Ultra subproject 68, instead of standard therapies for their psychiatric conditions (Def. No. 49, 50, 52, 53, 56–58, 61–64, 67, 69, 70, 74–76, 82–85, 88–91, 95, 96, 99–101, 119, 120).

p. The CIA concealed M-K-Ultra subproject 68 and failed to notify plaintiffs that they had been unwitting subjects of those brainwashing experiments (Def. No. 78–81, 106–118).

q. Defendant has admitted negligence in the CIA's M-K-Ultra brainwashing experiments (Def. No. 13–26, 121–29).

r. Each plaintiff was injured by exposure to one or more of these brainwashing techniques of depatterning with intensive electroshock of LSD and other drugs, psychic driving, partial sensory isolation, and continuous sleep experiments described in the application and financed by M-K-Ultra subproject 68. (Def. No. 104, 124, 128).

s. The brainwashing experiments financed by M-K-Ultra subproject 68 were unethical and irresponsible violations of recognized standards governing research with human subjects (Def. No. 123, 125–127).

t. The CIA violated accepted standards governing research involving human subjects by financing brainwashing experiments upon nonvolunteers in M-K-Ultra subproject 68 (Def. No. 123, 125–127).

The opening and closing sections of the book, which deal with the activities of Dr. al-Abub and terrorism in general, owe a great deal to the help of Ellen Mercer of the American Psychiatric Association in Washington. Having provided me with a complete set of Dr. Cameron's own publications, in all some 130 papers, authored and coauthored, Ms. Mercer provided a series of invaluable reports, many unpublished, which helped to put into context the work of the specialists working in or with intelligence agencies to combat terrorism. These reports included:

The Ethics of Terror. Professor Abraham Kaplan, Department of Philosophy, University of Haifa, Israel.

The Psychiatrist and the Terrorist. Professor John Gunn, Institute of Psychiatry, The Maudsley Hospital, London.

Ethics in Hostage Encounters. Professor Burr Eichelman, University of Wisconsin at Madison.

Victimization and Rehabilitative Treatment. Professor Martin Symonds, John Jay School of Law, Director of Psychological Studies, New York City Police Department.

Hostage Victims. Dr. Frank Ochberg, St. Lawrence Hospital, Lansing, Michigan.

The Hostage Situation: Law Enforcement Options. Captain Frank Bolz, chief negotiator, Hostage Negotiation Team, New York City Police Department.

Preparing Law Enforcement Personnel for Terrorist Incidents. Conrad Hassell, unit chief, Special Operations and Research Unit, FBI Academy, Quantico, Virginia.

Law Enforcement and Psychiatry: Forging and Working Alliance. Professor David Soskis, clinical associate professor of psychiatry, Temple University, Philadelphia, Pennsylvania.

Research in Terrorism. Professor William Reid, Nebraska Psychiatric Institute, University of Nebraska College of Medicine, Omaha, Nebraska.

Areas of Consensus: Areas of Ignorance. Brian Jenkins, program director, Security/Subnational Conflicts. The Rand Corporation, Santa Monica, California.

Psychodynamic Theory of Terrorist Behavior. Professor Jerrold M. Post, Department of Psychiatry and Behavioral Science, George Washington University.

Hizballah: The Moral Logic of Extraordinary Means. Professor Martin Kramer, Dayan Center, University of Tel Aviv, Israel.

The Logic of Terrorism. Professor Martha Crenshaw, Department of Government, Wesleyan University.

Messianic Sanctions for Terror. Professor David C. Rapport, Professor of Political Science, University of California, Los Angeles.

Ideology and Repentance: Terrorism in Italy. Professor Franco Ferracuti, professor of criminological medicine and forensic psychiatry, University of Rome School of Medicine.

Nationalism, Sectarianism and Political Violence. Joseph Montville, research director, Center for the Study of Foreign Affairs, Foreign Service Institute, U.S. Department of State.

Ideology and Rebellion: Terrorism in West Germany. Konrad Kellen, The Rand Corporation.

The Problems and Challenges of Research on Terrorism. Dr. Jo Groebel, Postgraduate Program in Communication Psychology, Rheinland-Pfalz, West Germany.

Militant Islamic Movements in Lebanon: Origins, Social Basis and Ideology. Professor Marius Deeb, The Center for Contemporary Arab Studies, Georgetown University, Washington.

Revolutionary Iran: Challenge and Responses. Professor Shimon Shapira, University of Tel Aviv, Israel.

These documents were supported by additional material from the files of the following Arab-language periodicals.

Interview with Husayn al-Musawi. *Al Nahar al-Arabi walduwali*, Beirut, June 10, 1985.

Interview with Abbas al-Musawi. *La Review du Lebanon*, Beirut, June 27, 1985.

Interview with Mahmud Nurani. *Monday Morning*, Beirut, January 14, 1985.

Interview with Husayn al-Musawi. *Kayan*, Tehran, July 29, 1986.

Interview with Sheykh Muhammed Fadlallah. *al-Ittihad al-usbu'l*, Abu Dhabi, January 30, 1986.

Grateful thanks are due to Ibraham al-Tafoli in Damascus who for a year monitored the Arab-language Press on my behalf.

Select Bibliography

Brown, J. R. C. *Techniques of Persuasion: From Propaganda t Brainwashing*. London: Penguin Books, 1963.

Colby, Kenneth Mark. *An Introduction to Psychoanalytic Re search*. New York: Basic Books, 1960.

Crowcroft, Andrew. *The Psychotic: Understanding Madness*. Lon don: Pelican Books, 1967.

Lifton, Robert Jay. *The Nazi Doctors: Medical Killing and th Psychology of Genocide*. New York: Basic Books, 1986.

Manchester, William. *The Glory and the Dream*. Boston: Little Brown & Company, 1973.

Mosley, Leonard. *Dulles: A Biography of Eleanor, Allen an John Foster*. London: Hodder & Stoughton, 1978.

Sargant, William. *Battle for the Mind*. Privately printed edition Ashford: The Invicta Press, 1984.

———— *The Mind Possessed*. Privately printed edition. Ashfor The Invicta Press, 1984.

———— *The Unquiet Mind*. Privately printed edition. Ashfor The Invicta Press, 1984.

Index

About the Author

GORDON THOMAS is the prize-winning author of *Desire and Denial*, *The Operation*, and *The Trial*, as well as more than twenty other books, which have sold more than thirty-five million copies in thirty-six countries. A former producer for the BBC, he is a veteran foreign correspondent and investigative journalist who has reported from many hot spots around the world. He is currently working on two books, one about China's recent upheaval, the other on the contemporary white slave trade.

We Deliver!
And So Do These Bestsellers.

Praise for Joseph Wambaugh

"Joseph Wambaugh's characters have altered America's view of police." —*Time*

"Wambaugh is a master artist of the street scene." —*Publishers Weekly*

"Wambaugh is a writer of genuine power." —*New York Times Book Review*

"Perhaps better than any other contemporary writer, Wambaugh is able to convey just what it is that makes cops different from the rest of us and, more important, why." —*Library Journal*

Nobody Writes About Cops Better Than Wambaugh
Don't Miss Any Of These Bantam Bestsellers